P9-EDL-455

NEW YORK CITY HANDBOOK

WITHDRAWN FROM FREE USE IN CITY CULTURAL
AND WELFARE INSTITUTIONS. MAY BE SOLD FOR
THE BENEFIT OF THE BROOKLYN PUBLIC LIBRARY
ONLY.

NEW YORK CITY HANDBOOK

CHRISTIANE BIRD

MOON
TRAVEL
HANDBOOKS

NEW YORK CITY HANDBOOK
FIRST EDITION

Published by
Moon Publications, Inc.
P.O. Box 3040
Chico, California 95927-3040, USA

Printed by
Colorcraft Ltd.

© Text and photographs copyright Christiane Bird, 1997.
All rights reserved.
© Illustrations and maps copyright Moon Publications, Inc., 1997.
All rights reserved.
Some photos and illustrations are used by permission
and are the property of the original copyright owners.

ISBN: 1-56691-103-6
ISSN: 1094-4400

Editor: Diane Wurzel
Map Editor: Gina Wilson Birtcil
Copy Editor: Gregor Krause
Production & Design: Carey Wilson, David Hurst
Cartography: Chris Folks and Mike Morgenfeld
Index: Emily Kendrick

Front cover photo: Chrysler Building, courtesy of The Stock Market, Pete Saloutos, photographer
All photos by Christiane Bird unless otherwise noted.

Distributed in the United States and Canada by Publishers Group West
Printed in China

All rights reserved. No part of this book may be translated or reproduced in any form, except brief extracts
by a reviewer for the purpose of a review, without written permission of the copyright owner.

Although the author and publisher have made every effort to ensure that the information was correct at
the time of going to press, the author and publisher do not assume and hereby disclaim any liability to any
party for any loss or damage caused by errors, omissions, or any potential travel disruption due to labor or
financial difficulty, whether such errors or omissions result from negligence, accident, or any other cause.

Please send all comments,
corrections, additions,
amendments, and critiques to:

**NEW YORK CITY HANDBOOK
MOON TRAVEL HANDBOOKS
P.O. BOX 3040
CHICO, CA 95927-3040, USA
e-mail: travel@moon.com
www.moon.com**

Printing History
1st edition—October 1997

CONTENTS

ABBREVIATIONS

AYH—American Youth Hostel
B&B—bed and breakfast
BYOB—bring your own bottle
d—double occupancy
DEC—Department of Environmental
    Conservation
Ln.—Lane
MAP—Modified American Plan
NYS—New York State

Pkwy.—Parkway
Pl.—Place
pop—population
RV—recreational vehicle
SRO—single room occupancy
Tnpk.—Turnpike
WW I—World War I
WW II—World War II

PRICE CATEGORIES

The price categories used in this book
correspond to the following dollar
amounts:

    Inexpensive—**$**; under $15
    Moderate—**$$**; $15-30
    Expensive—**$$$**; $30-50
    Very Expensive—**$$$$**; over $50

MAPS

MAP SYMBOLS

═══ Superhighway	⬭ Interstate	○ City / Town
══ Main Road	⬡ U.S. Highway	✕ Airport
── Other Road	◯ State Highway	▪ Sight
---- Tunnel	▨ Water	·········· Ferry

ACKNOWLEDGMENTS

A heartfelt thanks to the many people who helped me put together this book. Dozens of fellow New Yorkers made my job easier by providing me with background information and showing me around their corners of the city.

In particular, I would like to thank Kenneth Jackson of Columbia University whose marvelous lectures on the history of New York greatly influenced this book; Ted Gottfried, who took me on an expedition to the Rockaways; Robert Baron of the New York State Council on the Arts; Steve Zeitlin of City Lore, and everyone at the New York Convention and Visitors Bureau. A special thanks, too, to my friends Nancy Miller, Mark Kirkeby, Zi Pinsley, Peter Trachtenberg, Megan Ratner, Kathryn Paulsen, Ross Kramer, Marie Williams, Wendy Crumpler, Kim Larsen, and Barbara Feinberg, who patiently filled out my questionnaire on favorite New York City sites.

In addition, this book could not have been written without the support of my family, Jerry Brown, and the staff at Moon Publications. I am deeply indebted to my editors Don Root and Diane Wurzel for correcting my inconsistencies, tightening my prose, and shepherding this project through the editorial process.

LET US HEAR FROM YOU

Though we strive to be as accurate as possible, travel information changes rapidly, and various entries in this book may reflect that. A restaurant may have closed or changed its name. Perhaps your motel—mentioned in these pages as an amenable place—proved a nightmare of black velvet Elvis paintings and washcloths posing for bath towels. Or, conversely, maybe you enjoyed that roadside show of tap-dancing chickens and felt it should have been included.

Please send us letters sharing your experiences, your corrections, comments, or suggestions.

New York City Handbook
Moon Travel Handbooks
P.O. Box 3040
Chico, CA 95927-3040
e-mail: travel@moon.com

ABOUT THE BANNERS
The images at the start of a new section or neighborhood are banners.

p. 1	The first viewing of New York, 1642.
p. 27	A night at the Lyceum Theatre.
p. 44	"Steamship Row" (1830), on the site of the Old Custom House.
p. 63	A street vendor on Hester Street, 1870s.
p. 77	The corner of Broadway and Canal Street in 1835.
p. 87	Broadway at 14th Street, 1823.
p. 98	Vagrants lodging in cellars under Greenwich Street, 1869.
p. 112	The triangular intersection of Broadway and Fifth Avenue shortly before the Flatiron Building was built, 1884.
p. 124	House of Clement Clark Moore between Ninth and Tenth Avenues, 22nd and 23rd Streets, 1854.
p. 133	The old Reservoir on Fifth Avenue, 40th to 42nd Street, present site of the Public Library.
p. 157	Blackwell's (now Roosevelt) Island and the East River from 86th Street.
p. 172	Lacrosse game at the original Polo Grounds, just above Central Park at Fifth Avenue and 110 Street.
p. 188	A barbecue at Tammany Hall, Harlem, 1884.
p. 203	The Fulton Ferry slip (before Fulton's Ferry) in 1746.
p. 217	A horse and wagon delivering beer on Main Street, in Flushing, Queens, 1910.
p. 225	Jerome Park in the 1860s, now the West Bronx.
p. 223	A ship being held at Quarantine Point in the bay near Staten Island, late 1800s.

INTRODUCTION
HISTORY

New York is a city people love to hate. It's dirty, it's dangerous, it's crass, and it's loud. It's cynical, corrupt, cold, and uncomfortable. Worst of all, say out-of-towners, there's something un-American about it. All that pushiness, all that traffic, all those people actually choosing to live in ugly apartment buildings with no green front lawns or white picket fences in sight. This can't be the American Dream, or the United States as our forefathers meant it to be. No—New York may be a fine place to visit, but it's no place to live.

New Yorkers don't disagree. In fact, they'll enthusiastically endorse any negative a visitor comes up with, and add a few of their own. New York's transportation system sucks, its taxes are too high, its real estate prices are exorbitant, and poverty is rampant. The school system is falling apart, the middle class is being forced out, the job market is impossible, and everyone is only out for himself. No, New Yorkers sigh, wearily shaking their heads, New York is no place to live . . .

But then again—they arch their eyebrows—it is the *only* place to live.

Imagine New York in the early morning, when a pink light bathes the buildings, and the sky turns from black to baby blue. Imagine New York at rush hour when hundreds of thousands of workers whoosh energetically through the subways and streets. Imagine New York at midday, when the air crackles and pops with imagination and ideas and deals in the making. Imagine New York in the evening, when a quiet calm briefly descends and secrets are exchanged in shadow-filled bars and restaurants. And most of all, imagine New York at night, when the brilliant lights beckon, warding off the darkness, and everything seems possible.

There's no other place quite like New York City. Where else can you find teeming sidewalks at most any hour of the day and night? Where else can you meet people of a dozen nationalities in just a few blocks? Where else can you choose from among over 15,000 restaurants, 150 museums, 400 art galleries, 240 theaters, 50 dance spots, 60 live music spots, 90 institutions of higher learning, and thousands of shops and boutiques?

John Steinbeck may have said it best. New York "is a an ugly city," he wrote, "a dirty city. Its climate is a scandal. Its politics are used to frighten children. Its traffic is madness. Its competition is murderous. But there is one thing about it—once you have lived in New York and it has become your home, no other place is good enough."

Early New York

New York has always been different. It was the only American colony settled by the Dutch, and the only colony settled for economic rather than religious reasons. Ever since the 1600s, people have come to New York City to make money, and they've never been too scrupulous in making it. They've also never cared much about

New Amsterdam

who does the making. For all its occasional outbursts of ethnic and racial violence, New York has long been a tolerant and heterogenous city. As early as 1643, a Jesuit priest visiting the colony reported that among its 500 inhabitants, 18 languages were spoken.

New York City's first human inhabitants were the Algonquin Indians. Several subtribes and local groups, including the Reckgawawanc, Canarsee, and Matinecock, once roamed through the area, planting corn and tobacco and hunting bobcat and wild turkey. Their New York was a land of great abundance, filled with verdant forests and meadows, ice blue streams and ponds, plump fish and game. The upper part of Manhattan was rocky and thick with trees, the lower part grassy and rich with fruits and flowers.

In 1524, explorer Giovanni da Verrazano arrived, sailing into New York Harbor on the *Delfina.* "We found a very pleasant situation amongst some steep hills, through which a very large river, deep at its mouth, forced its way to the sea," Verrazano reported to King Francis I of France, financier of the voyage. "Therefore, we took the boat, and entering the river, we found the country on its banks well peopled, the inhabitants being dressed out with feathers of birds of different colors. They came toward us with evident delight, raising loud shouts of admiration . . ."

However, due to a sudden "violent contrary wind [that] blew in from the sea and forced us to return to our ship," Verrazano never set foot on New York, and King Francis never sent anyone back to explore its "great riches." Not until 1598 did a handful of Dutch traders working summers in Greenland first winter in Manhattan, ensconced in two small forts they built on the southern tip.

Between 1609 and 1611, Englishman Henry Hudson made two voyages to the New World aimed at finding a northwest passage to the Orient. On the first—backed by the Dutch West India Company—Hudson sailed into New York harbor and ventured halfway up the Hudson River before abandoning his quest and returning home. The following year he returned as captain of a British ship. This time he sailed into Hudson Bay, where the ship became icebound. Starving and doubting their captain's navigational abilities, the crew mutinied. They cast Hudson, his son, and several others adrift in a small boat, never to be seen again.

Though unsuccessful in his search for a northwest passage, Hudson proved instrumental in drawing Europeans to the New World. His reports to the Dutch West India Company described the area's abundant natural resources—including a wealth of beaver and mink—and soon a group of Dutch merchants established a trading post on lower Manhattan. The Dutch West India Company was run by the foremost traders of the day and was perhaps the greatest business enterprise ever; the company returned an average annual profit of 18% over 250 years.

Dutch New York

The Dutch named their new outpost Fort Amsterdam and built a fort on the site of what is now the former U.S. Custom House. In 1626, Peter Minuit was appointed first governor of the tiny colony—population 300—and almost immediately bought Manhattan Island from the Algonquins for trinkets worth about $24. The Algonquins considered it a good deal at the time. Having a different sense of ownership than did the Dutch, they thought they were selling only the right to use Algonquin land, not the land itself.

They would soon find out otherwise. Problems between the Algonquins and the Dutch arose quickly. First, Dutch cattle strayed into Indian cornfields, taking a toll on the crops. Then the Dutch tried to impose a tax on the Indians. In

1643, open warfare broke out. The colony, now known as New Amsterdam, applied to Holland for help, and it arrived in the form of arms and men. By 1645, the Indians were no longer an issue.

Unlike their dour fellow colonizers in New England, the Dutch were a fun-loving, easygoing bunch who had to be constantly reminded by their governors not to play tennis when they should be working and not to drink on Sunday when they should be listening to sermons. Both men and women smoked, and as one observer of the day noted, "All drink here from the moment they are able to lick a spoon." In 1644, the Dutch even issued their own Emancipation Proclamation, freeing the black slaves who had arrived in 1625 and 1626, and giving them their own farmland near what is now Greenwich Village. The Dutch themselves were afraid to settle that far north, due to the possibility of Indian attacks.

Dutch control of New York lasted 40 years, with the last and most flamboyant Dutch governor, Peter Stuyvesant, in power 1647-64. Nicknamed "Old Peg Leg," due to a leg lost in battle, Stuyvesant was an arrogant, quick-tempered man with a puritanical streak. He ordered the taverns closed on Sundays and tried to prevent a group of Portuguese Jews from settling in the colony—an action for which he was swiftly reprimanded by his bosses back in Amsterdam.

For all his failings, however, Stuyvesant was responsible for turning the colony into a semblance of a town. He straightened the streets, repaired the fences, and established a night watch. And he was one of the few Dutch colonists who wanted to fight off the English. The rest of the colony didn't much care; the English, who had by this time established a strong presence in New England, had promised the residents of New Amsterdam that if they surrendered, their lives would go on as before. That was just fine with the Dutch merchants. As long as they were making money, it made no difference to them who governed the colony.

Enter and Exit the English
The British took over New Amsterdam in 1664, renaming the city New York after the Duke of York, later crowned King James II. The Dutch system of government was replaced with the British one, but for most of the colonists, life did go on as before. The town continued to prosper and

grow, reaching a population of 25,000 in 1750. In the New World, only Philadelphia was bigger.

For the colonists of African heritage, however, life under British rule became increasingly difficult. Slavery was reinstated, and the slave trade encouraged; a slave market was set up on Wall Street. Some black families had their land confiscated; others lost it after passage of a 1712 law prohibiting blacks from inheriting land.

Elsewhere in the colonies, the initial rumblings of the American Revolution began. When word reached New York, the city first took a pro-Tory stance. Merchants intent on making money wanted nothing to do with war. As tensions escalated, however, New Yorkers changed their position. After 1753, they supported the Revolution completely, rioting against the Stamp Act and burning the British lieutenant governor in effigy.

The earliest battles of the Revolution were fought in New York City. Most notable among them was the Battle of Long Island, in which George Washington tried to defend what is now Brooklyn Heights from the British. Washington was trounced, but managed to retreat up Manhattan with a large enough army to continue the war. The battle also taught him an important lesson: he hadn't a prayer of defeating the professional British soldiers head-on, and would have to resort to guerrilla tactics.

New York remained in the hands of the British throughout the Revolutionary War, and served as an incarceration center. More men perished in the prison ships anchored in Wallabout Bay, just north of Brooklyn, than in all the war's battles combined.

After the war, in 1789, Washington was inaugurated as first president of the United States. The ceremony took place in New York City—in Federal Hall on Wall Street. The city had been designated the fledgling nation's first capital in 1785, and held the honor until 1790, when the federal government was transferred to Philadelphia.

Rise to Power
The years following the Revolution were critical ones for New York City. Between 1790 and 1830, the city gradually transformed itself from one of many important Colonial centers into the largest and wealthiest metropolis in the new republic.

The factors leading to New York's ascendancy were many, but probably the most important was the opening of the Erie Canal in 1825. The canal—stretching from the Hudson River to Lake Erie—established a water route to the West, thereby reducing the cost of transporting goods by a whopping 90%. Hundreds of thousands of small boats were soon plying the new route, carrying cargo to New York City for transfer onto oceangoing vessels. New York Harbor became one of the world's busiest ports, with grain elevators and warehouses sprouting up all along the docks.

About the same time, New York established the country's first regularly scheduled transatlantic shipping service. Previously, ships had sailed only when their holds were full. This innovation gave the metropolis a competitive edge for decades to come.

Manhattan's famous grid street system was established in 1811. All of the island that had not yet been settled was scored into 12 major avenues—each 100 feet wide—and 155 consecutively numbered streets. Most of the streets were 60 feet wide, but those that intersected the already established Broadway when it crossed an avenue were 100 feet wide. Later, when the subway system was built, stops were placed along many of the wider streets.

In 1842, New York opened the Croton Aqueduct Water System, then the world's largest water system. The $12-million project dammed the Croton River, 40 miles upstate, and brought water into the city through a series of reservoirs and aqueducts. New York thus became one of the first cities in the world to supply all its citizens—even the poorest—with clean fresh water. As a result, outbreaks of cholera and other epidemic diseases were drastically reduced. Today, New York still has one of the world's best water systems.

Slavery and Immigration

Reminiscent of its pre-Revolutionary War ambivalence, New York was slow to take a stand on the issues surrounding the Civil War. As a commercial city conducting lucrative business with the cotton-growing states, it often conveniently turned its back on the cruelties of slavery. In fact, New York State was one of the last of the Northern states to abolish slavery, only doing so in 1827.

Nonetheless, New York City had an active free black community that by the mid-1800s had established many prominent churches, schools, theaters, and other institutions. Many of the city's middle-class blacks were active in the Underground Railroad—the network of abolitionists who helped fugitive Southern slaves reach freedom in the North.

The pre-Civil War years also witnessed the influx of the first of the great waves of immigrants that swept into the city between the mid-1800s and the 1920s. From 1840 to 1855, over three million Irish and Germans arrived. Many of the Irish were escaping the potato famines, many of the Germans the failed Revolution of 1848.

When the Civil War began, New York officially supported the Union. But the citizenry remained divided. The city's newest immigrants particularly resented having to fight to free slaves, who might then come north and compete for jobs. In 1863, this deep-rooted discontent led to the Draft Riots, in which 2,000 people were injured or killed.

After the war, the infamous William Marcy "Boss" Tweed came to power in New York City. A tough street fighter, Tweed became America's first "political boss." He never held mayoral office, but he controlled the city from behind the scenes, through the Democratic machine known as Tammany Hall. During Tweed's corrupt reign, from 1866 to 1871, he and his henchmen pocketed as much as $200 million from padded or fraudulent city expenditures and tax improprieties. Eventually indicted, Tweed died in a Ludlow Street jail not far from his birthplace.

All That Glitters

By the late 1800s, New York was in its full glory. In 1892, 1,265 millionaires lived either in the city or its suburbs. In 1895, the city housed nearly 300 companies

Boss Tweed

BOB RACE

worth over one million dollars—more than the next six largest cities combined. In 1898, New York annexed Brooklyn, Queens, Staten Island, and the Bronx, thereby increasing its area from 23 to 301 square miles.

The rich and the powerful flocked to New York from all over the country, and the social elite were soon defined as the "Four Hundred"—the maximum number of guests who could squeeze into Mrs. Astor's Fifth Avenue ballroom. Investment bankers such as J.P. Morgan and August Belmont became household names, as did leaders of commerce and industry such as John D. Rockefeller, Andrew Carnegie, and F.W. Woolworth.

New York became the nation's cultural capital as well. Theaters sprang up along Broadway, and the Metropolitan Museum of Art and the Metropolitan Opera opened their doors in 1880 and 1890, respectively. Walt Whitman sang the city's praises in poems such as "Leaves of Grass" and "Crossing Brooklyn Ferry," and Henry James and Edith Wharton reported on the lives of the upper crust in books such as *Washington Square* and *The Age of Innocence.*

But the years surrounding the turn of the century also had a darker side. Between 1880 and 1919, a new wave of more than 17 million immigrants—this time mainly from Southern and Eastern Europe—swept into New York. In his 1890 book, *How the Other Half Lives,* Jacob Riis wrote, "A map of the city, colored to designate nationalities, would show more stripes than on the skin of a zebra, and more colors than any rainbow." Many settled in the Lower East Side, where they worked miserable, low-paying jobs in the garment industry. Overcrowding became a serious problem; by 1900, more than two-thirds of the city's residents were crowded into some 80,000 tenements in Manhattan and Brooklyn. The Lower East Side

had a population density of 209,000 people per square mile, equal to that of today's Bombay.

In 1904, Manhattan opened its first subway, long after London (1863) and shortly after Boston (1897). But New York's subway system would soon be distinguished for both its enormous size and its technological innovations. Within a year after opening, New York's subway—then just a single line running up Park Avenue, across 42nd Street, and up Broadway—was carrying over 600,000 passengers per day. By 1937, the city boasted over 700 miles of track handling 4.2 million passengers per day. Today, the subway system still has about 700 miles of track, but it handles only about 3.5 million passengers a day.

Prosperity
After WW I, the U.S. emerged as a world power, and nowhere was this newfound status more evident than in dazzling New York. Business and manufacturing flourished. The Jazz Age arrived and the liquor flowed. F. Scott Fitzgerald came to town, and Jimmy Walker was elected mayor. A dandified gentleman with a taste for the good life, Walker spent most of his time visiting nightclubs, sporting halls, and showgirls. Thanks to his late-night carousing, he rarely appeared at City Hall before 3 p.m., if at all. "No civilized man," he once said, "goes to bed the same day he wakes up."

The strict new immigration laws of 1921 and 1924 slowed the influx of foreigners to a trickle, but Harlem boomed as black Southerners fleeing poverty took refuge in the city. In 1910, Manhattan was home to about 60,000 blacks; by 1930, that number had tripled. Harlem became the center for African American culture, with the Harlem Renaissance attracting writers and intellectuals such as Langston Hughes and W.E.B. DuBois, and the jazz

BOB RACE

ROBERT MOSES, MASTER BUILDER

City Parks Commissioner Robert Moses—part civil servant, part evil genius—was one of the most unusual and controversial figures in New York's history. Though a nonelected official, he wielded enormous political power extending far beyond his office, the city, and even the state.

In power for 44 years (1924-68), Moses conceived of and executed major public works costing $27 billion, thereby shaping virtually the entire modern landscape of New York. He was responsible for all but one of the city's major expressways, most of Long Island's parkways and beaches, thousands of public housing units, and over 600 playgrounds and parks. Literally hundreds of major construction projects were completed during his tenure, among them the Henry Hudson, Bronx-Whitestone, Cross Bay, Throgs Neck, Verrazano Narrows, Marine Parkway, and Triborough Bridges; the Brooklyn-Battery Tunnel; Lincoln Center; the New York Coliseum; Shea Stadium; Co-Op City; the United Nations; the giant dams at the St. Lawrence and Niagara Rivers; and both the 1939 and 1964 World's Fairs.

According to biographer Robert Caro, Moses began his career as a visionary idealist yearning to bring about social change but ended it as a power-hungry tyrant who would stop at nothing to achieve his goals. To build his highways, he evicted over 250,000 people and destroyed scores of neighborhoods; the housing he designed for the poor was "bleak, sterile, cheap"; his World's Fairs cost the city hundreds of thousands of dollars; his highways sapped funding for the subways and created the mess of a transportation system New York suffers from today.

Writes Caro in *The Power Broker*, "Robert Moses was America's greatest builder. He was the shaper of the greatest city in the New World. But what did he build? What was the shape into which he pounded the city? . . . It is impossible to say that New York would have been a better city if Robert Moses had never lived. It is possible to say only that it would have been a different city."

Moses died in 1981 at the age of 92.

BOB RACE

clubs and theaters attracting the likes of Duke Ellington and Chick Webb.

All this high living crashed with little warning in October 1929, when the stock market collapsed. Overnight, the gaiety stopped and the Depression began. By 1932, one out of every four New Yorkers was unemployed, and scores of shantytowns called "Hoovervilles" dotted Central Park.

But the city didn't stay down for long. That same year, Fiorello La Guardia was elected mayor. La Guardia—regarded by many historians as the best mayor New York ever had—set about cleaning up corruption, imposing stiff taxes, and obtaining moneys through FDR's New Deal programs. Together with Parks Commissioner Robert Moses, La Guardia embarked on an enormous public works program that transformed the city both physically and economically. The nation's entry into WW II in 1941 also gave New York a much needed economic jolt.

During the war, Columbia University at 116th St. and Broadway was the site of a nuclear experiment conducted by Dr. Robert Oppenheimer. Code-named the "Manhattan Project," the experiment led to the creation of the world's first atomic bomb, dropped on Japan in Aug. 1945.

Post-War Decline

Despite the prosperity brought to New York by WW II, the city reached its economic peak relative to the rest of the country around 1940. Thereafter, certain trends already in effect began to undermine both New York and the entire Northeast. These trends would not become visible for many years, but they were there, slowly eating away.

In 1880, 16% of all U.S. production workers lived in the New York Metropolitan Region. By 1900, that figure had fallen to 14%, and by 1990, it had fallen to four percent. Between 1956 and 1985, the region lost over 600,000 industrial jobs, most in small, light-industrial businesses such as glass-making and textile manufacturing. Unlike most cities, New York has always been dominated by small businesses. Some of these companies left the city due to demographic shifts towards the South and West, others due to technological changes that allowed them to decentralize. Still others fled from the rising cost of doing business in New York.

During this same period, New York's once-thriving port also declined. The advent of containerships—which require large dockside cranes for loading—spelled its death. New York's old shipyards simply did not have the space needed to maneuver the cranes. In addition, the Brooklyn Naval Yard—a major employer since before the Civil War—closed in 1968.

With these economic shifts came considerable social unrest. The declining number of manufacturing jobs, coupled with continuing immigration of poor blacks and Puerto Ricans, resulted in racial disturbances and an increase in crime, which frightened the middle class. Between 1950 and 1970, over one million families left the city in the "Great White Flight," further eroding the once-stable tax base.

On the up side, New York's cultural scene was thriving. The Guggenheim Museum opened in 1959, followed by Lincoln Center in the mid-'60s. Broadway was producing one great hit after another—including *My Fair Lady* and *West Side Story*—and the publishing and television industries were booming. "Culture had become a commodity," wrote historian Harold Syrett, "and New Yorkers were its largest producers. Most other Americans had to be content with being consumers."

Fiscal Crisis and Rebound

Things came to a head in 1975. Cultural attractions aside, New York was all but bankrupt. Banks shut off credit, and the city, in desperation, turned to the federal government for help. The famous *Daily News* headline, "Ford to City: Drop Dead," caustically summed up Washington's stony response.

The city was temporarily rescued by the Municipal Assistance Corporation, put together by financier Felix Rohatyn and Gov. Hugh Carey to issue city bonds and thereby borrow money. Washington was impressed enough by this effort to finally extend the city a short-term loan of $2.5 billion.

The city's recovery was further aided in 1978 by the election of Mayor Ed Koch. A one-time liberal from the Bronx via Greenwich Village, Koch helped set the city back on track through budget cuts and austerity programs. Brash, shrewd, and outspoken, Koch managed to play the city's various interest groups off one another to the general public's advantage, winning the respect of many New Yorkers in the process. Much of the '80s' construction boom, which included Trump Tower and the World Financial Center, was attributed to his efforts. Unfortunately, so was the city's steadily increasing homeless population.

Koch was reelected twice. But by 1990, the city was fed up with his egotistical style, neglect of the poor, and insensitivity to racial issues. In his stead was elected David Dinkins, the city's first black mayor. The consummate party politician, Dinkins succeeded in implementing several important anticrime programs. But overall, his indecisive governing style did not sit well with most New Yorkers. In 1994, he was defeated by Rudolph Giuliani, a tough, former U.S. attorney who soon surprised the predominantly Democratic city by supporting Democrat Mario Cuomo instead of fellow Republican George Pataki in the 1994 gubernatorial election. Many later Giuliani decisions, such as his ouster of police commissioner William Bratton (apparently for outshining the mayor), have not proven as popular.

Today and Tomorrow

New York faces all the urban woes of most cities, and then some. As one of the largest and oldest industrialized cities, it's plagued with some of the largest and oldest problems. Poverty, crime, drugs, pollution, racial strife, a deteriorating infrastructure, a fleeing tax base, a skyrocketing real estate market, AIDS—all are urban ills that New York seems almost to have invented before passing them along all too generously to other cities. And none of these problems will be going away soon. The city has been running an enormous budget deficit for years, with no relief in sight. In addition, Gotham's job market—once a solid mix of manufacturing and business concerns—has been steadily bifurcating over the past two decades into service jobs paying too little for a mature adult to live on, and white-collar positions requiring highly advanced skills. In short, the middle class is being squeezed out of the city it created.

When describing New York City in 1900, Theodore Dreiser wrote, "The strong, or those who ultimately dominated, were so very strong, and the weak so very weak." Those same words still apply today, as the chasm between the haves and the have-nots continues to widen. According to the 1990 census, the mean income of the poorest 10% of Manhattan families was only about $3,000, while among the upper 10% it was nearly $200,000—66 times as high. In contrast, in 1980, the top 10th was only 48 times richer than the poorest 10th; in 1970, 39 times. Some Manhattanites routinely partake of $50 meals, while nearly 15,000 of the island's housing units lack complete plumbing and nearly 46,000 have no phones. In the other boroughs, poverty is even more widespread. One in every four New York City residents is poor—the highest percentage since the Depression.

With such statistics, it's not surprising that homelessness is a major problem. Some estimate the city's homeless population to be close to 300,000. And whereas a decade ago most New Yorkers were outraged by the plight of the homeless, now most pass by the down-and-out without taking notice. Feelings of guilt, annoyance, and helplessness—together with the sheer numbers of the homeless—have inured the middle-class to the destitute.

On a more positive note, New York City is less polluted today than it was a decade ago, due largely to increased public concern and federal mandates. Recycling is now in effect citywide, and the Hudson River is cleaner than it's been in years; fishing, never completely abandoned by the poor, is regaining popularity.

Crime in the city is also down. According to FBI statistics, New York doesn't even make the top-25 list of cities with the highest homicide rates anymore, and its overall crime rate is declining three to six times more rapidly than the

> *"Life in New York follows the neighborhood pattern. The city is literally a composite of tens of thousands of tiny neighborhood units. There are, of course, the big districts and big units: Chelsea and Murray Hill and Gramercy . . . But the curious thing about New York is that each large geographical unit is composed of countless small neighborhoods. Each neighborhood is virtually self-sufficient. Usually it is no more than two or three blocks long and a couple of blocks wide. Each area is a city within a city within a city. Thus, no matter where you live in New York, you will find within a block or two a grocery store, a barbershop, a newsstand . . ."*
>
> —E.B. WHITE

rest of the country's. The subways have become cleaner and safer—crime underground has dropped nearly 50% since 1990—and certain neighborhoods once written off as beyond hope are actually on the rebound.

Now is an especially exciting time here as the city teems with yet another enormous influx of immigrants. Many have been steadily arriving since the easing of immigration quotas in 1965; others have come since the end of the Cold War, or following political upheaval in their home countries. Some 90,000 documented immigrants enter the city each year, and one out of every three New Yorkers is foreign born.

These new immigrants are transforming the city. Between 1965 and 1990, the city's Chinese population more than quadrupled, to an estimated 250,000. Since 1989, the Russian presence has exploded from a small group of émigrés to a community of over 100,000. Many of the city's doctors and medical technicians now hail from India, Korea, or the Middle East, while many of its nurses come from the West Indies, Korea, or the Philippines. The Koreans have a corner on the fruit markets, while immigrants from India control the newsstands. Almost half of the city's cab drivers are from India, Pakistan, or Bangladesh; another third are from Eastern Europe and Russia.

More important than statistics, however, is the energy and spirit immigrants bring with them. Into a city that sometimes seems about to topple from the sheer weight of excess sophistication, solipsism, wealth, and hype, the immigrants bring a much-needed freshness. Some might be working menial jobs today, but rest assured that their children won't be working those menial jobs tomorrow. And as the immigrants and their offspring weave their way into the warp and woof of the city's fabric, they revitalize Gotham's brilliance and ensure its future.

For all its concrete and steel, New York is an ephemeral, shape-shifting city. See it in one light and its streets are paved with gold; see it in another, and it's the antechamber to hell. Hold on long enough, however, and the city will reveal to you neither splendor nor decay, but something resembling its eclectic, energetic, rainbow-hued soul, slipping around the corner just in front of you somewhere only to disappear again into the crowds.

THE BOROUGHS: AN OVERVIEW

New York City, official population 7.3 million, is made up of five boroughs—Manhattan, Brooklyn, Queens, the Bronx, and Staten Island—covering a total of 301 square miles. Only the northernmost borough, the Bronx, sits on the mainland; the rest of the city is spread out over a group of islands in New York Bay, where the Hudson River meets the Atlantic Ocean. Manhattan and Staten Island are islands in their own right. Brooklyn and Queens are on the western tip of Long Island.

Queens is the largest borough in area (118 square miles), followed by Brooklyn (78.5 square miles), Staten Island (61 square miles), the Bronx (43 square miles), and Manhattan (23 square miles). By population, Brooklyn takes top spot with 2.3 million residents, followed by Queens (1.9 million), Manhattan (1.5 million), the Bronx (1.2 million), and Staten Island (just 379,000).

Between Staten Island and Brooklyn runs the Verrazano Narrows, a strait separating the upper and lower parts of New York Bay. Manhattan lies in upper New York Bay and is separated from the mainland by the East River to the east, the Hudson River to the west, and the Harlem River and Spuyten Duyvil to the northeast. Technically, the East River isn't a river at all, but a strait running between Long Island Sound and New York Bay.

Manhattan

Manhattan is the epicenter of New York City. Its preeminent status among the boroughs is evidenced by the fact that when people speak of "the boroughs," they're usually referring to the *other* boroughs, outside Manhattan.

The island is 12 miles long and three miles wide and scored by a grid of streets (running east-west) and avenues (running north-south). "Downtown" generally refers to anything south of 14th St., "Midtown" to addresses between 34th and 59th Sts., and "Uptown" to areas above 59th Street. "Downtown" also translates as the hip, bohemian, and avant garde; "Midtown" as high-rise offices and the corporate world; and "Uptown" as either the sophisticated and the well-heeled or the ethnic worlds of the Harlems, depending on whom you're talking to. These shorthand definitions hardly do justice to

the island's complexities, but they're true enough to be part of every New Yorker's lexicon.

The East Side encompasses everything east of Fifth Ave.; the West Side, everything to the west. The East Side has the reputation of being stuffier, wealthier, and less interesting than the West, but again, this is a generalization of limited utility.

Virtually all of New York's world-famous tourist attractions are concentrated in Manhattan, including the World Trade Center, the Empire State Building, Rockefeller Center, Central Park, and the Metropolitan Museum of Art.

Brooklyn

A separate city until 1898, Brooklyn boasts its own civic centers, cultural institutions, downtown shopping district, and residential neighborhoods. Among its many visitor attractions are the Brooklyn Museum, Brooklyn Botanical Gardens, Brooklyn Academy of Music, Aquarium for Wildlife Conservation, and Coney Island boardwalk.

Queens

A largely residential borough that many Manhattanites once dismissed as a snore, Queens is now one of the most ethnically diverse sections of the city. Ethnic neighborhoods here include Greek Astoria, Latino Jackson Heights, and Asian Flushing. Flushing Meadow-Corona Park and Shea Stadium are among the borough's biggest attractions.

The Bronx

The only borough that's connected to the mainland, the Bronx holds some of the city's worst pockets of urban decay, along with its biggest parks—among them the Bronx Zoo, New York Botanical Garden, Van Cortlandt Park, and Pelham Bay Park. Yankee Stadium's here, too.

Staten Island

Largely residential, Staten Island is the most rural and isolated of the boroughs, and the only one whose residents speak longingly of seceding from New York City. Its major visitor attractions are historic Richmond Town, the Jacques Marchais Museum of Tibetan Art, and the Staten Island ferry.

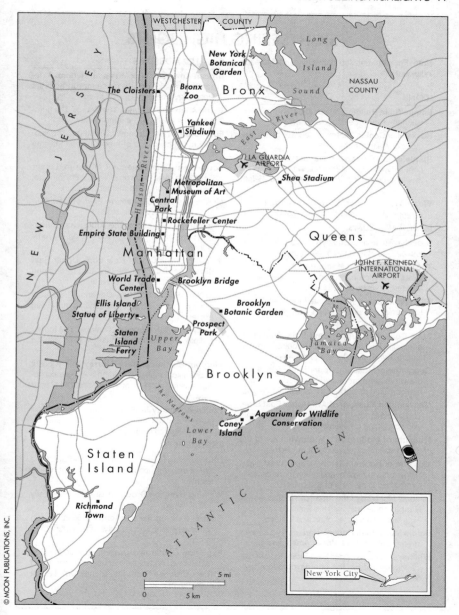

WESTCHESTER COUNTY

New York Botanical Garden

The Cloisters

Bronx Zoo

Bronx

Long Island

NASSAU COUNTY

Sound

Yankee Stadium

East River

LA GUARDIA AIRPORT

Shea Stadium

Metropolitan Museum of Art

Central Park

Rockefeller Center

Empire State Building

Hudson River

Manhattan

Queens

JOHN F. KENNEDY INTERNATIONAL AIRPORT

World Trade Center

Brooklyn Bridge

Ellis Island
Statue of Liberty

Brooklyn Botanic Garden

Prospect Park

Staten Island Ferry

Upper Bay

Jamaica Bay

NEW JERSEY

Brooklyn

The Narrows

Aquarium for Wildlife Conservation

Coney Island

Lower Bay

ATLANTIC OCEAN

Staten Island

Richmond Town

0   5 mi

0   5 km

New York City

© MOON PUBLICATIONS, INC.

SIGHTSEEING HIGHLIGHTS

Note: For more detailed information, refer to each individual site.

ICONS

Empire State Building, West 30s. Come at night, when the views are especially fine.

Rockefeller Center, Midtown. New York's most famous city within a city.

Statue of Liberty, Lower Manhattan. The eminent lady stands 151 feet tall, with a three-foot mouth, an eight-foot index finger, and a 25-foot waist.

World Trade Center, Lower Manhattan. Now equipped with an elaborate new visitors center.

MAJOR MUSEUMS

Brooklyn Museum, Brooklyn. Though often overlooked, one of the city's finest museums.

The Cloisters, Upper Manhattan. The Met's medieval art collection, housed in a monastic setting with terrific views of the Hudson.

Ellis Island, Lower Manhattan. More than 12 million immigrants once passed through here; now a state-of-the-art museum.

Frick Collection, Upper East Side. Former industrialist Henry Clay Frick's fabulous art collection, hung inside his elegant mansion.

Guggenheim Museum, Upper East Side. A top-drawer modern art museum, housed in a landmark building designed by Frank Lloyd Wright.

Metropolitan Museum of Art, Upper East Side. The granddaddy of New York City museums, with something for everyone.

Museum of Modern Art, Midtown. One of the world's foremost museums of modern art.

Museum of Natural History, Upper West Side. Dinosaurs, mammals, and much more; recently refurbished to the tune of $12 million.

National Museum of the American Indian, Lower Manhattan. A branch of the Smithsonian, holding a superb collection of art and artifacts.

Studio Museum of Harlem, Harlem. The nation's foremost museum of African American art.

Whitney Museum, Upper East Side. Another outstanding museum, this one devoted to American art.

SMALLER MUSEUMS

African American Wax Museum, Harlem. A delightfully quirky private museum run by artist Raven Chanticleer.

Edgar Allan Poe Cottage, The Bronx. The humble 1840s abode of the famed writer.

Forbes Galleries, Greenwich Village. The idiosyncratic collections of media tycoon Malcom Forbes.

Lower East Side Tenement Museum, Lower East Side. A re-creation of early immigrant life, housed in an original tenement building.

Merchant's House Museum, East Village. Furnished exactly as it was in 1835.

Museum of Chinese in the Americas, Chinatown. Intriguing exhibits focusing on personal stories.

Museum of the City of New York, Upper East Side. The history of the city, told through an eclectic collection of art and artifacts.

New York Hall of Science, Queens. The largest array of hands-on science exhibits in the Big Apple.

Noguchi Garden Museum, Queens. The former sculptor's studio, now a museum filled with his work.

Pierpont Morgan Library, Murray Hill. A posh, neoclassical mansion holding a superb collection of illuminated manuscripts and Old Master drawings.

Police Academy Museum, East 20s. Antique guns, Al Capone's marriage certificate, and "recently acquired contraband weapons."

EXPERIENCES

Birdwatching in the Ramble, Central Park. On a typical morning, about 35 different species can be seen.

Walking over the Brooklyn Bridge. Especially fine at twilight.

Central Park on the weekends. Fun in the sun with every size, shape, color, and make of humanity.

Exploring Chinatown. Jostling crowds, teeming restaurants, and exotic markets, including **Pearl River Chinese Products,** Chinatown's largest department store.

Coney Island, Brooklyn. A magnificent boardwalk, tawdry amusement rides, a bustling Russian community, and **Sideshows by the Sea**, presenting snake ladies, fire eaters, and escape artists.

Eating in the East Village. Restaurants, restaurants, and more restaurants, many of them ethnic and cheap.

Eating along Ninth Avenue. More ethnic noshing.

Fulton Fish Market, Lower Manhattan. Boisterous, smelly, and fishy—best before dawn.

Author Avenue, The Bronx. An old Italian enclave chock-a-block with restaurants, many of them ethnic and cheap.

Meandering through the West Village. Cozy shops and restaurants, jazz clubs, and historic buildings.

Mets' and Yankees' games. New Yorkers at their most serious.

SoHo on a weekend afternoon. The city's trendiest neighborhood, crowded with fashionables.

Riding the Staten Island Ferry, Lower Manhattan. Spectacular views 24 hours a day.

Times Square at night. More neon lights than anyplace else in America except the Las Vegas strip.

Weekend flea markets, Chelsea. One part treasure, one part junk.

Chess Shop, Greenwich Village. Where the obsessed go to play.

Leisure Time Bowling, Port Authority Bus Terminal, Midtown. An old-time bowling alley; one of the last in Manhattan.

ENVIRONMENTS

Aquarium for Wildlife Conservation, Brooklyn. Walruses, beluga whales, sharks, sea otters, dolphins, electric eels, stingrays . . .

Bronx Zoo. One of the world's largest zoos, housing over 4,000 animals; next door is the equally impressive **New York Botanical Garden.**

Brooklyn Botanic Garden. A beloved institution, spread out over 50 meticulously landscaped acres.

City Island, The Bronx. A little piece of nautical New England transported south.

Conservancy Garden, Central Park. A lovely, formal spot in bloom from early spring through late fall.

Gramercy Park, East 20s. An enclosed private park, surrounded by elegant townhouses.

The Promenade, Brooklyn. Great views of Manhattan.

Socrates Sculpture Garden, Long Island City, Queens. More great views of Manhattan, along with wacky works of sculpture.

Washington Square Park, Greenwich Village. Still the heart of New York's bohemia.

Woodlawn Cemetery, Bronx. Lush, rolling hills studded with the elaborate mausoleums of famous New Yorkers.

World Financial Center/Battery Park City Promenade, Lower Manhattan. An elongated park to one side, the whitecaps of the Hudson River to the other.

ENTERTAINMENT

Amateur Night at the Apollo, Harlem. A tradition since the 1930s.

Broadway plays, Midtown. A quintessential New York experience.

Jazz in Greenwich Village. Ditto.

Free performances in Central Park. Music, theater, and dance beneath the stars.

Poetry readings, music clubs, and Off-Off-Broadway theater, East Village. Where anything goes.

Russian nightclubs, Brighton Beach, Brooklyn. Non-stop vodka and dancing on the tabletops.

ONLY IN NEW YORK

Riverbank State Park, Harlem. A 23-acre state-of-the-art park built on top of a sewage treatment plant.

Broken Kilometer, SoHo. An enormous, darkened room filled with 500 polished brass rods and changing art exhibits.

Justice-of-the-peace weddings, Municipal Building, Lower Manhattan. As many as 14,000 couples get married here every year.

New York Panorama, Queens Museum of Art. A scale model of the city, showing some 895,000 buildings.

Night court, Criminal Courts Building, Lower Manhattan. Where arraignments take place after hours.

Russian and Turkish baths, East Village. Traditional Old World baths, filled with saunas, steam rooms, and massage rooms.

ORIENTATION

ACCOMMODATIONS

From Budget to Extravagant

Cheap sleeps are not readily available in New York City except to students and those willing to rough it, and even then the options are limited. An inexpensive hotel in the Big Apple costs $80-100 a night, while a moderately priced one, with standard "nothing special" rooms, costs $100-175. To add to the bad news, hotel rates in 1996 were the highest they've been in 15 years, and rose, on average, another 10% in the first quarter of 1997.

Nonetheless, relatively inexpensive hotel rooms can be found, especially if you reserve early enough. One good area in which to look is between 23rd and 34th Streets near Fifth Avenue (see "From Union Square to Murray Hill" and "Chelsea and the Garment District," in the Manhattan chapter). Though this is a desolate area late at night, it's centrally located and not particularly dangerous as long as you stay alert. Other good neighborhoods for relatively inexpensive lodging are the Theater District in Midtown and the Upper West Side.

At the other end of the economic scale, New York is a glittering wonderland, home to some of the world's grandest hotels. The Plaza, Pierre, Four Seasons, and St. Regis are among the reigning monarchs. Even if you can't afford to stay in these elegant hostelries—and at $350-500 a night, who can?—they're well worth stepping into for afternoon tea, a drink, or just a look-see.

Bed and Breakfast Inns

Though not necessarily cheaper than an inexpensive or moderately priced hotel, a B&B can be a good, friendly alternative. Some New York City B&Bs are the traditional kind—a room or two in a host's home. Others are entire apartments that you'll have completely to yourself. Double rooms usually run $70-90/night; unhosted apartments $90-150/night. The cheapest B&Bs are in the boroughs. Reservations should be made a few weeks in advance.

Several B&B registries operate in the city. **Urban Ventures,** tel. (212) 594-5650, is the oldest and most established with over 700 listings, all in Manhattan. The **Bed and Breakfast Network of New York,** tel. (212) 645-8134, has about 300 listings citywide, while **New World Bed and Breakfast,** tel. (212) 675-5600 or (800) 443-3800, has about 150. **City Lights Bed & Breakfast,** tel. (212) 737-7049, and **At Home in New York,** tel. (212) 956-3125, both match mostly artists and professionals with like-minded hosts.

Hostels, YMCAs, and Dorms

New York has an American Youth Hostel on the Upper West Side, as well as a number of independent hostels unaffiliated with AYH. Hostels can't be beat for budget travelers willing to live with the communal atmosphere. YMCAs, tel. (800) FIT-YMCA, are another alternative for the budget conscious. Rooms should be reserved about two months in advance, and rates include use of the athletic facilities.

In summer, clean and inexpensive rooms are also available in some of the city's university dorms.

Getting the Most for Your Money

Before you book, ask about discounts. Almost no one pays full rack rates in New York, and most hotels offer at least a corporate discount. Many business and luxury hotels also offer substantial weekend discounts—as much as a third off regular rates. Off-season or long-term packages are sometimes available as well.

Another option is to use a booking service. These companies buy large blocks of rooms at a discount and pass on the savings (as high as 40%) to consumers. Three of the best of these companies are Quikbook, tel. (800) 789-9887, Express Reservations, tel. (800) 356-1123, and the Hotel Reservations Network, tel. (800) 964-6835. Oxbridge Property Services, tel. (212) 840-8100, provides furnished apartments for stays of a week or more.

A welcome new service offered by the New York Convention and Visitors Bureau is the free **Peak Season Hotel Hotline,** tel. (800) 846-7666 or (212) 582-3352. In operation Sept. 1-Dec. 31—a traditionally busy period for New

York hotels—the hotline matches visitors with hotels in various locations and price ranges.

Keep in mind that in addition to the room rate, you'll also have to pay a hefty tax. Although New York State finally reduced hotel taxes by five percent in 1994, and New York City by another one percent later that same year, Gotham's hotel tax is still 13.25%, plus two dollars.

Be sure to book your accommodations well in advance, especially if you're hoping to stay in an inexpensive hotel. During the early summer and the Christmas holidays in particular, rooms go fast.

The prices quoted in this book are the current rack rates for a double room, but as these change frequently, the general categories of Cheap (under $60), Inexpensive (under $100), Moderate ($100-175), Expensive ($175-275), and Luxury (over $275) are also used.

FOOD

New York boasts about 15,000 restaurants. Some come and go almost overnight, while others have been around for decades. A few rules of thumb: The East Village is an excellent neighborhood for cheap eats and ethnic restaurants; SoHo, TriBeCa, and Columbus Ave. boast lots of trendy spots; and Midtown and the Upper East Side are home to some of the city's most venerable and expensive restaurants.

For coffee and dessert suggestions, see "Light Bites" under the district headings in the Manhattan chapter. A number of bars in New York are also good spots for casual meals; see "Watering Holes" under the district headings.

SERVICES

Emergencies

Dial 911 for emergency **police, ambulance,** or **fire department** response. If you're calling from a pay phone, you'll need a quarter. The sex crimes report line is (212) 267-7273. The crime victims hotline is (212) 577-7777.

Private hospitals with 24-hour emergency rooms include **St. Vincent's Hospital,** Seventh Ave. at 11th St., tel. (212) 604-7000; **Beth Israel Medical Center,** First Ave. at 16th St., tel. (212) 420-2000; **New York University Medical Cen-**

SECRET GARDENS AND SIDEWALK CAFES

SECRET GARDENS

Barolo, SoHo/Mod.-Exp.
Bell Cafe, SoHo/Inexp.
Trattoria Vente Tre, SoHo/Inexp.-Mod.
Provence, SoHo/Exp.
Miracle Grill, E. Village/Mod.
Yaffa Cafe, E. Village/Inexp.
Lanza, E. Village/Mod.
Chelsea Commons, Chelsea/Inexp.
Gascogne, Chelsea/Exp.
Luna Park, Union Sq./Mod.
Barbetta, Midtown West/Exp.
Tavern on the Green, Central Park/Exp.
Telly's Taverna, Astoria, Queens/Mod.

SIDEWALK CAFES

Felix's, SoHo/Exp.
Le Pescadou, SoHo/Exp.
Life Cafe, E. Village/Inexp.
7A, E. Village/Inexp.
Time Cafe, E. Village/Mod.
Mappamondo II, W. Village/Inexp.-Mod.
Coffee Shop, Union Sq./Mod.
Arizona 206 Cafe, Upper East/Mod.
Saloon, Upper West/Mod.
Cleopatra's, Upper West/Mod.

---

ter, First Ave. at 34th St., tel. (212) 263-7300; **St. Luke's-Roosevelt Hospital,** Ninth Ave. at 58th St., tel. (212) 523-4000; **New York Hospital,** York Ave. at 68th St., tel. (212) 746-5454; and **Mount Sinai Hospital,** Fifth Ave. at 100th St., tel. (212) 241-6500.

Post Offices

Many post offices are open weekdays 8 a.m.-6 p.m., and Sat. 8 a.m.-1 p.m., but hours vary from branch to branch. The city's main post office on Eighth Ave. at 33rd St. is open 24 hours a day, seven days a week. For general post office information, call (212) 967-8585.

Telephones

Public phones in various states of distress are available on many street corners, but when you do find one that works, there's often a queue. In Midtown, hotel phones are a good alternative.

For **directory assistance** in Manhattan, call 411. For directory assistance in the other boroughs, call (718) 555-1212.

Other useful numbers include **time,** tel. (212) 976-1616; **weather,** tel. (212) 976-1212; and **wake-up calls,** tel. (212) 540-WAKE (9253).

Restrooms

Public restrooms can be difficult to find in New York. The city plans to put public toilets on the sidewalks, but at the moment, your best bet is to duck into a major hotel, department store, or public institution such as a library. Restaurants are also worth a try, although they often reserve their facilities for patrons.

Some of the most accessible public restrooms in Manhattan are at the World Trade Center (Church to West Sts., concourse level), the New York City Housing Authority (5 Park Pl., bet. Broadway and Church, 2nd Fl.), Cooper Union (41 Cooper Square, near Third Ave. and 8th St., downstairs), the New York Public Library (Fifth Ave. and 42nd St., ground and third floors), the GE Building (30 Rockefeller Pl., concourse level), Citicorp Center (153 Lexington Ave., at 53rd St., lower level), Trump Tower (725 Fifth Ave., at 56th St., downstairs), the 92nd Street Y (1395 Lexington Ave., at 92nd St., ground level), and Mart 125 (260 W. 125th St., near Adam Clayton Powell Jr. Blvd., 2nd Fl., key available at any counter).

Gay and Lesbian Services

The **Gay and Lesbian Community Services Center,** 208 W. 13th St., bet. Seventh and Eighth Aves., tel. (212) 620-7310, hosts frequent events and meetings. Numerous organizations are also headquartered here, including the Lesbian Switchboard (Mon.-Fri. 6-10 p.m., tel. 212-741-2610), which lists up-to-the-minute information on everything from clubs to accommodations.

Services for the Disabled

New York is a difficult city for visitors with disabilities to navigate, but help is available. One source is the **Mayor's Office for People with Disabilities,** tel. (212) 788-2830, which puts out a free Access Guide. Another is **Hospital Audiences, Inc.,** tel. (212) 575-7676, which publishes a guide to the city's cultural institutions that includes information on elevators, ramps, Braille signage, services for the hearing impaired, and restroom facilities. For more general information, contact the **Society for the Advancement of Travel for the Handicapped,** 347 Fifth Ave., New York, NY 10016, tel. (212) 447-7284, a nationwide, nonprofit membership organization that collects data on travel facilities around the country.

Two hundred of the 500 volunteer "Big Apple Greeters" are specifically trained to help the handicapped enjoy the city. The Big Apple Greeter program, available free to all visitors, matches out-of-towners with New Yorkers eager to share their hometown. The Big Apple Greeters can also provide handicapped visitors with resource lists and answer questions regarding accessibility. For more information, call (212) 669-3602 or 669-8273.

All of New York's buses are wheelchair accessible, but only a handful of subway stations are. For more information, call New York City Transit, tel. (718) 596-8585, and request copies of the free brochures *Accessible Travel* and *Accessible Transfer Points Within the NYC Subway.*

INFORMATION

Tourist Information

The **New York Convention and Visitors Bureau,** tel. (212) 397-8222 or (800) NYCVISIT (800-692-8474), operates a visitor information center in the lobby of the well-marked Embassy Theater on Broadway between 46th and 47th Sts. (note: phone numbers may change in late 1997). The center is open 365 days a year, Mon.-Fri. 9 a.m.-6 p.m., Sat.-Sun 10 a.m.-3 p.m. Maps, hundreds of brochures, and calendars of events are available. The staff is multilingual. Also in the Embassy's lobby is the **Times Square Visitors Center,** tel. (212) 869-5453.

Smaller **visitor information booths** are located at 2 World Trade Center, Grand Central Station (42nd St. and Vanderbilt Ave.), and the JFK Airport International Arrivals building.

Publications

New York City has three major daily newspapers— *The New York Times,* the *Daily News,* and the *New York Post.* The *Times* is the country's unof-

BOB RACE

Among magazines, **New York, The New Yorker,** and the new **Time Out New York** cover the city extensively. *New York* is mostly lightweight mainstream patter, with entertaining articles, good reviews, and a solid events listing. *The New Yorker* is renowned for its acerbic, and usually deadly accurate, listings and reviews. *Time Out New York,* founded by the London-based magazine and guidebook company, features excellent round-up articles and a phenomenal listings section—the most comprehensive in the city.

More consciously hip is the monthly *Paper,* which does an especially good job of covering the ever-changing downtown nightlife scene. To find the latest alternative publications, visit **St. Marks Bookshop,** 31 Third Ave., near St. Marks Pl., tel. (212) 260-7853.

ficial paper of record, exhaustively covering the national and international scene. But it also contains good information on happenings around town, especially in its Friday "Weekend" section. The Sunday *Times* features an Arts & Leisure section offering extensive listings on events of all sorts, as well as a City section containing imaginative features on various aspects of city life.

You'd be coming away with a skewed view of New York, however, if you didn't also pick up occasional copies of the *Daily News* and the *New York Post.* Both tabloids, with their in-your-face headlines, do a much better job of covering local news than does the *Times.* The *Daily News* is also a good source for crisp, pithy features and reviews of local events. The *New York Post* often revels in sensationalism and right-of-center politics, but its "Page Six" gossip column is must reading for many New Yorkers, and many of its reviews are excellent. In addition, both papers feature a daily movie schedule, which the *Times* does not.

When it comes to "alternative" papers, the weekly **Village Voice** is the granddaddy. Though best known for its leftist politics, the Voice's strongest suit is its cultural coverage and events listings—among the city's most comprehensive. This is the paper to buy to find out what's happening where, whether you're interested in foreign films or jazz meets hip hop. As of recently, the *Voice* is free of charge and can be found in red boxes on street corners, or in bookstores, music stores, clubs, and delis.

Free neighborhood newspapers containing good listings and reviews are also plentiful. The best of these small papers, currently giving the *Voice* a run for its money, is the **New York Press.**

NEW YORK RADIO

FM STATIONS

WBAI/99.5. Independent station, diverse programming.

WBGO/88.3. Jazz, broadcast from Newark.

WBLS/107.5. Rap, house, soul, hip hop.

WCBS/101. Rock-and-roll oldies and top 40.

WFMU/91.1. Eclectic programming, listener-supported station.

WKCR/89.9. Columbia University's station. First-rate jazz.

WNEW/102.7. Modern rock.

WNYC/93.9. Classical music.

WPLJ/95.5. Top 40.

WQXR/96.3. Commercial classical music station.

WRKS/98.7, aka KISS. Urban contemporary.

WXRK/92.3, aka K-ROCK. Alternative rock; home to the infamous Howard Stern.

AM STATIONS

WINS/1010. News around the clock.

WLIB/1190. Caribbean music and black talk station.

WNYC/820. Excellent talk station; NPR's New York outlet.

WOR/710. Interviews and talk programs.

For books dealing exclusively with New York, including its history and culture, visit **New York Bound Bookshop,** 50 Rockefeller Pl., off Fifth Ave. and 51st St., tel. (212) 245-8503.

On-Line Sources
The most comprehensive on-line guides to New York City, listing thousands of events and visitor attractions, are **New York City Citysearch,** www.citysearchnyc.com, and Microsoft's **New York Sidewalk,** www.newyork.sidewalk.com. Other informative sites include **New York Now,** www.nynow.com, a savvy guide to downtown, and **New York City Reference,** www.panix.com clay/nyc/, which is not so much a traditional guide as it is a fascinating array of eclectic listings.

Budget Tips
New York is an expensive city, but there are ways to keep costs down:

• Stay in hotels a bit off the beaten track. Take advantage of hotel packages.

• Avoid routine purchases in Midtown. You'll get much better values in other parts of the city. Avoid those Midtown restaurants and stores that obviously cater to tourists—their prices are always inflated.

• Eat in ethnic restaurants. They're ubiquitous and often amazingly cheap; the East Village has an especially large supply.

• Watch the papers for free events. Top performers in many artistic disciplines often appear in public plazas or parks.

• Take advantage of free regularly scheduled activities, such as the tours offered by the New York Stock Exchange, Grand Central Terminal, and the 42nd Street Partnership; and the exhibits presented by the New York Public Library and Harlem's Schomberg Center. Many museums also offer free admission one night a week.

• Walk or take public transportation. New York is a great walking city, and public transportation is excellent.

• Take advantage of discount services. The TKTS booth in Times Square, at 47th St. and Broadway, tel. (212) 768-1818, sells half-price orchestra tickets to many Broadway shows. **Worldwide Cinemas,** 340 W. 50th St., near Eighth Ave., tel. (212) 246-1560, charges $3 for second-run movies.

• Explore the small music clubs that feature unknown performers. In New York, the unknowns are often well-known performers in their hometowns, and many small clubs charge little or no cover.

Tipping
A 15-20% tip is customary for waiters and taxi drivers. Hotel bellhops expect $1 a bag, porters $1 for hailing a cab, and room attendants $1 per person per night.

Safety
As in most big cities, crime in New York is a serious problem. But according to the FBI, New York is one of America's safest large cities. It didn't even make the top-25 list of cities with the highest homicide rates in 1996, and reported crime dropped by 43% between 1993 and 1997. Statistically, your chances of being mugged are less than 30,000 to 1. To avoid being that one:

• Act as if you know where you're going, especially when passing through empty neighborhoods. New Yorkers—forever blasé—keep up a brisk, disinterested pace at all times. If you spend too long ogling the sites or looking nervously about, you'll be targeted as an easy mark.

• Don't carry large quantities of cash or large bills, but do carry something; $20 is recommended.

• Ignore hustlers and con artists, especially the three-card-monte players and anyone who approaches you with an elaborate sob story.

• Avoid the parks at night, and be extra careful around transportation centers such as the Port Authority and Penn Station.

• Don't carry valuables in lightweight backpacks that can easily be slashed open. Carry handbags close to your body.

• When in rougher neighborhoods, stick to blocks where other people are in sight or at least where cars are passing by. At night, on empty streets, walk near the curb, away from dark overhangs.

- If you're mugged, hand over your valuables immediately—they're not worth dying for.

Climate

New York has plenty to offer any time of year, but the best times to visit are the spring, early summer, and fall, when temperatures are moderate and conducive to exploring the city on foot. Autumns are often especially wonderful, with deep cobalt blue skies and the excitement of a new season in the air. Winters in New York can be bitterly cold (in the 20s, with bone-chilling winds), summers stiflingly hot (in the 90s, with high humidity), and, though both have their charms—there's nothing like Manhattan after a snowfall or during an August thunderstorm—you do take your chances. On the other hand, the best times for inexpensive hotel packages are weekends in July and August and January and February.

GETTING THERE

By Air

New York is serviced by three airports. **John F. Kennedy International Airport** is about 15 miles from Manhattan in Queens. It's the largest of the three and handles primarily international flights. **La Guardia Airport,** also in Queens, is about eight miles from Manhattan and handles primarily domestic flights. **Newark Airport,** across the Hudson River in New Jersey, handles domestic and some international flights. Kennedy is generally the most congested of the three airports, Newark the least.

Both JFK and La Guardia are currently in the midst of extensive redevelopment programs, which can cause delays. By the end of the century, $4.4 billion will be spent at JFK and another $805 million at La Guardia. Improvements will include new roadways, terminals, and parking lots.

Public transportation from the airports into Manhattan and the other boroughs is excellent; call (800) AIR-RIDE for general information. A taxi ride into Manhattan from La Guardia takes 20-30 minutes and costs about $20-25, including tolls and tip. The ride from Kennedy takes 30-45 minutes and costs a flat fare of $30, plus tolls and tip. The 45-minute ride from Newark usually runs about $50. Cabs leave from well-marked stands staffed by dispatchers, just out-

side the flight arrival areas at all airports. Avoid the gypsy cab drivers hawking their services near the baggage-claim areas.

Carey Transportation, tel. (718) 632-0500, offers frequent bus service from La Guardia and Kennedy airports to Manhattan, Brooklyn, and Queens. The buses to Manhattan run every 20-30 minutes, cost $8.50-12, and make six stops: Grand Central Station at 42nd St. and Park Ave.; the Port Authority Bus Terminal at 42nd St. and Eighth Ave.; and four midtown hotels (the New York Hilton, the Sheraton Manhattan, the Crowne Plaza Manhattan, and the Marriott Marquis).

Olympia Trails, tel. (212) 964-6233, offers bus service between Newark Airport and Manhattan. Buses leave every 20-30 minutes, and make four stops in Manhattan: Grand Central Station at 42nd St. and Park Ave.; Pennsylvania Station at 34th St. and Eighth Ave.; the Port Authority terminal at 42nd St. and Eighth Ave.; and the World Trade Center at West St. near the Vista Hotel. Tickets cost $7. **New Jersey Transit,** tel. (201) 762-5100 or (212) 629-8767, also services Newark Airport from the Port Authority. Buses run every 15-20 minutes, and tickets cost $7.

By Train

Manhattan has two main railroad stations: **Pennsylvania Station** at 33rd St. and Seventh Ave.; and **Grand Central Station** at 42nd St. and Park Avenue. All **Amtrak** trains arrive and depart from Pennsylvania Station. For information, call (800) 872-7245 or (212) 582-6875. **New Jersey Transit,** tel. (201) 762-5100, and **Long Island Railroad,** tel. (718) 217-5477, also offer passenger-train service out of Pennsylvania Station. **Metro-North,** tel. (212) 532-4900, runs commuter trains to suburban New York and Connecticut from Grand Central. Both stations are well serviced by buses, subways, and taxis.

By Bus

The **Port Authority,** Eighth Ave. bet. 40th and 42nd Sts., is the world's largest bus terminal, serving both commuter and long-distance travelers. For bus information, call (212) 564-8484.

By Car

If you must drive into Manhattan, be prepared to pay a steep price for parking at a garage (often $7-12 per hour) or to spend 20 minutes or so looking for street parking. In contrast, street parking in most sections of the boroughs is generally available. When parking on the street, never leave *anything* on the seats; cars are broken into frequently.

Travel Seasons
New York has plenty to offer year-round, but the best times to visit are spring and fall, when temperatures are moderate and conducive to exploring the city on foot. Autumns are often especially wonderful, with deep cobalt blue skies and the excitement of a new season in the air. Winters in New York can be bitterly cold, summers stiflingly hot. Both have their charms—there's nothing like Manhattan after a snowfall or during an August thunderstorm—but you do take your chances. On the other hand, the best times for inexpensive hotel packages are weekends in July and August, January and February.

GETTING AROUND

Most of Manhattan is laid out in a grid pattern, which makes it easy to find your way around. Avenues run north-south, streets east-west, and most are one way. Fifth Ave., which more or less marks the center of the city, separates the East and West Sides. Street addresses are labeled accordingly (1 E. 50th St., 1 W. 50th St.), with the numbers increasing as you head away from Fifth. Broadway, following an old Algonquin trail, cuts through the city on a diagonal.

Those neighborhoods not laid out in a numbered grid pattern—essentially everything south of 14th St.—are considerably more difficult to navigate, and it helps to have a good map. The same applies in the other boroughs, where it's also a good idea to get exact directions to your destination before you set out.

By Subway
Despite their reputation and the constant complaints of commuting New Yorkers, the subways are the easiest and quickest way to get around

UNDERGROUND MUSICIANS

They say that Tony Bennett started his career down under, in the long bleak corridors of the New York subways. In this unlikely concert hall, you might hear the sad, sensuous notes of a Lester Young solo, or the mad, rushing arpeggios of a Bartok concerto. Who knows what future musical genius is now starting out down here.

But playing the New York subways is not as spontaneous as it seems. Since 1985, musicians have had to audition for the choicest spots, and only about 100 of the 300-plus acts that try out each year are granted a license. These musicians are then booked into two-week slots, just as if they were working regular jobs. Many also have other, more traditional gigs, and even a CD or two to their name. Making a living as a musician is tough, even after you've been "discovered."

Not to be completely outdone, independent performers—i.e., those without a license—do still play some of the subway's more out-of-the-way spots. They won that right several years ago when they took the Metropolitan Transit Authority to court. But they're not allowed to use the small amplifiers popular among their licensed colleagues, and they face constant police harassment.

town. Service is frequent—at least in Manhattan—and the trains run all night.

To ride the subways, you need either tokens—which can be purchased for $1.50 each at booths in the subway stations—or electronic fare cards, available at many stops. There has been talk of completely replacing tokens with fare cards but, as of this writing, no final decision has been made. Subway maps are usually posted in each station, and free copies are sometimes available at the token booths. You can also pick up a copy at the New York Convention and Visitors Bureau, 2 Columbus Circle, Eighth Ave. at 59th St., tel. (212) 397-8222.

Three subway lines service the city: the IRT runs north-south on either side of Manhattan; the IND runs along

Sixth and Eighth Aves.; and the BMT runs from lower Manhattan to Brooklyn and Queens. The subway lines used most frequently by visitors are the IRT No. 6 train, which makes local stops along the East Side of Manhattan, and the IRT No. 1/9 train, which makes local stops along the West Side. There's also a Grand Central-Times Square Shuttle connecting the east and west sides of the IRT at 42nd Street.

New Yorkers will delight in telling you stories about how dangerous their city's subway system is, but in reality, 3.5 million passengers travel the 700 miles of track every day without mishap. Still, crime is a serious problem and you should take certain precautions. Keep a close eye on your belongings, especially during rush hours when the crush of the crowd makes pickpocketing easy. Don't wear expensive jewelry. Avoid empty or near-empty cars, even during the day when the subways are theoretically the safest. During off hours, wait for your train in the well-lit "Off-Hour" waiting areas near the token booths. When your train comes, sit in the center car, which has a conductor and is usually the most crowded car on the train. Finally, although some New Yorkers ride the subways at all hours, it's not advisable to take them after midnight.

If you don't know how to get where you're going, call the **New York City Transit Authority** at (718) 330-1234, between 6 a.m. and 9 p.m., and they'll tell you the best route via subway or bus.

By Bus

Buses run 24 hours a day uptown along Tenth, Eighth, Sixth, Madison, Third, and First Aves., and downtown along Ninth, Seventh, Fifth, and Second Avenues. East-west crosstown service can be found along 14th, 23rd, 34th, 42nd, 57th, 65th/66th, 79th, 86th, and 96th Streets. Bus stops are usually located every two blocks, and signs or shelters mark the spots.

The fare is $1.50, payable with either exact change, a subway token, or the electronic fare card. Free transfers are available between uptown-downtown buses and crosstown buses, enabling you to make any one-way trip in Manhattan on a single fare. Good bus service is also available in the outer boroughs.

LOCATING CROSS STREETS

To find the nearest cross street of an avenue address, drop the last digit of the address number and divide by two. Then, add or subtract the number shown below. (For example, to find the cross street of 666 Fifth Ave., drop the last 6, divide 66 by 2 which is 33, and add 18 to get 51.)

Ave. A, B, C, D; add 3

First Ave.; add 3

Second Ave.; add 3

Third Ave.; add 10

Fourth Ave.; add 8

Fifth Ave.—
    up to #200; add 13
    up to #400; add 16
    up to #600; add 18
    up to #775; add 20
    #775 to #1286; do not divide by 2, subtract 18
    up to #1500; add 45
    up to #2000; add 24

Sixth Ave.; Subtract 12

Seventh Ave.—
    below 110th St.; add 12
    above 110th St.; add 20

Eighth Ave.; add 10

Ninth Ave.; add 13

Tenth Ave.; add 14

Amsterdam Ave.; add 60

Audubon Ave.; add 165

Broadway above 23rd St.; Subtract 30

Central Park West; divide full address by 10, add 60

Columbus Ave.; add 60

Convent Ave.; add 127

Lenox Ave.; add 110

Lexington Ave.; add 22

Madison Ave.; add 26

Park Ave.; add 35

Riverside Dr.; divide full address by 10, add 72

St. Nicholas Ave.; add 110

West End Ave.; add 60

York Ave.; add 4

CITY OF ISLANDS

Manhattan and Staten Islands are not the only islands of New York City. Dotting the rivers and harbor are many little outcroppings of land, some with complex histories. Only a few of these islands are open to the public; others house institutions such as hospitals or prisons, while still others are accessible only to wildlife, including rare birds such as herons, ibis, egrets, and even a few ospreys.

Hart Island

The city's potter's field since 1868, Hart Island is the final resting place of about 750,000 unknown or unwanted bodies. Approximately 2,800 new burials take place each year, and a crew of 15 to 30 prisoners from nearby Rikers Island handles the formalities. The bodies are buried in white-pine coffins made in six standard sizes; the smallest ones are for infants and body parts. New York is one of the only cities in the U.S. that has a potter's field; most cities cremate their unclaimed dead.

City Island

Known for its numerous seafood restaurants and small boatbuilding industry, City Island is a little piece of nautical New England transported south. See "Northwest Bronx," in the Other Boroughs chapter.

Rikers Island

Named after its original owner, Abraham Rycken, Rikers Island now houses a number of penal institutions. The largest is the Men's House of Detention, where about 5,000 prisoners are incarcerated. Built in 1935 to replace the old prison on Welfare Island (now called Roosevelt Island), Rikers was once regarded as a model penitentiary. Today it's seriously outmoded and overcrowded.

North Brother Island

Typhoid Mary was once quarantined on this now abandoned island that's become an important nesting ground for rare birds. An infected cook who worked in dozens of kitchens in the days before the nature of communicable diseases was completely understood, Typhoid Mary may have infected hundreds of people. She herself was a carrier who wasn't affected by the disease, and she didn't understand why she had to be quarantined. She fiercely attacked the officials who tried to confine her, and refused to give up her career as a cook. In 1923, after isolating Typhoid Mary in several different hospitals, the city gave her a one-room cottage of her own on North Brother Island. She lived here until 1938, when she died of a stroke at age 70. At the time of her death, she'd spent nearly half her life in confinement.

South Brother Island

Seven-acre South Brother Island is heavily wooded, privately owned, and a favorite nesting site of egrets.

Randalls Island

Like several other islands surrounding Manhattan, Randalls Island has at various times been the site of a potter's field, poorhouse, reform school, and insane asylum. In 1929, the island became the headquarters of the Triborough Bridge and Tunnel Authority, from where controversial City Parks Commissioner Robert Moses once ran his empire. Randalls Island is connected to Wards Island by landfill.

Wards Island

Used as a military base by the British during the Revolutionary War, Wards Island is now home to the Manhattan Psychiatric Center; the Manhattan Children's Treatment Center, which provides care to mentally impaired and disturbed children; and the Firefighters' Training Center.

Mill Rock Island

This one-time pirate's refuge got its name from a tide-powered mill that stood here in the early 1700s. During the War of 1812, a fort was built on the island; in the 1880s, the U.S. Army Corps of Engineers used it as a base to mix the explosives with which they blew up nearby Flood Rock. That explosion is said to have been the biggest ever before the atomic bomb. In 1953, the island was taken over by the Parks Department—supposedly because Commissioner Moses was worried that a commercial enterprise might erect a billboard there, blocking his views on the way to work.

Roosevelt Island

Today a planned residential community where no cars are allowed, Roosevelt Island—formerly known as Blackwell's Island and Welfare Island—was once the site of a grim and nasty penal institution notorious for its innovative tortures, including "cooler" rooms and the "water drop cure." Politician Boss Tweed served time here in 1873, and actress Mae West was imprisoned here for 10 days in 1927, for her scandalous play *Sex*. See the "Upper East Side," in the Manhattan chapter.

Governors Island

At various times the site of a sheep farm, quarantine station, racetrack, game preserve, the governor's "pleasure house," and a Civil War prison for Confederate soldiers, Governors Island is now a U.S. Coast Guard Station. The Coast Guard plans to leave by the end of 1998, however, and the island's future remains uncertain.

Liberty Island

Egg-shaped Liberty Island, where the Statue of Liberty stands, was once known as Bedloe's Island and used as a place of execution. One of the most famous men hung here was Albert E. Hicks, who in 1860 was shanghaied onto a sloop heading for Virginia. Five days later, the boat was discovered—empty—off the coast of New Jersey. Hicks, meanwhile, was sighted around Manhattan flashing wads of money. He was promptly arrested, and eventually confessed to killing the entire crew with an ax. The case attracted the attention of P.T. Barnum, who gave it even more notoriety by buying up Hicks's clothes and putting them on display. See "Lower Manhattan," in the Manhattan chapter.

Ellis Island

From 1892 to 1924, Ellis Island was the primary point of entry for immigrants to the U.S. The island's main building, fancifully equipped with red-brick towers topped with white domes, now houses a $150-million museum. Its cavernous halls still seem to echo with the voices of the 12 million terrified immigrants who once passed through here. See "Lower Manhattan," in the Manhattan chapter.

Hoffman and Swinburne Islands

These two manmade bits of land were constructed as a quarantine station in 1872. On Hoffman once stood the quarantine hospital; on Swinburne, the crematory. The station was abandoned in the 1920s when tough laws restricting immigration were passed. Now the islands are deserted and undeveloped, home to seagulls and cormorants.

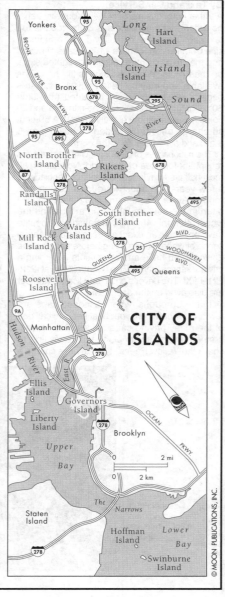

CITY OF ISLANDS

© MOON PUBLICATIONS, INC.

By Taxi and Car Service

Another notorious mode of New York City transportation that's nonetheless quite good is the taxi cab. The New York City Taxi and Limousine Commission licenses 11,787 cabs annually, and they're all painted yellow with lighted signs on their roofs. When the sign is lit, the cab is available and may be hailed anywhere. Fares begin at $2 when the meter is started, then jump 30 cents for each additional one-fifth mile and 20 cents for each minute of waiting time. A 50-cent surcharge per ride is added nightly 8 p.m.-6 a.m., and a 15-20% tip is the norm.

The nationalities of New York City's cab drivers reflect the fortunes of the world. Nowadays, almost half are from India, Pakistan, or Bangladesh; a few years ago, most were from Eastern Europe or Africa. Since many cab drivers haven't been in the country long, and are behind the wheel after only 40 hours of training, it's best to have patience, an exact address, and a general sense of where you're going before flagging one down. If you have any complaints regarding a driver's service, call the Taxi Commission at (212) 221-TAXI. The driver's photo and license number are displayed on the dashboard.

In the boroughs, where licensed cabs are few and far between, your best bet is to call one of the many private car services. Ask for recommendations at the place you're visiting or check the Yellow Pages. The services charge a flat rate that's usually reasonable, and pick you up wherever you wish.

By Foot

Walking is by far the best way to see Manhattan and many parts of the boroughs. In Manhattan, figure on needing about a minute for each north-south block, two minutes for each east-west one.

TOURS

No matter where your interests lie—in architecture, ethnic foods, or social history—chances are good you'll find a tour tailor-made for you. Walking tours are proliferating all over the city, with each one more imaginative than the next ("Famous Murder Sites," "Edith Wharton's New York," "Irish New York"). *Time Out New York* has the best listings; other resources include the weekend editions of the daily papers, *New York,* and *The New Yorker.*

City Tours

One of the best ways to get an overview of the city is to take a **Circle Line** cruise, tel. (212) 563-3200. The boats leave daily from Pier 83, W. 42nd St. and the Hudson River, April-December. Standard daytime cruises last three hours; "express" cruises last two. The fare is adults $17-20, children under 12 half price.

Visitors take in the sights aboard a double-decker tour bus.

Seaport Liberty Cruises, tel. (212) 630-8888, provides one-hour cruises past the Statue of Liberty, departing from Pier 16 at South Street Seaport; adults $12, children $6. **World Yacht,** tel. (212) 630-8100, departing from W. 41st St. at the Hudson, offers luxury dinner cruises with live entertainment and dancing. Prices start at $70 per person.

Gray Line Tours, 900 8th Ave., near 53rd St., tel. (212) 397-2600, offers over 20 different bus tours lasting anywhere from two hours to a full day. Tours are offered year-round, and foreign language tours are available. Prices start at $17.50; reduced rates for kids.

New York Double-Decker Tours, tel. (212) 967-6008, operates on a continuous loop seven days a week year-round, covering all major locations uptown and down. One fare of adults $17, children $10, allows unlimited boarding and reboarding for two days.

For a spectacular bird's-eye view of the city, try **Island Helicopter,** tel. (212) 683-4575. Flights leave daily from the heliport at 34th St. and the East River. Prices start at $44.

Shuttle Bus Plus offers van and bus tours of the Bronx, Brooklyn, and Staten Island that take in the major sights. Most of the tours last 3 1/2-4 hours, cost $25, and leave from both the West Side YMCA, 5 W. 63rd St., near Central Park West, tel. (212) 595-6608; and the Vanderbilt YMCA, 224 E. 47th St., near Lexington, tel. (212) 355-2980.

Walking Tours

The **Municipal Art Society,** 457 Madison Ave., near 51st St., tel. (212) 935-3960, runs an extensive series of walking tours almost daily year-round. Most focus on architecture and history; cost is $10. The society also offers occasional bus tours.

Big Onion Walking Tours, tel. (212) 439-1090, founded by two university American-history professors, offers some of the city's most fun and well-researched tours. Many concentrate on New York's immigrant history and on neighborhoods below 14th Street. The cost is adults $9, students and seniors $7. **Radical Walking Tours,** tel. (718) 492-0069, specializes in revolutionary and labor history; the cost is $6.

The 92nd Street Y, 1395 Lexington Ave., at 92nd St., tel. (212) 427-6000, leads many excellent walking and bus tours. They're very popular and must be signed up for weeks in advance. Tours start at $15.

Adventure on a Shoestring, tel. (212) 265-2663, is a membership organization offering a plethora of tours, most of which are open to the public. At $5 a pop, this is one of the cheapest ways to tour the city. You get what you pay for, however. Group size can be enormous—100-plus is not unusual. And while the organization's eccentric founder and most frequent tour leader, Howard Goldberg, can be entertaining, he often seems more interested in hearing himself talk than in imparting information.

Tours of Harlem are offered by a number of companies. **Harlem Spirituals,** tel. (212) 757-0425, specializes in visits to gospel services and soul-food restaurants; prices start at $30. **Harlem Your Way!,** tel. (212) 690-1687, offers daily walking tours of historic sites, as well as custom-made tours; prices start at $25. The **Penny Sightseeing Company,** tel. (212) 410-0080, features both walking and gospel tours; prices start at $18. **Shuttle Bus Tours,** tel. (212) 595-6608 or 355-2980, offers van and bus tours, some of which include stops at a gospel church or jazz club; $25-37.

Downtown, the **Lower East Side Tenement Museum,** 97 Orchard St., bet. Delancey and Broome, tel. (212) 431-0233, sponsors occasional walking tours of old immigrant neighborhoods, $10-12; and the **Museum of Chinese in the Americas,** 70 Mulberry St., at Bayard, tel. (212) 619-4785, offers occasional tours of Chinatown, also $10-12.

Outside Manhattan, the **Brooklyn Historical Society,** 128 Pierrepont St., at Clinton St., tel. (718) 624-0890, features imaginative tours taking in anything from genteel Brooklyn Heights to Caribbean-American Crown Heights. Tours start at $8. The **Bronx County Historical Society,** 3309 Bainbridge Ave., tel. (718) 881-8900, offers occasional tours as well.

Various **urban historians** with astounding knowledge of the city frequently conduct tours. Sometimes they work independently, sometimes through an institution. Their tours are often announced in the papers. A few names to watch out for include **Barry Lewis,** tel. (718) 849-0297, a preeminent architectural historian; **Val Ginter,** tel. (212) 496-6859, who specializes in jazz history, among other things; and **Joyce Gold,** tel. (212) 242-5762, who teaches the city's history at New York University. Also well worth watching out for is **Wild Man Steve Brill,** tel. (718) 291-6825, a self-taught naturalist who conducts frequent free tours through the city's parks.

Site Tours

Tours are also available at many specific Manhattan visitor attractions, including the Federal Reserve Bank and New York Stock Exchange (Lower Manhattan); Grand Central Station, the United Nations, NBC Studios, and Radio City Music Hall (Midtown); and Gracie Mansion (Upper East Side). For more information, see the listings for those sites in the corresponding neighborhood sections below.

DOVER PUBLICATIONS, INC.

OUT ON THE TOWN

Excellent entertainment listings can be found in *The New Yorker, New York, New York Free Press*, the *Village Voice*, the Sunday edition of the *New York Times*, and—especially—*Time Out New York*, which includes hundreds upon hundreds of listings. The *Voice, Time Out*, and *Free Press* do a very good job of covering downtown, while *The New Yorker* is the best source for capsule theater reviews. The most complete daily movie schedules are published by the *Daily News, New York Post, Village Voice*, and *New York Free Press*. For information on the volatile club scene—with its roving deejays, hip hop, soul, and techno parties—pick up *Time Out*, the *Free Press*, or the monthly *Paper*.

Unless stated otherwise, all the venues listed below are in Manhattan. For popular music, see also "Watering Holes and Lounges" in the specific neighborhood sections; some feature live local bands, especially on weekends.

POPULAR MUSIC VENUES

New York's largest venue is the 19,000-seat **Madison Square Garden,** Seventh Ave. bet. 31st and 33rd Sts., tel. (212) 465-MSG1 (-6741). Also home to the city's basketball and hockey teams, it's hardly an atmospheric spot, and usually not worth the very high admission price unless there's someone you've just got to see.

The 5,600-seat **Paramount,** a separate venue inside the Garden, is considerably more stylish and comfortable.

The grand, art deco **Radio City Music Hall,** 1260 Sixth Ave., at 50th St., tel. (212) 247-4777, sometimes presents popular music acts, as does the legendary **Carnegie Hall,** 154 W. 57th St., at Seventh Ave., tel. (212) 247-7800. The **Apollo,** 253 W. 125th St., near Adam Clayton Powell Jr. Blvd., tel. (212) 749-5838, presents R&B, soul, and rap, while on Wednesdays, the famed amateur-night tradition continues. Don't hesitate to venture up here at night—125th St. is always bustling.

The historic **Beacon Theater,** 2124 Broadway, at 74th St., tel. (212) 496-7070, is a convivial spot with an eclectic booking policy. **Town Hall,** 123 W. 43rd St., bet. Sixth and Seventh Aves., tel. (212) 840-2824, often presents jazz and world music.

ROCK AND ALTERNATIVE

East Village
The granddaddy of New York rock clubs is the ratty, hole-in-the-wall **CBGB & OMFUG,** 315 Bowery, at Bleecker, tel. (212) 982-4052, still going strong after more than 20 years. During the 1970s, the battle-scarred CBGB's—short for "Country, Bluegrass, Blues, and Other Music

for Uplifting Gormandizers"—was America's cradle of punk rock, home to such later legends as the Talking Heads, Television, and Patti Smith. Nowadays, an average of six fledgling bands are booked nightly; cover, $5-10.

Brownies, 169 Ave. A, at 10th St., tel. (212) 420-8392, is a comfortable, bare-bricked place featuring top local bands, along with the occasional "name"; cover, $3-10. The often packed **Coney Island High,** 15 St. Mark's Pl., near Third Ave., tel. (212) 674-7959, is a wacky, two-level funhouse offering a mix of indie rock, punk, and disco; cover $5-8. At the dark, black **Continental,** 25 Third Ave., at St. Mark's Pl., tel. (212) 529-6924, you'll hear local bands playing alternative, roots rock, or metal; cover, $3-10.

The **Acme Underground,** 9 Great Jones St., at Lafayette, tel. (212) 420-1934, offers a good P.A. system and some of the hottest young bands in town; cover $5-10. The scrappy **Pyramid Club,** 101 Ave. A, bet. 6th and 7th Sts., tel. (212) 473-7184, a major rock club in the '80s, now draws a predominantly gay crowd, and spins mostly industrial and dance music; cover, $3-10.

Just north of the East Village is **Irving Plaza,** 17 Irving Pl., at 15th St., tel. (212) 777-6800, an unusual venue with a wide balcony, large dance floor, and elaborate ornamentation left over from its days as a Polish dance hall. Many bigger-name rock and new-music groups play here, along with some reggae, blues, rap, and world bands; cover, $10-15. On Sunday nights, the Swing Dance Society, tel. (212) 696-9737, gathers here to dance to the hits of yesteryear; nonmembers welcome.

Lower East Side
Just south of the East Village, on the south side of Houston St., is the long, dark **Mercury Lounge,** 217 E. Houston, near Essex, tel. (212) 260-4700, featuring an antique wooden bar, exposed brick walls, heavy red drapes, and an excellent sound system. Some very hip rock and jazz acts play here; cover, $5-12. An excellent place to catch top up-and-coming bands at no cover is **Arlene Grocery,** 95 Stanton St., bet. Ludlow and Orchard Sts., tel. (212) 358-1633, housed in a former bodega.

SoHo and TriBeCa
Wetlands, 161 Hudson St., at Laight, tel. (212) 966-4225, is an oddly earnest ecologically minded place offering scads of free PC literature along with acts ranging from ska to psychedelic rock; cover $8-12. The hole-in-the-wall **McGovern's,** 305 Spring St., near Greenwich St., tel. (212) 627-5037, presents local rock and new-music bands; cover $3-8. The comfortable **New Music Cafe,** 380 Canal St., at W. Broadway, tel. (212) 941-1019, presents mostly mainstream rock-and-roll, some hip hop; cover $3-8.

Greenwich Village
Another music institution is the **Bottom Line,** 15 W. 4th St., at Mercer, tel. (212) 228-6300. A big and comfortable place packed with tables, the club has been around since 1974 when Dr. John opened the place, with Stevie Wonder sitting in. Since then, the legedary venue has presented an eclectic array of rock and jazz—everyone from Bruce Springsteen to the Sun Ra Arkestra; cover, $15-25.

Also in the neighborhood are the decades-old **Bitter End,** 147 Bleecker St., at Thompson, tel. (212) 673-7030, and the relatively new **Lion's**

Den, 214 Sullivan St., bet. Bleecker and W. 3rd St., tel. (212) 477-2782, two small and informal spots hosting mostly young traditional rock bands; cover, $3-6. The low-ceilinged, dark, and intimate **Cafe Wha?,** 115 MacDougal St., near W. 3rd St., tel. (212) 254-3706, presents rock, R&B, and soul.

Midtown

Downtime, 251 W. 30th St., near Eighth Ave., tel. (212) 695-2747, is an intimate, two-tiered music-industry hangout featuring mostly rock and blues downstairs, dance parties upstairs; cover, $5-10. The rustic, peanut-shell-strewn **Rodeo Bar,** attached to the Albuquerque restaurant, 375 Third Ave., at 27th St., tel. (212) 683-6500, presents local rock, blues, and country; no cover.

The **Supper Club,** 240 W. 47th St., bet. Broadway and Eighth Ave., tel. (212) 921-1940, is a classy renovated ballroom that frequently books large rock bands. **Roseland,** 239 W. 52nd St., tel. (212) 249-8870, once a grand old dance hall may now be faded and frayed, but it still features ballroom dancing on Thursday and Sunday. During the rest of the week, it's a dark, pulsating rock club with two stages and a young crowd; cover, $15-25.

Outside Manhattan

Many New Yorkers frequent **Maxwell's,** 1039 Washington St. in Hoboken, New Jersey, tel. (201) 798-4064. Just a short subway ride from Manhattan, the casual and unpretentious club features top up-and-coming bands, as well as occasional big names; cover $6-10. To reach Hoboken, catch the PATH train which runs underneath Sixth Ave. from the World Trade Center to 34th Street.

BLUES

Greenwich Village

Bringing in the best of the blues from the heartland is **Chicago B.L.U.E.S.,** 73 Eighth Ave., bet. 13th and 14th Sts., tel. (212) 924-9755, a laid-back, brick-walled joint; cover, $5-10. **Terra Blues,** 149 Bleecker St., near Thompson, tel. (212) 777-7776, is a small, upstairs club with picture windows overlooking the street. Most of

the bands are local favorites, but better-known acts appear from time to time; cover, $5-10.

Chelsea

Tramps, 45 W. 21st St., near Sixth Ave., tel. (212) 727-7788, is a big yet somehow still intimate club with a beautiful old wooden bar, a sizable dance floor, and a good Creole/Cajun menu. Nationally known blues and zydeco acts are often featured, along with world, rock, and rockabilly; cover, $5-20. Next door is Tramps Cafe, a smaller venue booking smaller acts.

Upper East Side

Manny's Car Wash, 1558 Third Ave., bet. 87th and 88th Sts., tel. (212) 369-BLUE (-2583), has a frat-house feel but presents top regional bands nightly; cover, $3-15.

JAZZ

New York is an international center for jazz, and top-caliber musicians can be heard in dozens of top-caliber clubs every night of the week. In general, such first-rate entertainment doesn't come cheap; many of the best clubs charge $15-30, plus a two-drink minimum. Cheaper venues do exist, however, typically booking lesser known but equally accomplished acts. You'll find most of New York's jazz clubs in Greenwich Village.

Greenwich Village

The oldest and arguably best jazz club in the city is the **Village Vanguard,** 178 Seventh Ave. S, at 11th St., tel. (212) 255-4037, a dark, wedge-shaped basement room filled with rickety tables and fading photographs. Established in 1934, the Vanguard has booked all the greats, from Miles Davis and Dinah Washington to Wynton Marsalis and Terence Blanchard; cover, $12-15, plus a two-drink minimum. On Monday nights, the 17-piece Vanguard Jazz Orchestra jams.

Just down the street from the Vanguard is **Sweet Basil,** 88 Seventh Ave. S, near Bleecker, tel. (212) 242-1785, a comfortable though oft-crowded spot featuring straight-ahead and mainstream jazz; cover, $15, with a two-drink minimum. On Monday nights, an electrified big band led by Miles Evans performs.

Between those two jazz institutions is **Smalls,** 183 W. 10th St., near Seventh Ave., tel. (212) 929-7565, a young and scrappy club featuring up-and-coming players who jam until dawn. No liquor is served, but there's free food and drink after 2 a.m.; cover, $10.

One avenue over is the pricey **Blue Note,** 131 W. 3rd St., near Sixth Ave., tel. (212) 475-8592, the city's premier jazz supper club. A large rectangular place all done up in glitzy blues, the club can seem annoyingly commercial. Come during a late weeknight set when the crowds are small and the intimacy level is high. After midnight, lesser-known players jam for a $5 cover. Otherwise, the cover runs a steep $25-60, plus a $5 minimum.

Also in Greenwich Village is **55,** 55 Christopher St., near Seventh Ave., tel. (212) 929-9883, a convivial hole-in-the-wall with live jazz as well as a great jazz jukebox; cover, $5, with a one-drink minimum. The friendly Spanish restaurant **Visiones,** 125 MacDougal St., at W. 3rd St., tel. (212) 673-5576, presents a wide spectrum of jazz, including the splendid Maria Schneider Orchestra on Monday nights; cover, $5-10. The dark, sardine-can **Arthur's Tavern,** 57 Grove St., near Seventh Ave., tel. (212) 675-6879, is another traditional jazz venue; no cover. **Zinno,** 126 W. 13th St., bet. Sixth and Seventh Aves., tel. (212) 924-5182, offers both first-rate jazz and top-notch Northern Italian food; cover $10-12.

On the border between Greenwich Village and East Village lies **Fez,** 380 Lafayette St., at Great Jones, tel. (212) 533-2680, a dark, low-ceilinged underground joint where one of the city's most unusual jazz events—the gathering of the Mingus Big Band—takes place once a week; cover, $20. The nearby **Louisiana Community Bar & Grill,** 622 Broadway, near Houston, tel. (212) 460-9633, is a long and lively restaurant/bar presenting free and often excellent jazz and blues 8 p.m.-midnight most nights.

The dark **Zinc Bar,** 90 Houston St., bet. La Guardia Pl. and Thompson St., tel. (212) 477-8337, is an oft-crowded cellar joint showcasing some of the top lesser-known jazz and Latin acts in town. Restaurants with a serious commitment to live jazz include **Knickerbocker Bar & Grill,** 33 University Pl., at 9th St., tel. (212) 228-8490, the steak house where Harry Connick, Jr., got his start; **Sweet Ophelia's,** 430 Broome St., at Crosby St., tel. (212) 343-8000, a classy soul-food restaurant that features many vocalists; and the **Cornelia Street Cafe,** 29 Cornelia St., bet. Bleecker St. and Sixth Ave., tel. (212) 989-9318), where small jazz groups often perform in the long, white-washed basement lounge.

TriBeCa

The quirky, bohemian **Knitting Factory,** 74 Leonard St., bet. Church and Broadway, tel. (212) 219-3055, features two bunkerlike performance rooms, an underground cafe, and 18 microbrews on tap. Best known for avant garde jazz, the Knitting Factory also books everything from alternative rock to poetry readings; cover, $7-15.

Midtown

Impresario Art D'Lugoff, former owner of the famed Village Gate in Greenwich Village (now closed), runs the

Village Gate 52nd Street, 240 W. 52nd St., tel. (212) 307-5252, a sleek, low-lit club with cabaret shows in the early evening and jazz and swing dancing from 10 p.m. to 2:30 a.m. On the menu you'll find everything from burgers to inventive entrees; $5 cover after 10 p.m. Also recently relocated to a sleek club in Midtown—this time from the Upper West Side—is **Birdland,** 315 W. 44th St., bet. Eighth and Ninth Aves., tel. (212) 581-3080. Featured are such top artists as Terence Blanchard and Bobby Watson; cover $10-20, with a $10 minimum.

Woody Allen blows clarinet with the **Eddy Davis New Orleans Jazz Band** every Monday at the posh Cafe Carlyle in the Carlyle Hotel, Madison Ave. at 76th St., tel. (212) 570-7189. Tickets cost $25 and $45. For traditional jazz and swing dancing, stop by the boisterous **Red Blazer Too Restaurant,** 349 W. 46th St., bet. Eighth and Ninth Aves., tel. (212) 262-3112.

Upper West Side

The **Iridium,** 44 W. 63rd St., at Columbus, tel. (212) 582-2121, is a trendy basement spot, wackily designed à la Dr. Seuss, that hosts top young jazz turks. Guitar legend Les Paul performs on Monday nights; cover, $15-30.

Harlem

The convivial **Showman's Cafe,** 2321 Frederick Douglass Blvd., near 125th St., tel. (212) 864-8941, presents some top acts, along with local favorites; cover ranges up to $5. For big bands, swing dancing, or an excellent gospel brunch, visit the nicely outfitted **Cotton Club,** 666 W. 125th St., bet. Broadway and Riverside, tel. (212) 663-7980 (no relationship to the famed club of the '20s); cover, $5-20.

At the lively **St. Nick's Pub,** 773 St. Nicholas Ave., at 149th St., tel. (212) 283-9728 or 234-3380, different house bands perform five nights a week; no cover or minimum. The **Lickety Split Lounge,** 2361 Adam Clayton Powell Jr. Blvd., at 138th St., tel. (212) 283-9093, is a neighborhood joint serving up spicy West Indian fare and live jazz several nights a week; cover $5, with a two-drink minimum. The vintage art deco **Lenox Lounge,** 288 Lenox Ave., bet. 124th and 125th Sts., tel. (212) 427-0253, presents top jazz artists on the weekends; cover $6, with a $10 minimum.

CLASSICAL

Classical music thrives in New York City, especially at the **Lincoln Center for the Performing Arts,** Broadway between 62nd and 66th Sts., which presents an astonishing 3,000 performances a year. On its north side is the 2,700-seat **Avery Fisher Hall,** tel. (212) 875-5030, home to the New York Philharmonic (Sept.-May), the Great Performers Series (Oct.-May), the Mostly Mozart Festival (July-Aug.), and the Jazz-at-Lincoln Center Series, run by Wynton Marsalis (Sept.-April). Ticket prices run $10-50, depending on the event, with $10-12 seats almost always available for the first two series. The Philharmonic also opens its rehearsals to the public once a week; tickets are $5. Call for more information.

Just north of Avery Fisher, above 66th St., is the 1,096-seat **Alice Tully Hall,** tel. (212) 875-5050, where the Chamber Music Society of Lincoln Center performs. Tickets run $15-40.

A dozen or so blocks from Lincoln Center is Manhattan's other major classical-music venue, **Carnegie Hall,** Seventh Ave. and 57th St., tel. (212) 247-7800. Saved from demolition by Isaac Stern and others in the early 1960s, this legendary hall was once home to the New York Philharmonic and remains a favorite spot among musicians of all persuasions. Tickets run $15-60.

Classical music can also be heard at a number of unusual venues around town. The **Metropolitan Museum of Art,** Fifth Ave. at 82nd St., tel. (212) 570-3949, offers a regular series in its Grace Rainey Rogers Auditorium, as well as less formal performances in such splendid settings as the Temple of Dundur or the Medieval Sculpture Hall. During the summer, the **Museum of Modern Art,** 11 W. 53rd St., near Fifth Ave., tel. (212) 708-9480, features an outdoor concert series in its sculpture garden. **Bargemusic,** at Fulton Ferry Landing in Brooklyn, tel. (718) 624-4061, is a large barge moored beneath the Brooklyn Bridge, where string quartets are accompanied by glorious views of Manhattan. Those on a tight budget should call or stop by the **Julliard School,** 60 Lincoln Center Pl., tel. (212) 769-7406, where the students and faculty members frequently perform in superb recitals costing little or nothing.

OPERA

On the west side of Lincoln Center is the grand **Metropolitan Opera House,** tel. (212) 362-6000, home of the Metropolitan Opera Company. A good seat here can cost $100 or more, but $15 seats are often available in the upper balcony (bring binoculars).

On the south side of the center is the **New York State Theater,** tel. (212) 870-5570, where the less exalted New York City Opera performs. Regular tickets run $25-50; $10 standing-room tickets and $15 seats are also usually available (again, bring binoculars).

The tiny **Amato Opera Company,** 319 Bowery, at Bleecker, tel. (212) 228-8200, puts on splendid weekend productions in a creaky turn-of-the-century vaudeville house. The $16 tickets are a great deal but must be reserved well in advance.

OTHER LIVE MUSIC

SoHo
S.O.B. (short for "Sounds of Brazil"), 204 Varick St., near Houston, tel. (212) 243-4940, is a stylish, multiethnic place emphasizing "tropical music," including African, Caribbean, reggae, Latin, and some jazz; cover: $8-20. Most of the well-known bands are dance-oriented, and the small dance floor stays packed with beautiful bodies. The Caribbean food is superb.

East Village
The **Sidewalk Cafe,** 94 Ave. A, at 6th St., tel. (212) 473-7373, bills itself as an "anti-folk" club but nonetheless features plenty of acoustic types; no cover, one-drink minimum.

Greenwich Village
In the heart of the Gansevoort Meat Market, you'll find the underground, steel-corridored **Cooler,** 416 W. 14th St., near Ninth Ave., tel. (212) 229-0785, a former meat locker that books rock, jazz, and world music; cover, $5-12.

Housed in a creaky old building once belonging to Thomas Paine is **Marie's Crisis Cafe,** 59 Grove St., at Seventh Ave., tel. (212) 243-9323, a lively piano bar where a predominantly gay crowd has been gathering to sing show tunes for over 50 years.

Murray Hill Area
Paddy Reilly's, 519 Second Ave., at 29th St., tel. (212) 686-1210, is a boisterous pub where the popular Irish band Black 47 has been playing one or two nights a week for years.

Midtown
O'Lunney's, 12 W. 44th St., bet. Fifth and Sixth Aves., tel. (212) 840-6688, is a casual restaurant with live country-and-western once a week; cover, $3. **Rainbow and Stars,** 30 Rockefeller Pl., bet. W. 49th and 50th Sts., tel. (212) 632-5000, adjacent to the Rainbow Room high above Midtown, is the city's classiest cabaret; cover, $40. In an old recording studio is swank **Le Bar Bat,** 311 W. 57th St., bet. Eighth and Ninth Aves., tel. (212) 307-7228, offering a mix of funk, soul, and pop; cover $10-20.

CLUBS

Since 1996, night life in New York has been under siege, due to a "quality of life" campaign waged by the Giuliani administration. Some long-established clubs, such as the Limelight, have been shut down; others, such as the Tunnel, have been toned down considerably. In their wake has come a new, more modest generation of clubs, which tend to be smaller and more mainstream than their predecessors.

Some of both New York's older and newer clubs are listed below, but as these can change overnight, be sure to check local listings before venturing out. A few other general rules:

Nothing really gets going until after midnight, and although arrogant door policies are often in effect, be patient—all but the snootiest of clubs eventually let almost everyone in. Be prepared to be searched at the door and to spend big bucks—in addition to a steep cover, you'll have to shell out $5-8 per drink. Admission prices are generally lower during the week than on weekends.

Some of New York's most interesting club events are independent roving parties, which *Time Out,* the *Free Press,* and *The Paper* chronicle in detail. These parties tend to take up residence in one location for six months or so, then move on. Among the longer lived of these are **Giant Step,** tel. (212) 714-8001, where jazz meets rap and hip-hop, and **Soul Kitchen,** tel. (212) 439-8133.

SoHo
One of the hottest club-lounges in town is dark, dramatic **Spy,** 101 Greene St., bet. Prince and Spring Sts., tel. (212) 343-9000, home to high ceilings and enormous sofas and chairs. Don't even *think* of venturing in here without plenty of attitude. **Don Hill's,** 511 Greenwich St., at Spring St., tel. (212) 334-1390, hosts some of the best deejays in town, spinning everything from jump-blues to hip hop; cover $10.

East Village
Webster Hall, 125 E. 11th St., near Third Ave., tel. (212) 353-1600, is a five-floored extravaganza with different themes for different nights. On weekends you might catch stiltwalkers, snake charmers, and flying trapeze artists, while on "Psychedelic Thursdays," deejays spin the classics; cover, $5-20.

Nearby is the even more cavernous **Palladium,** 126 E. 14th St., near Third Ave., tel. (212) 473-7171. Housed in what used to be the classical Academy of Music, the Palladium now churns out hip-hop to a young, multiethnic crowd; cover, $15-18.

Den of Thieves, 145 E. Houston St., bet. Eldridge and Forsythe Sts., tel. (212) 477-5005, is a hip storefront dive offering up a mix of funk, soul, reggae, and hip hop; no cover.

West Village
Among the best of the city's newer dance clubs is **Life,** 158 Bleecker St., at Thompson St., tel. (212) 420-1999, a glamorous, disco-fabulous affair a la a suburban hotel; cover $10-15. The one-of-a-kind **Night Strike** takes place Monday nights at Bowler Lanes, 110 University Place, bet. 12th and 13th Sts., tel. (212) 255-8188, one of only two bowling alleys left in New York; expect deejays

spinning house, techno, and R&B, plus bowling with glow-in-the-dark balls, pins, and shoes; cover, $5; shoe rental, $5.

The Gansevoort Meat Market is home to the velvet-draped **Hell,** 59 Gansevoort St., bet. Greenwich and Washington Sts., tel. (212) 727-1666, one of the city's newest lounges, and **Plush,** 431 W. 14th St., bet. Ninth Ave. and Washington St., tel. (212) 367-7035, a two-level nightspot with a lounge up above, dance floor below.

DOVER PUBLICATIONS, INC.

Chelsea
Housed in a warehouse on Chelsea's western fringe is the **Tunnel,** 220 12th Ave., at 27th St., tel. (212) 695-4682, a sort of dance club department store where different rooms offer techno, disco, alternative rock, and rap; cover $15-20. **ReBar,** 127 Eighth Ave., at 18th St., tel. (212) 627-1680, is a small, hot dance club offering a mix of funk, disco, hip-hop, reggae, and soul; cover, $10-15. The **Roxy,** 515 W. 18th St., at Tenth Ave., tel. (212) 645-5156, once solely a roller-skating rink, is now a rollerdisco. Some nights are gays only, other nights are mixed; cover, $12-20. Chic **Cheetah,** 12 W. 21st St., bet. Fifth and Sixth Aves., tel. (212) 206-7770, bills itself as the "fastest club in the world." Inside you'll find golden columns, lots of cheetah prints, a floor-to-ceiling waterfall, and a largely over-30 crowd.

Upper East Side
Decade, 1117 First Ave., at 61st St., tel. (212) 835-5979, is a posh supper and dance club catering to the over-30 crowd. Expect lots of make-up, jewels, champagne, and caviar.

Latin/Salsa
Two-story **Les Poulets,** 16 W. 22nd St., near Fifth Ave., tel. (212) 229-2000, is a disco presenting live Latin music, especially salsa and merengue. Les Poulets was the first club in the city to book Mark Anthony. Cover $5-20. A more sedate place to dance to the sounds of

Latin big bands is the classy **Latin Quarter,** 2551 Broadway, bet. 95th and 96th Sts., tel. (212) 864-7600, recently reoutfitted in a sublime pink-and-gray decor à la Miami; cover, $10-15. At the big, glitzy **Copacabana,** 617 W. 57th St., at 11th Ave., tel. (212) 582-COPA, all done up in tropical decor, you'll dance to first-rate Latin big bands on some nights, deejays spinning salsa and merengue on others; cover, $2-20.

THEATER AND PERFORMANCE ART

Theater productions in New York are listed as "Broadway," "Off-Broadway," and "Off-Off Broadway." The terms do not refer to geographic location, but to theater size and cost of production. "Broadway" shows are the big, expensive kind, playing to audiences of over 500; "Off-Broadway" are smaller shows, playing to audiences of 100 to 499; and "Off-Off Broadway" are the smallest of all, with audiences of fewer than 100. Broadway productions lean toward the mainstream, and Off-Broadway productions—which began in the 1930s as a rebellion against Broadway values—almost equally so. Off-Off Broadway theater was a 1960s' rebellion against the rebellion; its shows are often quirky and experimental.

For information on major shows and ticket availability, call the **NYC/ON STAGE hotline** at (212) 768-1818.

Broadway

Attending a Broadway show is a quintessential New York experience. No matter whether the play you see turns out to be a dazzler or a dud, there's nothing quite like hurrying down the neon-splashed streets of Times Square along with thousands of other theatergoers, most of whom always seem to be running late. Among Broadway's many gorgeous, historic venues—most located just off Times Square—are the **Shubert, Booth, Nederlander, Majestic, Belasco,** and **Lyceum.**

Tickets: Full-price tickets to Broadway plays usually run $45-65, athough some of the larger theaters offer $15 seats far in the back. Half-price orchestra-seat tickets (about $25, plus a $2.50 service fee) to same-day performances are sold daily at the **TKTS** booth, tel. (212) 768-

1818, located on the triangle formed by 47th St., Seventh Ave., and Broadway. The booth is open Mon.-Sat. 3-8 p.m. for evening performances; Wed. and Sat. 10 a.m.-2 p.m. for matinees; and Sun. 11 a.m.-closing for matinees and evening performances. The lines are often very long, but they move quickly. If you don't want to wait, come early, or—surprisingly enough—come late. Your selection will be more limited then, but there's often no wait at all after about 7 p.m.

TKTS also operates a booth in Lower Manhattan, on the mezzanine level of 2 World Trade Center. Here, tickets to evening performances are sold Mon.-Fri. 11 a.m.-5:30 p.m., Sat. 11 a.m.-3:30 p.m. Tickets to matinee performances are sold 11 a.m.-closing on the day *before* the performance.

Another similarly priced budget option is to pick up the **twofer** ticket coupons that can be found at bookstores, delis, and hotels all over town, as well as at the New York Convention and Visitors Bureau. "Twofers" allow you to buy two tickets for the price of one, and they're usually issued for old Broadway shows that have been around forever or are about to close.

Off and Off-Off Broadway

Many Off-Broadway theaters are in East- or Greenwich Village, or along Theater Row on 42nd St. bet. Ninth and Tenth Avenues. Off-Broadway tickets generally run $20-40, with discounted tickets also available through TKTS. Off-Off Broadway shows, which can cost as little as $7, tend to be produced in theaters below 14th Street. A number of these theaters consistently produce fine theater.

East Village: Foremost among Off-Broadway companies is the **Joseph Papp Public Theater,** 425 Lafayette St., near Astor, tel. (212) 260-2400, founded by the late Joseph Papp, who also fought long and hard to bring free **Shakespeare in the Park** to the city. The Public still puts on two free Shakespeare plays—featuring top actors—every summer in Central Park's Delacorte Theater, tel. (212) 539-8500 or 861-7277. Not far from the Papp Theater is a bastion of the avant garde: **La MaMa E.T.C.,** 74A E. 4th St., near Second Ave., tel. (212) 475-7710. It's a sprawling three-theater complex run by the innovative Ellen Stewart, one of the founders of the Off-Off Broadway movement. **Theatre for**

the New City, 155 First Ave., near 11th St., tel. (212) 254-1109, presents new and experimental drama, often at very low prices.

En Garde Arts, tel. (212) 941-9793, offers avant garde, site-specific theater at various outdoor locations throughout the city; productions in the past have included a roving drama through the Gansevoort Meat Market and a play about J.P. Morgan set on Wall Street. The **Bouwerie Lane Theater,** 330 Bowery, at Bond St., tel. (212) 677-0060, home to the Jean Cocteau Repertory Company, presents the classics in the old German Exchange Bank, built in 1876.

Greenwich Village: The **Circle Repertory Company,** 159 Bleecker St., bet. Thompson and Sullivan Sts., tel. (212) 239-6200, is one of the city's top theater ensembles, committed to presenting five new American dramas each year; playwrights connected to the theater include Lanford Wilson and Terrence McNally. The **Cherry Lane Theater,** 38 Commerce St., near Barrow St., tel. (212) 989-2020, is a small, appealing venue founded by Edna St. Vincent Millay and others in 1924. The delightful **Ridiculous Theater Company,** 1 Sheridan Square, near Seventh Ave., tel. (212) 691-2271, was founded by the late Charles Ludlam. It's a creaky, downstairs venue that's the irreverent home of parody, farce, and actors in drag.

SoHo: The avant garde **Performing Garage,** 33 Wooster St., bet. Grand and Broome, tel. (212) 966-3651, is home to the Wooster Group, one of the country's oldest experimental theater companies.

Chelsea and Union Square: The **Atlantic Theater Company,** 336 W. 20th St., bet. Eighth and Ninth Aves., tel. (212) 239-6200, housed in a converted church, is an acting ensemble that grew out of a series of workshops taught by David Mamet and William H. Macy in the mid 1980s. The **Vineyard Theatre,** 108 15th St., just off Union Square, tel. (212) 353-3874, is a nonprofit theater company that focuses on new voices for the New York stage; writers such as Nicky Silver, Brian Friel, and Paula Vogel have premiered works here.

Midtown: Playwrights Horizons, 416 W. 42nd St., near Ninth Ave., tel. (212) 279-4200, produces many plays that eventually move on to Broadway. The **Negro Ensemble Company,** tel. (212) 582-5860, founded in 1967, is one of the older African American companies around; it performs in various venues. **Naked Angels,** 311 W. 43rd St., tel. (212) 397-7841, is a not-for-profit company dedicated to original works and experimental theater; actors and playwrights connected with the theater include Matthew Broderick, Joe Mantello, Rob Morrow, and Marisa Tomei. The **Manhattan Theatre Club,** 131 W. 55th St., bet. Sixth and Seventh Aves., tel. (212) 581-1212, presents plays by both new and established playwrights, and sponsors a Writers-in-Performance series, featuring readings by well-known authors.

Performance Art

P.S. 122, 150 First Ave., at 9th St., tel. (212) 477-5288, housed in a former school, is a mecca for often highly imaginative performance art, as well as a center for avant garde dance. Other venues regularly presenting performance artists include the **Kitchen,** 512 W. 19th St., bet. Tenth and Eleventh Aves., tel. (212) 255-5793, a three-story emporium best known for its video series and avant garde music; the underground Alterknit Room at the **Knitting Factory,** 74 Leonard St., bet. Church and Broadway, tel. (212) 219-3055; **Sidewalk,** 94 Ave. A, near 6th St., tel. (212) 473-7373, a restaurant and "anti-folk" club; **Dixon Place,** 258 Bowery, near Houston, tel. (212) 219-3088, a creaky upstairs joint that also hosts many literary readings; and **P.S. 1,** 46-01 21st St., Long Island City, tel. (718) 784-2084, in Queens. **Exit Art,** 548 Broadway, tel. (212) 966-7745, and **HERE,** 145 Sixth Ave., at Dominick St., tel. (212) 647-0202, are gallery/performance spaces in SoHo.

The hip **Nuyorican Poets Cafe,** 236 E. 3rd St., bet. Aves. B and C, tel. (212) 505-8183, is a big, raw, high-ceilinged place best known for its Friday night poetry slams, in which poets compete with one another in front of an opinionated audience. The rest of the week, performance art and literary readings are frequently featured.

DANCE

New York is home to two major ballet companies, several smaller ones, and numerous modern-dance troupes. The **American Ballet Theater,** once directed by Mikhail Baryshnikov, performs at the Metropolitan Opera House in Lincoln Center, tel. (212) 362-6000, from May to July; tickets cost $21-120. The **New York City Ballet,** founded by George Ballanchine, performs at the New York State Theater in Lincoln Center, tel. (212) 870-5570, during the winter and spring; tickets cost $12-65.

Many of the city's other companies perform in three major venues. The gorgeous, Moorish-style **City Center,** 131 W. 55th St., bet. Sixth and Seventh Aves., tel. (212) 581-7907, annually hosts the **Dance Theater of Harlem,** the **Alvin Ailey Dance Company,** the **Paul Taylor Dance Company,** and the **Merce Cunningham Dance Company,** among others. The more intimate **Joyce Theater,** Eighth Ave. at 18th St., tel. (212) 242-0800, hosts the **Eliot Feld Ballet** and numerous touring dance troupes. The **Brooklyn Academy of Music** (BAM), 30 Lafayette Ave. in Brooklyn, tel. (718) 636-4100, presents a *Next Wave* series featuring avant garde dance companies from New York and around the world.

Two important smaller venues presenting experimental dance are the **Dance Theater Workshop,** 219 W. 19th St., bet. Seventh and Eighth Aves., tel. (212) 924-0077; and **P.S. 122,** 150 First Ave., at 9th St., tel. (212) 477-5288. **St.-Mark's-Church-in-the-Bowery,** 131 E. 10th St., at Second Ave., tel. (212) 674-8112, also offers an experimental dance program in its newly renovated main sanctuary.

COMEDY CLUBS

Caroline's, 1626 Broadway, at 49th St., tel. (212) 757-4100, is the glitziest and most expensive club around, booking big-name acts on a regular basis; cover is $7.50-17.50, with a two-drink minimum. Another well-established spot is **Dangerfield's,** 1118 First Ave., bet. 61st and 62nd Sts., tel. (212) 593-1650. Run by comedian Rodney Dangerfield, it showcases new talent and attracts a large tourist crowd; cover is $12-15, no minimum. **Stand-up New York,** 236 W. 78th St., tel. (212) 595-0850, is the sort of place where Robin Williams might drop in unexpectedly.

Top New York comics often appear at the dark and cozy **Comedy Cellar,** 117 MacDougal St., bet. W. 3rd St. and Bleecker, tel. (212) 254-3480; cover is $7-10, with a one-drink minimum. Among the best of the alternative comedy clubs, where the comics work less traditional material, are **Luna Lounge,** 171 Ludlow St., at Houston, tel. (212) 260-2323; and **Surf Reality,** 172 Allen St., at Stanton, tel. (212) 673-4182; the cover at both ranges up to $8.

CINEMA

As you'd expect, the city boasts a large number of commercial, multiplex theaters, most of which are owned by Cineplex Odeon or Loews. Revival and art-house theaters have died long and torturous deaths over the last decade, until now only a handful remain.

TeleTicket, tel. (212) 777-FILM (-3456), allows you to reserve movie tickets in advance by charging them over the phone to your credit card. This does avoid disappointment—first-run movies frequently sell out—but a service fee is charged.

For independent and foreign films, and retrospectives, the best place in town is the **Film Forum,** 209 W. Houston St., near Sixth Ave., tel. (212) 727-8110, equipped with three screens and a small coffee bar. Lincoln Center's **Walter Reade Theater,** on 65th St., bet. Broadway and Amsterdam, tel. (212) 875-5600, is another excellent venue for foreign films and retrospectives, while the **Public Theater,** 425 Lafayette St., near Astor, tel. (212) 260-2400, offers an unusual selection of art and experimental film classics.

The **Museum of Modern Art,** 11 W. 53rd St., bet. Fifth and Sixth Aves., tel. (212) 708-9480, features many classic films that are free with museum admission. In Astoria, Queens, the **American Museum of the Moving Image,** 35th Ave. at 36th St., tel. (718) 784-0077, has three full-size theaters presenting film in all its forms. Two smaller venues for avant garde films are the **Anthology Film Archives,** 32 Second Ave., at 2nd St., tel. (212) 505-5181; and the **Millennium Film Workshop,** 66 E. 4th St., near Second Ave., tel. (212) 673-0090.

The only truly magnificent movie theater left in Manhattan is the **Ziegfeld,** 141 W. 54th St., bet. Sixth and Seventh Aves., tel. (212) 505-

CINE, which has one of the largest screens in America and a deliciously ornate red-and-gold decor. Another unusual venue—this one minimalist—is the **Angelika Film Center,** 18 W. Houston St., at Mercer, tel. (212) 995-2000, which screens a mix of new and old films to a hip, downtown crowd, and features an extensive cafe.

Sony Lincoln Square, 1992 Broadway, at 68th St., tel. (212) 336-5000, is as much a Disneyfied theme park as it is a movie theater. Inside you'll find plenty of neon, classic movie sets, a gift shop selling movie memorabilia, 12 screens presenting first-run features, and an eight-story-high IMAX screen, to be viewed through 3-D spectacles!

ACTIVITIES

SHOPPING

Sometimes it seems as if all of New York City is one enormous shopping center, with new stores opening up and older ones closing down daily. Nevertheless, certain areas of town are particularly well known for their shops.

Fifth Avenue bet. 49th and 59th Sts., has long been home to many of the city's most famous and expensive stores, including Saks Fifth Avenue, Bergdorf Goodman's, and Tiffany's. In recent years, tourist meccas such as the Coca-Cola Company and Warner Brothers Studio store have also set up shop here. **Madison Avenue** bet. 59th and 82nd Sts. has many exclusive antique and designer shops. **Herald Square** at 34th St. and Sixth Ave., and **34th Street** bet. Fifth and Sixth Aves. feature more moderately priced stores such as Macy's, The Gap, and The Limited. **Columbus Avenue** bet. 66th and 86th Sts. offers a large number of stylish clothing stores, as well as gift and home-furnishings shops.

SoHo is known for trendy clothing stores and unusual gift shops, while the **East Village** has some of the most imaginative and reasonably priced stores in town. **Lower Fifth Avenue** below 23rd St. has an eclectic smattering of clothing shops, and the **Lower East Side** is a bargain-hunter's delight, especially for clothing, shoes, and linens.

Some specific areas on which to focus your shopping endeavors are listed below. For further shopping suggestions, see the "Shopping" entries in the individual neighborhood sections.

Antiques

Many of the city's oldest and most expensive antique stores line Madison Ave. above 59th St., while 60th St. bet. Third and Second Aves. recently developed into a center for more reasonably priced furnishings.

An eclectic array of antique shops can be found in SoHo along Lafayette and Wooster Sts.; and in the West Village, along Bleecker St. west of Christopher and on Hudson St. near Christopher. For bargains, try 9th St. in the East Village and the city's flea markets in Chelsea and SoHo.

Cameras and Electronics

Cameras and electronic equipment are available at excellent prices throughout the city, but avoid the tourist traps along Fifth Ave. and 42nd St., all of which have been "Going Out of Business" for years. The Tuesday editions of the *Daily News* and *The New York Times* carry advertisements from electronics retailers. **The Wiz** is a reputable chain with branches throughout the city. **J&R,** on Park Row, in Lower Manhattan, has a wide selection.

Clothing: New

On the Upper East Side, **Madison Avenue** above 59th St. is home to some of the world's most expensive designer shops. More reasonably priced stores are clustered near Bloomingdale's at **Lexington Avenue and 59th Street.** On the Upper West Side, **Columbus Avenue** between 72nd and 82nd Sts. has a large number of boutiques aimed at young professionals.

On **34th Street,** between Fifth and Sixth Aves., and around **Herald Square** at 34th St. and Sixth Ave., you'll find one store after another. Most are moderately to inexpensively priced. **Lower Fifth Avenue,** just west of Union Square, features many clothing boutiques catering to young professionals.

SoHo is filled with trendy clothing shops, most along Prince and Spring Streets. Ninth St. between First Ave. and Ave. A, in the **East Village,** and Ludlow St. south of Houston on the **Lower East Side** are home to some of the town's hippest young designers.

Clothing: Vintage and Discount
Most vintage clothing stores are in SoHo, the East Village, and Greenwich Village. **Orchard Street** on the Lower East Side offers many bargain-priced stores carrying both designer goods and casual wear.

The city's largest and best-known stores for discounted designer wear are **Century 21** near the World Trade Center, and **Loehmann's,** in Chelsea and the Bronx. Smaller stores featuring both discounted designer and casual wear include **Daffy's, Bolton's,** and **Hit or Miss;** all have multiple outlets in the city. The best place for really cheap secondhand clothes—some vintage, some not—is **Domsey's** in Brooklyn.

Shoes
Manhattan's two main thoroughfares for shoes are W. 8th St. between Fifth and Sixth Aves. in Greenwich Village; and West 34th St. between Fifth and Sixth Aves. near Herald Square. The former caters to young fashion mavens with money, the latter to office workers looking for bargains.

Business Hours
In general, most stores are open Mon.-Sat. from about 10 a.m. to about 6 p.m., and on Sunday afternoons. Many department stores stay open late on Thursday, and some on Monday as well. Stores in SoHo, the East Village, and along Columbus Ave. keep later hours, often opening at about noon and closing about 8 p.m.

SPORTS AND RECREATION

Baseball
New Yorkers take their baseball seriously, and even if you're not much of a fan, it's worth riding the subway out to Shea or Yankee Stadium just to take in the scene. The season starts in April and runs into October. Tickets are usually available at the box offices, at prices ranging $8-20.

Though there's currently much talk of building a new Yankee stadium—perhaps in Manhattan or (gulp) New Jersey—for the moment, the **New York Yankees,** who won the 1996 World Series, still play at 161st St. and River Ave., in the Bronx, tel. (718) 293-6000; take the No. 4 train to 161st St. and follow the crowd. Built by a brewery magnate in 1923, the stadium is sometimes called "the house that Ruth built," in honor of the man who hit 60 home runs here in 1927 alone. The **New York Mets** play in more modern and nondescript Shea Stadium, 126th St. at Roosevelt Ave. in Queens, tel. (718) 507-8499; take the No. 7 train to Willets Point-Shea Stadium and follow the crowd.

Basketball
The **New York Knicks** play out of Madison Square Garden, Seventh Ave. and 33rd St., tel. (212) 465-6741 or 465-JUMP (fan line), from late fall to late spring. Theoretically, ticket prices start at about $12, but that doesn't mean much as the games are usually sold out well in advance.

Football
Both New York teams, the **Giants** and the **Jets,** play across the river in Giants Stadium, Byrne Meadowlands Sports Complex, East Rutherford, New Jersey, tel. (201) 935-8222. Buses to the complex operate out of the Port Authority, but since tickets to Giants games are nearly impossible to get (there's a 10-year waiting list) and to Jets games nearly as bad, you'll probably end up staying in the city and watching them on TV.

Hockey
The **New York Rangers** play out of Madison Square Garden, Seventh Ave. and 33rd St., from late fall to late spring. For information, call (212) 465-6741. The **New York Islanders** play out of Nassau Coliseum, off Hempstead Turnpike in Uniondale, tel. (516) 587-9222. Train service to and from the stadium is available on the Long Island Railroad, tel. (718) 217-5477. Tickets to both teams' games run $15-50 and are generally available.

Horse Racing
The city's two racetracks run alternately. **Belmont Park,** Hempstead Turnpike and Plainfield

Ave., Belmont, Long Island, tel. (718) 641-4700, is by far the more attractive of the two, with a large grandstand, pretty pond, and red and white geraniums. Races run May through July and September through mid-October, every day except Tuesday. (In August, the entire industry migrates up to Saratoga Springs.) To reach Belmont, take the train from Pennsylvania Station; a roundtrip ticket costs about $7 and gets you $1 off the admission price.

The **Aqueduct Racetrack,** 108th St. and Rockaway Blvd., Jamaica, Queens, tel. (718) 641-4700, is a considerably smaller and seedier affair. Built in 1894, it's named for an aqueduct that once ran nearby. Races run late October to early May, every day except Tuesday. To reach Aqueduct, take the A or C train to the Aqueduct station.

Grandstand seating at both tracks costs $2, and bets start at $1. The 75-cent programs include explicit instructions on how to place a bet.

Tennis

The **U.S. Open** is held in late August and early September at the U.S. Tennis Association's Tennis Center in Flushing Meadows Park, Queens, tel. (718) 760-6200. Tickets start at about $12 and must be purchased three months in advance.

Bicycling

Although very crowded on nice weekends, one of the best places to ride bikes in New York is Central Park, where bikes can be rented at the **Loeb Boathouse,** near the Fifth Ave. and E. 72nd St. entrance, tel. (212) 861-4137. Other rental shops near Central Park include **Metro Bicycles,** 1311 Lexington Ave., at 88th St., tel. (212) 427-4450; and the **Pedal Pusher Bicycle Shop,** 1306 Second Ave., bet. 68th and 69th Sts., tel. (212) 879-0740. Rates run $6-8 an hour, $25-32 a day, and security deposits are required.

Boating

Paddling about on The Lake in Central Park is a popular pastime. Rowboats can be rented at the **Loeb Boathouse,** tel. (212) 517-4723, near the park's Fifth Ave. and E. 72nd St. entrance. Rates are $10 an hour, with a $30 deposit.

Fitness Classes

New York has a plethora of well-equipped health clubs offering a wide variety of fitness classes, but most are closed to visitors. One of the few exceptions is **Crunch,** where you can take a single aerobics or yoga class for about $15. Crunch has branches at 54 E. 13th St., bet. University and Broadway, tel. (212) 475-2018; 162 W. 83rd St., bet. Columbus and Amsterdam, tel. (212) 875-1902; 152 Christopher St., at Greenwich St., tel. (212) 366-3725; 404 Lafayette St., near E. 4th St., tel. (212) 614-0120; and 1109 Second Ave., bet. 58th and 59th Sts., tel. (212) 758-3434.

Single classes costing $10-15 each are also offered by **Steps,** 2121 Broadway, at W. 74th, tel. (212) 874-2410; and **West 72nd Street Studios,** 131 W. 72nd St., bet. Broadway and Columbus, tel. (212) 799-5433. The **Integral Yoga Institute,** 227 W. 13th St., bet. Seventh and Eighth Aves., tel. (212) 929-0585, offers single yoga classes for $8. A $26 day rate gives you access to the many cardiovascular machines and aerobics classes offered by **Equinox,** 897 Broadway, at 19th St., tel. (212) 780-9300; 2465 Broadway, at 91st St., tel. (212) 799-1818; 205 E. 85th St., at Third Ave., tel. (212) 439-8500; and 344 Amsterdam Ave., at 76th St., tel. (212) 721-4200.

Horseback Riding

Manhattan's oldest and largest riding center is **Claremont Riding Academy,** 173-177 W. 89th St., at Amsterdam, tel. (212) 724-5100, which rents horses with English-style saddles to ride in Central Park. The horses are well taken care of, and some are quite spirited. Rates run about $33 an hour, and lessons are also available.

Ice Skating

The city's most famous rink, often surrounded by spectators, is the sunken **Rockefeller Center Ice Rink,** Fifth Ave. and 50th St., tel. (212) 332-7654, where admission is adults $8-10 and kids under 12 $6-7 and rentals cost $4. The wonderful **Wollman Rink,** in Central Park near 64th St., tel. (212) 396-1010, with its great views of the city skyline, is much more low-key and about half the price. The **Chelsea Piers Sky Rink,** 23rd St. and the Hudson River, tel. (212) 336-6100, belongs to the brand new Chelsea Piers sports complex; admission is adults $9, kids under 12 $7; skate rental is $4.

Indoor Games

Indoor batting cages, basketball courts, in-line skating rinks, a gymnastics center, golf driving range, rock-climbing wall, health club, and spa are just some of the many attractions at the brand-new **Chelsea Piers Sports & Entertainment Complex,** 23rd St. at the Hudson River. For more information, call (212) 336-6666.

Over the past decade, many spiffy new **pool halls** have opened up in Manhattan. Among them are **Chelsea Billiards,** 54 W. 21st St., bet. Fifth and Sixth Aves., tel. (212) 989-0096; **Soho Billiards,** 298 Mulberry St., at Mott, tel. (212) 925-3753; and the **Amsterdam Billiard Club,** 344 Amsterdam, near 77th St., tel. (212) 496-8180. All have a multitude of tables and keep late hours. **Hackers, Hitters, and Hoops,** 123 W. 18th St., bet. Fifth and Sixth Aves., tel. (212) 929-7482, is equipped with batting cages, miniature golf, Ping-Pong, and more.

Only two bowling alleys exist in Manhattan. The **Leisure Time Bowling and Recreation Centre,** at the Port Authority, Eighth Ave. and 42nd St., tel. (212) 268-6909, is a well-kept place with 30 lanes and a bar. In Greenwich Village, **Bowlmor Lanes,** 110 University Pl., at 12th St., tel. (212) 255-8188, is an old-fashioned spot with 44 lanes and a bar and grill.

Jogging

New Yorkers jog in all sorts of places in all sorts of weather, but one especially popular route is the track around the recently renamed **Jacqueline Onassis Reservoir,** in Central Park, where the late former first lady herself often ran. The main entrance is at Fifth Ave. and E. 90th St.; one lap is about a mile and a half.

EVENTS

New York is a city of parades and festivals, the larger of which are usually announced in the daily papers. Or you can call the New York Convention and Visitors Bureau, tel. (212) 397-8222 or (800) NYCVISIT. Telephone numbers for smaller or more site-specific events are listed below.

January

On New Year's Day, the intrepid **Arctic Ice Bears** take a dip in the icy waters off Coney Island. Between mid-January and early February, the streets of Chinatown come alive with dragon dances, lion dances, and fireworks celebrating **Chinese New Year.** The two-day **Winter Antiques Show,** in the Seventh Regiment Armory, Park Ave. and 67th St., tel. (212) 472-1180, is a great excuse to see the building's grand, cavernous interior, designed by Stanford White and Louis Tiffany.

February

Black History Month is celebrated throughout the city with a variety of events, including concerts, films, exhibits, and lectures. For two days mid-month, dogs of every imaginable breed strut their stuff at the **Westminster Kennel Club Dog Show,** Madison Square Garden, Seventh Ave. and 33rd St., tel. (212) 465-6741. For one week mid-month, the **National Antiques Show** comes to Madison Square Garden.

March

Felines from around the world primp and preen at the two-day **International Cat Show,** Madison Square Garden, Seventh Ave. and 33rd St., tel. (212) 465-6741. The 17th marks the date of one of the city's biggest events and the oldest parade in the U.S.—the **St. Patrick's Day Parade,** first marched in 1752. A bright green stripe runs up Fifth Ave. from 44th to 86th Sts., and Midtown swells with thousands upon thousands of spectators and party animals, many of them teenagers from the suburbs who see the day as an excuse to get falling-down drunk. Meanwhile, throughout the city, Irish taverns celebrate St. Pat's with party favors and green beer, and many New Yorkers—Irish or not—don something green. Smaller St. Patrick's parades are held on Staten Island, tel. (718) 987-2300, and in Brooklyn, tel. (718) 499-9482, on the weekends before and after the 17th, respectively.

Greek Independence Day is celebrated on the 25th with a more sedate parade on Fifth Avenue. Madison Square Garden blooms with the **New York Flower Show.** At the end of the month, the **Ringling Brothers and Barnum & Bailey Circus** comes to Madison Square

Garden for its annual two-month stint; the animals parade into town around midnight through the Queens Midtown Tunnel. **New Directors, New Films,** a showcase of the films of young filmmakers, takes place at the Museum of Modern Art, tel. (212) 708-9500, the last week of March.

April

On Easter Sunday, citizens show off their spring finery in the **Easter Parade** on Fifth Ave. near St. Patrick's Cathedral (49th St.). This is not an organized event but a sort of free-for-all, in which participants dress to the hilt. On the Saturday before Easter, an **egg-rolling contest** for kids is held on the Great Lawn in Central Park, tel. (212) 408-0100. At the Brooklyn Botanic Garden, the two-day **Cherry Blossom Festival** celebrates both the flower and Asian culture through performances and traditional crafts demonstrations, tel. (718) 941-4044.

May

In mid-May, the colorful three-day **Ukrainian Festival** on 7th St. in the East Village, tel. (212) 674-1615, commemorates the Ukraine's conversion to Christianity. The enormously popular two-day **Ninth Avenue Food Festival,** between 36th and 59th Sts., features delectable edibles from around the world. The **Martin Luther King Jr. Day Parade** is held on Fifth Ave. on or around May 17.

Also mid-month, the city's Norwegian population celebrates its heritage by marching down Brooklyn's Fifth Ave. from 90th to 67th Sts. in a **Norwegian Day Parade,** tel. (718) 833-6300. Other ethnic festivals celebrated during the month include the **India Festival** at the South Street Seaport, tel. (212) 732-7678; the **Czechoslovak Festival,** held in the city's last beer garden, Bohemian Hall in Astoria, Queens, tel. (718) 274-4925; and the **Salute to Israel Parade,** which marks Israeli independence by marching down Fifth Avenue.

Over Memorial Day weekend, artists of varying talents pack the streets around Washington Square, selling their wares during the **Washington Square Outdoor Art Exhibition,** tel. (212) 982-6255. The same exhibition also takes place in the fall.

June

The city's enormous smorgasbord of free, and mostly outdoors, summer festivities begins in June. Events include dance, drama, opera, jazz, pop, and folk music. Among the top series are performances by the **Metropolitan Opera,** tel. (212) 360-8211, and the **New York Philharmonic,** tel. (212) 875-5709, held in parks throughout the city; the **SummerStage** series at the bandstand in Central Park, which features everything from dance and poetry to salsa and rock, tel. (212) 360-2777; the **Lincoln Center Out-of-Doors** performing arts festival, tel. (212) 875-5400; and the **Shakespeare in the Park** festival at the Delacorte Theater in Central Park, tel. (212) 861-7277 or 260-2400.

During the day-long **Museum Mile Festival,** all of the museums on Fifth Ave. from 82nd to 102nd Sts. are free to the public. The fabulistic **Mermaid Parade,** displaying eye-popping costumes down the boardwalk in Coney Island, is an event not to be missed, tel. (718) 372-5159. The 10-day **Festival of St. Anthony,** on Sullivan St. in Little Italy, is mostly a commercial affair, with booths selling games of chance, pizza, and ices. **Rose Day Weekend,** at the New York Botanical Garden in the Bronx, features tours, lectures, and demonstrations of horticultural crafts, tel. (718) 817-8705. In mid-June, Puerto Ricans celebrate their heritage with the boisterous **Puerto Rican Day Parade** on Fifth Avenue. In late June and early July, the 10-day **JVC Jazz Festival** takes place at various concert halls around the city and also offers a few free outdoor events, tel. (212) 501-1390. Late in the month, the **Lesbian and Gay Pride Day Parade** heads down Fifth Ave. to Greenwich Village.

July

On the Fourth of July, Macy's lights up the skies with spectacular **fireworks** over either the Hudson or the East River. One of the city's favorite concert series, the **Mostly Mozart Festival** at Lincoln Center, begins mid-month and lasts through August, tel. (212) 875-5400. Also at Lincoln Center in July and August is the **Serious Fun Festival,** a series that celebrates the avant garde performing arts. Throughout the month, accomplished Juilliard School musicians perform free **Summergarden Concerts** at the Museum of Modern Art, tel. (212) 708-9500.

Mid-month, the four-day **African Street Festival** offers sports, art, music, and food on Fulton St. in Brooklyn between Schenectady and Utica Aves., tel. (718) 638-6700. On the second Saturday, during the **Feast of Our Lady of Mt. Carmel** in East Harlem, a statue of Our Lady of Mt. Carmel is carried through the streets as churches ring their bells and street vendors hawk their wares, tel. (212) 534-0681. The highlight of the mid-month, week-long **Feast of the Gigolo** in Williamsburg, Brooklyn, comes when a platform weighing thousands of pounds and carrying an enormous tower is "danced" through the streets on the shoulders of 250 men, tel. (718) 384-0223. On the Saturday closest to the full moon, the **O-Bon Festival** comes to Riverside Park; featured is a ritual dance with drummers and kimono-clad dancers, tel. (212) 678-0305.

August

Harlem Week, which began as Harlem Day back in 1975, now lasts almost the entire month, and festivities run the gamut from fashion shows, open houses, and sports competitions to concerts, films, and food, tel. (212) 427-7200. Mid-month, Ecuador's independence from Spain is celebrated with an **Ecuadorian Festival** in Flushing Meadows-Corona Park, Queens, tel. (718) 520-5900. Also mid-month is the **India Day Parade,** when floats depicting landmark events in India's history parade down Madison Ave. between 34th and 21st Streets. Late in the month, the **U.S. Open Tennis Tournament** comes to Flushing, Queens, tel. (718) 760-6200.

September

Over a million spectators gather along Brooklyn's Eastern Parkway every Labor Day to watch the most fantastic of fantastic parades—the **West Indian American Day Carnival.** Steel bands ring out with calypso music, feathered dancers balance on stilts, and West Indians of all ages strut their stuff, many wearing costumes that have taken months to construct, tel. (718) 773-4052. Also on Labor Day is **Wigstock,** a take-off on Woodstock performed in drag, which takes place in Tompkins Square Park.

The first Saturday of the month marks the **Brazilian Carnival,** when W. 46th St. rocks with the samba, bossa nova, and dancing in the street. Also early in the month is the 10-day **Feast of San Gennaro,** the best-known Italian festival in the city. An effigy of the saint is paraded through the streets, but otherwise the celebration—complete with a small Ferris wheel—is a commercial affair with over 300 vendors.

A second **Washington Square Outdoor Art Exhibit** (see May) takes place early in September. Mid-month is the **"New York Is Book Country"** fest, when over 150 publishers and booksellers set up booths along Fifth Ave. in Midtown. The three-week **New York Film Festival,** previewing some of the ensuing year's finest films, starts mid-September at Alice Tully Hall, Lincoln Center, tel. (212) 875-5610; tickets should be ordered well in advance.

Other special events in September include the **Von Steuben Day Parade** on Fifth Ave., featuring the German Drum and Bugle Corps; and the **African American Day Parade,** held mid-month in Harlem, featuring hundreds of bands. On the last Sunday of September, Koreans celebrate the autumn moon during the splendid **Korean Harvest and Folklore Festival** in Flushing Meadows-Corona Park, Queens, tel. (718) 520-5900.

October

On or about Oct. 5, the **Pulaski Parade** on Fifth Ave. salutes Polish heritage. On or about Oct. 9, the **Hispanic Day Parade** celebrates the city's Latinos. And on or about Oct. 12, the popular **Columbus Day Parade** salutes the explorer and his Italian heritage.

The **Blessing of the Animals** is a singular event held at the Cathedral of St. John the Divine, Amsterdam Ave. at 112th St., tel. (212) 316-7400, on the feast day of Saint Francis of Assisi. Thousands of New Yorkers bring their animals in for a special mass.

October 31 marks the night of the granddaddy of the city's outrageous parades, the **Greenwich Village Halloween Parade.** Each costume seems more fantastic than the next as the procession wends its way downtown, ending with a party in Washington Square.

November

On the first Sunday of the month, the **New York Marathon** is run through all five boroughs. Early

*October's
Pulaski Parade*

in November, the week-long **National Horse Show** comes to Madison Square Garden, Seventh Ave. and 33rd St., tel. (212) 465-6741. On Thanksgiving, the traditional **Macy's Thanksgiving Day Parade** makes its way down Broadway. From just after Thanksgiving well into the New Year, many of the stores in the city deck out their windows for the holidays. Fifth Ave. is especially well decorated; check out Lord & Taylor, between 38th and 39th Sts., and Saks Fifth Avenue, between 49th and 50th Streets.

December
One afternoon in early December, a huge Christmas tree is raised and lighted at Rocke-feller Center, behind the skating rink. The **tree-lighting ceremony** is one of the city's signature events, drawing celebrities and dignitaries, tourists and, yes, even cynical native New Yorkers. Also during the month is the lighting of the **Chanukah Menorah** at Grand Army Plaza, Fifth Ave. and 59th St., and the **Kwanzaa Holiday Expo,** at the Javits Convention Center, 655 W. 34th St., tel. (212) 216-2000. **New Year's Eve** is celebrated with events including the traditional dropping of the Big Apple ball from the top of Times Tower, Times Square; a **midnight run** in Central Park; and family-oriented **First Night** events held at various locations throughout the city.

MANHATTAN

To many people, Manhattan *is* New York. On this small island, just 12 miles long by three miles wide, are crowded most of the city's skyscrapers, businesses, museums, theaters, hotels, restaurants, and famous sites. Though by far the smallest of the five boroughs in area, Manhattan is by far the largest in reputation.

Manhattan was settled from south to north, with the first Dutchmen arriving near what is now known as Battery Park in 1500. By 1650, the city had spread northward to include today's Financial District, and by 1800, Greenwich Village was a thriving community. Union Square

was established in the early 1900s. The wealthy began moving to the Upper East Side in the late 1800s, and the Dakota—New York's first grand apartment building—went up on the Upper West Side in 1884. Harlem existed as an independent farming community until 1873, when it was annexed to the borough.

Manhattan can be subdivided into a dozen or so large "neighborhoods" or districts, which are then sometimes divided again according to commerical activity or ethnic bent. Each neighborhood is distinctive from the rest, and all are worth a visit.

LOWER MANHATTAN

New York City began down here, on this tip of an island where the Hudson and East Rivers meet. This is where the Dutch West India Company established its first New World outpost, and where Peter Minuit "bought" Manhattan from the Algonquins for the grand sum of $24. This is where George Washington bade farewell to his troops at the end of the Revolutionary War, and where he was inaugurated as the first president of the United States. Here the New York Stock Exchange was born beneath a buttonwood tree, and here over 20 million immigrants entered the country on their way to new and often difficult lives as Americans.

Whispers of this early history still echo throughout Lower Manhattan, in sites tucked away among the glistening towers and stone fortresses of corporate and financial America. In this most compressed of cities, this is the most compressed of neighborhoods. Everything here—the old and the new, the glitzy and the drab—is squeezed together on narrow, crooked streets that seem to belong more to the past than to the present.

Unless they work down here, New Yorkers often seem to forget about this district—largely because it has few residential areas and shuts down for the most part at the end of the business day. The Alliance for Downtown New York, an informal organization made up of local businesses, is attempting to change all that through publicity, cultural events, and tours, and some progress has been made. In the meantime, however, savvy visitors will find this a fascinating neighborhood. Every corner has tales to tell.

Orientation

Lower Manhattan includes roughly everything south of City Hall. To take in all the sights here in one day would be extremely difficult—a trip to the Statue of Liberty and Ellis Island alone takes about four hours. But since everything's within walking distance of everything else, it's easy to pick out sights that interest you and skip the rest.

Highlights include the Statue of Liberty and Ellis Island boat tour (or the Staten Island Ferry—an excellent and significantly cheaper way to see the harbor), Wall Street and the New York Stock Exchange, the National Museum of the American Indian, and the South Street Seaport/Fulton Fish Market. Many area businesses and restaurants are closed weekends, but commercial attractions such as South Street Seaport remain open. Be sure to keep a map handy—it's easy to get lost down here.

Frequent guided tours of the district, offered by **Heritage Trails,** leave from the Federal Hall National Memorial, 26 Wall St., bet. Broad and William Sts., tel. (888) 487-2457. Cost for the most popular "Highlights of Downtown" tour, departing daily May-Oct. at 11 a.m., is adults $14, seniors $10, children 7-12 $7. Heritage Trails also publishes a self-guided tour ($4; available at Federal Hall), which directs visitors along 4.5 miles of sidewalk trails marked with red, blue, orange, and green dots.

BATTERY PARK, THE STATUE OF LIBERTY, AND BOWLING GREEN

At Manhattan's tip is Battery Park—a gentle, crescent-shaped park filled with curved pathways, statues, and sculptures. Built on landfill, it's lined by the wide **Admiral George Dewey Promenade.** Wooden benches along the Promenade make great places to relax in the sun and enjoy superb harbor views. At the park's south end is the **East Coast War Memorial,** featuring a giant bronze American eagle by sculptor Albino Manca and granite slabs engraved with the names of WW II casualties. At the north end, half submerged in the harbor, is the **American Merchant Marines Memorial,** an eerie Marisol sculpture of a drowning man reaching up to his comrades. Behind the sculpture is **Pier A,** the last remaining historic pier in New York, built in 1886.

Battery Park is part of "the Battery," the term used for the whole downtown tip of Manhattan. The name comes from the battery of cannons that once stood along Battery Place, on the park's north side. The Dutch erected the cannons to protect Fort Amsterdam, their original settlement, established in 1624-25. The fort was located where the former U.S. Custom House is today.

Castle Clinton

Though not much to look at now, this roofless red sandstone ring near the north end of the promenade was once an American fort protect-

Battery Park, built on landfill

NEIGHBORHOODS: AN OVERVIEW

New York City's neighborhoods are described below, in order from south to north.

Lower Manhattan

Also known as the **Financial District** and **Wall Street,** this is the city's oldest developed area. It's full of historic buildings and towering, glass-sheathed skyscrapers.

Chinatown, Little Italy, and the Lower East Side

Just north of the Financial District, and in startling contrast to it, is an area of low-slung brick buildings housing small apartments and bustling businesses. Chinatown is booming; Little Italy disappearing. The Lower East Side was once home to thousands of Eastern European Jews. It's now mostly Asian and Latino but is still known for its Jewish-owned discount shops.

SoHo and TriBeCa

Short for "**So**uth of **Ho**uston" (a major cross street) and "**Tri**angle **Be**low **Ca**nal," SoHo and TriBeCa were once commercial warehouse districts. SoHo was discovered by artists in the 1970s and is now a trendy hot spot filled with galleries, boutiques, restaurants, and bars. TriBeCa has some of the same, but remains largely undeveloped.

East Village

Since the 1960s, the scruffy East Village has been a haven for young artistic types. Despite encroaching gentrification, it's still the best place in the city for cheap coffeehouses, bars, and restaurants. **Alphabet City** is the term used for the eastern section of the East Village, where the avenues take on letter names—A, B, C, and D.

Greenwich Village

For decades a bohemian capital, Greenwich Village today is largely overrun with tourists and teens. Wonderful blocks rich with atmosphere still remain, however, especially in the West Village. West of the West Village is the **Meat District,** filled with warehouses and cobblestone streets.

Gramercy Park and Murray Hill

Though primarily quiet and sedate residential neighborhoods, both Gramercy Park and Murray Hill have their share of history and unusual attractions. Here you'll find **Little India,** centered on Lexington Ave. between 26th and 29th Streets.

Chelsea and the Garment District

Chelsea harbors many lovely residential blocks, a few deserted ones, a large gay community, a dwindling Latino one, and a steadily increasing number of trendy restaurants and shops. The **Flatiron District,** centered around the historic Flatiron building on 23rd St. and Fifth Ave., is also burgeoning with restaurants and shops. The small, wholesale **Flower District** is on Sixth Ave. between 26th and 28th Sts., and the sprawling **Garment District** starts just north of Chelsea.

Midtown

Most of Manhattan's skyscrapers are found in Midtown, along with most of its offices, major hotels, theaters, shops, restaurants, department stores, and visitor attractions. The **Theater District** is on the west side of Midtown and centers in Times Square. The **Diamond District** is on 47th St. between Fifth and Sixth Avenues.

Upper East Side

For the most part, this is a hushed and elegant neighborhood that's home to some of New York's wealthiest residents. Museums here include the Metropolitan Museum of Art and the Frick Collection.

Upper West Side

In some parts shabby and genteel, in other parts imposing and ornate, this neighborhood is home to many actors, writers, musicians, dancers, and intellectuals, as well as Lincoln Center and the Museum of Natural History.

Harlem

This is one of the city's most fascinating areas, both in terms of its African American history and its architecture. Highlights include the Apollo Theater and the Studio Museum of Harlem. **Morningside Heights,** home to Columbia University, is on the west edge of Harlem. **East Harlem,** predominantly Hispanic, lies east of Fifth Ave.; and **Washington Heights,** to the north, is home to the medieval Cloisters museum.

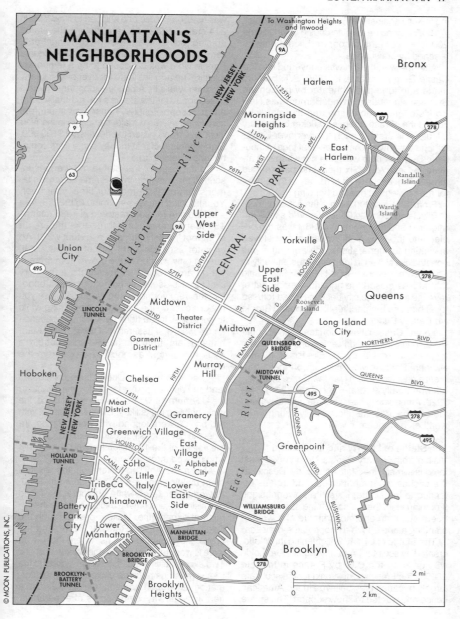

MANHATTAN'S NEIGHBORHOODS

To Washington Heights and Inwood

Bronx

Harlem

Morningside Heights

East Harlem

Randall's Island

Ward's Island

Upper West Side

CENTRAL PARK

Yorkville

Upper East Side

Union City

Hudson River

Queens

Midtown

Theater District

Roosevelt Island

Long Island City

Garment District

Murray Hill

Midtown

QUEENSBORO BRIDGE

MIDTOWN TUNNEL

Hoboken

Chelsea

Meat District

Gramercy

Greenwich Village

East Village

Alphabet City

Greenpoint

SoHo

Little Italy

Lower East Side

TriBeCa

Chinatown

WILLIAMSBURG BRIDGE

Battery Park City

Lower Manhattan

MANHATTAN BRIDGE

BROOKLYN BRIDGE

Brooklyn

BROOKLYN-BATTERY TUNNEL

Brooklyn Heights

LINCOLN TUNNEL

HOLLAND TUNNEL

NEW JERSEY / NEW YORK

0   2 mi

0   2 km

© MOON PUBLICATIONS, INC.

ing the city against the British. When it was built in 1807, it stood on an outcropping of land some 200 feet out in the harbor and could only be reached by drawbridge.

After the war, the fort was converted into the Castle Garden theater. In 1850, P.T. Barnum made a fortune at the theater by presenting Swedish singer Jenny Lind. Barnum was New York's original impresario and the man who coined the phrase "there's a sucker born every minute." He created such a fervor over Lind—hitherto unknown in America—that tens of thousands turned out to welcome her when she arrived in New York. Six thousand people paid three dollars each—a lot of money at the time—for the privilege of hearing her sing.

From 1855 to 1890, before the establishment of Ellis Island, Castle Clinton served as the Immigrant Landing Depot. In 1896 it was remodeled into the New York Aquarium. A beloved institution for generations, the aquarium was nonetheless closed in the 1940s due primarily to Parks Commissioner Robert Moses. Some said that Moses closed the aquarium as an act of revenge against the city because it had refused to let him use the park for his proposed Brooklyn-Battery Bridge.

Today, Castle Clinton houses a small bookstore, tourist information center, and ticket booth for the Statue of Liberty and Ellis Island. A small National Park Service museum on the monument's east side chronicles the Castle's history. It's open daily 9 a.m.-5 p.m., tel. (212) 344-7220. Admission is free, and free guided walking tours of the area are offered daily during warm weather, by request in winter.

The Statue of Liberty and Ellis Island

Visible from Battery Park is New York's most famous symbol, the Statue of Liberty. Despite all the cliches, sentimentalities, and ironies attached to the statue, it's still a powerful sight. If nothing else, there's something strangely eloquent about an enormous statue of a woman standing alone above a choppy blue-gray sea.

The Statue of Liberty Enlightening the World, created by sculptor Frédéric-Auguste Bartholdi, was given to the U.S. by France in the late 1800s. The French people paid for the sculpture largely because they believed in the American cause and wanted to show support. The statue was made in France and shipped to New York in 214 crates. But once here, getting the statue erected proved difficult. In 1876, its right arm, carrying the torch, was set up in Madison Square Park in what was supposed to be a temporary exhibit. The arm sat there for over seven years, however, while its American supporters tried to raise money for the statue's base. Finally, journalist Joseph Pulitzer, himself an immigrant from Hungary, ran a major campaign in the *New York World* and raised the necessary $100,000. Eighty percent of that money came from contributions of less than a dollar.

On the base of the Statue of Liberty is inscribed the passage from Emma Lazarus's famous poem: "Give me your tired, your poor, Your huddled masses yearning to breathe free . . ." The statue itself, restored in 1986, stands 151 feet tall and has a three-foot mouth, an eight-foot index finger, and a 25-foot waist. An elevator ascends to the top of the pedestal, but the only way up to the crown from there is via a narrow spiral staircase. It's a 22-story climb that is decidedly not for the claustrophobic, the very young, or the elderly. Unless you make it over on the first boat, expect long waits to get inside. If you don't have enough patience for the wait, rest assured that the views of Manhattan island from the base—while not bird's eye—are almost as good as those from the crown.

A half mile north of Liberty Island is Ellis Island, the primary point of entry for immigrants to the U.S. from 1892 to 1924. From a distance, the main building looks like a Byzantine castle, with red-brick towers topped with white domes. Inside, the cavernous halls still seem to echo with the voices of the 12 million terrified immigrants who passed through here.

After a $150-million restoration, the facility's main building opened as a museum in 1990. Powerful black-and-white photographs, taped oral histories, and other exhibits re-create the immigrant experience. Visitors pass through the Baggage Room, the Registry Room, and the physical examination rooms, where those who were ill were marked on the shoulder with chalk. Two excellent films are also shown; tickets to the free screenings must be picked up at the information desk upon entering. Outside, across a narrow waterway, stand acres of eerie abandoned red-brick buildings, once also used by the immigration service and now going to seed.

Ferries serve both the Statue of Liberty and Ellis Island on the same trip. The boats leave from the dock near Castle Clinton every half-hour 9:30 a.m.-4:30 p.m. during peak season, and every 45 minutes the rest of the year. For schedule information, call the Circle Line at (212) 269-5755. Admission to the monuments is free, but the ferry tickets cost adults $7, seniors $5, children 3-17 $3, under three free. Tickets go on sale at Castle Clinton at 8:30 a.m., and it's best to arrive early to avoid the inevitable long lines.

Staten Island Ferry

Few people—New Yorkers or tourists—ever get around to exploring Staten Island, but nearly everyone rides the Staten Island ferry. At 50 cents roundtrip, it's one of the best deals in the city. The views of Manhattan from the harbor are spectacular, especially at twilight when the sunset reflects off a hundred thousand windows, or at night, when the skyline lights up like a carnival midway. The sights inside the ferry are fun as well: New Yorkers of every ethnicity bump up against tourists of every nationality; an ageless shoeshine man toils tirelessly up and down the aisles; young musicians quietly strum guitars.

On your right, as you head toward Staten Island, are Ellis Island and the Statue of Liberty. On your left are Governors Island and the Verrazano-Narrows bridge. Governors Island, where 1,500 Confederate soldiers were imprisoned during the Civil War, became a U.S. Coast Guard Station in 1966. In 1995, the Coast Guard announced that it planned to leave the island by the end of 1998, and now its future remains up in the air. The city is considering various development projects, including public parks and luxury housing. In the waters far beneath the Verrazano-Narrows bridge is an odd artificial ledge, made up of the bricks and debris from hundreds upon hundreds of condemned tenement buildings torn down in the 1930s. Informally known as the Doorknob Grounds, the ledge is a spawning area for fish.

The Staten Island ferries, tel. (718) 390-5253, operate 24 hours a day, leaving from the southern tip of Manhattan every 15 minutes during rush hour, every half-hour during much of the day, and every hour at night. You pay nothing on the way over, 50 cents on the way back.

7 State Street

Across State St. from Battery Park is a lone Federal-style house almost strangled by the buildings towering around it. The house was built around 1800, when State St. was an elegant residential promenade. The columns on its curved wooden porch may have been made from ships' masts. During the Civil War, Union Army officers lived here, where they could keep an eye on their troops camped out in Battery Park.

The house is now the **Shrine of Saint Mother Elizabeth Ann Seton,** commemorating the first American-born saint (1774-1821). Once a resident of State St., Seton was canonized in 1975. Visitors are welcome inside, where a peaceful chapel invites contemplation.

New York Unearthed

Just behind the shrine, in the basement of one of the skyscrapers surrounding it, is a small, archaeological museum called New York Unearthed. The museum's actual address is 17 State St., but the entrance is in back, separate from the main building. Inside are pottery sherds, Native American artifacts, coins, jewelry, and more, arranged in a time line, as well as a hokey 10-minute video purporting to take you into the bowels of the earth. The museum, tel. (212) 748-8628, is run by the South Street Seaport. It's open Mon.-Sat. noon-6 p.m., closed Jan. 1-March 31. Admission is free.

Custom House/American Indian Museum

At State St. and Battery Pl. is the stunning former U.S. Custom House, a 1907 beaux arts masterpiece designed by Cass Gilbert. Standing on the site of New York's first European settlement, Fort Amsterdam, the Custom House now houses the George Gustav Heye Center of the Smithsonian's National Museum of the American Indian. Opened in late 1994, the center is a precursor to, and will eventually be a branch of, a larger American Indian museum slated to open in Washington, D.C., in 2001. Inside the center are displays holding some of the country's finest Native American art and artifacts, ranging in date of origin from 3200 B.C. to the 20th century. The maze of galleries surrounds a gorgeous elliptical rotunda lined with Reginald Marsh murals.

Also in the first-class museum are two sophisticated museum shops, a library, and a video room with daily screenings. The Heye Center, 1 Bowling Green, tel. (212) 668-6624, is open daily 10 a.m.-5 p.m. Admission is free.

Don't leave the museum without noticing the anthropomorphized sculptures of the four continents standing out front; under the circumstances, they're more than a little ironic. Designed by Daniel Chester French, who's best known for his Lincoln Monument in Washing-

ton, D.C., the sculptures show a personified young "America" of European ancestry holding a sheath of corn in her lap while an American Indian hovers uncertainly behind her. The area in front of the Custom House was also where Peter Minuit closed his $24 deal with the Algonquins.

Bowling Green

The Custom House sits on the southern edge of small, circular Bowling Green, the city's first park. Used initially as a cattle market and then as a parade ground, the park was leased out as a bowling green in 1733 for the fee of one pep-

percorn per year. A statue of King George III once stood in the park, but irate patriots tore it down on July 9, 1776. Parts of the statue were then melted down "to make musket balls so that his troops will have melted Majesty fired at them"; other parts were found in a swamp in Connecticut as recently as 1972.

Today, all that remains from Bowling Green's Colonial era is its encircling iron fence. Brought from England in 1771, the fence was erected to protect King George's statue and keep out "all the filth and dirt in the neighborhood."

Broadway

Broadway, the city's central and most idiosyncratic avenue, begins at the north end of Bowling Green. Once an Algonquin trail, it runs diagonally the entire length of Manhattan and on up into upstate, where it's known as Albany Post Road. A street of commerce, entertainment, and public ceremony, it's witnessed everything from Washington's first public reading of the Declaration of Independence, to Malcolm X's assassination 189 years later (at the Audubon Ballroom, Broadway and 166th Street).

One of Broadway's southernmost addresses of note is the former **Cunard Building,** at 25 Broadway, now a U.S. post office. Designed by Benjamin Morris in 1921, the building boasts a splendid domed lobby lined with frescoes of sailing ships, mermaids, and maps highlighting the voyages of Leif Eriksson, Sebastian Cabot, Christopher Columbus, and Sir Francis Drake. Unfortunately, poor lighting makes it all very difficult to see, and on top of that, the building is closed weekends.

Across the street from the Cunard Building is the small **Museum of American Financial History,** 24 Broadway, tel. (212) 908-4110. The museum is open Mon.-Fri. 11:30 a.m.-2:30 p.m. Admission is free.

BROAD STREET AREA

Stone Street

About two blocks southeast of Bowling Green (off Broad St.) is Stone St., a narrow, nondescript lane that in 1658 became the first paved street in Manhattan. Legend has it that the street's resident brewer, Oloff Stephensen van

Cortlandt, had the street paved at the urging of his wife and her friends, who hated the dust raised by the brewery's horses and carts. The job was completed in three years, with most of the work done by African slaves.

Fraunces Tavern

At the corner of Broad and Pearl Sts. is the red-brick, yellow-shuttered Fraunces Tavern, a 1907 reconstruction of the historic pub where George Washington bade good-bye to his troops in 1783. During the late 1700s, Fraunces Tavern was owned by Samuel Fraunces, whom many historians believe was a black French West Indian. If so, Fraunces, also known as Black Sam, would have been one of the most important African Americans of his day. Following Washington's election to the presidency, Fraunces was appointed steward of the presidential mansion.

Today the tavern is a dark and comfortable place not especially known for either the historical accuracy of its reconstruction (no one is sure what the original Fraunces Tavern looked like) or for its food. It does, however, house an informal museum with changing exhibits on early American history, and its tavern room is a nice place for a drink. The tavern, 54 Pearl St., tel. (212) 269-0144, is open Mon.-Fri. for breakfast, lunch, and dinner. The museum, tel. (212) 425-1778, is open Mon.-Fri. 10 a.m.-4:45 p.m., Sat. noon-4 p.m. Admission is adults $2.50, students and seniors $1, under seven free.

On the block surrounding the tavern is one of the few surviving groups of 18th- and 19th-century buildings in Lower Manhattan.

Vietnam Veterans' Plaza

One block east of the tavern sits the windswept Vietnam Veterans' Plaza, 55 Water St., where translucent blocks of glass are engraved with the heart-wrenching writings of Vietnam veterans. Worn down by the elements, the engravings are hard to read in more ways than one.

Hanover Square

A few blocks north of Fraunces Tavern, where Pearl St. meets William St., is Hanover Square. Today the square is just a small park with a few benches, but it once stood at the heart of a fine residential district whose most notorious resident was the Scotsman William Kidd. Captain Kidd, as he is more commonly known, was a privateer commissioned by the British crown to capture pirate ships. He was hung in England in 1701 for murdering his gunner. Hanover Square was also where William Bradshaw published the city's first newspaper, the *New York Gazette,* in 1725.

On the square's south side is a handsome dark-brown Italianate building with a blue awning. Known as the India House, it's been the home of Hanover Bank (1851-54) and the N.Y. Cotton Exchange (1870-85). Today it houses **Harry's at Hanover Square,** 1 Hanover Square, tel. (212) 425-3412, a clubby steak house for Wall Streeters.

Delmonico's
One block west of Hanover Square, at 56 Beaver St., is the former Delmonico's building, perched on a triangular plot of land between two narrow streets. New York's premier restaurant for generations, Delmonico's almost single-handedly changed America's eating habits. Before Delmonico's, the city's only eateries were grimy boardinghouses and rough-and-ready taverns, serving what Charles Dickens called "piles of indigestible matter." Then in 1827, a family of Swiss restaurateurs introduced to America the idea of fresh food served in a clean environment. It was a welcome innovation and Delmonico's took off. For 96 years, nearly everyone who was anyone ate here or at other locations later established farther uptown. Boss Tweed, Lillian Russell, Diamond Jim Brady, Jenny Lind, and Oscar Wilde— all were among the restaurant's patrons. The original Delmonico's restaurants shut down in 1923; a new restaurant is scheduled to open on the site in 1997.

WALL STREET

One block north of Hanover Square, Pearl St. bumps into that most famous of New York thoroughfares: Wall Street. Before heading west toward the canyon of financial buildings, look right, towards the East River, where the city's slave market once stood. Established by the British in the late 1600s to accommodate the Royal African Company's growing human cargo, this was once the busiest slave market outside of Charleston, South Carolina. In the early 1700s,

nearly 20% of New York City's inhabitants were slaves, and it was here they were examined and sold to the highest bidder.

The wall for which Wall Street was named was erected by the Dutch in 1653 to defend the city against an expected attack by the British (Britain and the Netherlands were at war at that time). All able-bodied men were called upon to dig a ditch from river to river and "prepare jointly the stakes and rails." The attack never did come, and the British tore down the wall in 1699.

If you've never seen it before, Wall Street will probably seem surprisingly narrow, dark, and short. Surrounded by towering edifices that block out the sun most of the day, the street stretches only about a third of a mile before bumping into the lacy, Gothic spires of Trinity Church.

Citibank and
Morgan Guaranty Trust
At 55 Wall St. is an impressive landmark building—now Citibank—lined with double tiers of Ionic and Corinthian columns. The Ionic ones were hauled here from Quincy, Massachusetts, by 40 teams of oxen. At 23 Wall St. is the Morgan Guaranty Trust building, erected by J.P. Morgan in 1913. About halfway down the length of the building are the pockmarks left by a 1920 explosion that killed 33 people and injured 400 others. The bomb—strapped to a driverless horse cart—may have been the work of anarchists intent upon attacking J.P. and capitalism, but nothing was proven one way or another.

Federal Hall National Memorial
Across the street from Morgan Guaranty Trust is the Federal Hall Memorial, 26 Wall St., at Broad, tel. (212) 825-6888. The fine Greek Revival building, fronted by a wide set of stairs, makes a perfect perch for watching the Wall Streeters and fellow tourists go by. Beside the stairs is a bronze statue of George Washington, who took his inaugural oath of office here in 1789. Back then, the English City Hall stood on this site, and Washington, dressed in a plain brown suit, spoke to the crowds from the building's second-story balcony.

The English City Hall also witnessed the 1735 libel trial of John Pete Zenger, publisher of the *Weekly Journal.* Zenger's acquittal established a precedent for freedom of the press, a con-

A DYING CANOPY OF GREEN

Street trees in New York City have always had a tough time of it. Their soil pits are often too compacted, their rooting spaces are tight, and their water supply is sporadic. They also have to put up with interminable indignities, including pollution, vandalism, dog urine, and the occasional gash inflicted by a passing car or bus.

In recent years, however, thanks largely to budget cuts, things have gone from bad to worse. Though the exact number of trees in New York is unknown, the Parks Department estimates that since the mid-1980s, the city's tree population has declined from around 700,000 to 500,000. Some 15,000-20,000 trees die each year, while only 9,000 new ones are planted. Norway maples and Callery pear trees, the most prevalent of the streets' 50-odd species, have been especially hard hit.

cept later incorporated into the Bill of Rights.

Inside today's Federal Hall—which was built in 1842, well after these historic events—are several small exhibits. One exhibit commemorates Washington's inauguration; the Bible that he used to take his oath of office is on display.

The Federal Hall Memorial is open Mon.-Fri. 9 a.m.-5 p.m. Admission is free.

New York Stock Exchange

Just south of Federal Hall Memorial, the enormous building resembling a Roman temple is the New York Stock Exchange, 20 Broad St., tel. (212) 656-5168. As a plaque on the building reads, the Exchange was founded in 1792 when a group of 24 brokers drew up a trading agreement beneath a buttonwood tree on Wall Street.

For all its grandeur, the Exchange has seen a lot of less-than-admirable human behavior in its day. In the 1860s, financial titans Jay Gould, Jim Fish, and Daniel Drew—with the help of bribed New York legislators—manipulated the market so that they could wrest control of the Erie Railroad from Cornelius "Commodore" Vanderbilt. In 1869, Gould and Fisk again used their financial wiles to try to corner the gold market; their effort failed, but it led to a 10-year panic that caused thousands of businesses to fail and the doors of the Exchange to close. In 1901, the struggle between J.P. Morgan and E.H. Harriman for control of Northern Pacific Railway led to another market collapse and nationwide panic. And in our own day, Ivan Boesky and Michael

Milken got their 15 minutes of infamy and time behind bars for securities violations.

Not surprisingly, tours of the Exchange don't delve into these sordid details. Instead, they begin with a series of bland exhibits describing how the stock market works. Then visitors are herded into a glassed-in balcony viewing area from which they can watch the frenzy of the trading floor below. A recorded voice explains what's going on as the traders rush to and fro, but it's not particularly illuminating or insightful. Even the Crash of 1929 is glossed over as a day of "reckless speculation" that, due to increased regulation, could never happen again.

Free tickets to the Exchange are given out weekdays, 9 a.m.-3:30 p.m., on a first-come, first-served basis.

Trinity Church

Trinity Church, at Wall St. and Broadway, tel. (212) 602-0872, is one of the oldest and wealthiest churches in Manhattan. The present building—the third Trinity Church to be built on the site—was designed by architect Richard Upjohn in 1846.

Up until 1892, Trinity was the city's tallest building, thanks to its 264-foot tower from which visitors could view the sea. The Gothic Revival church also boasts one of the first stained-glass windows installed in America.

Inside, a small museum documents this and other aspects of Trinity's history. Not to be found in the museum's chronology is the fact that during the 1800s, Trinity—which owned all the land west of Broadway between Fulton and Christopher Sts.—was the un-Christianlike slumlord of nearly 500 tenement buildings. The tenements were finally razed in the early 1900s, due to embarrassing publicity.

Trinity is surrounded by a pretty cemetery where some of New York's most illustrious early residents are buried. Among them are Alexander Hamilton, the first secretary of the treasury; Robert Fulton, inventor of the steamship; and

looking down Wall St. to Trinity Church

Charlotte Temple, whose seduction and abandonment by a British officer was romanticized in a popular novel of the day, *A Tale of Truth* by Susanna Rowson.

Trinity Church is open Mon.-Fri. 7 a.m.-6 p.m., Sat. 8 a.m.-4 p.m., Sun. 7 a.m.-4 p.m. The church's museum is open Mon.-Fri. 9-11:45 a.m. and 1-3:45 p.m., Sat. 10 a.m.-3:45 p.m., and Sun. 1-3:45 p.m.

North to Liberty Street

Across the street from Trinity Church is **Irving Trust Company,** 1 Wall Street. Known for its lush art deco lobby done up in red, orange, and gold mosaics, the 1932 building is well worth a quick look.

One block north of Trinity, at 120 Broadway, stands the massive, light gray **Equitable Building,** which shoots straight up for 40 stories, darkening all the streets around it. Though nothing special to look at, the building did New York and the entire country an enormous favor; its

heavy presence led to the nation's first zoning laws in 1916. The laws required that new buildings over a certain height be designed with tiered setbacks to let more light down into the streets. Hence, the wedding-cake look characteristic of many New York skyscrapers.

At 140 Broadway, in front of **Marine Midland Bank** (designed by Skidmore, Owings & Merrill), is a wide, empty plaza with the huge, 28-by-28-by-28-foot *Red Cube* at its center. The creation of sculptor Isamu Noguchi, the cube is so large that a building permit was required before it could be erected.

Just east of Marine Midland Bank and visible down Cedar St., is *Group of Four Trees,* a sculpture by Jean Dubuffet. Beside the sculpture is a sunken garden with meteoritelike sculptures designed by Noguchi; behind it is **Chase Manhattan Bank.** Completed in 1961, the bank was the first big office building built in the financial district after WW II. It helped spur the area's rapid development in the late 1960s.

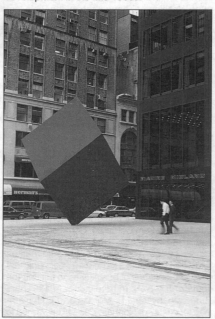

Noguchi's Red Cube

Federal Reserve Bank of New York

This massive, fortresslike structure of dark limestone fills an entire city block and safeguards one of the world's largest accumulations of gold—over 10,000 tons. Built in the style of an Italian Renaissance palace, the Federal Reserve is a "bank for banks," where cash reserves are stored. In addition, nearly 80 foreign countries keep gold bullion here, in thick-walled vaults five stories underground. As international fortunes change, the bars are simply moved from one country's pile to the next. Most of the gold was deposited here during WW II—when many European countries needed a safe storage site—and hasn't left the building since.

Tours of the Fed include an informative video and a look at the vaults. Some of the gold bars are reddish due to their copper content; some are especially shiny due to their silver content; and all seem fake, looking more like giant bricks of candy than precious metal. No one has ever attempted to rob the Fed, but if someone should, the entire building shuts down in 31 seconds. The guards are tested on their shooting ability monthly, and there's a shooting range in the building (not open to the public).

The Federal Reserve Bank is at 33 Liberty St., tel. (212) 720-6130. The free tours are offered Mon.-Fri., and reservations must be made at least a day—and preferably a week—in advance.

WORLD TRADE CENTER

Visible from all over downtown Manhattan are the twin, 110-story towers of Minoru Yamasaki's World Trade Center, bounded by Church, West, Vesey, and Liberty Streets. Erected between 1966 and 1970 by the New York and New Jersey Port Authority, the 1,350-foot-high towers were among the first modern skyscrapers built with weight-bearing walls instead of the steel frame construction popular since the late 1800s.

Entering the complex from the east on Church St., you'll climb a wide set of steps onto **Tobin Plaza,** where it's hard not to feel overwhelmed. The plaza is so stark, and the towers so tall, that human beings seem insignificant here—which is just one of the many complaints about the complex voiced by everyone from architectural critics to office workers. The complex is

sterile, people say, it's boring, and it doesn't fit in with the rest of downtown. And why didn't the New York and New Jersey Port Authority use its money to tackle the many problems of the harbor instead of investing it here? All those objections are valid, and yet, when you sit down near the plaza's fountain, and look up, up, up, the sight is startling—that anything manmade could be so tall.

The World Trade Center (WTC) is made up of seven buildings: the two towers (No. 1 to the north, No. 2 to the south), three office buildings, the Marriott Hotel, and the U.S. Custom House. In the center of the plaza are a fountain and a large bronze sculpture by Fritz Koenig that looks like a giant misshapen globe. Other sculptures dot the plaza, and in summer, many outdoor events—music, dance, comedy, and magic shows—are presented here. Schedules are available in the towers.

In February 1993, a bomb exploded in the subterranean parking garage of the World Trade Center, killing six people and trapping thousands of others in stalled elevators, darkened halls, and smoke-filled stairwells. The blast tore a 180-foot-wide crater into the complex, closing the towers for several months, the hotel for a year and a half, and the Windows on the World restaurant for three years. In 1994, Muslim terrorists were convicted of the crime.

On a lighter note, the WTC has attracted more than its share of daredevils. In 1974, French acrobat Philippe Petit used a crossbow to string a rope between the two towers and then walked across. In 1977, mountaineer George Willig scaled the outside of the South Tower, reaching the top in three and a half hours. At first, the city threatened to sue him for $250,000, but they settled upon a $1.10 fine—one cent for each floor.

The first stop for most visitors is the observation deck, on the 107th Floor of 2 WTC. A long line inevitably forms at the elevators, so check the sign posting the day's visibility to make sure it's worth the wait. On the best days you can see up to 55 miles, and if the weather is good, you can take the escalators up another 67 feet to the open rooftop above the 110th floor.

The observation deck was refurbished in early 1997 and is now known as the **Top of the World,** tel. (212) 323-2340. New additions include three theaters, two gift shops, a food court modeled after a subway car (way up here?), and 24 video monitors that provide descriptions in six languages of 44 New York landmarks. With the new additions have come new prices: admission is now a lofty adults $10, seniors $8, children $5. Open daily Sept.-May 9:30 a.m.-9:30 p.m., June-Aug. 9:30 a.m.-11:30 p.m.

The World Financial Center and Battery Park City

Taking the pedestrian bridge from the mezzanine level of the U.S. Custom House (6 WTC), you'll pass over West St. to the World Financial Center. A glittering complex of ultramodern office towers designed by Cesar Pelli and Associates, the center is also home to first-class shops and restaurants, a pleasant outdoor plaza, and the Winter Garden—a splendid glass-domed public space with enormous palm trees imported from the Mojave Desert. Both the plaza and the Winter Garden overlook the Hudson River, and the Winter Garden is the site of frequent free concerts. Call (212) 945-0505 for information.

Stretching from the World Financial Center south to Battery Park City is a breezy esplanade offering great river views. Along the way are playful sculptures, inviting benches, and pockets of green. Residential Battery Park City, however, is a disappointment. Largely built on landfill excavated during construction of the WTC towers, it's glitzy and sterile, with little to interest the visitor.

Fulton Street

Extending east from the World Trade Center is a short, narrow street filled with discount clothing stores and cheap eateries. The street is named after Robert Fulton, who invented the steamship in 1807 and started a ferry service between Manhattan and Brooklyn in 1814. Each of Fulton's ferries could accommodate 200 passengers and numerous horses and wagons, and could cross the river in eight minutes. At the east end of Fulton St., where it meets the East River, is the site of the old ferry terminal—now the Fulton Fish Market.

St. Paul's Chapel

On Broadway at Fulton St. is St. Paul's Chapel, tel. (212) 602-0874, dedicated in 1766. It's one of Manhattan's oldest buildings and the only one

built by the British. Designed by Thomas McBean, the Georgian church is surprisingly light inside, with pale pink and blue walls, white trim, and cut-glass chandeliers. A coronet atop the pulpit is thought to be the only emblem of British nobility in New York surviving in its original place.

George Washington worshipped at St. Paul's, in a pew on the north aisle now marked with an oil painting of the Great Seal of the United States. Behind the chapel is a pretty 18th-century cemetery.

St. Paul's is open Mon.-Fri. 9 a.m.-3 p.m., Sat. 8 a.m.-3 p.m. Free classical music concerts are presented most Mondays and Thursdays at noon; call (212) 602-0768 for details.

SOUTH STREET SEAPORT

Fulton St. meets the East River at South Street Seaport, one of the city's oldest and most historic areas. A thriving port during the 19th century, the seaport went into a steep decline in the 20th. In the early 1980s, the Rouse Company took over the place and filled it with commercial enterprises. As a result, the area's original atmosphere of cobblestone streets and 18th-century buildings is today marred by scores of restaurants and shops.

The Seaport's historic sites are scattered throughout the 11-block district. Many of the sites are free, but to get into the Seaport's four galleries and its 19th-century sailing ships—or to join a walking tour—you'll need to purchase a ticket at the **Seaport Museum Visitors' Center** on Schermerhorn Row (an extension of Fulton St.), tel. (212) 748-8600. The center is open daily 10 a.m.-5 p.m., with extended hours in summer; tickets are adults $6, seniors $5, students $4, and children $3.

Schermerhorn Row is the heart of the Seaport. Built in 1812, it's made up of pretty, Federal-style buildings that once housed warehouses and accounting offices. Around back, at 171 John St., is the **A.A. Low Building,** an elegant 1850 hall used as a countinghouse during the China trade. The building now houses **Norway Galleries,** showcasing changing maritime exhibits. Next door is the **Children's Center,** 165 John St., with hands-on exhibits for kids, while down the street is the **Boat Building**

Shop, John and South Sts., where boatwrights build and restore small wooden vessels.

Just beyond Schermerhorn Row are Piers 15 and 16, where a number of historic sailing ships are moored. The *Pioneer* is an 1885 schooner that cruises the harbor in summer; the *Peking* is a 1911 four-masted ship housing exhibits on maritime life. Not to be missed aboard the *Peking* is a fascinating documentary film about the ship's early journeys around stormy Cape Horn.

Also docked at Pier 16 are the modern boats of **Seaport Liberty Cruises,** tel. (212) 630-8888. The boats offer one-hour cruises past the Statue of Liberty; cost is adults $13, children $7.

Water Street

Many of the Seaport's other historic sites are along Water Street. The **Museum Gallery,** 213 Water St., specializes in exhibits on New York City history. Next door is **Bowne & Co., Stationers,** 211 Water St., a working 19th-century print shop. Down the street, between Beekman St. and Peck's Slip, is the **Seaman's Church Institute,** a large brick structure whose top floor resembles the hull of a steamship. Still in operation as a philanthropic society, the Seamen's Church once provided a safe haven for sailors who would all too often be shanghied out of the regular boardinghouses. At 273 Water St. is one of Manhattan's oldest buildings, dating to the 1770s. The now-neglected structure once housed **Sportsmen's Hall,** a place known for its "rat pits" where rats were pitted against bull terriers.

Fulton Fish Market

The best part of South Street Seaport is the Fulton Fish Market, where the best time to visit is about 4 a.m. That's when you'll see enormous tuna carcasses being carved into steaks, big piles of shiny flat fish getting dumped into vats, basketfuls of crabs scrabbling over each other, and burly Italian fishmongers wrangling with their wholesalers. But even if you get here later in the morning, you'll still get a sense of what this boisterous, smelly, fishy place is all about.

Adjacent to Pier 17, the Fulton Market dates back to at least 1822, when vendors selling everything from fish to meat to produce set up their stalls here. By 1834, the messy fish dealers had been exiled to their own shed on the water,

behind which floated vats filled with live fish. Use of these vats was discontinued in the early 1900s because of the East River's pollution. Today, ironically enough, most of the market's fish are trucked or flown in.

Up until recently, the fish market was largely controlled by organized crime. A 1995 crackdown by Mayor Giuliani, however, apparently dispersed such influences to the winds. "We say family down here," one fishmonger recently told the *Daily News.* "Brothers, sisters, sons. There are no gangsters here."

Tours of the market are given April-Oct. on the first and third Thursday of the month at 6 a.m. For information, call (212) 669-9416 or (212) SEA-PORT (732-7678).

AROUND CITY HALL

Woolworth Building

The Woolworth, 233 Broadway, bet. Barclay and Park Pl., stands at the edge of City Hall Park. Its glistening white walls and green copper roofs are probably best seen from a distance, where they can be appreciated in all their elegant 800-foot glory. But up close, the 1913 Cass Gilbert extravaganza is also a visual feast. Craggy-faced gargoyles peer down at you from the detailed Gothic exterior, while mosaic-covered ceilings grace the lobby. One lobby caricature shows the architect on the run, hugging a model of the building; another shows Frank Woolworth, king of the discount stores, counting out his nickels and dimes.

Woolworth, a farmer's son, began as a salesman earning $8 a week. By the time he built his $13.5 million headquarters here, however, he was able to pay for it in cash. Completed in 1913, "the Cathedral of Commerce" was the world's tallest building when it opened. President Wilson did the inaugural honors via telegraph from Washington, by pressing a button that illuminated the building's 80,000 lightbulbs.

Park Row and Newspapering

The diagonal street across from the Woolworth Building is Park Row, once the center of New York's newspaper industry. From the 1850s well into the 1920s, as many as 12 papers were published here, including Joseph Pulitzer's *New*

THE "GREAT NEGRO PLOT"

The tragic "Great Negro Plot" of 1741, which resulted in 33 needless deaths, was supposedly hatched in a seedy Irish pub in Lower Manhattan. Hughson's Tavern, once located on Broadway near today's City Hall Park, had an unsavory reputation as a gathering place for sailors and prostitutes. After several mysterious fires erupted in the city, Mary Burton—an indentured servant working at the tavern—testified in court that the fires had been set by slaves who met with her employers at the bar. They were plotting to burn the entire city, she said, free all slaves, declare Hughson king, and divide the white women among the black men. On the basis of Burton's testimony alone, the Hughsons, their daughter, a prostitute, and four slaves were found guilty and hung or burned at the stake.

But Burton's conspiracy charges didn't end there. Over the next few months, she began to point her finger wildly in all directions. Hysteria gripped the city as she accused first one slave and then another, then identified a white schoolteacher as the mastermind behind the plot. Only after she had accused several other white men in even more prominent positions did the judge declare it time to have "a little relaxation from this intricate pursuit." But by then, for many, it was far too late. Sixteen blacks and four whites had been hung, 13 blacks had been burned at the stake, and 70 blacks had been deported.

finest Federal-style buildings in New York. Inside the surprisingly small building is an unusual circular staircase that "hangs" with no visible signs of support. Open to the public are the Rotunda and the Governor's Room, which is lined with portraits by John Trumbull.

The steps of City Hall always seem to be thronged with newspeople interviewing the mayor or some other politician. Visitors are welcome Mon.-Fri. 10 a.m.-3 p.m.

Tweed Courthouse

Behind City Hall, at 52 Chambers St., is Tweed Courthouse. The building was named for William Marcy "Boss" Tweed, the corrupt Tammany Hall official who embezzled millions of dollars from the city. The courthouse was Tweed's most notorious project. It was projected to cost the city $250,000, but ultimately cost over $13 million thanks to exorbitant bills submitted by Tweed-controlled contractors. For just three tables and 40 chairs, the city paid $179,729. For carpets, $350,000. For brooms, $41,190. And then there were the gaudy courthouse thermometers—11 of them, each five feet long and one foot wide, with cheap paper fronts. Their cost: $7,500.

The Tweed Ring was exposed in 1871, the same year the building was completed. The "Boss" was tried in his own courthouse and sentenced to 12 years in prison for fraud, but the Court of Appeals reduced that sentence to one year on a legal technicality. In 1875, Tweed was arrested again on other charges of theft. While in prison awaiting trial, he escaped to Spain. There he had the bad luck to be recognized from a Thomas Nast caricature, and soon was returned to the Ludlow St. jail. He died there on April 12, 1878, at the age of 55.

Half-empty for years, the three-story Tweed Courthouse is now being renovated. Its lobby, lined with WPA murals, will soon be open weekdays to the public. The renovation has fueled the Tweed legend; it was recently discovered that the supposedly solid-brass elevators the city paid for are merely brass plated.

York World, Horace Greeley's *New York Tribune,* Charles Anderson Dana's *New York Sun,* and *The New York Times.* The original home of the *Times,* 41 Park Row, still stands.

Tributes to newspapering still dot the immediate area. A statue of Benjamin Franklin stands at the corner of Park Row and Spruce Street. A statue of Horace Greeley—abolitionist, feminist, and coiner of the phrase "Go West, young man"—presides over the northeast quadrant of City Hall Park. The former 20th-century headquarters of the *New York Sun* is at the corner of Broadway and Chambers St., where a bronze clock still reads, "The Sun It Shines for All." This building was also once home to the nation's first department store, founded by A.T. Stewart in 1846. Initially ridiculed for the department-store concept, Stewart later became one of America's richest men.

City Hall Park

This busy park was once a cow pasture, then a gathering place for Revolutionary-era political meetings. Now it's the site of City Hall, one of the

North of City Hall Park

At the north end of City Hall Park is the **Surrogate's Court and Hall of Records,** 31 Chambers St., at Centre—a glorious, ostentatious building in the traditional beaux arts style. To its east is the skyscraping 1913 **Municipal Building,** designed by McKim, Mead & White. The building houses many city offices, including those of the justice of the peace, where as many as 14,000 couples are married every year. Photographers and flower vendors mill about the lobby, eager to help the happy couples celebrate their new status.

Brooklyn Bridge

South of the Municipal Building is the entrance ramp to one of the city's most spectacular sights, the Brooklyn Bridge. Nothing can compare to walking over this soaring span—intricate as a spider's web—with the roar of the traffic below you, the lights of Manhattan behind, and the mysteries of Brooklyn ahead. The best time to cross is at sunset, when the rays of the sun reflect off the steel cables and wires.

Design of the bridge was begun by John A. Roebling and completed by his son, Washington. Construction took 14 years, and the bridge finally opened in 1883. The world's first steel suspension bridge, it was built largely by Irish immigrants working for 12 1/2 cents an hour.

From the beginning, the bridge's construction was plagued with tragedy. Only three weeks after the city approved the elder Roebling's plans, his foot was crushed by the Fulton Ferry. He died of gangrene a few weeks later. His son, then age 32, took over the project, but soon fell prey to caisson disease—known today as the bends. At the time, the dangers of rapid decompression were not yet understood, and Roebling and his employees spent hours working in the caissons (huge upside-down boxes filled with compressed air) far beneath the river. In the end, as

DOVER PUBLICATIONS, INC.

many as 110 workers may have suffered or died from the disease.

When Roebling became too sick to work on site, he supervised the project from his Brooklyn Heights apartment, watching via telescope. His wife Emily became his emissary, carrying messages between Roebling and his foremen. By the time the bridge was finished, Emily was an engineer in her own right. A plaque in her honor can be found on the bridge, near the Brooklyn side.

Tragedy at the bridge didn't end with its completion. On the day of the grand opening, some 20,000 people crowded onto the span. Someone panicked, and in the resulting stampede, 12 people were killed. Future New York governor Al Smith, watching from the shore, said that the blue sky was suddenly filled with hats and umbrellas fluttering down into the river.

Next came the publicity stunts. In 1884, P.T. Barnum led 24 elephants across the bridge to prove that it was safe. In 1886, a stuntman named Steve Brodie "jumped" off the bridge. Some said he never actually took the plunge, that a dummy was used in his stead. But Brodie nonetheless became a celebrity, living off his stunt for the rest of his life. He lectured, appeared in museums, and opened a saloon that became a tourist attraction. To "pull a Brodie" still means to have pulled off an impossible feat.

African Burial Grounds

On the east side of Broadway, about one block north of City Hall Park (between Reade and Duane), is a new office building with an interesting history. In 1991, when workers were first digging the building's foundation, they unearthed one of the most exciting archaeological discoveries in Manhattan in recent decades—the African Burial Ground.

This centuries-old boneyard dates to about 1755. At that time, blacks were not allowed to join the city's churches and so were buried outside the city limits. Scholars studying old city maps believe that the graveyard may once have covered nearly six acres and held the remains of 20,000 free and enslaved African Americans.

After the discovery of the graveyard, the new office building's site was adjusted, and more scholarly digging began. Excavating about 14,000 square feet, archaeologists discovered about 390 bodies, all buried east to west, with their heads toward Africa. Many were buried with seashells, and some in the remnants of British uniforms. During the Revolutionary War, the British offered freedom to any slave who joined in their cause.

A plaque and enclosed field of green now mark the excavation site near the corner of Elk and Duane Streets. Interested visitors can also stop by the African Burial Grounds' information office in the new U.S. Custom House, 6 World Trade Center, tel. (212) 432-5707. In the office are numerous photos of the excavation site and documentary films that can be viewed free of charge. Open Mon.-Fri. 1-5:30 p.m.

Foley Square

Just north and slightly east of City Hall Park is another government hub, this one dominated by two imposing courthouses and lots of criss-crossing traffic. The neoclassical **U.S. Court-house,** designed by Cass Gilbert in 1936, is the building with the incongruous 32-story tower on top. Facing it is the 1926 **New York County Courthouse,** whose inside rotunda is covered with worn WPA murals depicting "Law Through the Ages." Both buildings are open to the public, and if you've a hankering to see a trial, ask the guards at the doors which rooms are in session.

Foley Square is named after Thomas Foley, a Tammany Hall politician who conducted business out of his saloon—the last one of which was located in today's square. Foley was said to have had a soft heart. Above one of his saloons he kept a dozen beds for derelicts, whom he also fed for free. And he once borrowed over $100,000 to help the bankrupt husband of an old neighbor.

The Tombs

One block north of Foley Square, at 100 Centre St., is the forbidding New York Criminal Courts Building, an imposing gray hulk that makes even the innocent feel guilty. On one side of its columns are inscribed the stern words, "Where Law Ends There Tyranny Begins"; on the other, the daunting "Only the Just Man Enjoys Peace of Mind."

Both prison and courthouse, the Criminal Courts Building works around the clock in its disheartening, seemingly futile attempt to cope with the city's staggeringly high arrest load. Inside, Room 218 is the site of **Night Court,** a depressing yet eerily fascinating place where arraignments take place after hours. Night court is open to the public.

The building's lugubrious nickname, the "Tombs," actually refers to its 1835 predecessor, which stood about a block away. Built in a sort of recessed pit in an Egyptian Revival style, the first Tombs was designed to hold only about 350 prisoners, but often had a population exceeding several thousand. Officially, only prison officials and politicians were invited to witness the Tomb's frequent hangings, but the public would crowd onto the roofs of nearby buildings to join in the fun.

SHOPPING

One of the city's largest and best discount clothing stores, **Century 21,** is across from the World Trade Center at 22 Cortlandt St., near Broadway, tel. (212) 227-9092. The store features designer wear and offers an especially good men's department.

J&R, 23 Park Row and adjoining buildings, near City Hall, tel. (212) 238-9000, was once just a record store. It's still one of the city's best stores for recordings of any kind, but it now also sells computers, audio equipment, and appliances.

ACCOMMODATIONS

Moderate-Expensive

Near the South Street Seaport is **Manhattan Seaport Suites,** 129 Front St., near Wall St., tel. (212) 742-0003 or (800) 77-SUITE. The lobby is worn and the furnishings are nondescript, but the suites are relatively large and equipped with kitchenettes; $195 d, $215-235 for a one-bedroom suite that accommodates four.

Near the World Trade Center is the 503-room **Marriott Financial Center,** 85 West St., tel. (212) 385-4900 or (800) 242-8685, featuring splendid harbor views, an indoor swimming pool, and a well-equipped health club. The Marriott is expensive during the week but offers more moderate weekend rates; $245-265 d, about a third off on weekends.

Expensive-Luxury
The ultramodern **Millenium Hilton,** 55 Church St., at Fulton, tel. (212) 693-2001 or (800) 445-8667, is the towering black column rising directly across from the World Trade Center. Rooms are tastefully outfitted with maple furnishings and marble bathtubs, but the hotel's finest attraction is its sky-lit pool area overlooking historic St. Paul's Chapel; $270-290 d, about a third off on weekends.

FOOD

American
Moderate: At the foot of Brooklyn Bridge is Manhattan's oldest restaurant building. It's now home to the casual **Bridge Cafe,** 279 Water St., near Dover, tel. 227-3344, serving standard but tasty fare. The **Liberty Cafe,** tel. (212) 406-1111, on the third floor of Pier 17 at the Seaport, offers good food and stellar views of the Brooklyn Bridge.

THE $19.90s LUNCH

During the 1992 Democratic Convention, some of the city's top restaurants—including the '21' Club, Lutece, and Four Seasons—celebrated the extravaganza by offering a $19.92 prix fixe luncheon. The program proved so popular that it's been repeated every summer since, with the luncheons' cost increasing one cent each year. In 1996, for example, over 100 top restaurants offered the $19.96 prix fixe lunch during the last week in June, with many extending the program throughout the summer. It's a great way to sample the city's poshest eateries. Contact the New York Convention and Visitors Bureau for details.

Expensive: Morton's of Chicago, 90 West St., bet. Albany and Liberty Sts., tel. (212) 732-5665, is a handsome new steak house. Excellent seafood is also on the menu.

International
Moderate-to-Expensive: Reopened in 1996, the jazzy new **Windows on the World,** 107th Fl., 1 World Trade Center, tel. (212) 524-7000, has updated both its style and its image. The menu now features innovative dishes from around the world, in several price ranges. And then, there's that view . . .

Italian
Moderate-to-Expensive: The elegant, Old World **Ecco,** 124 Chambers St., bet. W. Broadway and Church, tel. (212) 227-7074, is a Northern Italian favorite.

Seafood
Inexpensive: Jeremy's Ale House, 254 Front St., near Dover, tel. (212) 964-3537, is known for its fish and chips.

Moderate: Sloppy Louie's, 92 South St., at Fulton, tel. (212) 509-9694, is a historic fish house now become dishearteningly touristic.

Light Bites
Both the Statue of Liberty and Ellis Island have decent, albeit overpriced, cafeterias. In the Wall St. area, a good choice for gourmet sandwiches and coffees is **Dean & DeLuca Wall Street,** 1 Wall St. Court, tel. (212) 514-7775, just south of the corner of Wall and Pearl (closed weekends). The **McDonald's** at 160 Broadway, near Liberty, tel. (212) 385-2063, is no ordinary fast foodery: a white-gloved doorman stands on duty and the tables are topped with fresh flowers. The usual McDonald's fare is served, along with a nice variety of upscale desserts and coffees. Farther north, on the plaza at 140 Broadway, at Liberty, food vendors sell everything from hot dogs to chicken fajitas on weekdays during good weather.

The basement mall at the World Trade Center holds a number of fast-food eateries and restaurants. At the Seaport, the third floor of **Pier 17** is filled with fast-food joints, while the **Fulton Market** building features both indoor and outdoor cafes.

Near City Hall is **Ellen's Coffee Cafe,** 270 Broadway, at Chambers, tel. (212) 962-1257, an upscale coffee shop frequented by politicians. Ellen's is owned by Ellen Hart Sturm, a former Miss Subways whose face once graced placards on the IRT, BMT, and IND lines.

Watering Holes and Lounges
Near South Street Seaport is **North Star Pub,** 93 South St., at Fulton, tel. (212) 509-6757, housed in an old brick building that was once a gathering place for slave runners. The pub offers a large selection of beers and English-style pub food.

Nearby is **Jeremy's Ale House,** 254 Front St., near Dover, tel. (212) 964-3537, featuring "oyster shots" (raw oysters with Tabasco, tomato sauce, and beer).

At the World Trade Center, **Tall Ships** bar at the Vista Hotel, tel. (212) 938-9100, is a favorite watering hole among Wall Streeters. **Windows on the World,** 107th Fl., 1 World Trade Center, tel. (212) 524-7000, features several bar areas and a "smoking lounge."

HARPER'S WEEKLY

CHINATOWN, LITTLE ITALY, AND THE LOWER EAST SIDE

No region of New York has been home to more immigrants than the East Side between the Brooklyn Bridge and Houston Street. Various ethnic groups have lived here over the years, including the Irish, Germans, and freed blacks in the mid-1800s; and the Chinese, Italians, and especially the Jews in the late 1800s and early 1900s. Around the turn of the century, over 700 people per acre lived on the Lower East Side, making it the second most crowded place in the world, after Bombay.

Today the district is still home to small enclaves of Jews and Italians, but it is the Asian population that has exploded. And a number of Latinos and West Africans have also moved in. On an island quickly becoming homogenized by white-collar professionals, this is one of the few districts left where you can see and feel the immigrant vibrancy that once characterized much of Manhattan. Jewish delis bump up against Spanish bodegas; West African grocery stores stand next to Chinese restaurants.

Orientation

Chinatown, Little Italy, and parts of the Lower East Side are the sorts of neighborhoods where you can have a great time wandering haphazardly about, going nowhere in particular. Especially in traditional Chinatown, the streets teem with jostling crowds and exotic markets. Chinatown's central street is Mott, just below Canal. What's left of Little Italy is centered along Mulberry St. just north of Canal. Orchard St., lined with discount clothing shops, is the best place to get the flavor of the Lower East Side.

Chinatown can be visited at any time; afternoons and evenings are best for Little Italy. Orchard St. shops are at their liveliest on Sunday afternoons, but for serious shopping, go during the week. Don't visit the Lower East Side on Saturdays, when many shops close for the Jewish Sabbath. All three neighborhoods are close to each other, though the easternmost sections of the Lower East Side are a hike.

CHINATOWN

The Chinese didn't begin arriving in New York until the late 1870s. Many were former transcontinental railroad workers who came to escape the violent persecution they were encountering on the West Coast. But they weren't exactly welcomed on the East Coast either. Pushed out of a wide variety of occupations, they were forced to enter low-status service work—part of the reason they established so many laundries.

CHINATOWN, LITTLE ITALY, AND THE LOWER EAST SIDE

© MOON PUBLICATIONS, INC.

Then came the Exclusion Acts of 1882, 1888, 1902, and 1924. Those acts prohibited further Chinese immigration—including the families of those who were already here—and denied Chinese the right to become American citizens. Chinatown became a "bachelor society" almost devoid of women and children. The Exclusion Acts were repealed in 1943, but even then only 105 Chinese per year were allowed to enter the country.

As a result, Chinatown was for many years just a small enclave contained in the six blocks between the Bowery and Mulberry, Canal and Worth Sts. (now known as "traditional Chinatown"). Not until 1965, when racial quotas for immigration were abolished, could the Chinese establish a true community here. Since then, Manhattan's Chinese population has grown to an estimated 100,000.

This enormous new influx has created tension. In the last five years especially, strains have developed between the established Cantonese community and the latest group of immigrants, the Fujianese, who come from Fujian Province on the southern coast of mainland China. Many of the Fujianese are here illegally, having been smuggled in on overcrowded vessels, and they work desperately at meager wages to pay back their exorbitant $30,000-50,000 smuggling fees.

Chinatown has also witnessed the rebirth of the nonunion garment factory. New York's garment manufacturers began moving into Chinatown in the 1970s, when it became apparent that it was less expensive to produce clothing here than in Asia or the Caribbean. Look up from many streets, especially on the fringes of Chinatown, and you'll see clouds of steam escaping from third-story sweatshops. Also note the bright red sheets of paper plastered on buildings here and there—Help Wanted posters for the garment industry.

Chatham Square/Kim Lau Square

At the southeastern entrance to traditional Chinatown, where 10 streets meet (!), is Chatham Square, also known as Kim Lau Square. The first name comes from the Earl of Chatham, William Pitt, an Englishman who supported American opposition to the Stamp Act. The second comes from the Kim Lau Memorial Arch in the middle of the square. Erected in 1962 in memory of the Chinese Americans who died in WW II, the arch is named after Lt. Kim Lau. Lieutenant Lau was flying a training mission over a residential district when his plane developed engine trouble. He ordered the rest of the crew to bail safely out while he stayed with the plane, guiding it away from city streets and crashing to his death in the ocean.

To the east side of the square at Division St. is Confucius Plaza, where a statue of the philosopher is dwarfed by a high-rise apartment building—one of the few new buildings in Chinatown.

First Shearith Israel Cemetery

Slightly south of Chatham Square along St. James Place is a small cemetery dating back to 1683—the oldest artifact in New York City. Buried here in the "Jew Burying Ground" are 18 Revolutionary War-era soldiers and patriots, and the first American-born rabbi. Like the African burial grounds further downtown (see "Around City Hall" under "Lower Manhattan," above), this cemetery was once well outside the city limits, and funeral parties had to be escorted here under armed guard.

By the time the 23 Jews who later established this cemetery arrived in Manhattan in 1654, they had already been thrown out of Spain and Brazil. Dutch governor Peter Stuyvesant didn't want them here either, but when he wrote to the Dutch West India Company, asking permission to throw them out, he was firmly reprimanded. First of all, his employers replied, we're a corporation, and these Jewish merchants and traders can help us make money; secondly, we have a number of important Jewish stockholders.

Nearby Churches

Just south of the cemetery on St. James Place is the pretty **St. James Church,** built in 1827 for an Irish Roman Catholic congregation. Former New York governor Al Smith was born nearby and received what little formal education he had at the church's Hall of St. James School next door. Around the corner on Oliver St. is the **Mariner's Temple Church,** built in 1844. Originally a mission for sailors and derelicts, the Mariner's Temple is now home to a largely Asian American congregation and a powerful African American gospel choir.

Fujianese East Broadway

Before heading west into traditional Chinatown, you might want to head northeast along E. Broadway to the Manhattan Bridge. The bridge once served as a dividing line between the area's Chinese and Jewish neighborhoods, but is now in the center of the new Fujianese community. In a three-block circumference around the bridge, you'll find Fujianese rice-noodle shops, herbal-medicine shops, outdoor markets, and hair salons. Many of these businesses have the word "Fu"—meaning "lucky"—in their names, but thus far at least, things are noticeably scruffier and poorer here than in traditional Chinatown.

At the corner of E. Broadway, Eldridge, Division, and Market Sts. are dozens of employment agencies where undocumented Fujianese men linger, hoping for work. Most will eventually be hired at low-level restaurant jobs paying $800-1200 a month for a 70-hour work week, and most will use all but a fraction of their earnings to pay off the smugglers, or "snakeheads," who got them into the country in the first place.

Doyers Street

Returning to Chatham Square, cross over to the odd elbow-shaped street just to the north. Some say that more people have died at this "Bloody Angle"—a *New York Post*-coined nickname— than at any other intersection in America.

For much of the 1900s, Doyers St. was the battleground of the Hip Sing and On Leong tongs. Similar to criminal gangs, the tongs fought for control of the opium trade and gambling racket. The On Leongs were the more powerful of the two tongs at first. But then, around 1900, a man named Mock Duck appeared. A loner who wore chain mail and a silver-dollar belt buckle, he liked to psyche out his enemies by squatting in the middle of the street, closing his eyes, and firing his guns in all directions. With Mock Duck as their leader, the Hip Sings took over Pell and Doyers Sts., and the On Leongs retreated to Mott.

The tong wars continued off and on through at least the 1940s, with vestiges continuing into the present day. Nearby Pell St. is still the headquarters of the Hip Sing Business Association. And as recently as 1992, members of the Flying Dragons—a youth gang said to be controlled by the Hip Sing—could be found loitering on the street. Crackdowns from police have changed that for the moment, although as far as the visitor is concerned, it hardly matters. Its drug trafficking notwithstanding, Chinatown has long been one of the city's safest neighborhoods.

During the 1890s, one of the favorite pastimes of some Caucasians was to go "slumming" in Chinatown. The more hardcore visited the then-legal opium dens—often just darkened rooms with mattresses—while the more mainstream signed up for expensive tours given by a man named Chuck Connors. Connors—a lively character who is said to have coined such phrases as "the real thing" and "oh, good night"—liked to terrify his tourists by pointing to innocent passersby and saying they were ax murderers or drug lords.

One of the stops on Connors's tour was **5-7 Doyers,** where he would stage a mock kidnap-ping, and rescue, of one of his tourists. The Chinese eventually threw Connors out of Chinatown for giving them a bad name, and in the early 1900s, 5-7 Doyers became the first Chinese theater in New York.

Today, the section of Doyers south of the Bloody Angle often feels gray and deserted, as if filled with ghosts from its violent past. The section north of the angle, however, is lined with busy barber and beauty shops.

Pell Street
Even more barber and beauty shops are situated along Pell St., which accounts for its nickname, "Haircut Street." Many of these small establishments have an old-fashioned feel, with candy-striped barbershop poles rotating out front.

At 16 Pell St. is the headquarters of the **Hip Sing Business Association,** housed in a red-and-gold building with a green awning. A few doors down, at 4 Pell St. is a **Buddhist Temple,** here for the benefit of the tourist trade. Bus tours come to the temple; most worshipping Chinese do not. The more authentic Buddhist temples are modest affairs, hidden well away from prying eyes.

Edward Mooney House
At 18 Bowery, at the corner of Pell St., stands the oldest dwelling in New York, built in 1785 by a butcher and amateur racehorse-breeder named Edward Mooney. The building was used as a private residence until the 1820s; after that, it became a tavern, store, hotel, pool parlor,

Chinatown is chock-a-block with food shops.

restaurant, and Chinese club room. It currently houses a bank.

Chinatown Video Arcade

A couple of blocks away, at 8 Mott St., is Chinatown Video Arcade—an L-shaped dive usually filled with Chinese teenagers. The "Chinatown Museum" was once housed here, and though it's recently been closed, two of its odder exhibits live on in the video arcade. One is a dancing chicken, who, as the sign reads, "may or may not dance and it depends on her mood" when a quarter is put into her rather dirty cage and she's fed. The other is "Bird Brain," a chicken who may or may not play tic-tac-toe when she's fed. "Large Bag of Fortune Cookies If You Beat the Chicken" reads the sign on the bird's cage.

Church of the Transfiguration

The church at 25 Mott St. is one of the oldest in New York, built by the English Lutheran Church in 1801 and sold to the Roman Catholic Church of the Transfiguration in 1853. Over the years, it has helped many immigrants adjust to life in the New World. First those immigrants were primarily Irish, then Italian, then Chinese. The future Cardinal Hayes was educated here, Mother Cabrini ministered here, and Jimmy Durante—whose dad was a Mott St. barber—worshipped here. Today, the church offers services in Cantonese, Mandarin, and English.

North on Mott Street

Mott is the oldest Chinese-inhabited street in the city. A man named Ah Ken moved in here in 1858, and New York's first Chinese grocery store, Wo Kee, opened here in 1878.

At **41 Mott St.** is a tall white building marked with large golden Chinese characters, and topped by the only remaining wooden pagoda-roof in Chinatown; such roofs were outlawed in the early 1900s as fire hazards. The **Chinese Community Centre**, 62 Mott St., is run by the Chinese Consolidated Benevolent Association (CCBA). The CCBA was established in 1883 by wealthy merchants who spoke English and served as unofficial "mayors" for the neighborhood. These merchants were exempt from the Exclusion Acts and were allowed to bring their families into the country. Today, the CCBA is closely aligned with the Taiwan government.

The **Eastern States Buddhist Temple of America,** 64 Mott St., tel. (212) 699-6229, is another temple aimed primarily at tourists, with $1 fortunes for sale near the front. Yet here you'll also find many Chinese, resting on the wooden pews after a hard afternoon's shopping. Some buy joss (incense) sticks which they place at a pretty altar covered with golden Buddhas and offerings of fresh fruit.

Near where Mott meets Canal is the intricate but somewhat crooked **Golden Dragon** neon sign, "famous" for lighting up on both sides.

Museum of Chinese in the Americas

Recently renovated, the small but fascinating Museum of Chinese in the Americas, 70 Mulberry St., at Bayard, tel. (212) 619-4785, centers around a permanent exhibit entitled "Where Is Home?" Encased in a large structure reminiscent of a glowing lantern, the exhibit features personal stories, photographs, mementos, and poetry culled from 16 years of research in the Chinese community. Among the topics explored are women's roles, religion, the Chinese laundry, and the "bachelor society."

The museum is on the fourth floor of an 1891 red-brick building that was once a school. On sale in the project's bookstore is an excellent "Chinatown Historical Map & Guide" ($4), which provides insights into the neighborhood's history, as well as tips on what to order in Chinese restaurants, where to shop, and what to buy. The bookstore also carries about 80 other titles by or about Asian Americans.

Hours are Tues.-Sun. 10:30 a.m.-5 p.m.; admission adults $3, students and seniors $1, children under 12 free. The museum also sponsors occasional walking tours. As you enter or leave the museum, keep an eye out for flyers; this is the best place in the city to find out about Asian American cultural events.

Columbus Park

On Mulberry St., a half-block south of the museum, is Chinatown's only park, created in the late 1890s through the heroic efforts of Jacob Riis and other early social reformers. Before the park was constructed, Riis—then working as police reporter—called this dilapidated stretch of the city "the worst pigsty of all"; he reported a stabbing or shooting here at least every week.

FROM POND TO SLUM

Collect Pond—early Manhattan's largest body of water—once covered a large chunk of Chinatown between present-day Franklin and Worth, and Lafayette and Baxter Streets. Though full of fish when the Dutch arrived, the pond was nearly exhausted by the mid-1700s. Then, around 1800, the city began filling it in with mounds of dirt and garbage; by 1807, a 15-foot-high pile of nasty-smelling refuse towered in its middle. Finally, in 1808, the city built a canal to drain the pond into the sea. That paved-over canal later became Canal Street.

Though advised against it, developers started building on the newly drained land without waiting for it to settle. The new homes were no sooner completed than they began to crack and tilt. No one with money would move in, and the area quickly evolved into Manhattan's first and arguably most notorious slum ever—Five Points. Named after the five streets that once intersected where Columbus Park is today, the neighborhood housed over 40,000 people in less than half a square mile. Most of its residents were desperate immigrants earning $1 a day and freed blacks earning even less. Local lore had it that policemen were afraid to enter the area except in squads of 10, and some said that at least one murder a day was committed there.

Wrote Charles Dickens in 1842, after his ill-fated trip to New York (he hated everything about it): "What place is this, to which the squalid street conducts us? A kind of square of leprous houses . . . reeking everywhere with dirt and filth . . . See how the rotten beams are tumbling down, and how the patched and broken windows seem to scowl dimly, like eyes that have been hurt in drunken frays."

Desperate living conditions gave rise to dangerous gangs, among them the Forty Thieves, the Dead Rabbits ("dead" meant "best," "rabbit" meant "tough guy"), the Plug Uglies, and the Shirt Tails. The latter, as might be expected, wore their shirts outside their pants, while the Plug Uglies wore big plug hats stuffed with leather and wool. The gangs' weapons of choice were clubs, bats, and hobnail boots.

Recent scholarship indicates, however, that Five Points had another side to it. In 1996, archaeologists examining remnants concluded that the neighborhood had also been home to a large, family-oriented population.

To get an idea of what living conditions in this then-Italian neighborhood were like, take a look at the "rear tenements" on Mulberry St., just below Bayard. These tenements were built *in between* two rows of other tenements, and most of their rooms had no windows or airshafts.

Though more concrete than greenery, Columbus Park is usually filled with Chinese kids at play and old women gossiping under rice-paper umbrellas. On the weekends, Chinese fortune-tellers often set up shop.

Mulberry Street
At the southernmost end of Mulberry across from the park is a row of funeral parlors that many Chinese who dabble in gambling go out of their way to avoid. No use courting bad luck. Heading north on Mulberry St. to Canal St., you'll pass some of the many outdoor markets that crowd the streets of Chinatown. These oft-mobbed stands sell everything from baby shrimp to Chinese broccoli at bargain prices. Yet the storeowners in traditional Chinatown—where the demand for space is ferocious—pay more rent per square foot than do the owners of Tiffany & Company in Midtown.

Canal Street
You'll find it all on this most remarkable of streets—fruits and vegetables, plastic toys, burglar alarms, car stereos, art supplies, Asian banks, and hordes and hordes of people. It's easy to spend hours here just meandering about, soaking it all in.

Most overwhelming at first are the fish stores near Baxter St., where enormous piles of fish seem to stare balefully at you as you pass by. Live carp, bass, eel, crabs—they're all here, some shipped in from as far away as Hong Kong, some from the Fulton Fish Market just down the street.

Next you'll notice the enormous number of banks. At the intersection of Mott and Canal Sts. alone stand four behemoths: Chase, Chemical, Abacus, and United Orient. Some say that banks in Chinatown now outnumber restaurants, and although that seems hard to believe, the banks' presence is indicative of the enormous investments from Hong Kong, Taiwan, and China that have flooded New York in recent years. In keeping with Chinese tradition—which puts a high value on savings—the banks in Chinatown stay open evenings and weekends. Employees in some branches speak seven dialects.

Shopping

Some of Chinatown's oldest stores are on Mott Street. **Quong Yuen Shing,** 32 Mott St., is a small 1890s store filled with ceramic dishes, figurines, and beautiful wood-and-glass cabinets.

Also on Mott are **Kam Kuo Food Corp.,** 7 Mott St., tel. (212) 233-5387, one of several new and very well stocked food markets that have opened in Chinatown in recent years; **Kam Tat Trading Co.,** 54 Mott St., one of the many herb shops in Chinatown; and **Ten Ren Tea Co.,** 75 Mott St., near Canal, tel. (212) 349-2286, a spiffy and very friendly store selling dozens of exotic teas.

Near the north end of Columbus Park is **Ping's Dried Beef,** 58 Mulberry St., tel. (212) 732-0850, a dark and uninviting store that's been in Chinatown for over 20 years. The well-known shop uses an original recipe from a school in Guangzhou (Canton) to preserve its products. Besides dried beef, the store sells pork and liver sausages, pressed duck, and Chinese bacon. The narrow **Chinese American Trading Company,** 91 Mulberry St., tel. (212) 267-5224, stocks cooking utensils, dishes, and other Chinese products.

Canal St. is known for its bargain-priced department stores. **Kam Man,** 200 Canal St., bet. Mott and Mulberry, tel. (212) 571-0330, is a modern food emporium offering a wide selection of Chinese foods, herbs, and cooking utensils. **Pearl River Chinese Products,** 277 Canal St., at Broadway, tel. (212) 219-8107 (with branches at 13 Elizabeth St. and 200 Grand St.), is the largest department store in Chinatown and a fascinating place to explore. On sale are Chinese musical instruments, paper lanterns, kites, dried herbs, clothing, and lots of merchandise from the People's Republic. Similar to Pearl

River, but less discovered, is **Phoenix Emport,** 51 Mott St., tel. (212) 608-6670.

Farther west on Canal, near W. Broadway, you'll run into a stretch of odd, informal stores selling a combination of hardware, industrial ware, machine parts, and junk. Boxes of *stuff* line the sidewalks, and unless you're a mechanic of some kind, you'll probably have a hard time figuring out what's what. On the south side of Canal is the venerable **Pearl Paint Company,** 308 Canal St., near Broadway, tel. (212) 431-7932. The grand five-story emporium is the world's largest art and graphics discount center, with more than 100 clerks on duty at all times.

Entertainment

A number of Asian American performing-arts groups are based in the area. Some of the better-known groups include **Chen and the Dancers,** 70 Mulberry St., tel. (212) 349-0126; the **Asian American Dance Theater,** 26 Bowery, tel. (212) 233-2154; and the **Chinese Music Ensemble,** 224 Centre St., tel. (212) 925-6110.

Accommodations

Moderate: The shiny, new **Holiday Inn Downtown,** 138 Lafayette St., at Howard, tel. (212) 966-8898 or (800) HOLIDAY, offers a modern second-story lobby accessible by escalator, 223 nondescript rooms, and an on-site Chinese restaurant. Despite the location, most of the guests are occidental; $150-171 s or d.

Food

Chinatown is home to over 300 restaurants serving various cuisines including Hunan, Szechuan, Shanghai, Cantonese, Vietnamese, and Thai. You can't go wrong with most of the restaurants here, especially those catering to a large Asian clientele. All are inexpensive to moderately priced.

Chinese: Several excellent choices on Mott St. include **Wong Kee,** 113 Mott near Hester, tel. (212) 966-1160, serving Cantonese food; **Tai Hong Lau,** 70 Mott, near Bayard, tel. (212) 219-1431, serving unusual Hong Kong-style cuisine; and **69 Mott Street** at Bayard, tel. (212) 233-5877, known especially for its roast pork and soups. Bustling **Joe's Shanghai,** 9 Pell St., bet. Bowery and Mott St., tel. (212) 233-8888, offers some of the best and freshest food in Chinatown. Good noodles can be had at **Hong Fat,**

63 Mott, bet. Bayard and Canal, tel. (212) 349-4735; and **New Chao Chow,** 111 Mott, bet. Canal and Hester, tel. (212) 226-2590, where you may be asked to share a table.

The popular **Great Shanghai Restaurant,** 27 Division St., near E. Broadway, tel. (212) 966-7663, serves a little bit of everything, and it's all first-rate. The modern, bilevel **Nice Restaurant,** 35 E. Broadway, near Catherine, tel. (212) 406-9510, is known for its fresh Hong Kong-style Chinese food. For spicy Szechuan, try the tiny **Little Szechuan,** 31 Oliver St., bet. Madison and Henry, tel. (212) 349-2360. Delicately flavored Fujianese cuisine is offered by **Long Shine Restaurant,** 47 E. Broadway, bet. Market and Catherine, tel. (212) 346-9888.

Other Asian Fare: Fresh and healthy Vietnamese fare is the specialty at the unassuming **Nha Trang,** 87 Baxter St., bet. Bayard and Canal, tel. (212) 233-5948. Some of the city's best Thai food can be found at **Thailand Restaurant,** 106 Bayard St., at Baxter, tel. (212) 349-3132. For Malaysian and Indonesian food, try **Malaysia and Indonesia,** 18 Doyers St., near the Bowery, tel. (212) 267-0088.

Dim Sum: Chinatown is home to a number of cavernous, gaily decorated restaurants serving dim sum from mid-morning until late afternoon, and fixed-priced banquets thereafter. The latter usually cater to groups of eight or more, so if you come at night, bring lots of friends. One of the largest and best of these banquet halls is **Golden Unicorn,** 18 E. Broadway, at Catherine, tel. (212) 941-0911, where waiters use walkie-talkies to communicate. Other excellent choices include **Silver Palace,** 52 Bowery, bet. Canal and Hester, tel. (212) 964-1204; the **Triple Eight Palace,** 88 E. Broadway, bet. Catherine and Market, tel. (212) 941-8886; and **HSF,** 46 Bowery, near Canal, tel. (212) 374-1319, where explanations of dim sum are available for the uninitiated.

Treats: Chinatown is also filled with bakeries. Some are big and modern, others are holes-in-the-wall with atmosphere in spades. One of the oldest is the creaky, 70-odd-year-old **Nom Wah Tea Parlor,** 13 Doyers St., near Pell, tel. (212) 962-6047. Near where Pell meets Mott is Nom Wah's antithesis, the cheery **May May Bakery,** 35 Pell St., tel. (212) 267-0733. Try the moon cakes, almond cookies, "cow ears" (chips of fried dough), or pork buns. Just off Mott St. on Mosco

St. is a dilapidated red shack where the "egg-cake lady," Mrs. Tam, sells nuggetlike cakes to a large following. Also, don't miss the **Chinatown Ice Cream Factory,** 65 Bayard St., near Mott, tel. (212) 608-4170, where you can buy every flavor of ice cream from ginger to mango.

LITTLE ITALY

In contrast to Chinatown, Little Italy is but a shadow of its former self. The Italian population here reached its zenith between 1890 and 1924. Today only about 10% of the neighborhood's residents are of Italian ancestry, and the heart of its dining and shopping district has shrunk to just three short blocks. Even on those blocks, the buildings tend to be owned by Asian Americans, who—knowing a good thing when they see it—rent to Italian Americans on the understanding that the buildings be used to perpetuate the tourist trade.

Despite all of this, little pockets of the Italian community can still be found here and there throughout downtown. This is especially evident during warm weather when older Italian women dressed in black set up folding chairs along Mott St., in sections of Greenwich Village around Sullivan St., and in SoHo east of Lafayette.

Mulberry Street
Most of what is left of Little Italy is along Mulberry St. just above Canal Street. Here, Italian restaurants and cafes line the street, with tables and striped umbrellas set out in warm weather. It's all very touristy, but it's also a lot of fun, with mustachioed waiters gesticulating wildly like caricatures of themselves, and lots and lots of bright, garish colors.

Not far from the intersection of Canal St., at 109 Mulberry St., is the **Church of the Most Precious Blood,** its pretty courtyard often filled with birds. Though usually shuttered and empty, the church is the center of the feast of San Gennaro, held for 10 days around Sept. 19. San Gennaro is the patron saint of Naples, and his blood—kept in a church in his home city—is said to turn to liquid on his feast day. During the festival, the streets of Little Italy are filled with bright lights, tacky games of chance, and food stands, very few of which sell Italian food.

Umberto's Clam House

On April 7, 1972, at 5:20 a.m., gangster "Crazy" Joe Gallo was shot to death in an Italian fishhouse at 129 Mulberry Street. The reputed leader of organized crime, and the man thought to be responsible for two of the mob's most famous hits—Albert Anastasia in 1957 and Joe Colombo in 1971—Gallo had been out celebrating his 43rd birthday with his new bride and 10-year-old stepdaughter.

The Gallo party arrived at Umberto's a little after 4 a.m. and sat in the back, with Joey facing the door, naturally. But his vigilance wasn't enough. A balding man wearing a tweed overcoat stepped in through the rear and fired more than a dozen shots at Gallo. While everyone else hit the floor, he staggered out into the street and fell down dead.

Bullet marks were still visible on Umberto's stainless steel kitchen door, until the restaurant closed in early 1997. The police never arrested anyone for the shooting, but they believe that Gallo was killed by followers of Joe Colombo, intent upon revenge.

Banco Stabile

On the corner of Mulberry and Grand Sts. stands the 1865 Banco Stabile. In the early 1900s, about 70% of all Italian immigrants prepaid their tickets to and from the U.S. through this Italian bank. These immigrants were sometimes called "Birds of Passage," because they spent half the year working in the New York garment industry, the other half in Italy, planting and harvesting the vineyards. Since an immigrant was charged a $25 tax if he or she returned home before three years were up, these Birds of Passage often traveled **with**out **p**apers—hence the slur "wop."

Old St. Patrick's Cathedral

On Mott near Prince St., on the fringes of SoHo, is Old St. Patrick's Cathedral. The predecessor to the famous St. Patrick's Cathedral on Fifth Ave., this 1809 Gothic structure was once the cathedral of the see of New York. Behind the church is a walled cemetery (usually locked) where Pierre Toussaint is buried. Toussaint was a Haitian born into slavery who later became the first black American candidate for sainthood.

Around the corner from the cathedral is the unusual **Elizabeth Street Garden,** 210 Elizabeth St., tel. (212) 941-4800, filled with enormous pieces of weathered statuary. The outdoor sculpture garden is maintained by the gallery across the way.

Ravenite Social Club

Also removed from the heart of today's Little Italy is Ravenite Social Club, 247 Mulberry St., near Prince Street. Inside the brick storefront with American flags in its windows is a social club for mobsters. Before he was put behind bars, John Gotti—nicknamed the Dapper Don— hung out here with his henchmen, playing cards, watching TV, and shooting the bull. Today, it's still not unusual to see Cadillacs and limos pulled up to the door.

Shopping

Across from the Banco Stabile is the city's mother lode of great Italian food stores, including the **Italian Food Center,** 186 Grand St., tel. (212) 925-2954, stocked with a wide variety of wares; **Alleva Dairy,** 188 Grand St., tel. (212) 226-7990, said to sell two tons of cheese a week; and **Piemonte Ravioli,** 190 Grand St., tel. (212) 226-0475, known for its homemade pasta. Also at the corner is **Rossi & Co.,** 191 Grand St., tel. (212) 966-6640, a variety store where you can buy everything from a Mussolini T-shirt to opera CDs.

Though becoming increasingly Chinese, Mott St. north of Canal St. still holds a number of traditional Italian shops. For Italian cheese, try **DiPalo's Fine Foods** 206 Grand St., at Mott, tel. (212) 226-1033. For excellent breads, head for **Parisi Bakery,** 198 Mott St., tel. (212) 226-6378.

Food

Though Little Italy is generally *not* the place to go for good Italian food, it does hold some bargain-priced eateries, cheery cafes, and a few noteworthy dinner houses.

Inexpensive-to-Moderate: Da Nico, 164 Mulberry St., bet. Grand and Broome, tel. (212) 343-1212, specializes in excellent coal-oven pizza and savory roasted meats and fish. **Benito I,** 174 Mulberry St., bet. Grand and Broome, tel. (212) 226-9171, serves good, traditional Sicilian food. And though not Italian, the **Road to Mandalay,** 380 Broome St., at Mulberry, tel. (212) 226-4218, deserves mention for its flavorful Burmese fare.

Expensive: One of Little Italy's best restaurants is **Il Cortile,** 125 Mulberry St., near Hester, tel. (212) 226-6060, specializing in Northern Italian cuisine. Also very good is **Taormina,** 147 Mulberry St., bet. Hester and Grand, tel. (212) 219-1007, once mobster John Gotti's favorite spot.

Light Bites: For an afternoon snack, try the cozy, tile-floored **Cafe Roma,** 385 Broome St., at Mulberry, tel. (212) 226-8413, a wonderful espresso-and-pastry cafe that was once a hangout for opera singers. Another good choice is the flashy **Ferrara's,** 195 Grand St., near Mulberry, tel. (212) 226-6150.

Watering Holes and Lounges
Mare Chiaro, 176¹/₂ Mulberry St., near Broome, tel. (212) 226-9345, is an Old World, out-of-time bar where, as one journalist recently commented, you might find the owner dancing in his underwear or the proprietress smoking a cigar. It's recently been discovered by the literary set,

---

HORSEPOWERED POLLUTION IN THE 1800s

New York today may not seem like the cleanest of cities, but before you voice a complaint, consider the way it was back in the late 1800s. Back then, the 120,000-some horses in the city left about 1,300 tons of manure a day on the streets. The city employed only a handful of street cleaners, and "that foul aliment" was allowed to accumulate in huge piles, breeding "pestilential vapours" and millions of flies. In addition, whenever one of the poor, overworked horses expired, it was simply left to rot by the side of the road. In 1880 alone, New York City removed 15,000 dead horses from its streets.

Reported *Harper's Weekly* on February 26, 1881: "The condition of the streets of New York during the present winter has been frightful beyond all precedent even for the dirtiest city in the U.S. . . . The thaw that followed aggravated the evil, and today the city lies ankle-deep in liquid filth through which the pedestrians are obliged to wade and flounder. There is no such thing as picking one's way, for with a few exceptions, one spot is as bad as another and everybody plunges in and ploughs through it without regard to the consequences."

---

who crowd the place after work and on the weekends. Across from the grand, baroque, former police headquarters on Centre Street (now luxury condominiums) is **Onieal's Grand Street Bar,** 174 Grand St., bet. Mulberry and Court St., tel. (212) 941-9119. In the 1940s, *Daily News* photographer Arthur Felig, better known as Weegee, hung out here while waiting to follow police sirens to nasty crime scenes. Nowadays, the clientele tends to be younger, trendier, more sheltered, and more upscale.

THE BOWERY

Heading east, you'll bump into one of the city's most famous thoroughfares—the gray, neglected Bowery. Though long associated with alcoholism and abject poverty, the Bowery has a long and singular history that predates New York.

Named after the Dutch word for farm *(bouwerie),* the street was first an Indian path, then a trail leading to Peter Stuyvesant's farm in what is now the East Village. Later in the 18th century, the Bowery became part of the Boston Post Road and was lined with a number of fine homes and estates, as well as roadside taverns. George Washington often drank at the Bullshead Tavern, 146 Bowery, since torn down.

By the mid-1800s, the Bowery had become a glittering strip of lowbrow theaters where rowdy audiences roared out their laughter or jeers. Extravagant productions were the order of the day, with dozens of horses or full-rigged ships often appearing on stage. The Bowery Amphitheater (37 Bowery) presented the nation's first blackface minstrel show, while the National Theater (104 Bowery) produced a long serial play about a mythic street fighter named Mose. Mose could lift streetcars off their tracks, blow wind into ships' sails, and jump from Manhattan to Brooklyn in a single bound.

Around 1880, the Bowery began changing again. Cheap boardinghouses, gin mills, missions, and brothels began replacing the theaters, and the down-and-out began replacing the working class. Crime became rampant, and the street slowly slid into poverty and despair. By 1907, an estimated 25,000 homeless men were living in the flophouses and missions here. (The Bowery has always been the province of men: in

1907, 115 stores on the Bowery sold menswear; none carried women's apparel.)

The Bowery continued to be known as a haven for the down-and-out until well into the 1960s, but today, all the bars are gone and less than a half-dozen flophouses remain. The Bowery's adjoining streets above Houston St. are rapidly becoming gentrified, while the Bowery above Canal St. is becoming part of Chinatown.

The Bowery around Broome St. is the city's lighting district, filled with shops selling lamps and lampshades of every conceivable variety. Farther north, around Rivington St., is the kitchen-supplies district, where restaurants come to buy silverware, utensils, and the like.

At the corner of the Bowery and Grand St. is **Bowery Savings Bank,** a grand building with a magnificent domed interior and glass skylight. The building was designed by McKim, Mead & White in 1894. At the corner of the Bowery and Hester St. is a giant, swirling 1977 mural—complete with a dragon, gambler, and man with a wok—entitled "Wall of Respect for the Working People of Chinatown."

THE LOWER EAST SIDE

East of the Bowery is the Lower East Side, where a once-thriving Jewish community has dwindled away. In 1892, some 75% of New York's Jews lived here; by 1916, that figure had dropped to 23%. Today, the figure is less than one percent. Only about 10,000 Jewish residents remain here; most of the neighborhood's population is now Puerto Rican or Asian. Nonetheless, many older Jews in other parts of the city still regard today's windswept and largely abandoned Lower East Side as a sort of spiritual center, coming here to shop for religious articles or to eat a kosher meal. Yiddish signs still dot the streets; Orthodox Jews dressed in traditional clothes still own many of the stores.

The Jewish people began arriving on the Lower East Side in the late 1800s, many finding work either as peddlers or in the garment industry. Sweatshops—so named because their stoves had to be kept on at all times to heat the flatirons—sprang up throughout the neighborhood, employing both on-premises laborers and outside workers who took enormous piles of piecework home with them to sew by candlelight. Children were often employed along with adults, the pay was extremely low (about $12.50 a week in 1905), and suicide was not uncommon.

Nonetheless, the Lower East Side possessed extraordinary vitality and intellectual life. Many actors, artists, and writers came out of the neighborhood, including Eddie Cantor, Fannie Bryce, Al Jolson, Jacob Epstein, and Abraham Cahan. Writes Michael Gold in *Jews Without Money:* "I can never forget the East Side street where I lived as a boy . . . Always these faces at the tenement window. The street never failed them. It was an immense excitement. It never slept. It roared like a sea. It exploded like firecrackers . . . Excitement, dirt, fighting, chaos! . . . The noise was always in my ears. Even in sleep I could hear it; I can hear it now."

Delancey and Allen Streets

The Lower East Side's major east-west cross-street is Delancey. Once bustling with people and peddlers, this wide thoroughfare is now primarily an entrance ramp to the Williamsburg Bridge. Cheap clothing stores and fast-food joints still line it in spots, but like so many streets on the Lower East Side, it has an abandoned, underpopulated feel. As you head east on Delancey, you'll pass over Allen St., another wide, scruffy boulevard. In the late 1800s, it was notorious for its "creep houses"—brothels equipped with sliding panels so that thieves could slip in and rob customers.

Orchard Street

For decades, this major shopping strip was jammed with pushcarts selling fruits, vegetables, knishes, bagels, hardware, and work clothes. Often the first stop for immigrants after Ellis Island, it was known for cut-rate bargains. Many of the city's most successful retailers, including Brooks Brothers, got their starts here. Today, Orchard St. is still known for bargains. On a sunny Sunday afternoon, its sidewalks teem with shoppers and shopkeepers, who spread out their merchandise on outdoor tables and racks. Most of the stores sell clothing—both designer goods and casual wear—and linens, with the stores below Delancey somewhat more upscale than the ones above. Be prepared to bargain.

Lower East Side Tenement Museum

This museum re-creating early immigrant life is housed in an 1863 tenement building at 97 Orchard St., bet. Delancey and Broome, tel. (212) 431-0233. It's a deliberately dark and oppressive place; the building originally had no windows, except in front, and no indoor plumbing. Declared illegal in 1935, it was sealed up and forgotten about until 1988, when historians looking for a structurally unaltered tenement building stumbled upon it.

Today, the museum's ground floor is devoted to temporary exhibits, while the upstairs rooms have been left more or less as they were when the house was occupied. Still eerily visible on one wall are the scribblings of an early garment worker, listing the numbers of skirts, dresses, and "jackets #2" he or she had cut or sewn. Plans are in the works to develop the upstairs into a "living history" display with interpreters in period dress, but at the moment, the rooms can only be seen via guided tour.

Across the street from the museum is **Gallery 90,** 90 Orchard St., which serves as an informal visitor center. It also holds a wonderful miniature model of an inhabited tenement building. The museum and the gallery are open Tues.-Fri. 11 a.m.-5 p.m., Sun. 11 a.m.-6 p.m.; call for tour information. Admission is adults $7, seniors $6, students $5. The museum also sponsors frequent walking tours of the area.

Eldridge Street Synagogue

About four blocks south of the Tenement Museum, at 12 Eldridge St., bet. Division and Canal, is the 1886 Eldridge Street Synagogue. The first synagogue in New York built by Eastern European Jews, it's a large and startlingly elaborate building with beautifully carved wooden doors. Due to a dwindling congregation, the main sanctuary was sealed in the 1930s and not entered again for 40 years. In the early 1990s, restoration work began, and the synagogue now houses the **Eldridge Street Project,** tel. (212) 219-0903, an exhibition space. Hours are Tues.-Thurs. and Sunday 11 a.m.-4 p.m. Admission is free.

Across the street from the synagogue are excellent examples of the early "Old Law" tenement buildings that were erected in the city between 1879 and 1901. Laid out in a dumbbell

shape—their facades and backs bumping up against each other with just a one-foot-wide air shaft in between—these apartments had virtually no light and only one bathroom per floor, to be shared by about 30 people. In 1901, a new building code improved these conditions somewhat, but by that time, some 1,196 dumbbell tenements had already been built on the Lower East Side.

Jewish East Broadway

Heading east, at 175 E. Broadway (at Rutgers), you'll come to the former headquarters of the Yiddish *Jewish Daily Forward.* Founded in 1897 and edited by Abraham Cahan, the *Forward* published writers such as Isaac Singer and Sholom Aleichem, as well as a famous popular column called the Bintel Brief ("Bundle of Letters"). This column, responding to letters from readers, offered advice on everything from what to do about children who ridiculed the Old Country to how to cure the common cold.

The *Jewish Daily Forward* is still being published uptown, but its old headquarters is now home to various Chinese associations. A barely visible sign up top reads "Forverts," while a much more visible one above the door reads "Jesus Saves" in Chinese.

Seward Park Library, 192 E. Broadway, and the **Educational Alliance,** 197 E. Broadway, both contributed significantly to the success of Jews in the New World. The library had an enormous selection of Yiddish books and a rooftop reading garden built to accommodate its thousands of book-hungry immigrant readers. The Alliance served as a sort of settlement house where the uptown German Jews, often embarrassed by the peasant habits of their newly arrived kinspeople, helped to "Americanize" them.

Between Jefferson and Montgomery Sts. are a number of small storefront synagogues, many with Yiddish signs out front. Most of these small Orthodox congregations are Hasidic.

"If you live in New York, even if you're Catholic, you're Jewish."

—LENNY BRUCE

BOB RACE

selling discounted women's designer clothes. For more information on shopping in the area, stop by the **Orchard Street Shopping District Center,** 261 Broome St., bet. Orchard and Allen, tel. (212) 226-9010, open Sun.-Fri. 10 a.m.-4 p.m. Free Sunday shopping tours leave from Katz's Deli, at the corner of Ludlow and E. Houston Sts., every Sunday April-Dec. at 11 a.m.

Clotheshorses might want to stroll down **Ludlow St.,** just off Houston St., where some of the city's younger and more outrageous fashion designers have set up shop. On **Essex St.** are numerous small Jewish stores selling religious books and supplies such as yarmulkes, *talith* (prayer shawls), and menorahs. Allen St. was once known for its many brass shops. One of them—the hodgepodge **Brass Antique Shoppe**—still stands, at 32 Allen St., bet. Hester and Canal, tel. (212) 925-6660.

Food Shops
Guss Pickles, 35 Essex St., tel. (212) 254-4477, is a boisterous storefront selling sour, half sour, and hot pickles in huge outdoor plastic vats, along with sauerkraut, pickled tomatoes, and horseradish. The store's strong garlicky smell wafts halfway down the block, and there's usually a long line of pickle aficionados waiting out front.

Just off Essex are **Gertel's,** 53 Hester St., tel. (212) 982-3250, the area's major bakery; **Kadouri Import Co.,** 51 Hester St., tel. (212) 677-5441, a Middle Eastern shop selling a wide variety of spices; and **Kossar's Bialystoker Kuchen Bakery,** 367 Grand St., tel. (212) 473-4810, famed for its fresh onion and garlic bialys and bagels.

On Essex between Delancey and Rivington is the indoor **Essex Street Market.** Created in the 1930s after Mayor La Guardia banned pushcarts from the streets, it's now run-down but worth a quick look.

Another thoroughfare lined with some wonderful old Jewish shops is Rivington Street. **Shapiro's House of Kosher and Sacramental Wines,** 126 Rivington St., tel. (212) 674-4404, offers short "tours" and free syrupy samples on Sundays. At **Streit's Matzoth Company,** 150 Rivington St., tel. (212) 475-7000, you can sometimes see the flat breads being made. West of Essex is **Economy Candy,** 108 Riv-

Henry Street
At 263-267 Henry St., east of Montgomery St., stand the attractive red-brick **Henry Street Settlement Houses,** founded by Lillian Wald in 1827. Wald was an important social reformer, credited with starting both the school nurse and school lunch programs. She built her houses here largely because many tenement buildings once stood across the street. Then, as now, the houses functioned as a neighborhood safety net, offering a wide range of social services aimed at children, young mothers, and the elderly.

Next door to the settlement houses is a bright red, meticulously kept firehouse—**Engine Co. 15,** where William Marcy "Boss" Tweed got his start. Another block east is **St. Augustus Church,** where Tweed supposedly watched his mother's funeral from the balcony while on the run from the law.

Shopping
Orchard St. holds a number of popular stores, among them **Lace-Up Shoe Shop,** 110 Orchard St., at Delancey, tel. (212) 475-8040, a good stop for discounted designer shoes; and **Forman's,** 82 Orchard St. (with branches at 78 Orchard and 94 Orchard), tel. (212) 228-2500,

ington St., tel. (212) 254-1531, an unassuming store selling great marzipan and halvah along with kosher marshmallows and huge bags of nuts.

The dividing line between the Lower East Side and the East Village is Houston (pronounced "How-ston") St., home to the famous Katz's Deli (205 Houston), as well as to several traditional food shops. **Russ & Daughters,** 179 E. Houston, bet. Allen and Orchard, tel. (212) 475-4880, is a bustling place filled with smoked fish and dried fruits, all arranged in neat rows; while **Yonah Schimmel's,** 137 E. Houston St., bet. Second and First Aves., tel. (212) 477-2858, is a rickety old storefront selling some of the best knishes in New York. Visible across the street from these shops, on the rooftop of 250 E. Houston, is a 15-foot statue of Lenin, his hand raised to the sky. Toppled by an angry crowd in Moscow in 1991, the statue was transported here by an art collector in 1993.

Accommodations
Inexpensive: A five-minute walk east of SoHo is **Off-SoHo Suites,** 11 Rivington St., bet. Chrystie and the Bowery, tel. (212) 979-9808 or (800) OFF-SOHO, a clean and friendly hotel featuring large, homey suites with kitchenettes and marble bathtubs (these are subject to being shared with the suite next door). Adjoining the narrow, mirror-lined lobby is a spartan cafe done up in gray and white, and a 24-hour self-service laundry room (since the hotel is located on a somewhat marginal street, you may wish to cab it late at night—if so, the hotel offers a discount car service); $89 s or d; maid service an extra $10/day.

Food and Watering Holes
The Lower East Side is famous for its Jewish delicatessens. **Katz's,** 205 Houston St., at Ludlow, tel. (212) 254-2246, is a huge, cafeteria-style place where you take a number at the door; overhead hang WW II-era signs reading "Send a salami to your boy in the Army." **Ratner's,** 138 Delancey St., bet. Norfolk and Suffolk, tel. (212) 677-5588, is a longtime favorite best known for its blintzes, egg creams, and brusque waiters.

Ludlow St., a hip nightlife mecca, is home to several laid-back hole-in-the-wall bars. Most notable among them is **Max Fish,** 178 Ludlow St., tel. (212) 529-3959, a long, comfortable watering hole drawing an artsy crowd. **Ludlow Bar,** 165 Ludlow St., tel. (212) 353-0536, a scruffy, step-down joint, often offers live local bands until the wee hours. Filled with nightcrawlers after midnight is the comfy, sofa-filled **Den of Thieves,** 145 E. Houston St., bet. Eldridge and Forsythe Sts., tel. (212) 477-5005.

BOB RACE

SOHO AND TRIBECA

SoHo—short for **So**uth of **Ho**uston—is the city's trendiest neighborhood. Within its 25 upscale blocks, bounded by Houston and Canal Sts., Lafayette St. and W. Broadway, glitter over 200 art galleries, five museums, 180 restaurants and bars, and 300 shops.

Once a quiet residential suburb, SoHo began developing in the early- to mid-1800s, when a number of expensive hotels opened up, along with brothels and dance halls. By the 1870s, however, most of this activity had moved to more fashionable digs uptown, leaving SoHo to turn to the industrial sector. Foundries, factories, warehouses, and sweatshops sprang up all over the district. Frequent fires started by machinery sparks soon gave the district the nickname, "Hell's Hundred Acres."

The factories flourished until the mid-1900s. By the 1960s, most of them were gone and artists began moving in. Attracted to the area by its low rents and high-ceilinged spaces—perfect for studios—they illegally converted the commercial buildings into living spaces, secretly adding plumbing and adequate heating. Soon thereafter, the art galleries began arriving, and then the shops and restaurants. Almost overnight, SoHo became fashionable again, so much so that the artists who started it all could no longer afford the high rents.

Recently, prognosticators have been sounding the death knell for SoHo's art gallery scene as well. A number of major gallery owners—in-cluding Mary Boone and Paula Cooper—have moved their prestigious operations out of the area, to resettle on 57th Street or in Chelsea. They'll be missed, but for the moment, rumors of SoHo's imminent demise as an art center are greatly exaggerated.

Besides, SoHo's cast-iron buildings—many freshly painted—remain its greatest treasure. Originally envisioned as a cheap way to imitate elaborate stone buildings, the cast-iron facades were prefabricated in a variety of styles—including Italian Renaissance, French Second Empire, and Classical Greek—and bolted onto iron-frame structures. An American invention, the cast-iron building was erected primarily in New York, with SoHo boasting the largest collection.

Orientation
SoHo is the perfect neighborhood for just wandering about—it's compact and filled with sights. **Broadway and West Broadway** are the main thoroughfares. West Broadway, originally built to help ease Broadway's traffic congestion, is lined with some of the most prestigious addresses in SoHo. Every weekend its sidewalks swell with hordes of fashionable people—many of them European—and artists hawking their wares. At the north end of the street, near Houston, and again farther south, near Grand, are numerous inviting, albeit pricey, restaurants, offering outdoor tables in good weather.

Prince and Spring Streets hold an enormous array of upscale shops, galleries, restaurants, and bars, along with a few old spots predating the SoHo scene. The intersections of Prince and Spring Sts. with W. Broadway could be called the heart of modern-day SoHo. West of W. Broadway, and east of Lafayette St., Prince St. takes on its older Italian feel. Children play in the street and old women gossip on the stoops, as the smell of fresh-baked bread wafts up and down the street.

To get the full effect of SoHo, come on a weekend afternoon—when the streets are jammed with beautiful people—or at night, when hip bars and restaurants—both upscale and down—attract the high life.

ARCHITECTURE

Many of SoHo's finest cast-iron gems can be found along Broadway. Foremost among them is the Italianate **Haughwout Building,** 488 Broadway, at Broome. The magnificent edifice is five stories tall and nine bays wide on the Broadway side, and sports 92 windows all flanked by Corinthian columns. Built for a merchant who once provided china to the White House, the store was the first in the city to install a passenger elevator.

Farther north is the magnificent **Singer Building,** 561 Broadway, designed by the innovative architect Ernest Flagg in 1904. It's decked out with red terra cotta panels, delicate wrought-iron detailing, and large plate-glass windows. Also be sure to note the facade of the **Guggenheim Museum SoHo,** 575 Broadway.

For a glimpse of what all of SoHo looked like before the trendy shops and art galleries moved in, head down to the lower end of dark, narrow Greene Street. Many of the cast-iron buildings here are still equipped with their old loading platforms, built waist-high so that horse-drawn wagons could pull right up and unload. At 28 and 30

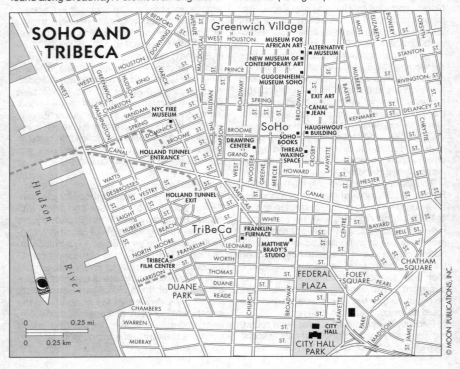

SOHO AND TRIBECA

© MOON PUBLICATIONS, INC.

COCKROACHES

Much to its residents' dismay, New York is home to four kinds of cockroaches—the brown German, the one-to-two-inch-long American, the striped brown-banded, and the stocky Oriental. All are much despised, but it is the German who elicits the foulest expletives, inhabiting dark crevices in kitchens and bathrooms from the dingiest East Village dive to the most luxurious Upper East Side condo.

New Yorkers have sense enough to know that it's impossible to eradicate *Blatella germanica*. The bugs have been around for about 350 million years, after all, and can survive on next to nothing, including salts from tennis shoes, grease spots on a wall from cooking, and starch on postage stamps. In one laboratory experiment, a cockroach colony lived two and a half years without any protein at all. Then, too, a female cockroach needs but one sex act a year to store enough male seed to reproduce 35,000 more cockroaches.

So instead of eradication, New Yorkers have to content themselves with pest control. In the past, this has meant chemical sprays and fumigations. In today's more environmentally aware times, the most popular methods are bait traps, boric acid, and—the Tokay gecko. This small blue-skinned lizard with orange spots measures between six inches and two feet long, and loves to eat cockroaches. A nocturnal creature, it's rarely seen during the day, but has an odd, distinctive bark that's sometimes heard at night.

BOB RACE

Greene, below Grand, is the so-called **"Queen of Greene Street,"** an ornate Second Empire building painted pale gray. On the southwest corner of Greene and Broome is the once-elegant **Gunther Building,** 469 Broome St., now in dire need of a facelift.

Charlton-King-Vandam Historic District

Just west of Sixth Ave., this three-block district including Charlton, King, and Vandam Sts. was once home to Richmond Hill, a fine mansion built on a crest overlooking the Hudson. George Washington established his headquarters here during part of the Revolutionary War, and later, Vice Pres. John Adams and his wife Abigail took up residence. In 1793, Aaron Burr bought the place and entertained lavishly up until his notorious duel with Alexander Hamilton in 1804.

After the duel he was indicted for murder and fled to Philadelphia.

In 1817, his career in ruins, Burr sold Richmond Hill to John Jacob Astor, who moved the mansion (which was eventually demolished) and leveled off the crest. Speculators then built the lovely rows of Federal-style houses that still line the streets today. The best preserved street is Charlton.

MUSEUMS

Art Museums

Heading south down Broadway from Houston St., the first museum you'll come to is the **Alternative Museum,** 594 Broadway, bet. Houston and Prince, tel. (212) 966-4444. Situated on the fourth floor, the museum presents works of noncommercial artists in galleries named after Gandhi, John Brown, and Josephine Baker. Its shows are usually political, multicultural, experimental, and first-rate. Hours are Tues.-Sat. 11 a.m.-6 p.m. Suggested admission is $3. A number of other galleries are also in the building.

Directly across the street from the Alternative Museum is the **Museum for African Art,** 593 Broadway, tel. (212) 966-1313, which presents excellent changing exhibits on Africa's ancient and tribal cultures. The museum, done up in deep yellows and blue-greens, was designed by architect Maya Lin. Up front is an interesting gift shop. Hours are Tues.-Fri. 10:30 a.m.-5:30 p.m., Sat.-Sun. noon-6 p.m. Admission is adults $4; students, seniors, and children $2.

On the same block is the spacious **New Museum of Contemporary Art,** 583 Broadway, tel. (212) 219-1355, one of the oldest and best-known exhibition spaces in SoHo. Founded in 1976 by Marcia Tucker, a former curator of the Whitney Museum, the museum presents innovative and often risky shows by contemporary artists from all over the world. Hours are Wed.-Fri. and Sun. noon-6 p.m., Sat. noon-8 p.m. Suggested admission is adults $4; students, artists, and seniors $3. Free for children under 12, and for everyone Sat. 6-8 p.m.

At the intersection of Broadway and Prince is the **Guggenheim Museum Soho,** 575 Broadway, tel. (212) 423-3500, the downtown branch of the uptown landmark (see "Upper East Side," below). Specializing in "art of the 21st century," the museum is all light and air, with one high-ceilinged room leading into the next. On the ground floor is an extensive gift shop. Hours are Sun., Wed.-Fri. 11 a.m.-6 p.m., Sat. 11 a.m.-8 p.m. Admission is adults $6, students and seniors $4, children under 12 free.

Children's Museum of the Arts, 72 Spring St., tel. (212) 274-0986, is a hands-on experimental museum designed to expose kids to the visual and performing arts. In the "Artist's Studio," youngsters can try their hand at sand painting, origami, sculpture, and beadwork. The museum is open Tues.-Fri. noon-6 p.m., Sat.-Sun. 11 a.m.-5 p.m. Admission is $5 on the weekends, $4 weekdays; seniors and children under 18 months free.

New York City Fire Museum

Technically outside of SoHo to the west is the New York City Fire Museum, 278 Spring St., bet. Varick and Hudson, tel. (212) 691-1303. Housed in an actual firehouse that was active up until 1959, the museum is staffed by ex-firefighters. It's filled with intriguing items, including a 1790 hand pump, a lifesaving net (which "caught you 75% of the time"), gorgeous 19th-century fire carriages, engraved lanterns, evocative photographs, helmets and uniforms, and wooden buckets. The firemen love to talk to visitors—they'll give you a personalized tour filled with anecdotes if they're not too busy. The museum is open Tues.-Sun. 10 a.m.-4 p.m. Suggested admission is adults $4; children under 12, $1.

ART GALLERIES AND ALTERNATIVE SPACES

Below, find a small sampling of SoHo's many art spaces, most of which are open Tues.-Sat. from about noon to about 6 p.m. To find out about others, or about who's exhibiting where, pick up a copy of the *Art Now Gallery Guide,* available at many bookstores and galleries. Other good sources for listings are *New York, The New Yorker, Time Out New York,* the *Village Voice,* and the Sunday Arts & Leisure section of *The New York Times.* Many of the more established galleries are at the northern end of SoHo; those farther south tend to be younger and more experimental.

West Broadway

The building at 420 W. Broadway, near Prince, is home to a number of galleries, including the renowned **Leo Castelli,** tel. (212) 431-5160, and **Sonnabend,** tel. (212) 966-6160. Castelli was largely responsible for the meteoric rise of such artists as Andy Warhol, Jasper Johns, Roy

The New York City Fire Museum was once a functioning fire station.

SoHo street scene

Lichtenstein, and Robert Rauschenberg. Across the street is the similarly preeminent **Witkin Gallery,** 415 W. Broadway, tel. (212) 925-5510, exhibiting the work of top contemporary photographers, as well as historical prints by the likes of Ansel Adams.

At 393 W. Broadway, near Spring, is an extended exhibition by Walter De Maria, funded by the Dia Center for the Arts. Installed in 1979, De Maria's **Broken Kilometer** is an enormous, darkened room filled with 500 polished brass rods, each measuring two meters in length and five centimeters in diameter. Around the room's perimeter hang changing exhibitions. The gallery, tel. (212) 925-9397, is open Wed.-Sat. noon-6 p.m. A few doors down is **O.K. Harris,** 383 W. Broadway, tel. (212) 431-3600, one of SoHo's first art galleries, run by Ivan Karp.

Greene and Wooster Streets
The building at 142 Greene St., bet. Houston and Prince Sts., houses **Sperone Westwater,**

tel. (212) 431-3685, and **John Weber,** tel. (212) 966-6115. Sperone Westwater is known for exhibiting modern Italian painters such as Sandro Chia and Francesco Clemente. John Weber is known for its conceptual and minimalist art, including works by Sol LeWitt and Alice Aycock.

On Wooster near Houston is the **New York Earth Room,** 141 Wooster St., tel. (212) 473-8072. Another extended exhibit by artist Walter De Maria, this 250-cubic-yard room is filled with a 22-inch-deep layer of fragrant, dark topsoil, along with changing exhibitions of contemporary art. Though it may sound crazy, it works. The room is open Wed.-Sat. noon-6 p.m.

Several blocks farther south is the **Drawing Center,** 35 Wooster, bet. Broome and Grand, tel. (212) 219-2166, an airy, first-rate exhibition hall dedicated to drawing as a major art form. Hours are Tues.-Fri. 10 a.m.-6 p.m., Sat. 11 a.m.-6 p.m.; admission is by donation.

At 38 Greene St., near Broome, is the **Artist's Space,** tel. (212) 226-3970, an alternative arts space that has focused on emerging artists since 1973. Hours are Tues.-Sat. 10 a.m.-6 p.m.

Broadway
Castelli Graphics, 578 Broadway, bet. Houston and Prince, tel. (212) 941-9855, exhibits the work of top contemporary photographers such as Mary Ellen Mark and Jan Groover. **Max Protetch,** 560 Broadway, at Prince, tel. (212) 966-5454, is known for its architectural drawings and models.

Exit Art, 548 Broadway, bet. Prince and Spring, tel. (212) 966-7745, is a 17,000-square-foot alternative space that holds two exhibit areas, a cafe, store, and performance space. Shows tend to be experimental and focus on both new and established artists.

Housed in a former warehouse once dedicated to its namesake is the **Thread Waxing Space,** 476 Broadway, bet. Broome and Grande, tel. (212) 966-9520. Experimental art exhibits, poetry readings, and performance art are featured.

SHOPPING

Most SoHo stores are open from about noon to about 9 p.m.

Antiques and Furnishings
A good dozen unusual antique shops are on Lafayette St. between E. Fourth St. (above Houston) and Spring. Among them are **Urban Archaeology,** 285 Lafayette St., tel. (212) 431-6969, specializing in artifacts from demolished buildings; and **Lost City Arts,** 275 Lafayette St., tel. (212) 941-8025, selling everything from barber chairs to street signs.

Books and Cards
Rizzoli's, 454 W. Broadway, bet. Houston and Prince, tel. (212) 674-1616, is a sleek, upscale bookstore with piped-in classical music. For secondhand books, try **SoHo Books,** 351 W. Broadway, near Broome, tel. (212) 226-3395. **A Photographer's Place,** 133 Mercer St., near Prince, tel. (212) 966-2356, offers a large selection of photography books, magazines, and postcards.

Kate's Paperie, in the Singer Building, 561 Broadway, at Prince, tel. (212) 941-9816, is an upscale stationery shop filled with handmade paper products. Art postcards are available at **Art Market,** 75 Grand St., near Greene, tel. (212) 226-4370, which stocks more than 10,000 cards; and at **Untitled,** 159 Prince St., near W. Broadway, tel. (212) 982-2088, also with a good selection.

Clothing and Accessories
Prince St. from W. Broadway east holds a number of up-to-date clothing stores, including **French Connection,** 435 W. Broadway, at Prince, tel. (212) 219-1197; and **Agnes B.,** 116 Prince St., tel. (212) 925-4649. **Harriet Love,** 126 Prince St., tel. (212) 966-2280, is a classic, albeit pricey, gem carrying fashions from the turn of the century to the 1950s. On the west side of W. Broadway is **Stella Dallas,** 218 Thompson St., bet. Prince and Houston, tel. (212) 674-0447, specializing in the '40s' look.

Spring St. is also lined with dozens of upscale shops. Among those you'll pass heading east from W. Broadway are **Agatha Paris,** 158 Spring, tel. (212) 925-7701, stocked with a whimsical assortment of costume jewelry, especially charms; and **Putumayo,** 147 Spring, tel. (212) 966-4458, selling women's clothing made of natural fabrics.

Alice Underground, 481 Broadway, bet. Broome and Grand, tel. (212) 431-9067, sells vintage clothing at relatively reasonable prices; styles range from Victorian to funk. One of the neighborhood's oldest and most beloved of stores is **Canal Jean,** 504 Broadway, tel. (212) 226-1130. This cavernous warehouse, housed in a classic cast-iron building, offers an enormous, jumbled selection of bargain-priced jeans, T-shirts, and vintage coats.

Crafts, Toys, and Gifts
The irrepressible **Keith Haring Pop Shop,** 292 Lafayette St., near Prince, tel. (212) 219-2784, sells T-shirts, posters, hats, refrigerator magnets, inflatable baby dolls, and more, all designed by the late artist. **Boca Grande,** 89 Spring St., near Crosby, tel. (212) 966-7716, features colorful handmade gift items from Latin America. The delightful **Bazaar Sabato,** 54 Greene St., near Broome, tel. (212) 941-6152, is filled with brightly colored Mexican handicrafts.

One of the city's most wonderful toy stores is **Enchanted Forest,** 85 Mercer St., just south of Spring, tel. (212) 925-6677. Made up to look like a magical rain forest, the store attracts as many adults as children. **After the Rain,** 149 Mercer St., near Prince, tel. (212) 431-1044, specializes in kaleidoscopes.

Other Shops
Evolution, 120 Spring St., bet. Greene and Mercer, tel. (212) 343-1114, is an odd natural history store where you can pick up a giraffe skull or wild boar tusk. **Terra Verde,** 120 Wooster St., near Prince, tel. (212) 925-4533, "NYC's original ecological department store," sells "cruelty-free" cosmetics, chemical-free linens, and the like.

Broadway Panhandler, 477 Broome St., bet. Wooster and Greene, tel. (212) 966-3434, sells discounted cookware, while **Vesuvio,** 160 Prince St., tel. (212) 925-8248, is a 70-odd-year-old Italian bakery with dozens of round loaves of bread in its window.

Flea Market
On weekends 9 a.m.-5 p.m., **SoHo Antiques Fair and Collectibles,** a large flea market, sets up shop in the empty lot at Broadway and Grand St., tel. (212) 682-2000. Admission is $1.

TRIBECA

If you follow W. Broadway south out of SoHo and over Canal St., you'll enter TriBeCa. Looking west from Canal, you can see the entrance to the **Holland Tunnel,** often backed up with traffic at the end of the day. TriBeCa, short for *Tri*angle *Be*low *Ca*nal, encompasses about 40 blocks between Canal, Chambers, West, and Church Streets. The district is often considered a second-tier SoHo, with plenty of fashionable restaurants, galleries, and cast-iron treasures. Yet large sections of TriBeCa remain empty and windswept, filled with half-deserted buildings and quiet blocks. TriBeCa's character is different than SoHo's—much of it still feels like industrialized, 19th-century New York.

Like SoHo, TriBeCa's main thoroughfares are Broadway and W. Broadway, though some of its best unrestored cast-iron buildings are on side streets, especially White Street.

West Broadway Art

Soho Photo, 15 White St., at W. Broadway, tel. (212) 226-8571, is a cooperative photography gallery showcasing the works of its 100-plus members; hours are Fri.-Sun. 1-6 p.m., Tues. 6-8 p.m.

Franklin Furnace, 112 Franklin St., at W. Broadway, tel. (212) 925-4671, was founded by artist Martha Wilson in 1976, with the goal of collecting and preserving artist-designed books and other "multiples" (magazines, pamphlets, etc.) published after 1960. The Franklin Furnace now houses over 18,000 works, available to anyone who wants to read them. The center also stages frequent exhibits and performance-art events.

Mathew Brady's Studio

The scruffy, five-story, cast-iron building at 359 Broadway, at Franklin, once housed the photographic studios of Mathew Brady. The famed 19th-century photographer, best known for his pictures of Lincoln and the Civil War, began his career in 1844, only five years after the daguerreotype was invented. In 1861, Lincoln said of him, "Brady and the Cooper Union speech made me president of the United States." Nonetheless, Brady went bankrupt in 1873, and died a pauper. A faint sign advertising his studio can still be seen high up on the south wall.

TriBeCa Film Center

At the corner of Greenwich and Franklin Sts. is TriBeCa Film Center, housed in the landmark 1905 Martinson Coffee Company warehouse. The center was started in 1989 by actor and director Robert DeNiro, who wanted to create a site where filmmakers could conduct meetings, screen films, and talk business over lunch.

The center's **TriBeCa Grill** is usually filled with more celebrity watchers than celebrities, but the famous do occasionally turn up here. Upstairs, off-limits to the public, are screening and business rooms, the headquarters of Miramax Films, and the New York offices of producers Stephen Spielberg and Ron Howard, among others.

Harrison Street and Duane Park

At Greenwich and Harrison Sts. are the **Harrison Houses,** a lovely group of nine restored Federal-style homes. Several were designed by John McComb Jr., New York's first architect. East of the houses, at the northwest corner of Harrison and Hudson Sts., is the former **New York Mercantile Exchange,** a five-story brick building with gables and a tower. At the turn of the century, $15,000 worth of eggs would change hands in an hour on the building's trading floor. TriBeCa is still the city's distribution center for eggs, cheese, and butter; a few remaining wholesalers can be found around Duane Park, one block south.

ACCOMMODATIONS

Expensive: SoHo's first hotel, the 370-room **SoHo Grand,** 310 W. Broadway, at Grand, tel. (212) 965-3000 or (800) 965-3000, opened in summer 1996. Sleekly done up in industrial metals downstairs and oversized lamps, columns, and sofas upstairs, the hotel has become a chic, minimalist haven for well-heeled fashionables. The custom-designed guest rooms feature muted greys, two-line phones, and—in many cases—excellent views. Adjoining the lobby is a classy, high-ceilinged bar; the on-site Canal House serves innovative international fare. Rooms run $209-349 s, $229-369 d.

FOOD

American

Inexpensive: The 24-hour **Moondance Diner,** 80 Sixth Ave., at Grand, tel. (212) 226-1191, offers gourmet sandwiches. It's most crowded in the early mornings, after the clubs let out. For vegetarian fare, try the casual-chic **Bell Caffe,** 310 Spring St., bet. Hudson and Greenwich Sts., tel. (212) 334-BELL (-2355).

Moderate: Jerry's, 101 Prince St., bet. Mercer and Greene, tel. (212) 966-9464, is an upscale diner with red leather booths and an eclectic menu. The light and airy **Spring Street Natural,** 62 Spring St., at Lafayette, tel. (212) 966-0290, features lots of plants, big windows, and solid vegetarian fare. Over 100 wines can be sampled at the sleek **SoHo Kitchen and Bar,** 103 Greene St., bet. Prince and Spring, tel. (212) 925-1866, which also serves run-of-the-mill pastas, pizzas, and burgers.

Expensive: The snug **Cub Room,** 131 Sullivan St., near Prince, tel. (212) 677-4100, is trendy yet comfortable, with an unusual menu and a large classy bar opening onto the street; adjoining the main restaurant is a moderately priced cafe. **Zoe,** 90 Prince St., bet. Broadway and Mercer, tel. (212) 966-6722, is another handsome and very popular spot known for its open kitchen and California-style cuisine. Robert DeNiro's brick-walled **TriBeCa Grill,** 375 Greenwich St., at Franklin, tel. (212) 941-3900, may attract hordes of celebrity watchers, but the food and service are nonetheless surprisingly good.

French Bistros

SoHo is home to a number of popular bistros that double as late-night hot spots.

Moderate: The fun and hospitable **Lucky Strike,** 59 Grand St., bet. Wooster and W. Broadway, tel. (212) 941-0479, was one of the first of these hip, downtown joints. It's been around for years now, but still attracts a very lively crowd, especially after midnight when the young, the beautiful, and the hopeful gather to exchange glances. **La Jumelle,** 55 Grand St., bet. Wooster and W. Broadway, tel. (212) 941-9651, is a quieter cousin to Lucky Strike, and catches the spillover crowd.

Expensive: The dark and stylish **Raoul's,** 180 Prince St., bet. Sullivan and Thompson, tel. (212) 966-3518, has long been a downtown mecca and with good reason; the food and ambience are top-notch. **Felix's,** 340 W. Broadway, at Grand, tel. (212) 431-0021, with its stunning door-windows opening onto the street, is kitty-corner to Lucky Strike and is like a grown-up, more pretentious version of the same. A more sedate favorite is **Provence,** 38 MacDougal St., at Prince, tel. (212) 475-7500, a "rustic" spot with a cozy garden out back. Tiny **Le Pescadou,** 16 King St., at Sixth Ave., tel. (212) 924-3434, specializes in fresh fish.

one of SoHo's many eateries

French/Continental
Expensive: A longtime favorite among night-crawlers is the chic, art deco **Odeon,** 145 W. Broadway, at Thomas, tel. (212) 233-0507, serving consistently good food in a lively, downtown setting.

Very Expensive: Bouley's, voted New York's No. 1 restaurant several years in a row by the Zagat Survey, shut down in mid-1996 with a promise to reopen, bigger and better than ever. The new Bouley's International will open in spring 1998 in two adjoining buildings, at 36-38 Hudson St., at Duane. One building will house a casual cafe, a formal restaurant, and a cooking school. The second building will house all the kitchens.

Chanterelle, 2 Harrison St., near Hudson, tel. (212) 966-6960, is an ultra-elegant spot serving nouvelle cuisine to an art-world crowd.

Italian
Inexpensive-to-Moderate: Casual **Il Corallo Trattoria,** 176 Prince St., bet. Thompson and Sullivan, tel. (212) 941-7119, serves tasty pastas and pizza. **Trattoria Vente Tre** 23 Cleveland Pl., near Lafayette St., just below Spring, tel. (212) 941-0286, offers hearty original dishes in a garden setting.

Moderate-to-Expensive: Rosemarie's, 145 Duane St., bet. W. Broadway and Church, tel. (212) 285-2610, is a snug hideaway serving homemade fare. **Barolo,** 398 W. Broadway, near Spring, tel. (212) 226-1102, features one of the prettiest gardens in the city, but the food is only mediocre—stick to drinks and dessert.

Southern
Moderate: Brother's Barbeque, 225 Varick St., near W. Houston, tel. (212) 727-2775, is a casual joint serving first-rate ribs, barbecued chicken, and all the Southern trimmings.

Other Ethnic
Inexpensive: The **Abyssinia,** 35 Grand St., at Thompson, tel. (212) 226-5959, is an African restaurant where diners perch on three-legged stools, handicrafts hang from the walls, and the food is spicy and delicious. The homey **Lupe's East L.A. Kitchen,** 110 Sixth Ave., at Watts, tel. (212) 966-1326, serves first-rate East L.A.-style Mexican food.

In TriBeCa, the **Thai House Cafe,** 151 Hudson St., at Hubert, tel. (212) 334-1085, features tasty weekday lunch specials.

Moderate: Playful **El Teddy's,** 219 W. Broadway, bet. Franklin and White, tel. (212) 941-7070, adorned with glass mosaics, serves good Tex-Mex and excellent margaritas. The dark and creaky **Cafe Noir,** 32 Grand St., at Thompson, tel. (212) 431-7910, offers spicy French-Moroccan cuisine, served *tapas* style; up front is a narrow bar, often crowded with young Europeans.

Expensive: Cool, happening **Pravda,** 281 Lafayette St., bet. Houston and Prince, tel. (212) 226-4696, is the place to go for innovative Russian-influenced fare accompanied by martinis and celebrity watching.

Light Bites
At the north end of SoHo you'll find **Kelley & Ping,** 127 Greene St., bet. Prince and Houston, tel. (212) 228-1212, a simple but excellent combination Asian grocery shop and noodle parlor; and **Dean & DeLuca,** 560 Broadway, at Prince, tel. (212) 431-1691, a sleek food emporium housing both a cafe and an extensive market.

At the south end of SoHo is the cozy **Cupping Room,** 359 W. Broadway, near Broome, tel. (212) 925-2898, especially good for afternoon snacks. Many New Yorkers go out of their way to visit **Eileen's Special Cheesecake,** 15 Cleveland Pl., near Lafayette St., just below Spring, tel. (212) 966-5585 (take-out only).

Housed in an old TriBeCa warehouse is the homey, ramshackle **Biblio's Bookstore and Cafe,** 317 Church St., near Canal, tel. (212) 344-6990, serving fresh baked goods.

Watering Holes and Lounges
The classic bar in SoHo is **Fanelli's,** 94 Prince St., at Mercer, tel. (212) 226-9412, an 1876 pub complete with beveled glass doors, tiled floors, and heavy dark wood. In the back are worn wooden tables where passable bar food is served.

The **Broome Street Bar,** 363 W. Broadway, at Broome, tel. (212) 925-2086, also lined with dark wood, features a long bar up front and a casual dining area in back. The creaky **Ear Inn,** 326 Spring St., near Greenwich, tel. (212) 226-9060, claims to have the oldest liquor license in New York State. It was once a hangout for poets and bohemians but now attracts a more generic crowd. On the Eastern fringe of SoHo is **Milano's,** 51 Houston St., bet. Mulberry and Mott, tel. (212) 226-8632, a long, narrow dive with one of the best jukeboxes in town.

Two of the neighborhood's trendier spots are the **Merc Bar,** 151 Mercer St., near Houston, tel. (212) 966-2727, done up in sleek, modernized Adirondackanna; and the **Buddha Bar,** 150 Varick St., near Vandam, tel. (212) 255-4433, filled with plush booths and golden Buddha statuettes. At both, the dreaded velvet rope, guarded by a doorman, sometimes blocks ordinary mortals from entering.

Classic TriBeCa bars include **Puffy's Tavern,** 81 Hudson St., at Harrison, tel. (212) 766-9159, a one-time artists' hangout now attracting everyone from bankers to bikers; and **Walker's,** 16 N. Moore St., at Varick, tel. (212) 941-0142, an 1890s' saloon serving tasty pub grub and Guinness on tap. The **Raccoon Lodge,** 59 Warren St., bet. Church and W. Broadway, tel. (212) 766-9656, is a big, scruffy place with a good pool table.

Of the restaurants listed above, the **Cub Room, Lucky Strike, La Jumelle, Felix's, Cafe Noir,** and **Raoul's,** all have lively bar scenes. The bar at the **SoHo Grand Hotel** also draws a crowd.

THE EAST VILLAGE

Musicians in post-punk, artists in retro, and pouty young fashionables in vinyl and faux fur— such are some of the types you'll find in the East Village. But it'd be a mistake to think that the neighborhood is only the province of the young and flamboyant. Over the last few decades, each generation has left a number of its own nonconformists in this gray, eclectic, and well-worn part of town.

For much of its existence, the East Village was simply an extension of the Lower East Side. Though favored by the well-to-do in the mid-1800s, by the turn of the century most of its residents were German Lutheran immigrants. By WW I, those Germans had been replaced by Poles, Ukrainians, Greeks, Jews, and Russians—some of whom still live in the neighborhood. Not long thereafter, a sizeable Latino population moved in, settling in the easternmost stretches. They, too, are still here.

In the 1950s, artists, writers, radicals, and counterculturists began arriving. Many were fleeing the rising rents in Greenwich Village, and they transformed the East Village into a distinct neighborhood with a character all its own. First on the scene were artists such as Willem de Kooning, Paul Georges, and Joan Mitchell, followed quickly by writers such as Norman Mailer, W.H. Auden, and Allen Ginsberg. Next came the beatniks, and then the hippies and the yippies, the rock groups and the punk musicians, the artists and the fashion designers.

Only in the early 1980s did the East Village begin to gentrify. Young professionals moved in, bringing with them upscale restaurants and shops. This trend has slowed since the recession of the late 1980s, but the East Village today is a mix between the cutting edge and the mainstream, the cheap hole-in-the-wall joint and the trendy hot spot. Performance artists and community activists rub shoulders with tourists and businesspeople. Owners of hip boutiques share sidewalk space with the homeless. Drug dealers skulk outside the doors of pricey restaurants.

Nightlife is a key component of East Village character. The neighborhood is home to scores of restaurants and bars, along with fly-by-night music clubs and performance spaces.

Orientation

The East Village encompasses everything east of Fourth Ave. between E. Houston and 14th Streets. Some blocks are crowded with business establishments, others with dull, crumbling buildings. East of First Ave., the avenues take on lettered names—A, B, C, and D; this area is also known as Loisaida (a phonetic corruption of "Lower East Side") or Alphabet City. Avenues A and B have for the most part been gentrified, but C and D have many rough spots and are best avoided unless you have a specific address in mind. The most interesting streets for aimless wandering are Second and First Aves., Ave. A, St. Mark's Pl., and 9th and 7th Streets.

ALONG SECOND AVENUE

St. Mark's-in-the-Bowery

Historic St. Mark's Church, 131 E. 10th St., at Second Ave., stands near the former site of Peter Stuyvesant's farm. Its hodgepodge of architectural styles includes a 1799 base, an 1828 Greek Revival steeple, and an 1854 cast-iron Italianate porch.

Buried in the bricked-in graveyard surrounding the church is "Petrus Stuyvesant" himself, the last and most colorful of the Dutch governors. By all accounts a crusty, often forbidding man, Stuyvesant spent the last of his years stomping around his farm on his wooden leg.

Some say Stuyvesant's ghost still haunts the graveyard. A tapping noise, like that made by the famous leg, has been heard from deep inside his tomb, and an angry wraith, resembling the dead man, has been seen limping around among the headstones. Several times, the church bells have supposedly tolled without being touched by human hands.

Also once buried in St. Mark's cemetery was Alexander Stewart, the founder of the modern department store. But in 1878, body-snatchers dug up his body—buried 12 feet down under three heavy slabs—and held it for ransom. Two years went by before Stewart's widow, worth millions, finally coughed up $20,000 for her husband's remains. The corpse was reburied in Garden City, an early planned suburb on Long Island that Stewart had financed. His new tomb was equipped with a burglar alarm.

Today, St. Mark's is known primarily for its poetry readings, performing-arts presentations, and leftist politics. In the 1950s, the Beat poets gave frequent readings here and, until his death in April 1997, Allen Ginsberg was a fixture. An annual poetry fest is held on New Year's Day. The interior of the church is open Mon.-Fri. 9 a.m.-4 p.m., Sun. 9 a.m.-1 p.m. For information call (212) 674-6377 (parish office), 674-0910 (poetry project), or 674-8112 (dance project).

Renwick Triangle

A half-block west of St. Mark's on 10th St. is Renwick Triangle, which holds 16 gorgeous Italianate brownstones designed by the then-young architect James Renwick. Renwick also designed St. Patrick's Cathedral on Fifth Ave. and Grace Church on Broadway. Just up from Renwick Triangle, at 21 Stuyvesant St., is the elegant, red-brick **Stuyvesant-Fish Residence,** which the great-grandson of Peter Stuyvesant built as a wedding present for his daughter Elizabeth.

Emma Goldman's Home

At 208 E. 13th St., bet. Second and Third Aves., is a six-story apartment building that was once a gathering place for radicals and intellectuals. Anarchist Emma Goldman lived here from 1903 to 1913, making it one of the most permanent of

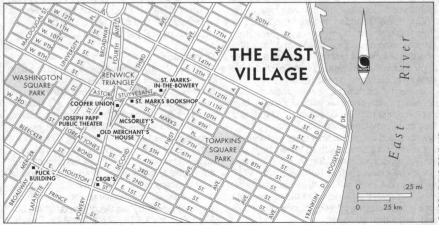

© MOON PUBLICATIONS, INC.

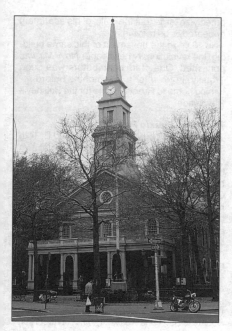

Dutch governor Peter Stuyvesant is buried near St. Mark's-in-the-Bowery.

the many addresses she occupied in the East Village and Lower East Side. Goldman was frequently evicted because of her politics.

While living here, Goldman began publishing her journal, *Mother Earth,* named after "the nourisher of man, man freed and unhindered in his access to the free earth!" In 1906, her former lover Alexander Berkman took up a troubled residence with her. Berkman had just been released after serving a 14-year prison term for the attempted assassination of industrialist Henry Clay Frick, and had a hard time readjusting to day-to-day life. Goldman had assisted him in plotting the murder.

South on Second Avenue
From the turn-of-the-century through the 1930s, Second Ave. between 14th St. and Houston was lined with lively Yiddish theaters. All are now gone, but the movie theater at the corner of 12th St. was once the **Yiddish Art Theatre,**

and still boasts a magnificent domed ceiling, recently restored.

On the same block as the theater is the tiny **Ukrainian Museum,** 203 Second Ave., tel. (212) 228-0110. Though of limited appeal, the museum does house a nice collection of embroidered clothing and *pysanky* (painted Easter eggs), as well as changing exhibits and a small gift shop. It's open Wed.-Sun. 1-5 p.m.; admission is $2.

At the southeast corner of 10th St. is **Second Avenue Deli,** its sidewalk studded with the names of stars of the Yiddish theater. Across the street, between 9th St. and St. Mark's Pl., are two grand terra cotta buildings from the 1880s: **Stuyvesant Polyclinic,** 137 Second Ave.; and **Ottendorfer Library,** 135 Second Avenue. The Ottendorfer, its facade adorned with miniature books, globes, and sage old owls, was the first building in the city built specifically for use as a public library.

Bill Graham's famous **Fillmore East** once rocked the corner of Second Ave. and 6th Street. Over the years, the theater hosted everyone from Janis Joplin and Jimi Hendrix to Jefferson Airplane and The Doors. In 1994, the city renamed the corner "Bill Graham's Way," in honor of the rock-and-roll promoter, who died in a helicopter crash in 1991.

The Gershwin Family
The second floor of the well-kept red brick building at 91 Second Ave., bet. 5th and 6th Sts., was an early home of the Gershwin family. George was 12 and Ira was 14 when they moved in. While living here, Mrs. Gershwin bought the family its first piano, which was hoisted into the apartment through a window. No sooner had it arrived than George sat down at the keys and began teaching himself to play. Six years later, he published his first song.

Murder on Second Avenue
The building at 79 Second Ave. once housed the BiniBon restaurant, site of a famous murder that had an interesting prologue. When Norman Mailer was writing *The Executioner's Song,* he befriended an inmate named Jack Henry Abbott. Abbott, in prison for robbery and murder, had written a series of letters to the author about life behind bars. Mailer loved Abbott's letters, and turned them over to Random House, who pub-

lished them in 1978 under the title *In The Belly of the Beast.* With Mailer's help, Abbott was paroled three years early. He came to New York, where he was interviewed by *Good Morning America* and feted by the intelligentsia. Then, on July 17, 1981, in the BiniBon restaurant, a waiter named Richard Adan told Abbott that the restaurant's restroom was for employees only. Enraged, Abbott stabbed him to death and fled. He is now back in prison, serving a 15-year sentence.

AROUND ST. MARK'S PLACE

Raucous and run-down in spots, outrageously entertaining in others, St. Mark's is the heart of the East Village. Punked-out artists and rock musicians, students and tourists, drug dealers and the down-and-out, all jostle each other, while the stores on either side sell everything from gourmet pretzels to frightening-looking leather goods. To get the full effect of the craziness, come after 10 p.m. on a weekend night.

In the 19th century, St. Mark's was a fashionable street with elegant residences set back from the sidewalks. Author James Fenimore Cooper lived at 6 St. Mark's Pl. for a while, and several Eastern European social clubs were headquartered here.

St. Mark's is at its raunchiest between Second and Third Avenues. One of its noisiest addresses is the **community center,** 23 St. Mark's Pl., whose stairs are always draped with black-leathered people—both young and middle-aged. The building once housed The Dom, a huge dance hall and bar where Andy Warhol presented "The Exploding Plastic Inevitable," starring Lou Reed and the Velvet Underground. The rock club called the Electric Circus also occupied the site for a number of years.

W.H. Auden's Digs

Between Second and First Aves., St. Mark's becomes residential. Poet W.H. Auden lived in a fourth-floor apartment at 77 St. Mark's Pl. from 1953 to 1972. A plaque by the door commemorates the man and quotes the line: "If total affection cannot be, let the more loving one be me." In contrast to those noble sentiments, Auden lived in considerable filth, amidst piles of dirty plates and a cockroach population reputedly so large that the walls of his apartment appeared to be moving.

In 1917, in the basement of this same building, the revolutionary newspaper *Novy Mir* was published. One of its contributors was Leon Trotsky, in town for a few months before returning home to Russia in time for the Bolshevik Revolution.

Tompkins Square Park

This small park bounded by E. 7th and E. 10th Sts., and Aves. A and B, was the scene of a violent confrontation almost a decade ago. During the 1980s, the park was a squalid haven for the homeless as well as a marketplace for drugs. One hot August night in 1988, a dozen cops on horseback rode in to shut the park down. The homeless and their advocates protested in a four-hour-long riot that left at least 50 people injured. Acts of police brutality were recorded on video by a local artist, and 121 people filed complaints against the police department.

Rioting took place again the following summer and the summer after that. Finally in 1991, amid much local protest, Mayor Dinkins padlocked the park for renovations. Today, Tompkins Square is quiet and well kept, with playgrounds, benches, and a dog run . . . as well as a midnight curfew and a marked police presence.

As the park has become more gentrified, so has Ave. A. Once considered the fringe of East Village, the thoroughfare is now home to a mix of hole-in-the-wall bars and upscale restaurants.

The General Slocum Memorial

At the north end of the park is a small weathered statue of a boy and girl looking at a steamboat. The statue is a memorial to the disastrous General Slocum fire, which took place onboard an excursion boat in the East River on June 15, 1904. Some 1,300 German Lutherans, en route to their annual picnic died when the boat exploded near a dangerous passage known as Hell Gate. The remaining German community, which lived near the park, was so devastated that they abandoned the neighborhood. Many moved uptown into the East 80s.

Charlie Parker Place

In 1951, jazz great Charlie Parker moved into 151 Ave. B, a small, solid building on the east side of Tompkins Square Park. With him were his girlfriend, Chan, and her daughter, Kim. "I like the people around here," he said once to biographer Robert Reisner. "They don't give you no hype."

While here, Parker kept his life middle-class and respectable, greeting Chan's relatives in a suit and tie, and taking walks in the park with Kim. Later, Chan said that if it hadn't been for his talent, race, and drug addiction, Charlie could have lived out his days on Ave. B as a "happy square."

The city renamed this block "Charlie Parker Place" in 1993.

Little Ukraine

Some dub 7th St. between Second and Third Aves. "Little Ukraine," and it's true that the Ukrainian community here is thriving. But for the tourist, there's not much to see. **Surma,** 11 7th St., tel. (212) 477-0729, is a Ukrainian shop selling books, records, and crafts. Across from it is **St. George's Ukrainian Catholic Church,** a large domed church built in 1977. Every May, the church puts on a splendid Ukrainian Festival, featuring traditional foods and crafts.

McSorley's Ale House

At 15 7th St. stands the famed McSorley's Ale House, tel. (212) 473-9148, established in 1854. Engineer Peter Cooper once drank here, as did *The New Yorker* writer Joseph Mitchell, who wrote of the alehouse in his book, *McSorley's*

Wonderful Saloon. McSorley's only opened its doors to women in the early 1970s, and then only under court order.

Outside, you'll see barrels and an aging green-and-gold sign. Inside, the pub sports a potbelly stove, old gas lamps, a carved mahogany bar, and pressed tin ceilings. Memorabilia collected by old John McSorley hangs everywhere, but the old neighborhood drinking crowd is gone, replaced primarily by boisterous twenty-something males. The best time to come is lunch, when you can take a look around while munching on a ploughman's lunch of bread and cheese. Ale is the only beverage served, and it comes two glasses at a time, light or dark.

THE BOWERY AND ASTOR PLACE

Playing the Bowery

At 315 Bowery, at Bleecker, stands the famed, hole-in-the-wall nightclub **CBGB & OMFUG** (short for Country, Blue Grass, Blues and Other Music For Uplifting Gourmandizers), tel. (212) 982-4052. Here in the 1970s flourished an underground rock scene of the kind which seems impossible today. The club opened in 1974 with Richard Hell, bass player for the group Television (the nation's "first psychosexual rock group"). That set the tone for years to come. Everyone played here, including the Ramones, Patti Smith, and David Byrne. The club endures to this day.

McSorley's Ale House was a male-only preserve until the early 1970s.

Next door to CBGB's is the tiny, ornate **Amato Opera House,** 319 Bowery, tel. (212) 228-8200, which during the 19th century was a vaudeville stage. Across the street is **Bouwerie Lane Theater,** 330 Bowery, tel. (212) 677-0060, an elaborate cast-iron building that once housed the German Exchange Bank.

McGurk's Suicide Hall
On the east side of the Bowery, just below E. 1st St., is the shell of a four-story building that once housed McGurk's, a hangout for sailors and longshoremen during the late 1800s. The establishment was nicknamed "Suicide Hall" because of the many prostitutes who killed themselves here. McGurk's was also known for its headwaiter, Short-Change Charley (who used knockout drops on his rougher customers), and its no-nonsense bouncer, Eat-'Em-Up Jack McManus.

Merchant's House Museum
The classic Greek Revival home at 29 E. 4th St., just west of the Bowery, was once one of many elegant residences lining this block. Today it's the Merchant's House Museum, tel. (212) 777-1089. Inside, the house is furnished exactly as it was in 1835 when merchant Seabury Tredwell and his family lived here. On display are the family's entire belongings, including the framed diplomas of the Tredwell daughters and trunks filled with sumptuous satin clothes. On the second floor is a secret trapdoor that may once have led to an underground tunnel. The museum is open Sun.-Thurs. 1-4 p.m. Admission is $3.

Joseph Papp Public Theater
Two blocks north of the Old Merchant's House stands an imposing, columned building with colorful banners beckoning out front. Once the Astor Library, this is now the Joseph Papp Public Theater, 425 Lafayette St., tel. (212) 260-2400, where various plays and movies are always on tap.

Until his death in 1991, Papp was one of America's most important theater producers. Best known as founder of the New York Shakespeare Festival, he was also the man who first produced *Hair, A Chorus Line,* and 15 other plays that later moved to Broadway.

Astor Place
Adjoining the Public Theater is a windy, disjointed plaza centering around the "Alamo," a big black cube by artist Bernard Rosenthal. Precariously balanced on one corner, the cube is supposed to rotate when pushed, but that's easier

JOHN JACOB ASTOR

Both the Astor Library and Astor Place were named after John Jacob Astor, once the richest man in the United States. A poor German immigrant with an obsessive passion for money, Astor made his fortune first in the fur trade and then in the New York real estate market. On his deathbed he was reportedly so weak that he was fed on breast milk—thought to be extra nutritious—and tossed in a blanket 10 minutes a day for exercise. Nonetheless, money was still foremost in his mind and one day as he was being tossed, he urged one of his rent agents to collect from an impoverished widow. The man pleaded with him—saying that the widow needed more time—but Astor would not hear of an excuse. Eventually the agent went to Astor's son, who gave him the money. "There," said the dying Astor as the agent handed him the overdue rent, "I told you she would pay if you went the right way to work with her."

said than done. The plaza also holds a cast-iron reproduction of one of the original subway kiosks that once stood all over the city.

No longer standing is the highbrow Astor Place Opera House, which once lorded over the west side of the plaza. In 1849, the Opera House's management sparked the bloody Astor Place riots by hiring English actor George Macready rather than Irish-American actor Edwin Forrest to play Hamlet. When Forrest's loyal, working-class Irish fans heard the news, they took to the plaza in protest. A crowd of 12,000 gathered, and the police—then a private organization paid by the wealthy—appeared. They opened fire, killing about 30 people and wounding about 120 others.

Cooper Union

The largest brownstone in New York City is Cooper Union, located in the triangle between Astor Pl. and Third and Fourth Avenues. The 1859 building was financed by Peter Cooper, a remarkable engineer who—among many other things—made a fortune in the iron industry, designed the first American locomotive, invented gelatin and a self-rocking cradle, and helped develop Morse's telegraph. The son of a poor storekeeper, Cooper built his Union to house a free school of practical arts and sciences. Still in operation today, Cooper Union was also the first coeducational, racially integrated school in the country.

Downstairs inside Cooper Union is the Great Hall, where Abraham Lincoln made his famous "Might makes right" speech that won him the Republican presidential nomination in 1860. Abolitionists Henry Ward Beecher, Frederick Douglass, and William Cullen Bryant also spoke here, as did every president following Lincoln up through Woodrow Wilson, and President Clinton.

A statue of Peter Cooper stands on the building's south side. Across the street, at 36 Cooper Square, are the offices of the *Village Voice,* founded in 1955.

SHOPPING

Books and Newspapers

One of the city's best bookstores, **St. Marks Bookshop** is no longer on its namesake street but just around the corner at 31 Third Ave., tel. (212) 260-7853. Open daily until midnight, the store has an especially fine selection of fiction and alternative publications.

On the southwest corner of Second Ave. and St. Mark's Pl. is **Gem Spa** newsstand, a dilapidated joint famous for egg creams. Made of very cold milk, seltzer water, and chocolate syrup, egg creams were once a staple in this part of town.

Clothes

Love Saves the Day, 119 Second Ave., at 7th St., tel. (212) 228-3802, is the stuffed-to-the-rafters, secondhand clothing (etc.) store where Rosanna Arquette bought her jacket in the movie *Desperately Seeking Susan.* **Trash and**

Cooper Union was the first coeducational, racially integrated school in the U.S.

Vaudeville, 4 St. Mark's Pl., tel. (212) 982-3590, is an over-the-top spot selling everything from studded halter tops to rock-and-roll gear from the 1960s. **Screaming Mimi's,** 382 Lafayette St., near E. 4th St., tel. (212) 677-6464, is known for '50s-, '60s-, and '70s-era duds. **Kanae + Onyx,** 75 E. 7th St., tel. (212) 254-7703, sells sleek, slinky fashion.

Crafts and Gifts

The bright and colorful **Back From Guatemala,** 306 E. 6th St., bet. First and Second Aves., tel. (212) 260-7010, is filled with ethnic clothing, jewelry, masks, and crafts, mostly from Central America. For eclectic gifts, try **Howdy Do,** 72 E. 7th St., tel. (212) 979-1618; **Made in Detroit,** 335 E. 9th St., tel. (212) 995-2592; **Mostly Bali,** 324 E. 9th, tel. (212) 777-9049; and **Dinosaur Hill,** 302 E. 9th, tel. (212) 473-5850—four unusual shops selling exactly what their names imply.

Health and Beauty

The traditional **Tenth Street Russian and Turkish Baths,** 268 E. 10th St., bet. First Ave. and Ave. A, tel. (212) 473-8806, is filled with saunas, steam rooms, and massage rooms. At one time, many such establishments existed in the East Village, but this is the last one left. Some days are coed, others for men or women only.

The 1851 **Kiehl's,** 109 Third Ave., near 13th St., tel. (212) 677-3171, is an old-fashioned chemist's where you can buy a full line of natural, handmade beauty products.

Music

Sounds, 20 St. Mark's Pl., bet. Third and Second Aves., tel. (212) 677-3444, is stocked with a good selection of alternative music and used CDs. **Fat Beats,** 323 E. 9th St., tel. (212) 673-3883, carries a mix of new hip hop, reggae, and breakbeat vinyl. **Footlight Records,** 113 E. 12th St., bet. Fourth and Third Aves., tel. (212) 533-1572, carries a good selection of show tunes, jazz, and used CDs. **Finyl Vinyl,** 204 E. 6th St., near Second Ave., tel. (212) 533-8007, features records from the '30s to the '70s.

Other Shops of Interest

Little Rickie's, 49¹/₂ First Ave., near E. 3rd St., tel. (212) 505-6467, is a wonderful offbeat shop

selling everything from rattlesnake eggs and tequila suckers (with worms inside) to "Make-Your-Own African-American Art" and "Baby Lenin" pins. **Surma,** 11 7th St., bet. Third and Second Aves., tel. (212) 477-0729, is a Ukrainian shop selling books, records, and crafts. **Jam Paper And Envelope,** 111 Third Ave., near 13th St., tel. (212) 473-6666, stocks a wide array of budget-priced stationery.

Ninth Street east of Second Avenue is lined with one tiny, eccentric, harum-scarum shop after another. Names and ownerships change seemingly overnight; for sale are antiques, home furnishings, vintage clothing, fashions by young designers, books, pottery, herbs, and crafts. **Seventh Street** east of Second Avenue and **Avenue A** are also good streets for shopping.

FOOD

American

Inexpensive: The informal **Life Cafe,** 343 E. 10th St., at Ave. B, tel. (212) 477-8791, is a long-time neighborhood favorite featuring vegetarian and Tex-Mex fare. **Around the Clock,** 8 Stuyvesant St., near 9th St. and Third Ave., tel. (212) 598-0402, is a 24-hour joint serving standard burgers, sandwiches, and the like. For unusual, flavorful health-food fare, try the snug **Caravan of Dreams,** 405 E. 6th St., at Ave. A, tel. (212) 254-1613. **7A,** 109 Ave. A, at 7th St., tel. (212) 673-6583, has a nice selection of salads, sandwiches, and more substantial entrees.

Moderate: Miracle Grill, 112 First Ave., at 7th St., tel. (212) 254-2353, features tasty Southwestern cuisine and a scruffy but romantic garden.

Asian

Inexpensive: Dojo's, 24 St. Mark's Pl., near Second Ave., tel. (212) 674-9821, is a popular spot offering a mix of Japanese and vegetarian fare. **Mingala Burmese Restaurant,** 21 E. 7th St., near Third Ave., tel. (212) 529-3656, serves good food in a comfortable setting adorned with Burmese handicrafts.

Moderate: The small and friendly **Siam Square,** 92 Second Ave., at 9th St., tel. (212) 505-1240, features good Thai food at very reasonable prices. **Iso,** 175 Second Ave., at 11th

St., tel. (212) 777-0361, serves first-rate sushi along with imaginative Japanese dishes. **Shabu Tatsu,** 216 E. 10th St., bet. Second and First Aves., tel. (212) 477-2972, is an oft-crowded cook-it-yourself Japanese barbecue place.

Eastern European
The East Village is especially known for its cheap, Eastern European fare. Some legendary Second Ave. spots include **Second Avenue Deli,** 156 Second Ave., at 10th St., tel. (212) 677-0606, a classic Jewish delicatessen; recently renovated **Veselka,** 144 Second Ave., at 9th St., tel. (212) 228-9682, a good stop for borscht, pirogis, and scrumptious poppyseed cake; and the 24-hour **Kiev,** 117 Second Ave., at 7th St., tel. (212) 674-4040, serving creamy cheese blintzes and the like. **Odessa,** 117 Ave. A, bet. 7th and 8th Sts., tel. (212) 253-1470, is the place to go for heaping platters of Ukrainian food; **Christine's,** 208 First Ave., at 12th St., tel. (212) 254-2474, serves classic Polish fare.

Eclectic
Inexpensive: The sprawling **Yaffa Cafe,** 97 St. Mark's Pl., near First Ave., tel. (212) 674-9302, serves a little bit of everything. The food's only fair, but the funky, artsy garden out back is delightful.

Moderate: The friendly **Two Boots,** 37 Ave. A, bet. 2nd and 3rd Sts., tel. (212) 505-2276, serves first-rate, often spicy fare from the lands shaped like "Two Boots"—Italy and Louisiana. **Time Cafe,** 380 Lafayette St., at Great Jones, tel. (212) 533-7000, attracts a trendy, sleek clientele with its imaginative and vaguely organic menu.

Indian
Inexpensive-to-Moderate: The East Village is also known for its Indian restaurants, most of which lie along the south side of 6th St. bet. First and Second Avenues. The lines waiting to get into these restaurants can be long, and most require that you BYOB.

Mitali, 334 6th St., tel. (212) 533-2508, is one of the oldest, most expensive, and best of the group. It also serves beer. **Gandhi,** 345 6th St., tel. (212) 614-9718; and **Sonali,** 326 6th St., tel. (212) 505-7517, are the best of the cheaper spots. **Bombay,** 320 6th St., tel. (212) 260-8229,

often hosts live music. **Haveli,** 100 Second Ave., tel. (212) 982-0533, is more upscale than the others, yet prices remain moderate.

Italian
Moderate: Cheery, old-fashioned **Lanza,** 168 First Ave., bet. 10th and 11th Sts., tel. (212) 674-7014, is a popular eatery decorated with bright oil paintings of Italy. Out back is a pleasant garden. The modern, step-down **Spaghetteria,** 178 Second Ave., near 12th St., tel. (212) 995-0900, features excellent pasta and other entrees. **John's,** 302 E. 12th St., near Second Ave., tel. (212) 475-9531, serves huge portions of Southern Italian food in a dark, romantic setting complete with wine bottles draped with candle wax.

Latin/Caribbean
Moderate: Authentic Mexican food can be found at **Pedro Paramo,** 430 E. 14th St., bet. First Ave. and Ave. A, tel. (212) 475-4581, a cheery restaurant done up in pink and white. **Maryann's,** 300 E. 5th St., at Second Ave., tel. (212) 475-5939, is one of a chain of three interesting and very popular spots also serving tasty Mexican fare. The lively **Boca Chica,** 13 First Ave., at 1st St., tel. (212) 473-0108, offers imaginative Latin dishes. Across the street is **Baby Jakes,** 14 First Ave., tel. (212) 254-2229, a friendly, dilapidated storefront eatery selling cheap, fresh New Orleans fare.

Seafood
Inexpensive: Cucina di Pesce, 87 E. 4th St., bet. Second and Third Aves., tel. (212) 260-6800, serves good Italian seafood.

Moderate-to-Expensive: The upscale **Pisces,** 95 Ave. A, at 6th St., tel. (212) 260-6660, offers unusual seafood dishes, as well as outdoor tables in good weather.

Southern/Soul/Creole
Inexpensive-to-Moderate: Good Southern/Creole food is the specialty at the tiny, lively **Great Jones Cafe,** 54 Great Jones St., bet. Bowery and Lafayette, tel. (212) 674-9304. The cafe turns into a hip hangout after midnight. The enormous **Acme Bar & Grill,** 9 Great Jones St., bet. Broadway and Lafayette, tel. (212) 420-1934, features Southern fare and a boisterous late-night drinking crowd.

Other Ethnic

Moderate: Jules, 65 St. Mark's Pl., bet. First and Second Aves., tel. (212) 477-5560, is a lively French bistro often presenting jazz quartets.

Moderate-to-Expensive: The stylish and very popular **First,** 87 First Ave., at Fifth St., tel. (212) 674-3823, lined with burnished steel and comfy gray booths, serves an eclectic international fare that's part Asian, part Mexican, part Italian, and part French.

Light Bites

One of the oldest and largest pastry shops in the East Village is the century-old **Veniero's,** 342 E. 11th St., near First Ave., tel. (212) 674-7264, featuring classic Italian treats. Around the corner is the **Black Forest Pastry Shop,** 344 E. 11th St., at First Ave., tel. (212) 254-8181, known for German delicacies. Across First Ave. is **De Robertis,** 176 First Ave., at 11th St., tel. (212) 674-7137, a cheery Italian shop with a handful of tables and wonderful window displays. **Caffe Della Pace,** 48 E. 7th St., at Second Ave., tel. (212) 529-8024, is modern and very good.

Watering Holes and Lounges

One of the best scruffy East Village bars is **2A,** 25 Ave. A, at 2nd St., tel. (212) 505-2566, which features a small, laid-back drinking scene downstairs and a comfortable lounge area upstairs. The intimate, tiled **WCOU,** First Ave. and 7th St., tel. (212) 254-4317, is a good place for a quiet drink. During happy hour, 5-8 p.m., all drinks are half-price.

Holiday Cocktail Lounge, 75 St. Mark's Pl., near First Ave., tel. (212) 777-9637, is a classic East Village dive where white-haired Ukrainian bartenders serve cheap drinks to surly old poets and cynical young musicians. Also a classic is **Vazac's,** 108 Ave. B, at 7th St., tel. (212) 473-8840, or "7B," equipped with a horseshoe-shaped bar that's been featured in a number of movies, including *Crocodile Dundee* and *The Victim.* **McSorley's Old Ale House,** 15 E. 7th St., bet. Second and Third Aves., tel. (212) 473-9148, is one of New York's oldest bars, but its callow fraternity crowd—drinking as much as they can as quickly as they can—makes it a place to avoid.

KGB, 85 E. 4th St., bet. Second and Third Aves., tel. (212) 505-3360, is a former speakeasy now filled with eclectic Soviet souvenirs and lovely wooden furniture. Especially popular among writers and editors, it hosts frequent readings and literary get-togethers. The friendly **Telephone Bar & Grill,** 149 Second Ave., bet. 9th and 10th Sts., tel. (212) 529-5000, sports bright red English-style phone booths out front. **Joe's Bar,** E. 5th St., bet. Aves. A and B, is small, dark, and casual. Inside the Time Cafe restaurant is **Fez,** 380 Lafayette St., at Great Jones, tel. (212) 533-2680, an upscale Moroccan-style bar sporting exotic fabrics and tile. Sleek **Vain,** 9 Ave. A, near 1st, tel. (212) 253-1462, serves 18 varieties of cocktails, including ones made with cinnamon schnapps.

And then there's the sleek retro-hip **Bowery Bar,** 358 Bowery, at 4th St., tel. (212) 475-2220, straight out of the '50s. Though also an upscale

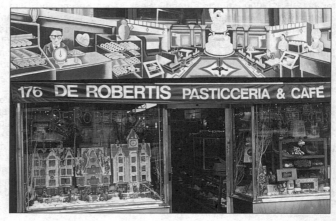

coffee and pastries, East Village style

restaurant, the place is especially known for its back room bar and garden, usually packed with beautiful people and impossible to get into. Other crowded hot spots are the **Temple Bar,** 332 Lafayette St., bet. Bleecker and Houston, tel. (212) 925-4242, a lush hideaway with Oriental rugs and expensive drinks; and **Tenth Street Lounge,** 212 E. 10th St., bet. Third and Second Aves., tel. (212) 473-5252, sporting a circular bar and dim red lighting.

Among gay bars, **The Bar,** 68 Second Ave., at 4th St., tel. (212) 674-9714, is a worn, scruffy joint with a devoted following, including many ACT-UP activists. **Cake,** 99 Ave. B, bet. 6th and 7th Sts., tel. (212) 674-7957, reputedly hosts some of the raunchiest queer parties in town. **Meow Mix,** 269 Houston St., at Suffolk St. tel. (212) 254-1434, is a funky lesbian hangout that hosts many theme parties and all-women bands.

A number of East Village restaurants mentioned above, including **Great Jones Cafe,** and **Acme Bar & Grill,** also have lively bar scenes. See also "Entertainment" under "Out on the Town," in the Introduction.

DOVER PUBLICATIONS, INC.

GREENWICH VILLAGE

It's easy to knock Greenwich Village. Once a hotbed of radical and artistic activity, its narrow winding streets now sometimes seem too tame, its restored buildings too cute, its shops and boutiques too artsy and out of sync with sleek, modern times. Only the well-to-do can afford to live here now, and nearly all the dingy old dives have gone safely commercial and mainstream. Worst of all, the streets are always filled with busloads of tourists and bands of roving teenagers looking for wild, sinful times.

And yet—Greenwich Village cannot be dismissed that easily. For all its patina of tourism and well-fed complacency, it still has a bohemian soul lurking somewhere underneath. You can feel it sometimes in the old jazz clubs, or in Washington Square on a windy afternoon, or in the faces of some of the older residents, who saw it all happen, not so long ago.

History
Once an Algonquin settlement, Greenwich Village was settled by Dutch tobacco farmers in the late 1600s and by English landowners in the early- to mid-1700s. By the 1790s, however, the large estates were breaking up as many New Yorkers came north to escape the yellow-fever epidemics in Lower Manhattan. During the epidemics, the city erected barricades along Chambers St. to prevent people from returning to the infected areas, and Greenwich Village started filling up with stores, banks, and other businesses.

Over the next few decades, as the city spread north along Broadway, Greenwich Village turned into a low-rent backwater that attracted immigrants. First came the Irish in the 1850s, then the African Americans after the Civil War, and the Italians in the 1890s.

Around 1910, artists and writers also discovered the low rents, and soon the area was teeming with artistic and political activity. Max Eastman founded his radical paper, *The Masses;* tea rooms, literary bars, and basement poetry clubs sprouted up; and theater groups flourished. Among the Village residents during this period were Eugene O'Neill, Edna St. Vincent Millay, Bette Davis, Sherwood Anderson, Theodore Dreiser, John Dos Passos, and e.e. cummings. Greenwich Village's tolerance of "the Third Sex," as gays and lesbians were discreetly called, also dates from this period.

In the 1960s, folk clubs, antiwar rallies, and the Civil Rights movement brought to the Village another wave of new settlers, including Bob Dylan and Jimi Hendrix, Abbie Hoffman and Jerry Rubin. In 1969, the Village's Stonewall Riots marked the beginning of the national gay-rights movement.

Orientation
Greenwich Village stretches from Houston St. north to 14th St., and from Fourth Ave. west to the Hudson River. The neighborhood west of Seventh Ave. is generally referred to as the West Village. Nearly every street has something interesting to offer, and you can't go wrong just wandering about. Be sure to bring a map, however—there's no grid system here and even the locals

get confused. First-time visitors will probably want to concentrate on Washington Square and on Bleecker, Christopher, and Bedford Streets.

Touring is best here in afternoon and early evening, but it's also well worth returning at night, especially if you're interested in jazz. The Village holds many of the city's top jazz clubs, including the Village Vanguard—arguably the best jazz joint in New York (see "Jazz" under "Out on the Town" in the Introduction).

WASHINGTON SQUARE AND THE SOUTH VILLAGE

Though nothing special to look at, Washington Square Park is the heart of the Village. On a sunny day you'll find everyone here, from kids hotdogging on skateboards and students strumming guitars, to die-hard Hare Krishnas spreading the word and old men taking in the sun. At the park's southwest corner are stone chess tables

a young New Yorker at Washington Square Park

where the click-clack of the pieces never seems to stop; at the northwest end is the dog run, where dogs of every conceivable shape and size dash madly to and fro. On the sidewalks surrounding the park are the joggers and—especially at night—the drug dealers. Periodically, the police do a sweep, but the dealers always return, seeping back like water leaking out of a dam.

Once marshland, the eight-acre park was purchased by the city near the end of the 18th century to be used as a potter's field. During the yellow fever epidemic of 1797, at least 660 people were buried here; in 1965, a Con Ed excavation unearthed a sealed tomb containing 25 skeletons that date back to that time. In the late 1700s, the park was used as a public hanging ground, with many of the doomed coming from the state penitentiary that once stood above Christopher St. at the Hudson River. Physical evidence of those days still exists: in the park's extreme northwest corner is an enormous tree bearing the sign, "The Hangman's Elm." According to *The New York Times,* the sign is accurate.

In 1826, the square was turned into a parade ground. But the heavy artillery on display sometimes sank into the graves below, so the following year, the parade ground was turned into a park. Elegant townhouses went up all around, and by the 1830s, Washington Square was considered to be the city's most fashionable residential neighborhood.

New York University (NYU) erected its first building on the park in 1837, and now occupies much of the park's periphery. Most of the old townhouses have been replaced by institutional buildings, the genteel old families by students.

Washington Arch

The park's biggest landmark is the marble arch marking the north entrance. Eighty-six feet tall, the arch replaces a temporary wooden one erected in 1889 to commemorate the centennial of George Washington's inauguration. Citizens liked the wooden arch so much that they decided to have it remade in marble. The designer was architect Stanford White, and the sculptor was A. Stirling Calder (father of famous mobile sculptor Alexander Calder).

In 1916, a group of Villagers led by a woman named Gertrude Drick climbed a now-sealed staircase inside the arch to read a Greenwich

Village declaration of independence, which proclaimed that the neighborhood was seceding from the rest of the city. Among Drick's party were artists John Sloan and Marcel Duchamp. The group partied until dawn by the light of red Chinese lanterns. Prior to this, Drick had already established herself as a bit of an eccentric by passing out black-bordered calling cards wherever she went. The cards bore the single word "Woe"; when asked why, Drick would reply, "Because woe is me."

Washington Square North

The beautiful red-brick Greek Revival townhouses on the north side of Washington Square date back to the early 1830s. The house at 1 Washington Square N was home, at different times, to novelists Edith Wharton and Henry James, who once described the neighborhood as "the ideal of quiet and of genteel retirement." James was born in 1843 just off Washington Square at 21 Washington Pl., and he set his novel *Washington Square* at his grandmother's house, 19 Washington Square North. Neither of these two buildings still stands.

The painter Edward Hopper lived at 3 Washington Square N—once known as the "Studio Building"—from 1913 until his death in 1967. Other notables claiming this address at one time or another included painter Rockwell Kent, literary critic Edmund Wilson, and writer John Dos Passos, who started his novel *Manhattan Transfer* in this building in 1922.

Washington Mews

Just north of Washington Square N, off University Pl. to the east, runs a picturesque cobblestone alley lined with stucco buildings. Once stables for the residents of Washington Square Park, Washington Mews is now a row of highly coveted homes and NYU buildings. Political journalist Walter Lippman lived at 50 Washington Mews from 1923 to 1926.

MacDougal Alley

Just north of Washington Square Park, off MacDougal St. to the west, is another picturesque alleyway, this one full of crooked houses, old-fashioned streetlamps, and birdhouses. The building at the rear of the alley (No. 19) was once the studio of Gertrude Vanderbilt Whit-

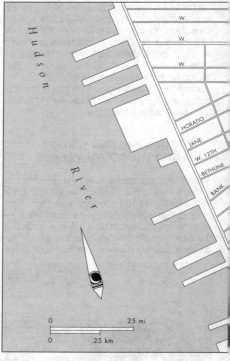

ney, the heiress, sculptor, and art patron who founded the Whitney Museum of Art.

Washington Square South

Most of the buildings along Washington Square S belong to NYU. One outstanding exception is **Judson Memorial Church,** whose amber Romanesque bell tower lends an air of European elegance to the park. The 1888 church was designed by architect Stanford White. Today the church is known for its political activism and arts-oriented congregation.

Before being replaced by the NYU student center, 61 Washington Square S was known as the "House of Genius." Numerous writers lived there over the years, including Willa Cather, Stephen Crane, John Dos Passos, Theodore Dreiser, O. Henry, and Eugene O'Neill. Before being replaced by NYU Law School, 43 Washington Square S was home to Marxist journalist

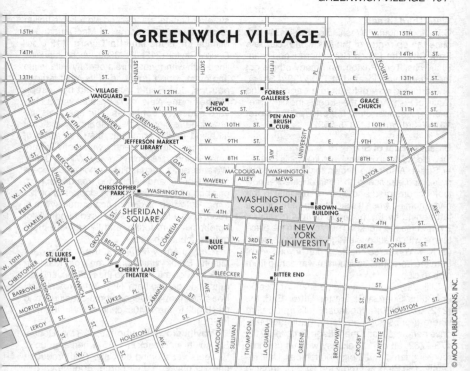

GREENWICH VILLAGE

© MOON PUBLICATIONS, INC.

John Reed. While living there, Reed married Louise Bryant, and in 1917, they traveled to Russia to witness the Bolshevik Revolution first-hand.

At 70 Washington Square S is NYU's **Elmer Bobst Library,** an enormous red-granite building. Just behind it is the I.M. Pei apartment complex, **Washington Square Village.**

To reduce costs, many of the NYU buildings erected during the 1830s were made of stone cut by convicts in Sing Sing. When members of the Stone-Cutters Guild heard of this arrangement, they paraded through the park in one of the city's first demonstrations of organized labor. The Stone-Cutters Riot, as it was later called, lasted four days, ending only when the National Guard was called in.

Triangle Shirtwaist Fire

Another important event in labor history is recorded by a plaque mounted high on the Brown Build-

ing, 29 Washington Pl., at Greene, just east of the park. It was in this building, on the afternoon of March 25, 1911, that 146 garment workers— mostly young Italian and Jewish women—lost their lives in a tragic fire. The women were working for the Triangle Shirtwaist factory, then located on the building's top three floors. When the fire broke out, the workers found their one exit door bolted on the outside by a management intent on keeping them from leaving early. Some of the women burned to death; most jumped to it.

Incredible though it may seem today, the fire wasn't particularly severe as fires in those days went. But it generated much publicity—largely because the women had gone on strike two years before to protest their poor working conditions—and led to the enactment of the city's first fire and safety codes. The Triangle Shirtwaist Company was indicted, but acquitted, of all responsibility for the tragedy.

West Third Street

One block south of Washington Park is W. 3rd, once the epicenter of the folk world. **Gerde's Folk City,** the famed club where Bob Dylan, Phil Ochs, Tom Paxton, and many others got their starts, was located at 130 W. 3rd Street. The address now belongs to a bar called the Kettle of Fish. Across the street is the city's premier jazz supper club, the pricey **Blue Note,** 131 W. 3rd, tel. (212) 475-8592.

Bleecker East of Sixth

Two blocks south of Washington Park is Bleecker Street. Also once known for its vibrant folk music and jazz scene, this part of Bleecker now looks bedraggled and worn, especially in the early morning when it's still strewn with garbage left behind by the previous night's revellers. Even worse are weekend nights, when the place teems with a raucous bridge-and-tunnel crowd (as New Yorkers so charitably dub anyone who's from the boroughs or suburbs) wandering from club to club.

Still, Bleecker St. should be seen. At Bleecker and La Guardia Pl. are the **Bitter End,** tel. (212) 673-7030, a legendary folk-music club where groups such as Peter, Paul and Mary once performed; and the **Village Grill,** tel. (212) 473-9762, an old speakeasy with tin ceilings, revolving fans, and a big wooden bar. Until recently, 160 Bleecker (now the CVS pharmacy) was home to the **Village Gate,** a sprawling basement club where big names such as Miles Davis, Charles Mingus, B.B. King, and Tito Puente once played. In 1895, a young Theodore Dreiser lived upstairs at this address in what was then the flea-bitten Mills House. Beds in the 1,500-room hotel went for 25 cents a night.

(For information on Bleecker St. west of Sixth Ave., see "Bleecker West of Sixth" under "West to Hudson Street," below.)

MacDougal Street

The old **San Remo** bar, where literary giants such as James Baldwin and James Agee hung out, once stood at 93 MacDougal, at Bleecker. Also a regular at the San Remo was poet Maxwell Bodenheim, who wrote, "Greenwich Village is the Coney Island of the soul."

Heading north on MacDougal, you'll pass a myriad of small funky jewelry and T-shirt shops, storefront falafel stands, and old reliable Italian restaurants. At the corner of MacDougal and Minetta Ln. is the **Minetta Tavern,** 113 MacDougal St., tel. (212) 475-3850, whose interior is lined with wonderful murals of early Village life and memorabilia from one of its most famous patrons, Joe Gould. As profiled by Joseph Mitchell in the *New Yorker,* Gould was a Harvard-educated bohemian who spent his life prowling the city streets in search of material for his 11-million-word opus, the *Oral History of Our Times.* He was friendly with many literary types, including Malcolm Cowley, William Carlos Williams, and e.e. cummings (who wrote a poem about Gould), and he cadged free drinks from one and all while expounding eloquently on his tome. But when he died in an insane asylum in 1958, only a few of his supposed hundreds of notebooks were found, and those were more or less unpublishable.

Pretty, narrow **Minetta Lane** is named for Minetta Brook, which once ran from Madison Park through the Village to the Hudson, and still runs underground here. New Amsterdam's first free black farmers began homesteading along this brook in the 1640s, on land given them by the Dutch.

Provincetown Playhouse, 133 MacDougal St., got its start back in 1915, when a group of Villagers vacationing on Cape Cod produced one-act plays on their porch. Eugene O'Neill was the group's most famous member, and most of his work from 1916 through the 1920s was produced here first. The Provincetown is now being restored and will reopen as an education performance space for young audiences, young playwrights, and community groups performing O'Neill's work.

NORTH TO 14TH STREET

Eighth Street

To the immediate north of Washington Park runs 8th Street. Once a highlight of Greenwich Village, 8th St. is now best known for its impossible number of shoe stores, grungy boutiques, and cheap food joints. The street hit rock bottom in terms of atmosphere in 1994-95, but residents are now working to clean the place up and progress has been made.

Eighth Street has been a Village tourist attraction since the late 1940s, when straight couples came to dance at the Bon Soir or the Village Barn, and gay men hung out at a bar called Mary's. In 1970, Jimi Hendrix brought attention to the street when he built his splendid **Electric Lady Studios,** shaped like a giant guitar, into a row of brownstones at 52 W. 8th. Hendrix recorded some 600 hours of tapes at his studio, but he died the following September—from inhalation of vomit following barbiturate intoxication—before anything was released. Today, the building's ground floor is still rounded like a guitar, and there's a shiny *Electric Lady* plaque at the door.

The building at 5 W. 8th St. was once the **Marlton Hotel,** where nightclub comedian Lenny Bruce stayed during his highly publicized obscenity trial in 1964. Arrested for an "obscene" performance at the Cafe Au Go Go on Bleecker St., he was eventually found innocent. He died less than two years later in Hollywood.

Across the street from the old Marlton, in what is now the New York Studio School, was the first home of the **Whitney Museum of American Art.** Gertrude Vanderbilt Whitney founded the museum in 1931, with her own collection of over 500 works by artists such as Edward Hopper, Joseph Stella, Charles Demuth, Thomas Hart Benton, and Isamu Noguchi. The museum was in this pinkish art deco building for almost 20 years before moving uptown.

Grace Church

If you continue east on 8th St. to the shopping mecca of Lower Broadway, then look north, you'll see that Broadway takes an enormous swerve to the left at 11th Street. That's because in 1847, a stubborn old farmer named Hendrick Brevoort refused to let the city's new grid street system cut through his property. It would have meant the death of his beloved gardens and his favorite elm tree.

At the curve today stands **Grace Church,** a lovely, lacy, Gothic Revival cathedral built by Brevoort's son-in-law James Renwick. Then a young construction engineer who had never studied architecture, Renwick entered a contest for the church's design, and won.

On Feb. 10, 1863, Gen. Tom Thumb and Lavinia Warren Bumpus were married at the church, much to the chagrin of many of its parishioners who regarded the P.T. Barnum-planned stunt as beneath the church's dignity. Nonetheless, when the wedding took place, over 1,200 of these same parishioners pushed and shoved and climbed up on the pews to get a better view of the little people.

Lower Fifth Avenue

Fifth Ave. begins at Washington Square Park. One block north, at the southwest corner of Fifth Ave. and 8th St., stands the lovely, art deco **1 Fifth.** During the 1920s, a women's political group called the "A Club" met here. The club's eclectic membership included Rose O'Neill, who later invented the Kewpie doll, and Frances Perkins, who later served as secretary of labor under Franklin Delano Roosevelt.

Other venerable clubs are still based in the area. The **Pen and Brush Club,** 16 E. 10th St., at Fifth Ave., is the oldest professional-women's organization in the U.S., founded in 1893. The **Salmagundi Club,** 57 Fifth Ave., near 11th St., is the nation's oldest artists' club, founded in 1870.

The streets bet. Fifth and Sixth Aves. in this part of town are among the prettiest in the city; 9th, 10th, and 11th Sts. in particular are lined with one gorgeous brownstone after another, many with colorful windowboxes out front.

Poet Marianne Moore lived at 35 W. 9th St. from 1966 until her death in 1971 at the age of 84. Mark Twain lived at 14 W. 10th St. from 1900 to 1901. He was famous by then and subjected to a constant stream of strangers filing by his door, asking for autographs and handshakes. Dashiell Hammett was living at 28 W. 10th St. in 1951 when he was sent to prison for 22 weeks for refusing to testify about the Civil Rights Congress, a leftist organization of which he was a member.

The Weathermen Blow-Up

At 18 W. 11th St. is a handsome 19th-century townhouse with an oddly modern, triangular front of red brick and glass. That's because on March 6, 1970, the radical group the Weathermen accidently blew off the front part of the building while concocting bombs in the basement. Three Weathermen died in the accident, but Cathlyn Wilkerson—whose parents owned the building—and her friend Kathy Boudin escaped and vanished. Wilkerson turned herself in 10 years later and served 11 months in prison for negligent homicide. Boudin was captured in 1981 in connection with a Brinks armored-truck holdup in which three people were killed. She was sentenced to 20 years to life.

Forbes Magazine Galleries
On the ground floor of the Forbes Building are the Forbes Magazine Galleries, 62 Fifth Ave., near 12th St., tel. (212) 206-5548. The museum is best known for its fabulous collection of Faberge eggs—perfect in their miniature beauty—but you'll also find much else of interest. Highlights include over 500 toy boats, 12,000 toy soldiers, lots of historical documents, and a weird and wacky trophy section called the "Mortality of Immortality." Everything was collected by idiosyncratic media tycoon Malcolm Forbes, and the whole place feels like the giant playhouse of a precocious kid.

The galleries are open Tues.-Wed., Fri.-Sat. 10 a.m.-4 p.m. Though only 900 tickets are handed out a day, there's usually no problem getting in. Tickets are free.

Jefferson Market Library was originally a courthouse.

New School
One block west of the Forbes Building is the New School, 66 W. 12th St., tel. (212) 229-5600, an adult educational institution known for its excellent social-sciences department and eclectic course offerings. Worth a quick look is the school's impressive lobby mural, *The Coming Together of the Races,* by Mexican artist José Clemente Orozco.

Sixth Avenue
Near the northwest corner of Sixth Ave. and 10th St. are two unusual residential courtyards, cut off from the streets by iron gates. The utilitarian **Milligan Place,** off Sixth Ave. just north of 10th St., was built in 1852, supposedly to house the waiters of the Brevoort Hotel. The more picturesque **Patchin Place,** off 10th St. just west of Sixth Ave., comes from the same time period and the same architect, Aaron Patchin.

Poet e.e. cummings once owned 4 Patchin Pl., living there from 1923 until his death in 1962. During much of that same time, writer Djuna Barnes rented a tiny apartment at 5 Patchin Place. Legend has it that cummings used to stand below the then-elderly Barnes's window every morning and shout up, "Djuna, are you dead yet?" As fate would have it, cummings died first.

Jefferson Market Library
Reigning over Sixth Ave. and 10th St. are the Gothic turrets and towers of Jefferson Market Library. Designed by Frederick Clarke Withers and Calvert Vaux in 1876, the stunning maroon-and-white building was originally a courthouse and part of a complex that also included a jail, firehouse, and market. The jail was later replaced by the Women's House of Detention, where jazz great Billie Holiday was once imprisoned for the possession of marijuana. The market's former site is now a community garden bursting with color in the spring.

WEST TO HUDSON STREET

West to Waverly Place
Heading west of Sixth Ave. on Christopher St. to Waverly Pl., you'll pass a picturesque elbow-shaped street on the left lined with 1840s' row houses. Originally a stable alley, **Gay Street** was

later home to African Americans, many of whom worked as servants for the families on Washington Square. Waverly Pl. was named after Sir Walter Scott's best-selling novel, *Waverley.*

At the intersection of Christopher, Waverly, and Grove is an odd, three-sided building called the **Northern Dispensary.** When it was built in 1831, it was one of the city's first free hospitals and was then at the city's northernmost edge—hence the name. Edgar Allan Poe was treated here for a cold in 1837. The building is now vacant.

Just around the corner to the north, at 193 Waverly Pl., is anthropologist Margaret Mead's old residence. A single mother, Mead lived with her daughter in this handsome four-story townhouse from 1955 to 1966.

Christopher Park/Sheridan Square

Just west of the dispensary, at Christopher St. and Seventh Ave. S, is scruffy Christopher Park, often mistaken for Sheridan Square. The latter is just southeast of Christopher Park at the triangle where Washington Pl., Barrow, Grove, and West 4th Sts. meet. The confusion is understandable—Christopher Park is more central and marked by a statue of Gen. Philip Sheridan. Sheridan was a Union general best remembered for the unfortunate, often misquoted line, "The only good Indians I saw were dead."

Next to the general is a George Segal sculpture depicting two gay couples—one male and standing, the other female and sitting on a bench. Erected in 1991, the statue commemorates the Stonewall Riots, which took place across the street at the Stonewall Inn on June 27, 1969. (The original Stonewall Inn was at 51 Christopher St. and is now gone; the bar called Stonewall at 53 Christopher is just a namesake.)

The night began with what the cops later said was a routine raid of a bar that was serving alcohol without a liquor license. But the gay men inside the Stonewall didn't see it that way. All too used to being unfairly harassed by the police, they resisted arrest. Friends in neighboring bars called out their support, and beer bottles began to fly. Eventually, 13 protestors were arrested, but that was almost beside the point. More significantly, the riots marked the first time that gays had collectively engaged in civil disobedience. The next night, an even bigger group of protestors gathered; the modern gay-rights movement had begun.

At night, and especially on the weekends, Sheridan Square and the adjoining blocks of Seventh Ave. S swell with out-of-towners and visitors of all types—young and middle-aged, gay and straight, white and black. Many popular bars and music clubs (see "Watering Holes" under "Food," below) are located in the immediate area.

Thomas Paine's Home

Across the street from Christopher Park, at 59 Grove St., is the former home of Thomas Paine, the Revolutionary War-era author of *Common*

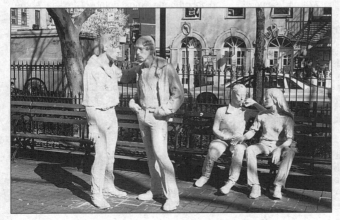

A George Segal sculpture commemorates the Stonewall riots.

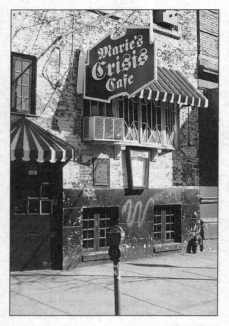

Tom Paine's old home is now a gay piano bar.

Sense, The Crisis, and *The Rights of Man.* It was Paine who wrote the famous words, "These are the times that try men's souls."

Born to Quaker parents in England, Paine immigrated to the U.S. in 1774 and served in the Revolutionary army. He moved into this house in 1808, at the age of 71. By then Paine was a difficult and crusty man, and also an atheist—a fact his straight-laced neighbors could not forgive. Upon his death in 1809, only six mourners attended his funeral and his request to be buried in a Quaker graveyard was denied.

Paine's house—marked with a plaque—is now a venerable gay piano bar called **Marie's Crisis Cafe,** tel. (212) 243-9323, named partly as a tribute to Paine.

Bleecker West of Sixth

Bleecker St. west of Sixth Ave. is much different than Bleecker St. to the east. Between Sixth and Seventh Aves., the thoroughfare is lined with old-fashioned food shops that hark back to the days when this was a largely Italian neighborhood. Between Seventh and Eighth Aves. are numerous gift and antique shops, many of them quite expensive (see "Shopping," below).

Bleecker ends at **Abingdon Square** at Eighth Avenue. If you were to head even farther west on Bethune or W. 12th St., you'd come to **Gansevoort Meat Market.** Largely deserted by day, the market is at the north end of the meatpacking district, and is surrounded by greasy cobblestone streets and half-abandoned buildings. The place only comes alive in the wee hours, when trucks pull up with their wares, transvestites cruise the streets, and hip denizens of the night—often arriving by cab—slip into the neighborhood clubs.

Christopher Street

Built along a path that the Algonquins once used to carry lobsters and oysters inland from a cove on the Hudson, Christopher St. was a working-class address for most of its modern existence. For years, longshoremen working the nearby Hudson River piers lived here with their families. But long before Stonewall, the street also had a thriving, underground gay nightlife. Gay bars such as the Colony operated as early as the 1940s. And by the early 1970s, the street's gay nightlife had become known around the world.

Christopher St. is still the center of gay New York, but this is changing. Because gays no longer feel as shunned by the rest of the city as they once did, they're moving into other neighborhoods—most notably Chelsea. At the same time, straight tourists—who no longer feel as threatened by gay life—are taking good looks around. "Sometimes I feel like this is kind of like a gay Jurassic Park," one gay Christopher St. habitue recently told *The New York Times.*

Walking west on Christopher from Seventh Ave., you'll pass provocatively named leather and clothing shops such as **Boyz, Leather Man,** and **Oh Boy.** West of Hudson St., outside tourist territory, are many of Christopher St.'s rougher gay bars.

Bedford Street

One of the prettiest and oldest areas in the Village is centered around Bedford St., just south of Christopher. Much of the property around here once belonged to Aaron Burr; his former coach-

The beautiful city, the city of hurried and sparkling
waters! the city of spires and masts!
The City nested in bays! my city!
The city of such women, I as mad with them! I will
return after death to be with them!
The city of such young men, I swear I cannot live
happy without I often go talk, walk, eat, drink,
sleep with them!

—WALT WHITMAN

house is now a bar and restaurant called **One If By Land, Two If By Sea.** It's at 17 Barrow St., near Seventh Ave., tel. (212) 228-0822.

At 102 Bedford is a small building known as **"Twin Peaks"** because of its two odd, very steep roofs. The roofs were the brainchild of designer Clifford Daily, who built the 1926 additions onto the formerly ordinary 1830 house because he felt that "the Village is growing into a desert of mediocrity with nothing of inspiration."

Right next to Twin Peaks, at 17 Grove St. (at Bedford), is a lovely wooden clapboard house. Built in 1822 by William Hyde, a window-sash maker, it's still superbly well preserved.

At 77 Bedford, at the corner of Commerce St., is the oldest existing house in the Village, the 1799 **Isaacs-Hendricks House.** At 75½ Bedford is the so-called **Narrowest House in New York.** Though not much to look at, it was poet Edna St. Vincent Millay's home in the 1920s.

Commerce Street

One of the shortest streets in the city is Commerce, which runs a graceful arch from Seventh Ave. S to Barrow Street. At the curve is the **Cherry Lane Theater,** 38 Commerce St., tel. (212) 989-2020, founded by Edna St. Vincent Millay and others in 1924. Experimental in nature at first, the Cherry Lane is now an Off Broadway theater with an excellent reputation.

At 39 and 41 Commerce St. (where Commerce meets Barrow) are two delightful **Twin Houses,** separated by a shared garden. Legend has it they were built by a sea captain for his two feuding daughters; the more mundane land records say they were built by a local milk merchant.

Hudson Street and Grove Court

Just north of where Barrow meets Hudson is the **Church of St. Luke's-in-the-Fields,** 479-485 Hudson. Once literally surrounded by fields, the church was built in 1821 as an uptown chapel of Wall Street's Trinity Church. Author Bret Harte lived in St. Luke's Parish House as a boy in the 1840s.

Directly across the street from St. Luke's, on Grove St., is Grove Court, a picturesque little courtyard lined with white shutters. Built in 1854 for workers, the courtyard was not always as serene as it is today. Among its early nicknames were "Mixed Ale Alley" and "Pig's Alley."

St. Luke's Place

Heading south on Hudson St. you'll come to St. Luke's Pl., a picturesque 1850s' block lined with Italianate row houses on one side, St. Luke's Park on the other. The charming but corrupt Jimmy Walker, mayor of New York City from 1926 to 1933, once lived at 6 St. Luke's Pl.; two "lamps of honor" mark the spot. Other former residents of the street include Sherwood Anderson, who lived at No. 12 in 1923; Theodore Dreiser, who began *An American Tragedy* while living at No. 16 in 1922-23; and Marianne Moore, who lived at No. 14 with her mother in the earliest years of her career, 1918-29.

SHOPPING

Antiques

Bleecker St. is known for antique stores. Among them are **American Folk Gallery,** 374 Bleecker, tel. (212) 366-6566; **Old Japan, Inc.,** 382 Bleecker, tel. (212) 633-0922; and **Susan Parrish,** 390 Bleecker, tel. (212) 645-5020, selling American country and folk. At 506 Hudson Street, near Christopher, is **Uplift Lighting,** tel. (212) 929-3632, specializing in art deco fixtures. Along Broadway between Union Square and 8th Street, find a good half-dozen antique furniture shops, some of which cater only to wholesalers.

Arts and Crafts
American Indian Community House Gallery, 708 Broadway, 2nd Fl., near Waverly, tel. (212) 598-0100, is the city's only Native American-owned and -operated gallery. **Common Ground,** 19 Greenwich Ave., bet. Christopher and W. 10th Sts., tel. (212) 989-4178, features a first-rate selection of Native American jewelry, rugs, and the like. **Russian Arts,** 451 Sixth Ave., near W. 10th St., tel. (212) 242-5946, is one of the many tiny Russian crafts shops that have opened in post-Cold War New York City.

Books
Oscar Wilde Memorial Bookshop, 15 Christopher St., near Sixth Ave., tel. (212) 255-8097, was established in 1967, and is said to be the world's oldest gay bookstore. **Three Lives & Co.,** 154 W. 10th St., bet. Sixth and Seventh Aves., tel. (212) 741-2069, is one of the city's top literary bookstores, and hosts frequent readings by well-known authors.

Other independent Village bookstores of note include **Biography Bookshop,** 400 Bleecker St., at 11th St., tel. (212) 807-8655, specializing in biographies, memoirs, and letters; the literary **Shakespeare & Co.,** 716 Broadway, tel. (212) 529-1330; and **East West Books,** 78 Fifth Ave., at 14th St., tel. (212) 243-5994, specializing in Eastern and New Age philosophy books. Chain stores include **B. Dalton's,** Sixth Ave. and 8th St., tel. (212) 674-8780, open Mon.-Sat. until 11 p.m., and Sun. until 6 p.m.; and **Tower Books,** 383 Lafayette St., tel. (212) 228-5100.

Clothing
Vintage clothing stores abound in Greenwich Village. **Star Struck,** 43 Greenwich Ave., near W. 10th St., tel. (212) 691-5357, carries a good selection of old coats, and creaky **Antique Boutique,** 712 Broadway, near Astor, tel. (212) 460-8830, is a great emporium selling everything from vintage cocktail dresses to leather jackets. **Reminiscence,** 74 Fifth Ave., near 13th St., tel. (212) 243-2292, is the place to go for reasonably priced retrowear.

Andy's Chee-Pees, 691 Broadway, near W. 4th St., tel. (212) 420-5980; and **Cheap Jack's,** 841 Broadway, near 12th St., tel. (212) 777-9564, both offer heaps of *stuff.* You might find some gems, but you'll have to dig.

More up-to-date styles are offered by **Urban Outfitters,** 360 Sixth Ave., near Waverly, tel. (212) 677-9350, a trendy store featuring natural-fabric fashions for both men and women, along with home furnishings and gifts. Over-the-top **Patricia Field,** 10 E. 8th St., near Fifth Ave., tel. (212) 254-1699, is the place to go for outré fashion and clubwear.

Along 8th St. is a mother lode of shoe shops.

Games and Fun Stuff
The famed **Chess Shop,** 230 Thompson St., just south of W. 3rd St., tel. (212) 475-9580, may sell all sorts of chessboards and pieces, but more importantly, endless chess games are always in session. Players of all levels are welcome. **Game Show,** 474 Sixth Ave., bet. 11th and 12th Sts., tel. (212) 633-6328, is well stocked with games for all ages. **Abracadabra,** 10 Christopher St., near Gay, tel. (212) 627-5745, features an enormous number of rubber Halloween masks and wacky gag gifts.

Gourmet Treats
Balducci's, 424 Sixth Ave., at 9th St., tel. (212) 673-2600, is a legendary Village food shop selling gourmet treats of every conceivable variety. On Bleecker St. bet. Sixth and Seventh Aves. are **Murray's Cheese Shop,** 257 Bleecker St., tel. (212) 243-3289, selling cheeses from around the world; **A. Zito & Sons,** 259 Bleecker St., tel. (212) 929-6139, Frank Sinatra's favorite bakery; **Faicco's Pork Store,** 260 Bleecker St., tel. (212) 243-1974, especially known for its homemade sausages; and the **Bleecker Street Pastry Shop,** 245 Bleecker St., tel. (212) 242-4959.

McNulty's Tea and Coffee, 109 Christopher, near Bedford, tel. (212) 242-5351, is an aromatic haven over 100 years old. **Li-Lac Chocolates,** 120 Christopher, tel. (212) 242-7374, sells luscious homemade sweets.

Music
Tower Records, 692 Broadway, at E. 4th St., tel. (212) 505-1500, offers an overwhelming array of recordings from rock to classical to everything in between. The store opened in 1983, and was largely responsible for transforming this one-time no-man's-land between the two villages into a distinct shopping strip. Tower is open until midnight every night, and

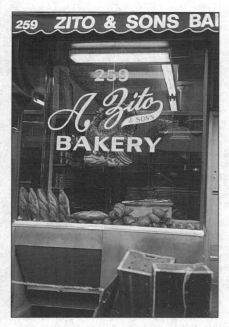

Frank Sinatra's favorite bakery

Tower Video and **Tower Books,** both at 383 Lafayette St., tel. (212) 505-1166 and 228-5100, respectively, are directly behind the main store. **Revolver Records,** 45 W. 8th St., near Sixth Ave., tel. (212) 982-6760, carries lots of rock and is the premier bootleg shop in town. **Bleecker Bob's,** 118 W. Third St., near MacDougal, tel. (212) 475-9677, an old Village favorite, is now something of a tourist trap.

Other Shops
More Bleecker St. stores include the nationally renowned **Matt Umanov Guitar Store,** 273 Bleecker St., bet. Sixth and Seventh Aves., tel. (212) 675-2157; and **Aphrodisia,** 264 Bleecker St., tel. (212) 989-6440, stocked with an enormous number of herbs, oils, and New Age remedies. **Condomania,** 351 Bleecker St., near Christopher, tel. (212) 691-9442, is the place for condoms and erotica.

Bigelow Pharmacy, 414 Sixth Ave., tel. (212) 533-2700, is New York's oldest continuously operating pharmacy; the official historic landmark was established in 1838, and still sports its original oak fittings and gaslight fixtures. **Star Magic,** 745 Broadway, near 8th St., tel. (212) 228-7770, with branches all over the city, sells a fascinating selection of space-age gifts, including science kits, mobiles, prisms, kaleidoscopes, and books.

Flea Market
On weekends, the empty lot next to Tower Records, 692 Broadway, at E. 4th St., hosts a small flea market selling new and used clothing. Farther west, the **P.S. 41 Flea Market** operates Saturdays only, on Greenwich Ave. at Charles Street.

ACCOMMODATIONS

Inexpensive
Stepping into the beaux arts **Larchmont Hotel,** 27 W. 11th St., bet. Fifth and Sixth Aves., tel. (212) 989-9333, is like stepping into a private home. Umbrellas are standing in the tiled foyer; someone is asleep on the loveseat in the tiny lobby.

A much-needed addition to Greenwich Village, the Larchmont was an SRO hotel from the late 1940s to the early 1990s. Now completely renovated, it offers 77 attractive rooms with rattan furnishings, good lighting, and clean, shared bathrooms down the hall. $60-70 s, $85-99 d; includes continental breakfast.

Moderate
Though small, the lobby of the family-owned **Washington Square Hotel,** 103 Waverly Pl., bet. MacDougal St. and Sixth Ave., tel. (212) 777-9515 or (800) 222-0418, is stunning—all black and white tiles, lacy iron grillwork, gilded adornments, and Audubon prints. The rooms aren't bad either, and neither is CIII, a stylish on-site restaurant lined with jazzy paintings. Combine all this with moderate prices and a terrific location, just off Washington Square, and you have one of the best bargains in the city. $90-110 s, $115-120 d; includes continental breakfast.

Dorms
From mid-May to mid-August, **New York University** rents out rooms on a weekly basis

(three-week minimum, 12-week maximum) at rates ranging from $110 for a simple single to $260 for a double with a kitchen and bath. Call (800) 771-4NYU, ext. 81, after Jan. 1 for the following summer.

FOOD

American

Inexpensive: One of the best places for a burger is the **Corner Bistro,** 331 W. 4th St., at Jane and Eighth Ave., tel. (212) 242-9502, a dark pub with creaky wooden booths.

Inexpensive-to-Moderate: For home cooking, try **Aggie's,** 146 W. Houston St., at Mac-Dougal, tel. (212) 673-8994, a modern, upscale luncheonette. Near Sheridan Square is **Boxers,** 190 W. 4th St., tel. (212) 633-2275, a hearty spot serving pub food.

Moderate: The warm and posh **Grange Hall,** 50 Commerce St., near Hudson, tel. (212) 924-5246, features a wonderful Depression-era mural and an imaginative menu. **Anglers & Writers,** 420 Hudson St., at St. Luke's Pl., tel. (212) 675-0810, specializes in homemade foods, country charm, and books and fishing paraphernalia à la Hemingway. The casual **Cornelia Street Cafe,** 29 Cornelia St., bet. Bleecker and W. 4th St., tel. (212) 989-9318, presents poetry readings and jazz concerts in its big downstairs room. The **Paris Commune,** 411 Bleecker St., bet. W. 11th St. and Bank, tel. (212) 929-0509, is a snug bistro that's an especially good place for Sunday brunch. For steaks, try the **Old Homestead,** 56 Ninth Ave., near 14th St., tel. (212) 242-9040, a classic eatery with a huge brown-and-white cow above its door.

Expensive: One of the city's top restaurants is the sleek and fashionable **Gotham Bar and Grill,** 12 E. 12th St., near Fifth Ave., tel. (212) 620-4020, winner of numerous awards for both its design and food.

French/Continental

Moderate: Caffe Lure, 169 Sullivan St., bet. Houston and Bleecker Sts., tel. (212) 473-2642, is a stylish bistro, very reasonably priced. On an empty street in the meatpacking district is the 24-hour bistro/diner **Florent,** 69 Gansevoort St., bet. Greenwich and Washington, tel. (212) 989-5779. It's best in the wee hours when the club crawlers descend.

Moderate-to-Expensive: The charming, lace-curtained **Cafe de Bruxelles,** 118 Greenwich Ave., near 13th St., tel. (212) 206-1830, features first-rate Belgian fare. For continental cuisine, try **Marylou's,** 21 W. 9th St., bet. Fifth and Sixth Aves., tel. (212) 533-0012, a comfortable spot in the basement of an elegant townhouse.

Expensive: The low-key, low-ceilinged **Cafe Loup,** 105 W. 13th St., near Sixth Ave., tel. (212) 255-4746, is a Village institution serving a wide range of especially fresh French fare.

Italian

Inexpensive: The city's best pizzeria is **John's,** 278 Bleecker St., near Seventh Ave., tel. (212) 243-1680. Its New York-style pies are thin, crispy, and low on grease; sold by the whole pie only, no slices. Expect long lines unless you come during the off hours. **Arturo's,** 106 W. Houston St., at Thompson, tel. (212) 677-3820, also serves good pizza, and is especially popular among students and young professionals.

Inexpensive-to-Moderate: The tiny, bustling **Mappamondo,** 11 Abington Square, at Eighth Ave., tel. (212) 675-3100, and **Mappamondo Due,** 581 Hudson St., at Bank, tel. (212) 675-7474, serve an interesting variety of pastas.

Moderate: Grand Ticino, 228 Thompson St., near W. 3rd St., tel. (212) 777-5922, is a Village institution, a creaky basement joint that was featured in the movie *Moonstruck.*

Moderate-to-Expensive: Cent'Anni, 50 Carmine St., bet. Bleecker and Bedford, tel. (212) 989-9494, is an excellent, modern trattoria serving a wide range of fresh and tasty dishes.

Expensive: A longtime favorite among connoisseurs of Italian food is **Il Mulino,** 86 W. 3rd St., bet. Thompson and Sullivan, tel. (212) 673-3783.

Latin/Caribbean

Inexpensive: For huge portions of Mexican food, try **Benny's Burritos,** 113 Greenwich Ave., at Jane, tel. (212) 727-0584.

Moderate: Caribe, 117 Perry St., at Greenwich, tel. (212) 255-9191, is a friendly slice of the Caribbean transported to the West Village. **Mi Cocina,** 57 Jane St., at Hudson, tel. (212) 627-8273, serves authentic Mexican food in a simple, brick-walled setting.

Southern

Inexpensive-to-Moderate: For many years the **Pink Teacup,** 42 Grove St., near Seventh Ave., tel. (212) 807-6755, was one of downtown's only soul food restaurants.

Other Ethnic

Moderate: Ginger Toon, 417 Bleecker St., at Bank, tel. (212) 924-6420, serves excellent Thai food to a largely Thai crowd. For some of the freshest sushi in town, try **Japonica,** 100 University Pl., at 12th St., tel. (212) 243-7752. **El Faro,** 823 Greenwich St., bet. Horatio and Jane, tel. (212) 929-8210, is a dark and old-fashioned spot offering excellent Spanish cuisine. **Gus' Place,** 149 Waverly Pl., near Sixth Ave., tel. (212) 645-8511, is an airy eatery serving tasty Greek and Mediterranean food. The new and popular **Tapestry,** 575 Hudson St., bet. Bank and 11th Sts., tel. (212) 242-0003, serves American-style *tapas* in a festive, candle-lit setting. Come here to sample a wide array of unusual small dishes.

Light Bites

Just east of Washington Square are a number of good coffee shops, including the **Waverly Coffee Shop,** 19 Waverly Pl., tel. (212) 674-3760, and **Pane & Cioccolato,** 10 Waverly Pl., tel. (212) 473-3944. **Mamoun's Falafel** on MacDougal St. north of Bleecker offers good, cheap takeout.

Bleecker and MacDougal Sts. are known for their many Italian coffee and pastry shops. Among the best are **Cafe Borgia,** 185 Bleecker St., tel. (212) 674-9589; **Cafe Dante,** 79 MacDougal St., tel. (212) 982-5275; and **Caffe Reggio,** 119 MacDougal St., tel. (212) 475-9557. **French Roast,** 78 W. 11th St., at Sixth Ave., tel. (212) 533-2233, is a new and popular spot serving both sandwiches and desserts. **Tea and Sympathy,** 108 Greenwich Ave., at 13th St., tel. (212) 807-8329, features a British-style afternoon tea.

Watering Holes and Lounges

Sturdy old **White Horse Tavern,** 567 Hudson St., at 11th St., tel. (212) 243-9260, was once a writer's hangout; Dylan Thomas drank himself to death here. Now the tavern caters mostly to a collegiate crowd. Outdoor picnic tables are set up in summer.

Chumley's, 86 Bedford St., bet. Barrow and Grove, tel. (212) 675-4449, is an old speakeasy/restaurant where writers John Dos Passos and Theodore Dreiser once drank. It's unmarked, but not hard to find. The big, worn **Cedar Tavern,** 82 University Pl., bet. 11th and 12th Sts., tel. (212) 741-9754, was once frequented by Jackson Pollock and other abstract expressionists. It's still a good place for a beer, but avoid the food.

To the west, the **Art Bar,** 52 Eighth Ave., near Horatio, tel. (212) 727-0244, is downtown grunge in front, aging Victorian parlor in back. The place is laid-back and relaxed, but with an edge. **Automatic Slim's,** 733 Washington St., at Bank, tel. (212) 645-8660, is a tiny, high-ceilinged joint with blues posters on the walls, and tasty Cajun dishes on the menu. The narrow, atmospheric **Fannie's,** 765 Washington St., at W. 12th St., tel. (212) 255-5101, sports an outdoor terrace and a basement bar where live blues bands sometimes perform.

In the Gansevoort Meat Market, you'll find the raucous **Hogs & Heifers,** 859 Washington St., near Gansevoort St., tel. (212) 929-0655, its crowds spilling out onto the streets, and **Hell,** 59 Gansevoort St., bet. Greenwich and Washington Sts., tel. (212) 727-1666, a new, SoHo-esque lounge all done up in chandeliers and velvet drapes. **Plush,** 431 W. 14th St., bet. Ninth Ave. and Washington St., tel. (212) 367-7035, is half dance club, half atmospheric lounge filled with oversized banquettes. All are best visited late at night.

Among gay bars, the **Duplex,** 61 Christopher St., at Seventh Ave., tel. (212) 255-5438, is a bustling two-story cabaret offering food, drink, and a downstairs piano bar. Across the street sprawls the **Monster,** 80 Grove St., tel. (212) 924-3557, featuring a drag cabaret. Two popular lesbian bars, drawing largely professional crowds, are **Henrietta Hudson,** 448 Hudson St., at Morton, tel. (212) 924-3347; and **Crazy Nanny's,** 21 Seventh Ave. S, at Leroy, tel. (212) 366-6312.

Among the restaurants mentioned above, the **Corner Bistro, Grange Hall, Marylou's,** and **Florent** all have lively late-night scenes. See also "Out on the Town," in the Introduction.

FROM UNION SQUARE TO MURRAY HILL

The East Side between 14th and 42nd Sts. is mostly residential, and lacks both the history of Lower Manhattan and the energy of the Villages. But it does have a considerable quiet charm and a number of quirky attractions sandwiched between the brownstones and apartment buildings.

Various neighborhoods make up this section of the East Side. **Union Square** begins at 14th St. and Broadway. **Madison Square,** which replaced Union Square as the city's commercial and theater center in the late 1800s, begins at 23rd St. and Broadway. East of those two neighborhoods is **Gramercy Park,** a residential square centered at 20th St. and Irving Place. **Murray Hill** lies between Madison and Third Aves., and 34th and 42nd Streets. It's a well-heeled neighborhood named for Quaker Robert Murray, who owned all the land in the area during the Revolutionary War era. Legend has it that Murray's wife, Mary Lindley, helped George Washington win the war by detaining the British officers for tea while the Americans escaped up the West Side to Harlem Heights.

Lately it has become fashionable to refer to the area around the Flatiron building at 23rd St. and Fifth Ave. as the **Flatiron District.** No one seems to be sure exactly what this new area encompasses, but it apparently takes in slices of the Union Square and Madison Square areas, as well as a hunk of Chelsea to the west. Whatever the exact boundaries, it's frequently referred to as one of the city's hottest new neighborhoods.

UNION SQUARE

Less than a decade ago, this small green square between 14th and 17th Sts., just east of Broadway, was dirty and neglected—a haven for drug dealers and petty criminals. Many of its buildings were deteriorating, others were abandoned.

Today the square has been transformed into a bustling urban center complete with sleek megastores, upscale restaurants, fashionable bars, and a farmers' **Greenmarket,** tel. (212) 477-3220, operating on Monday, Wednesday, Friday, and Saturday mornings.

Laid out as a park in 1815, Union Square was first the province of prominent local families such as the Roosevelts, who lived nearby. Then in the mid-1800s, the city's entertainment and commercial industries moved in. The famous Academy of Music (now the Palladium nightclub) started up on 14th St., and department stores went up all along Broadway from 8th to 23rd Streets. This commercialism was short lived, however. By 1900 both the theaters and the shops had moved uptown, to Madison

Square at 23rd St., and Union Square had become home to garment factories and immigrant workers. Many of the fine old homes were converted into tenement buildings.

From the 1910s until after WW II, Union Square was a center for political demonstrations. Socialists, communists, and the "Wobblies" (members of the Industrial Workers of the World) protested here, while many left-wing organizations had headquarters on or near the square. One of the most dramatic protests took place on Aug. 22, 1927, the night anarchists

Nicola Sacco and Bartolomeo Vanzetti were executed. The police had machine guns mounted on a roof overlooking the square, but the demonstration remained peaceful.

Andy Warhol's Factory

The sixth floor of the narrow Moorish-accented building at 33 Union Square W, bet. 16th and 17th Sts., was once home to Andy Warhol's Factory, frequented by the likes of Lou Reed, John Cale, and Nico of The Velvet Underground; Truman Capote; and John Lennon. Here Warhol

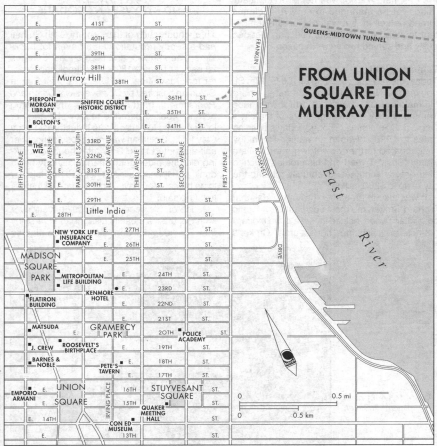

made many of his underground films, including *Blow Job, Flesh,* and *I, Man,* featuring a woman named Valerie Solanas.

Solanas went on to found SCUM, or the Society for Cutting Up Men. As she wrote in her manifesto, "there remains to civic-minded, responsible, thrill-seeking females only to overthrow the government . . . and destroy the male sex." One day in June 1968, Solanas went by the Factory to see Warhol. He was on the phone, but she waited patiently until he got off and then shot him four times in the chest. At the hospital, Warhol was declared clinically dead, yet he managed to survive. Solanas turned herself in, but was declared incompetent to stand trial. Nonetheless, she pleaded guilty and served two years in prison.

Tammany Hall

Today, the red-brick building at 100 E. 17th St. houses the New York Film Academy, where filmmakers learn their craft. But it was once Tammany Hall, the headquarters of the city's Democratic machine. Though today's building dates to 1928, it was in an earlier Tammany Hall, located farther downtown, that William Marcy "Boss" Tweed and his cronies hatched their greedy schemes, eventually robbing the city of up to $200 million.

It was also in an earlier Tammany Hall that Richard Croker, the most powerful Democratic boss after Tweed, helped invent a more modern get-rich-quick scheme: "honest graft." Croker's colleague George Washington Plunkitt described the concept best when he wrote, without any sense of irony: "There's the biggest kind of a difference between political looters and politicians who make a fortune out of politics by keepin' their eyes wide open." At the height of his career, Croker, who never held political office, owned a $180,000 house, an upstate farm, and a string of thoroughbreds—all supposedly earned on a $25,000-a-year salary.

14TH STREET AND STUYVESANT SQUARE

Throughout much of this century, 14th St. has had a seedy reputation as a haven for hucksters, peep shows, and porn shops. Even as far back as the late 1800s, the street was a center for prostitution. In 1892, anarchist Emma Goldman, inspired by Dostoyevsky's *Crime and Punishment,* tried her hand at streetwalking here in order to earn the money she and her lover needed to assassinate industrialist Henry Clay Frick. Goldman was none too adept at her self-appointed task. Only after hours of walking did one older gentleman finally buy her a drink, and then he slipped her $10 and told her to go home. "You haven't got it, that's all there is to it," he said.

Much of this seedy quality still hovers over 14th St., but it's steadily disappearing. A shiny new Bradlees discount store now dominates

A Salvation Army band plays 14th Street.

the southern end of Union Square, while many other new shops have opened nearby.

West of Union Square in what is technically considered Chelsea, 14th St. is crammed with discount stores catering to a largely Hispanic clientele. For years, these stores have been frenetic with activity, but recently, they, too, have started to lose their vitality. See the wig stores, plastic toy vendors, and clerks sitting on ladders—shouting out the day's bargains—while you still can.

Con Ed Museum
On the ground floor of the Consolidated Edison Building is a small energy museum that will probably appeal most to scientifically minded older children. The museum, 145 E. 14th St., near Third Ave., tel. (212) 460-6244, explains how electrical equipment works, and outlines the history of electricity in the U.S. (New York was the first city in the world to have commercial electrical service.) Hours are Tues.-Sat. 9 a.m.-5 p.m. Admission is free. At night, the big, bold tower of the Con Ed Building is strikingly illuminated in blue and white, serving as a landmark for blocks around.

Stuyvesant Square
Between 15th and 17th Sts., and Third and Second Aves., is a small, somewhat neglected park, once part of Dutch governor Peter Stuyvesant's farm. On the park's west side, at 15th St., is the **Friends' Meeting House,** a lovely red-brick Greek Revival building. Back in the 1800s, in order to obtain the quiet that they needed for their meetings, the Friends used to spread six inches of tanbark on the street to muffle the sound of horses' hooves.

Across the street from the meeting house is **St. George's Episcopal Church,** 209 E. 16th St., an impressive Romanesque Revival complex. It's sometimes called "J.P. Morgan's church" because the wealthy financier worshipped here. Also once affiliated with St. George's was baritone soloist Harry T. Burleigh. Born the son of slaves, Burleigh helped popularize the African American spiritual. People would come from all over the city to hear him sing. Burleigh also composed more than 300 songs, and helped Czech composer Antonin Dvorak adapt traditional black melodies into his New World Symphony. Dvorak lived nearby at 327 E. 17th St. from 1892 to 1895; his statue stands in Stuyvesant Park.

IRVING PLACE TO GRAMERCY PARK

Washington Irving's "Home"
Though the plaque on the pretty building at 40 Irving Pl., at 17th St., states that Washington Irving once lived here, he never actually did. The street was named after the author, however, as was the high school across the street, which sports a grim bust of Irving out front.

It is to Washington Irving that we owe our impressions of Dutch New York. Irving immortalized the fat, loll-about burghermeisters and their bossy, red-cheeked wives in his satiric 1821 tome, *A History of New-York, from the beginning of the World to the end of the Dutch Dynasty: Containing, among many surprising and curious matters, The Unutterable Ponderings of Walter The Doubter, The Disastrous Project of William The Testy, and The Chivalric Achievements of Peter The Headstrong, The Three Dutch Governors of New-Amsterdam: Being the only authentic history of the times that ever hath been published.*

Pete's Tavern
Founded in 1864, Pete's Tavern, 129 E. 18th St., at Irving Pl., tel. (212) 473-7676, bills itself as the city's oldest bar. The creaky joint was once a favorite hangout of short-story writer O. Henry, who lived across the street at 55 Irving Place. Henry—whose real name was William Sydney Porter—had previously served time in Texas for embezzlement. Supposedly he wrote his famous short story, "The Gift of the Magi," in a booth at the back. Pete's is open for lunch and dinner, but go for the atmosphere and drink, not the food.

Gramercy Park
At the north end of Irving Pl., bet. 20th and 21st Sts., is Gramercy Park, bought and laid out in 1831 by lawyer and real estate developer Samuel Ruggles. As fashionable today as it was back then, the park consists of both stately buildings and an enclosed green to which only the residents have access. Outsiders have to

Writer O. Henry once frequented Pete's Tavern.

content themselves with peering in through an eight-foot-high iron fence.

At 3 and 4 Gramercy Park W are two somber 1840 brownstones sharing an ornate cast-iron veranda. Actor John Garfield was residing here in 1952, when he died in his sleep at the age of 39. At 34 Gramercy Park E is a turreted red-brick building that was probably the city's first housing cooperative. Famous residents here over the years have included actors James Cagney and Margaret Hamilton. The building boasts one of the city's few remaining birdcage elevators. At 36 Gramercy Park E is a Gothic apartment house guarded by two near-life-size silver-plated knights. Actor John Barrymore lived here with his first wife in the mid-1920s.

In 1925, John Steinbeck lived in a small, dingy room on the sixth floor of 38 Gramercy Park North. He'd been working as a reporter for the *New York World,* but got fired. After that he holed up in his room, living on sardines and crackers and writing around the clock. Also on

the north side is the genteel **Gramercy Park Hotel,** 2 Lexington Avenue. Humphrey Bogart lived in the hotel in 1926, just after marrying his first wife, and critic Edmund Wilson lived here with novelist Mary McCarthy in the early 1940s. Writer S.J. Perelman died in his apartment in the hotel in 1979, at the age of 75.

Gramercy Park South

The square's most impressive buildings stand on the south side. At 15 Gramercy Park S is the **National Arts Club,** a formidable Gothic Revival brownstone that was once home to New York governor Samuel Tilden. Tilden is best remembered as the man who lost the 1876 presidency to Rutherford Hayes by only one electoral vote. But he was also responsible for Boss Tweed's downfall. After Tweed was arrested, Tilden had steel doors installed in his windows and an escape tunnel dug to 19th St. in case of repercussions. The building became the National Arts Club in 1906. Club members have included George Bellows, Alfred Stieglitz, and Frederic Remington.

Across the street at 16 Gramercy Park S is the **Players Club,** an extravagant, columned building with large flags out front. The building was purchased by the great thespian Edwin Booth in 1888, who turned it into a home for a group of actors. The brother of Lincoln-assassin John Wilkes Booth, Edwin Booth ironically was the president's favorite actor. After the assassination, Edwin holed himself up in the club and refused to come out. A crowd of thousands gathered in Gramercy Park to show him their support. Today, a statue of Booth playing Hamlet stands in the park, facing his former home. Recent members of the Players Club have included Laurence Olivier and Frank Sinatra.

Kenmore Hotel

A few blocks north of Gramercy Park is the old Kenmore Hotel, 145 E. 23rd St., at Lexington, where young writer Nathanael West worked as night manager in 1927-28. West spent his nights reading the classics and entertaining his friends, who included Dashiel Hammett and S.J. Perelman.

The hotel stands on the former site of the building where writer Stephen Crane lived in 1893, sharing a small studio with three friends. The four were so poor that they only had enough clothes for one of them to look for work at a time. Crane worked on *The Red Badge of Courage* while living there.

In 1994, federal agents seized the Kenmore—by then a dilapidated, crime-infested residence—and arrested 18 people in one of the city's largest drug busts ever. Today, the building is being cleaned up and converted into studio apartments.

Police Academy Museum

Several blocks east of Gramercy Park is the New York City Police Academy, 235 E. 20th St., bet. Third and Second Aves., tel. (212) 477-9753, usually buzzing with fresh-faced kids in blue. On the second floor of the Academy is an informal museum filled with fascinating displays. One is devoted to antique firearms, including a palm-size pistol, a long-barreled "game getter," and a .410-caliber cane, circa 1895. Another explains how fingerprints are used in crime detection, and another chronicles New York's mobsters. Al Capone's baptism and marriage certificates are on display, along with his machine guns and 75-diamond belt buckle.

Most intriguing of all is an exhibit entitled "Recently Acquired Contraband Weapons: Youth Gang Weapons." Here you'll see a cement-filled blackjack, a nail ring with a sharp blade, a dagger disguised as a fountain pen, and a baseball bat with horseshoes attached. The bat's wielder apparently wanted the police to believe that his victim had been kicked to death by a horse.

The museum is open Mon.-Fri. 9 a.m.-3 p.m. Admission is free.

BROADWAY AND LOWER FIFTH AVENUE

During the late 1800s, the stretch of Broadway between 8th and 23rd Sts., and especially between Union and Madison Squares, was known as **Ladies Mile** because of the many fashionable department stores located there. The original stores themselves are now long gone, but their fine cast-iron buildings remain. Many are covered with black grime, but if you look carefully, it's easy to imagine the elegant emporiums they once were. Two of the street's finest cast-iron buildings stand opposite each other

on Broadway south of 20th Street. On the east side, at 900 Broadway, is an 1887 McKim, Mead & White creation notable for its lovely brickwork; on the west side, at 901 Broadway, is the former home of Lord & Taylor, cast in a deluxe French Second Empire style. At 881-887 Broadway, at the southwest corner of 19th St., stands the former Arnold Constable Dry Goods Store, topped with an immense mansard roof.

Running alongside Broadway is lower Fifth Ave., which like many other parts of the Flatiron District was gray and neglected a decade or so ago. Then, in the early- to mid-1980s, publishing and advertising companies looking to escape exorbitant midtown rents began moving in, and trendy shops soon followed.

Theodore Roosevelt's Birthplace

The handsome four-story brownstone at 28 E. 20th St., near Broadway, is an exact replica of Theodore Roosevelt's birthplace. It was rebuilt by Roosevelt's family and friends just after his death in 1919 and only a few years after the original building was torn down in 1916. Now a museum, it's filled with thousands of engrossing photographs and the world's largest collection of Roosevelt memorabilia, including TR's christening dress, his parents' wedding clothes, and much original furniture.

In the museum you'll learn that the first American Roosevelts came to Manhattan from Holland in the 1640s, and made their fortune in the glass import trade. Theodore was born in this house in 1858, and grew up a sickly, asthmatic child. In addition to his political achievements, he also spent years in North Dakota raising cattle, served as New York's first police commissioner, led the Rough Riders at San Juan Hill, wrote over 50 books, shot game in Africa for the Smithsonian, and raised a large family. "No president has ever enjoyed himself as much as I," he once said.

The museum, tel. (212) 260-1616, is open Wed.-Sun. 9 a.m.-5 p.m. Admission is $2.

Flatiron Building

Where Fifth Ave. and the Ladies Mile meet 23rd St. is one of Manhattan's most famous and idiosyncratic landmarks. The Flatiron Building, more formally known as the Fuller Building, was designed by Chicago architect Daniel H. Burnham in 1902. Its nickname comes from its narrow

The Flatiron Building is only six feet wide at its northern end.

triangular shape, only six feet wide at the northern end. H.G. Wells once described it as a "prow . . . ploughing up through the traffic of Broadway and Fifth Avenue in the afternoon light." The portrayal is apt.

Gusty winds often swirl around the Flatiron's northern end, where men used to gather to watch the billowing skirts of the lady shoppers. Policemen shooed the men away, giving rise to the old expression, "23 skiddoo."

Madison Square

Between 23rd and 26th Sts., and Fifth and Madison Aves., is Madison Square. Once a marsh, potter's field, and parade ground, the square became fashionable in the mid-1800s. In those days, expensive hotels stood along its west side, the old Madison Square Garden stood to the north, and the Statue of Liberty's torch-bearing right arm stood in the center of the square, awaiting funding for the monument's base.

Today all those buildings—and the arm—are gone, but other graceful structures have taken their place. The park is well worn, but remains pleasant and relaxing. A statue of William Henry Seward, the U.S. senator and secretary of state best remembered for purchasing Alaska from Russia, guards the southwest entrance.

On the park's east side, along Madison Ave., are several impressive buildings. Between 23th and 25th Sts. is the 1932 **Metropolitan Life Insurance Company,** an enormous art deco building made of limestone that seems to change color with the day. On the north corner of 25th St. is the 1900 **Appellate Division of the New York State Supreme Court,** covered with an impossible number of marble sculptures. Taking up the whole block between 26th and 27th Sts. is the **New York Life Insurance Company,** an elaborate 1898 wedding-cake extravaganza designed by Cass Gilbert, the architect of the Woolworth Building.

LITTLE INDIA

Though now much smaller than the rapidly growing Indian communities in Queens, Little India—centered on Lexington Ave. between 27th and 29th Sts.—is still frequented by women in saris doing their weekly shopping. The area offers some excellent Indian restaurants and food shops, a few Indian music-and-video stores, and a dwindling number of shops selling sari silks.

MURRAY HILL

Pierpont Morgan Library

This elegant neoclassic gem, 29 E. 36th St., at Madison Ave., tel. (212) 685-0610, was designed by McKim, Mead & White in 1906 as John Pierpont Morgan's personal library and art gallery. Now a museum, it retains its original elaborately carved wooden ceilings, medieval tapestries, renaissance paintings, and domed rotunda.

At the heart of the museum's collection are Morgan's priceless illuminated manuscripts and Old Master drawings. Compelling traveling exhibitions—ranging from illustration to photography—are often on display as well. In recent years, the museum has doubled its exhibit space

THE STANFORD WHITE SCANDAL

New York's first Madison Square Garden, built in 1890 and demolished in 1925, once stood where the New York Life Insurance Company stands today. Designed by architect Stanford White, the sports arena was a sumptuous affair, complete with turrets, towers, and a revolving golden statue of Diana on top. In addition, the building housed an upscale restaurant, theater, and roof garden, and it was in the roof garden that Stanford White was murdered by the husband of his former mistress, Evelyn Nesbit.

A pretty chorus girl from Pittsburgh, Nesbit was only 16 when White fell in love with her and took her to his studio. Already well known for his philandering, he had love nests all over town, including one at 22 W. 24th St. (the building still stands), which he had lined with mirrors and hung with a red velvet swing. He liked his girlfriends to swing in the nude above him while he watched from the bed.

Nesbit, intent on finding a rich husband, soon left White, and in 1905 married millionaire Harry Kendall Thaw. But Thaw seemed obsessed with White, asking her about him again and again, until the evening of June 25, 1906, when they were all in the roof garden together. Then he pulled out a gun and shot White three times in the back of the head.

Thaw was found unfit to stand trial, due to what his lawyer called "dementia Americana," a mental disease supposedly afflicting husbands trying to defend their wives' honor. Thaw was sent to an insane asylum instead, where he stayed until 1915. Nesbit, divorced, starred in a silent film about the scandal (called *The Girl in the Red Velvet Swing*), and joined a traveling cabaret show. Later, she became a heroin addict and worked in a Panamanian brothel. She died in 1966.

and opened a glass-enclosed garden court where classical-music concerts are sometimes presented. The museum also offers a very pleasant cafe and a gift shop stocked with unusual books and gifts.

Hours are Tues.-Fri. 10:30 a.m.-5 p.m., Sat. 10:30 a.m.-6 p.m., Sun. noon-6 p.m. Suggested admission is adults $5, students $3, children under 12 free.

Notable Residences
Many of the streets in Murray Hill have their share of fashionable residences. Two addresses especially worth looking out for are the ornate mansion at 233 Madison Ave., at 37th St., now the Polish Consulate; and 148 E. 40th St., now a converted carriage house. Also of prime interest is the **Sniffen Court Historic District,** 150-158 E. 36th St., bet. Lexington and Third Avenues. Built in the mid-1850s by a man named John Sniffen, the 10 brick carriage houses are all delightfully converted and preserved.

SHOPPING

Books
Two blocks south of Union Square is **Strand Book Store,** 828 Broadway, at 12th St., tel.

The Strand stocks some two million books.

(212) 473-1452. By far the city's largest secondhand bookstore, it claims to stock some two
million books on eight miles of shelves. Some
New Yorkers seem to spend their entire lives
here, browsing, browsing, browsing. The store is
open until 9:30 p.m. every evening.

The **Barnes & Noble** flagship, in operation
decades before the current crop of megastores,
is located at Fifth Ave. and 18th St., tel. (212)
807-0099. Travel lovers should stop by the
Complete Traveller Bookstore, 199 Madison
Ave., at 35th St., tel. (212) 685-9007.

Clothing

Fifth Ave. is the place to shop for clothes in this
area. **Matsuda,** 156 Fifth Ave., bet. 20th and
21st Sts., tel. (212) 645-5151, features high-
priced, avant garde Japanese clothing. **Daffy's,**
111 Fifth Ave., at 18th St., tel. (212) 529-4477;
and **Bolton's,** 4 E. 34th St., near Fifth Ave., tel.
(212) 684-3750, are known for discounted designer fashions. **Emporio Armani,** 110 Fifth
Ave., at 16th St., tel. (212) 727-3240, is an expensive designer showroom. **J. Crew** has a
new branch at 91 Fifth Ave., at 19th St. tel.,
(212) 255-4848.

Food Shops

In Little India, a number of food stores waft
their luscious smells out onto the street. Foremost among them is the venerable **Kalustyan's,**
123 Lexington Ave., tel. (212) 685-3451. The
first store to import Indian foodstuffs into the
city, the bustling shop sells everything from
homemade *labne* yogurt to Afghan nan bread
to stuffed pita pockets to go. **Foods of India,**
121 Lexington Ave., tel. (212) 683-4419, carries
an especially good supply of cooking utensils.

Health and Beauty

Carapan, 5 W. 16th St., near Fifth Ave., tel.
(212) 633-6220, is an airy New Age spa offering
shiatsu, aromatherapy, and herbal facials. **La
Casa de Vida Natural,** 41 E. 20th St., near
Park, tel. (212) 673-2272, is a reasonably priced
day spa and skin care center specializing in traditional Puerto Rican methods. If you're looking to get pierced, the **Gauntlet,** 144 Fifth Ave.,
near 19th St., tel. (212) 229-0180, is the best-
known place in the city.

Other Shops

The beguiling **ABC Carpet and Home,** 888
Broadway, tel. (212) 473-3000, arranged more
like a luxurious living room than a shop, sells
everything from painted country furniture to
French antiques. **Fishs Eddy,** 889 Broadway,
tel. (212) 420-9020, is known for its bargain-
priced china. **Paragon Sporting Goods,** 867
Broadway, tel. (212) 255-8036, is the city's top
sporting-goods department store.

Wonderfully creaky and affordable, the 1898
B. Shackman's, 85 Fifth Ave., at 16th St., tel.
(212) 989-5162, sells such essentials as Victorian paper dolls and miniature toys. The **Wiz** is
a reputable chain of electronics stores with
branches all over the city, including 337 Fifth
Ave., at 33rd St., tel. (212) 447-0100, and 17
Union Square W, at 15th St., tel. (212) 741-
9500. The **Compleat Strategist,** 11 E. 33rd St.,
near Fifth Ave., tel. (212) 685-3880, sells games
for players of all persuasions.

In Little India, **Little India Emporium,** 128
E. 28th St., near Lexington, tel. (212) 481-0325,
sells foodstuffs on the ground floor and sari silks
and costume jewelry on the second.

ACCOMMODATIONS

Cheap

A surprising new addition to this part of town is
the friendly **Murray Hill Inn,** 143 E. 30th St.,
bet. Lexington and Third Ave., tel. (212) 545-
0879. Opened in spring 1997, this former apartment building on a quiet residential street offers 50 small but spic-and-span rooms at budget
rates. All rooms have cable TV, daily maid service, and shared bathrooms. $50 s, $65 d.

A bunk in a dorm-style room at the irrepressible **Gershwin** (see "Inexpensive," below) goes
for a mere $22 a night. Some dormitory rooms
accommodate four people, others eight. The
shared bathrooms are reasonably clean.

Inexpensive

The high-spirited **Gershwin Hotel,** 7 E. 27th
St., bet. Fifth and Madison, tel. (212) 545-8000,
aswirl with artwork and budget travelers from
around the world, is a sort of cheaper, more
modern version of the classic Chelsea Hotel
(see "Chelsea and the Garment District," below).

Here you'll find a lobby brimming with color, rooms of all shapes and sizes, a gallery with changing exhibits, a rooftop bar in summer, and a cafe where jazz trios and East Village bands perform. Private room rates are $70-120 s or d.

Even more exuberant than the Gershwin is **Hotel 17,** 225 E. 17th St., bet. Second and Third Aves., tel. (212) 475-2845, which bills itself as "New York's most notorious night-time drama." The hostelry of choice among club hoppers and drag queens, Hotel 17 offers such over-the-top amenities as in-house makeovers and rooftop fashion shows. Meanwhile, the rooms are as basic as it gets. $80 s, $90 d.

Moderate

Around the corner from the Gershwin is **The Carlton,** 22 E. 29th St., at Madison Ave., tel. (212) 532-4100 or (800) 542-1502, a striking beaux arts edifice partially built of rose-colored brick. The large, well-kept lobby gleams with polished windows, mirrors, and brass; rooms are attractive and well kept. Adjoining the lobby is a small cafe. $119-169 s, $129-189 d.

A new **Quality Hotel,** 161 Lexington Ave., at 30th St., tel. (212) 545-1800, opened in early 1997 in what was once an SRO hotel. The small, square rooms, papered in royal blue, have a cozy but somewhat slapped-together feel, and only time will tell whether they'll be maintained in their current pristine state. $99-139 s, $119-149 d; the $99 rooms share baths.

A second **Quality Hotel,** 3 E. 40th St., at Fifth Ave., tel. (212) 447-1500 or (800) 228-5151, is located directly across from the New York Public Library. The decor here is modern nondescript, but the hotel is a good choice on the weekends, when rates drop to $109 s or d. In contrast, weekday rates are a high $162-180 s, $177-195 d.

Once an inexpensive hotel with imaginative decor, the 65-room **Howard Johnson on Park Avenue,** 429 Park Ave. S., near 29th St., tel. (212) 532-4860 or (800) 258-4290, has gone uphill in price and downhill in service. Housed in a former private mansion, it still features its dark woods and faux antiques but is now in need of renovation. Nonetheless, the place is still a good deal during the off-season, when prices dip to the lower end of its price scale. $105-199 s, $115-249 d.

The **Gramercy Park Hotel,** 2 Lexington Ave., at 21st St., tel. (212) 475-4320 or (800) 221-4083, may be more than a bit worn, but it still has a gracious old-New York feel. The rooms are large and airy, and downstairs reigns a '50s-era cocktail lounge that attracts all ages. The hotel is a favorite among publishing types and rock musicians. $135 s, $145 d.

Expensive

Housed behind a discreet gray facade with huge dark windows that allow insiders to see out but prevents outsiders from seeing in is the posh **Morgans,** 237 Madison Ave., at 38th St., tel. (212) 686-0300. Started by Ian Schrager and the late Steve Rubell—of Studio 54 fame—the place is so hip, it doesn't even hang a sign out front. Not surprisingly, rooms are sleek and luxurious. On site is a 24-hour spa. $215-235 s, $255-375 d.

The atmospheric opposite of Morgans is charming **Shelburne Murray Hill,** 303 Lexington Ave., at 37th St., tel. (212) 689-5200 or (800) ME-SUITE. Downstairs, find an especially attractive lobby filled with baroque antiques, and an especially helpful staff. Upstairs, find very spacious suites with two double beds and well-equipped kitchens. The blue and gold furnishings are plush, yet comfortable. On site is a well-maintained health club. $189 s, $219-239 d; weekend rates $139 s, $175 d.

FOOD

American

Moderate: Open in the summer only is **Luna Park,** 1 Union Square E, tel. (212) 475-8464, a lively eatery set in Union Square Park. Stick to the sandwiches; the entrees are mediocre and overpriced. **America,** 9 E. 18th St., bet. Fifth Ave. and Broadway, tel. (212) 505-2110, is a huge, cheery hangar of a place serving an astonishing array of mouthwatering foods from the 50 states. **Albuquerque Eats,** 375 Third Ave., at 27th St., tel. (212) 683-6500, specializes in tasty Tex-Mex fare. **Brew's,** 156 E. 34th St., near Lexington Ave., tel. (212) 889-3369, is a comfortable old-fashioned pub with red-checked tablecloths.

Expensive: The playful, high-ceilinged **Mesa Grill,** 102 Fifth Ave., at 15th St., tel. (212) 807-7400, offers first-rate Southwestern delights.

The best thing about the sleek barge-restaurant, the **Water Club,** 500 E. 30th St., at the East River, tel. (212) 683-3333, is its splendid view, but the food's good as well. **An American Place,** 2 Park Ave., at 32nd St., tel. (212) 684-2122, is a swank neo-art deco eatery with acclaimed cuisine. **Granville,** 40 E. 20th St. near Park Ave. S., tel. (212) 253-9088, is a classy, two-story hot spot.

Asian

Inexpensive: Sam's Noodles, 411 Third Ave., at 28th St., tel. (212) 213-2288, offers a nice array of noodle dishes from various parts of Asia. Next door to the Irving Plaza, a music club, is the **Galaxy,** 15 Irving Pl., at 15th St., tel. (212) 777-3631, an intimate hot spot bestrewn with tiny ceiling lights. On the menu is imaginative Asian-influenced fare; try the spring rolls.

Moderate: The stylish **Zen Palate,** 34 Union Square E, at 16th St., tel. (212) 614-9291, offers a mix of innovative Asian and vegetarian fare. **Tatany,** 380 Third Ave., bet. 27th and 28th Sts., tel. (212) 686-1871, serves some of the best sushi in town.

Eclectic

Expensive: A longtime favorite among restaurant critics and New Yorkers alike is **Union Square Cafe,** 21 E. 16th St., near Fifth Ave., tel. (212) 243-4020, a gracious and hospitable place serving an imaginative mix of Italian, French, and American cuisine.

French

Expensive: Les Halles, 411 Park Ave. S, bet. 28th and 29th Sts., tel. (212) 679-4111, is a boisterous French bistro and butcher shop with meats hanging in the windows. Directly across the street is its quieter but still bustling sister restaurant, **Park Bistro,** 414 Park Ave. S, bet. 28th and 29th Sts., tel. (212) 689-1360. Both serve good, authentic fare.

Indian

Inexpensive: Tasty Indian fast food can be picked up at **Curry in a Hurry,** 119 Lexington Ave., at 28th St., tel. (212) 683-0900, housed in a bright turquoise building. Another excellent choice is **Joy,** 127 E. 28th St., tel. (212) 685-0808, a spic-and-span cafeteria-style eatery always crowded with Indians.

Moderate: Annapurna, 108 Lexington Ave., bet. 27th and 28th Sts., tel. (212) 679-1284, is one of the neighborhood's oldest and best spots. **Muriya,** 129 E. 27th St., near Lexington Ave., tel. (212) 689-7925, specializes in Mughali fare. For vegetarian dishes, try the stylish **Mavalli Palace,** 46 E. 29th St., tel. (212) 679-5535.

Italian

Inexpensive: Pasta Presto, 613 Second Ave., bet. 33rd and 34th Sts., tel. (212) 889-4131, is one of a chain serving standard but reliable pasta dishes.

Moderate: Trattoria Siciliana, 517 Second Ave., bet. 28th and 29th Sts., tel. (212) 684-9861, is a sleeper of a snug Italian eatery well worth discovering.

Latin/Caribbean

Moderate: Though now close to a decade old, the **Coffee Shop,** 29 Union Square W, at 16th St., tel. (212) 243-7969, is still a fashionable hot spot serving Brazilian-accented food.

Expensive: Lola, 30 W. 22nd St., bet. Fifth and Sixth Aves., tel. (212) 675-6700, features spicy Caribbean food in a sophisticated setting; on Sundays, a gospel brunch is served. **Patria,** 250 Park Ave. S, at 20th St., tel. (212) 777-6211, serves nouveau Latin American fare in a sleek, high-ceilinged setting.

Southern/Soul/Creole

Inexpensive-to-Moderate: For tasty Southern fare, try **Live Bait,** 14 E. 23rd St., bet. Broadway and Madison Ave., tel. (212) 353-2400, a comfortable dive with a waitstaff of aspiring models.

Other Ethnic

Moderate: One of the city's few Turkish restaurants is the comfortable **Turkish Kitchen,** 386 Third Ave., bet. 27th and 28th Sts., tel. (212) 679-1810. **Tibetan Kitchen,** 444 Third Ave., bet. 30th and 31st Sts., tel. (212) 679-6286, features vegetarian dishes that sound more interesting than they taste.

Expensive: One of Manhattan's few Greek restaurants is **Periyali,** 35 W. 20th St., bet. Fifth and Sixth Aves., tel. (212) 463-7890, acclaimed for its authentic fare.

Light Bites

Union Square area: City Bakery, 22 E. 17th St., bet. Fifth Ave. and Broadway, tel. (212) 366-1414, is a good place for gourmet lunches and baked goods, while **Friend of a Farmer,** 77 Irving Pl., bet. 18th and 19th Sts., tel. (212) 477-2188, serves hearty soups and sandwiches. Farther north is **La Boulangerie,** 49 E. 21st St., near Park Ave., tel. (212) 475-8582, especially good for salads and fresh baked breads.

Fifth and Sixth Aves.: Fifth Ave. eateries include **Seattle Coffee Roasters,** 150 Fifth Ave., bet. 19th and 20th Sts., tel. (212) 675-9700, serving reasonably priced sandwiches as well as desserts; and **Eisenberg's,** 174 Fifth Ave., near 22nd St., tel. (212) 675-5096, one of the few old-time sandwich shops left in the city. Next door to Lola (see "Latin/Caribbean," above) is **Lola Bowla,** 30 W. 22nd St., tel. (212) 675-5544, specializing in one-bowl Asian and Italian food.

Farther Uptown: Sarge's, 548 Third Ave., near 36th St., tel. (212) 679-0442, is the best-known deli in the area. **Chez Laurence,** 245 Madison Ave., at 38th St., tel. (212) 683-0284, is a good spot for sandwiches and dessert.

Watering Holes and Lounges

One of the most stunning historic bars around is the **Old Town,** 45 E. 18th St., bet. Broadway and Park Ave. S, tel. (212) 529-6732, complete with high ceilings, mosaic floors, and a gorgeous back bar. Upstairs is a casual dining room serving passable food.

Also unique is the bar at the **Gramercy Tavern,** 42 E. 20th St., tel. (212) 477-0777, a spacious, ritzy, old-New York sort of place. Near Union Square is **119,** 119 E. 15th St., near Irving Pl., tel. (212) 995-5904, a grungy but comfortable dive with a pool table in front, dart boards in back, and a handful of creaky booths in between. The historic **Pete's Tavern,** 129 E. 18th St., at Irving Pl., tel. (212) 473-7676, is somewhat touristy, but soaked in the ale of time.

The genteel **Gramercy Park Hotel,** 2 Lexington Ave., at 21st St., tel. (212) 475-4320, offers a cozy, worn-around-the-edges cocktail lounge that seems frozen in the '50s. The Irish **Abbey Tavern,** 354 Third Ave., at 25th St., tel. (212) 532-1978, features roomy booths, a boisterous bar, and tasty pub food.

Among the restaurants mentioned above, **Galaxy, Luna Park, Live Bait, Granville** and the **Coffee Shop** all have late-night bar scenes. Adjoining Albuquerque Eats is the **Rodeo Bar,** presenting free live bands nightly.

CHELSEA AND THE GARMENT DISTRICT

The West Side between 14th and 42nd Sts. is not the most tourist-oriented of neighborhoods. Part residential, part industrial, this section of the city has no major public spaces. But it does have a solid, gritty feel and its share of one-of-a-kind attractions, including cutting-edge arts organizations and the Empire State Building.

Chelsea, roughly stretching between 14th and 28th Sts., Sixth Ave. and the Hudson River, is one big residential neighborhood, made up of brownstones, row houses, tenements, and apartment buildings. Most of the area was once owned by Capt. Thomas Clarke, whose grandson, Clement Charles Clarke, laid out a residential district here in the early 1800s. Clement Charles was also a scholar who wrote the *Compendious Lexicon of the Hebrew Language* and the famous poem beginning, "Twas the night before Christmas."

Chelsea began to change character in the mid-1800s, when the Hudson River Railroad was built along Eleventh Avenue. With the railroad came breweries, slaughterhouses, warehouses, and immigrant laborers desperate for work. Most of the earliest immigrants were Irish. They were followed by Greeks, who clustered around Eighth Ave., and Hispanics, many of whom still live in the area. Meanwhile, the eastern section of Chelsea retained a more genteel character, becoming a theater district in the 1870s and 1880s, and a short-lived center for the movie industry around the time of WW I.

Today, Chelsea is in a state of flux. Still large-ly middle- and working-class, it has also begun attracting affluent professionals and a large gay population, drawn to the area by its tranquility and relatively moderate rents. Trendy stores and restaurants have moved in, along with advertising and publishing companies. East of Seventh Ave., Chelsea is considered part of the Flatiron District, one of the city's hottest new neighborhoods (see introduction to "From Union Square to Murray Hill," above).

Chelsea ends and the historic Garment District begins somewhere around 28th St., where the streets change from residential to commercial. The heart of today's Garment District is farther north, however, around Seventh Ave. and 35th Street. Chelsea can be visited at almost any hour, while weekdays are the best time to roam the Garment District.

Back in the late 1800s, all of this area was known as the Tenderloin, or "Satan's Circus," and it was filled with brothels, saloons, clip joints, dance halls, and raucous restaurants. As a song from the period went:

"Lobsters! Rarebits! Plenty of Pilsener beer
Plenty of girls to help you drink the best of
*   cheer*
Dark girls, blonde girls, and never a one
*   that's true*
You get them all in the Tenderloin when
*   the clock strikes two."*

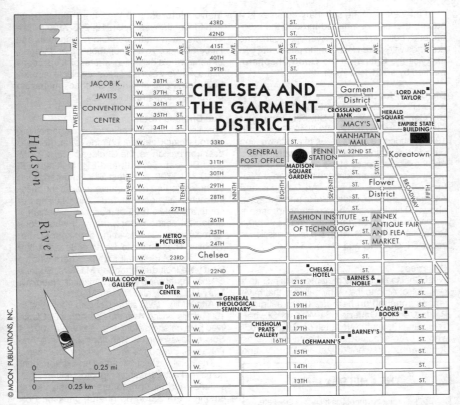

CHELSEA WEST

West 20th Street

One of Chelsea's prettiest blocks is W. 20th St. between Eighth and Ninth Avenues. The house with the curved bay windows at 402 W. 20th St. was designed by Charles Gilbert in 1897. At 404 W. 20th St. you'll find the area's earliest Greek Revival house, while at 406-418 W. 20th is Cushman Row—a group of charming brick houses named after its developer, dry-goods merchant Don Alonzo Cushman.

In 1951, Jack Kerouac lived at 454 W. 20th St., near Tenth Ave., while writing his novel *On the Road.* He wrote most of the book in about 20 days, typing almost nonstop at his kitchen table while a roll of paper fed continuously into his

typewriter. The roll eliminated the need for the time-consuming task of putting individual sheets of paper into the machine.

Other especially pretty residential streets in Chelsea are W. 21st and W. 22nd Sts. between Eighth and Tenth Avenues.

General Theological Seminary

The block bounded by Ninth and Tenth Aves. between 20th and 21st Sts. is home to the General Theological Seminary, a peaceful, campuslike enclave of ivy-draped buildings that look as if they belong more in rural England than in urban New York. Charles Clement Moore, who taught Hebrew and Greek here, donated the land on which the seminary stands. Most of the seminary's Gothic buildings were built in the late 1800s.

In the center of the seminary complex is a square that can be entered through the modern brick building on Ninth Avenue. Most of the buildings within are closed to the public, but you can visit the **Chapel of the Good Shepherd,** marked by a 161-foot tower.

Dia Center for the Arts

Another "alternative" arts center in Chelsea is the Dia Center, 548 W. 22nd St., bet. Tenth and Eleventh Aves., tel. (212) 989-5912. Founded in 1974 to support a select group of artists working outside the mainstream, the foundation has a major exhibition space at this address and sponsors two quasipermanent exhibits by artist Walter De Maria in SoHo (see "Art Galleries and Alternative Spaces" under "SoHo and TriBeCa," above). The foundation also plans to open a second major exhibit space on 22nd St. in 1997. Hours are Thurs.-Sun. noon-6 p.m. Admission is adults $4, students and seniors $2.

Galleries

West Chelsea is rapidly metamorphosing into a new SoHo. Among the many galleries that have recently opened up here are the prestigious **Paula Cooper Gallery,** 534 W. 21st St., bet. Tenth and Eleventh Aves., tel. (212) 255-1105, whose clients include such heavyweights as Jonathan Borofsky and Elizabeth Murray; and

---

THE CHELSEA PIERS

The largest gymnastics facility in the state, the largest rock-climbing wall in the northeast, the longest indoor running track in the world, a huge fitness center, a golf driving range, an ice-skating rink, a full-service marina, restaurants, and a 1.2-mile public esplanade all opened at the Chelsea Piers in the fall of 1995. The piers date back to 1910 when they served as "the most extensive and complete steamship terminal in this country," as the *Times* once put it. But they fell into disuse and disrepair with the building of the Midtown piers and the coming of transatlantic jet travel. The recent rehab project cost over $60 million.

To reach the Chelsea Piers, head west on 23rd St. to the Hudson River. For more information, call (212) 336-6666.

Metro Pictures, 519 W. 24th St., bet. Tenth and Eleventh Aves., tel. (212) 206-7100, which exhibits such names as Cindy Sherman and Robert Longo. To find out about other galleries, or about who's exhibiting where, pick up a copy of the *Art Now Gallery Guide,* available in many bookstores and galleries. Or check magazine or Sunday newspaper listings.

The Chelsea Hotel

With its deep maroon paint job accented by numerous black gables, chimneys, and ornate cast-iron balconies, the Chelsea Hotel, 222 W. 23rd St., bet. Seventh and Eighth Aves., tel. (212) 243-3700, is a West Side landmark. One of the city's first cooperative apartment buildings when it opened in 1884, the Chelsea became a hotel in 1905 and almost immediately began attracting writers, many of whom took up residence. Plaques at the door honor Dylan Thomas, Thomas Wolfe, Brendan Behan, Arthur Miller, and Mark Twain, while others who've lived here include Edgar Lee Masters, Eugene O'Neill, Tennessee Williams, Vladimir Nabokov, Mary McCarthy, and Nelson Algren.

Arthur Miller lived at the Chelsea from 1962 to 1968, while writing *After the Fall.* Arthur C. Clarke lived here on and off for years, and wrote *2001: A Space Odyssey* in his 10th-floor apartment. And William S. Burroughs wrote *Naked Lunch* here.

The hotel has also attracted an extraordinary number of actors, painters, photographers, musicians, and film producers over the years, among them Sarah Bernhardt, Jackson Pollock, Willem de Kooning, Larry Rivers, Jane Fonda, Robert Mapplethorpe, Milos Forman, and Peter Brook. Andy Warhol filmed part of his movie *Chelsea Girls* here in 1966, and musician Virgil Thompson lived on the hotel's ninth floor for over 40 years.

In the late 1960s, the Chelsea became a favorite stopover for rock stars passing through town. Among those who overnighted were Janis Joplin, Jimi Hendrix, the Grateful Dead, the Mamas and the Papas, Leonard Cohen, and Patti Smith. Bob Dylan wrote *Sad-Eyed Lady of the Lowlands* while staying at the Chelsea.

But perhaps the hotel's most notorious couple was Sid Vicious, lead singer for the Sex Pistols, and his girlfriend Nancy Spungen. The two were living here in 1978 when Nancy was found

Everyone from writer Arthur Miller to rocker Sid Vicious once lived at the Chelsea Hotel.

in her negligee beneath the bathroom sink, stabbed to death with a hunting knife. Vicious was indicted for the murder but died of a heroin overdose before he could stand trial. Alex Cox documented the events in his film *Sid and Nancy,* part of which was shot at the Chelsea. The hotel has since gotten rid of Room 100, where the murder was committed.

Artists, tourists, and well-heeled pseudobohemians still live and stay at the Chelsea, whose lobby is hung floor-to-ceiling with artwork by present and former tenants. The rooms are relatively big and reasonably priced, but the place is well worn and without amenities.

CHELSEA EAST

Sixth Avenue
A continuation of the Ladies Mile (see "Broadway and Lower Fifth Avenue" under "From Union Square to Murray Hill," above), Sixth Ave.

bet. 17th and 23rd Sts. is flanked by impressive cast-iron buildings, considerably larger than the ones on Broadway. Dirty and underused until just a few years ago, the buildings now house several new megastores. At night their newly painted and brightly lit facades cast mysterious shadows onto the street.

Today's Man, 625 Sixth Ave., bet. 18th and 19th Sts. was once B. Altman's, built in the 1870s. Across the street, at 620 Sixth Ave. where Bed Bath and Beyond is today, once housed Siegel-Cooper, the world's largest store when it opened in the late 1890s. Farther north at 655 Sixth Ave., bet. 20th and 21st Sts., is an especially lovely building equipped with columned turrets at either end and an immense, inscribed pediment. It was once home to the Hugh O'Neill Store, a dry goods emporium. Another unusual Sixth Ave. address is 47 W. 20th St., a gothic-style church designed in 1846 by architect Richard Upjohn. Until recently, the church housed the nightclub **Limelight.**

The Flower District
In the early morning, the area around 28th St. and Sixth Ave. is all abustle with flowers of red, orange, blue, purple, yellow, and white. Later in the day, the stores cater to the retail market, setting up small forests of green along the sidewalks.

The city's wholesale Flower District may be small, but it's been centered on these streets since about 1870, when Long Island growers brought their flowers to the foot of E. 34th St. at the East River. Recently, rising rents have been threatening to drive the market elsewhere, but thus far, the vendors have managed to hold their own.

Fashion Institute of Technology
On Seventh Ave. between 26th and 28th Sts. is a gray, boxy complex of buildings known as F.I.T. *The* school in the city for young fashion designers, the institute often features unusual exhibits that are open to the public. When an exhibit is up, the galleries at the Shirley Goodman Resource Center, Seventh Ave. at 27th St., tel. (212) 760-7760, are open Tues. 10 a.m.-9 p.m., Wed.-Sat. 10 a.m.-5 p.m. Admission is free.

Penn Station and Vicinity
On Seventh Ave. at 32nd St. is the entrance to the ugly underground Pennsylvania Station, topped with the equally ugly Madison Square

Garden. There's no reason to visit either place unless you're taking a train, have tickets to a game, or want to take a look at Maya Lin's "Eclipsed Time" clock, installed in 1994 on the station's lower level. Lin is the architect who, as a 21-year-old undergraduate at Yale in 1980, created the winning design for the Vietnam Veterans Memorial in Washington, D.C. She spent five years working on the Penn Station project, and her sculpture, hovering in the ceiling above commuters' heads, looks like a glowing flying saucer with numerals etched along its edges. Time is marked by a slowly moving shadow.

West of Penn Station, on Eighth Ave. between 31st and 33rd Sts., is the glorious, block-long **General Post Office,** designed by McKim, Mead & White in 1913. Lined with tall Corinthian columns, the post office is all that the train station is not, and a proposal is in the works to convert it into the next Pennsylvania Station. The original Penn Station, located where the present Madison Square Garden is now, was also designed by McKim, Mead & White, and was said to have been their masterpiece. Its demolition in 1968 spawned the birth of today's landmark-preservation movement.

The Garment Worker *honors the district's labor force.*

THE GARMENT DISTRICT

Centering around Seventh Ave. in the mid-30s is the Garment District, now sporting the more tony "Fashion Center" label. Once stretching roughly between Fifth and Ninth Aves., 25th and 42nd Sts., the district—like the American garment industry itself—has shrunk considerably in recent years. Now it reaches only between 34th and 42nd. Nonetheless, this is still the country's largest clothing-manufacturing district and constitutes an important part of New York's economy. About $10 billion a year in clothing is designed, cut, and sewn here. In the Fashion Center are 450 buildings with 5,000 fashion-trade tenants, including 4,500 factories.

The garment industry moved to Seventh Ave. from the Lower East Side around the time of WW I. It's always been predominantly Jewish-run, but the labor force has become increasingly Hispanic and Asian. Traditionally, the southern part of the district was devoted to the fur industry, the area around 34th St. to children's clothing, and the area north of 36th St. to women's apparel.

Visiting the Garment District on a weekday morning you'll see long lines of double-parked trucks, brawny men wheeling clothing racks, and young fashion assistants hustling to and fro with large boxes and bags. The industry's showrooms are closed to the public, but you can get a good sense of the place just by wandering the streets. Especially interesting are the many millinery, trimming, and fabric outlets—most catering to the trade only—along 37th and 38th Streets.

A long-overdue monument honoring the industry's thousands of workers stands in front of 555 Seventh Ave. at 39th Street. Cast in bronze by artist Judith Weller in 1984, *The Garment Worker* was sponsored by several dozen companies in the area, and depicts a Jewish tailor at his sewing machine.

Macy's and Herald Square

"The World's Largest Department Store" dominates Herald Square, a small gray triangle of land where Sixth Ave., Broadway, and 34th St. intersect. In the middle of the square stands a memorial to the *New York Herald,* once published here.

Macy's—rescued from bankruptcy in 1994 by its merger with Federated Department Stores—boasts about 170 departments stocking half a million items, from sneakers to bed linens, furs to baked goods. Ten stories high and a full block wide, the store was founded in 1858 by Rowland Hussey Macy, a Quaker from Nantucket. Macy went to sea at the age of 15 and returned four years later with $500 and, legend has it, a red star tattooed on his hand—now Macy's logo. Six times Macy tried to establish a shop, and six times he failed. Then he started Macy's.

One block south of Macy's, where its arch rival Gimbel's once stood, is a 90-store complex known as **Manhattan Mall.** Built largely of glass, it's equipped with playful glass elevators and pink and green lights. Also lining the square are the huge megastores **Daffy's, Toys 'R Us,** and **HMV Music.**

Just north of Herald Square, where Broadway meets 36th St., is **Crossland Bank.** Though nothing special to look at from the outside, the building's interior is an astonishing visual delight, with a graceful elliptical lobby and a gorgeous oval skylight. South of Herald Square, below 34th St., is another gray triangle of land holding a statue of journalist Horace Greeley. Surrounding Greeley is a small park, usually filled with pigeons and the down-and-out.

Empire State Building

One of the world's most famous buildings, this landmark at 350 Fifth Ave., at 34th St., is best visited at night, when the city lights lie strewn at your feet. There are fewer visitors then, too, and it's easy to imagine yourself back in the early 1930s, just after the Empire State went up. The building was erected during the Depression in an astonishing 14 months, at the rate of 4 1/2 stories a week.

For years, the art deco Empire State, built on the former site of the Waldorf-Astoria hotel, was the world's tallest building. That's no longer true, yet the Empire State—extensively reno-

the Empire State Building, still the world's quintessential skyscraper

vated in 1993—remains the quintessential skyscraper. The landmark holds 73 elevators, 6,500 windows, 3,500 miles of telephone and telegraph wire, 1,860 steps, and two observation decks, one on the 86th floor, the other on the 102nd.

In 1933, Irma Eberhardt became the first person to commit suicide by jumping off the Empire State. That same year, the classic film *King Kong* was made, showing a giant ape climbing up the skyscraper. In 1945, a B-25 bomber smacked into the building's 79th floor, killing 14 people. And in 1986, two parachutists jumped from the 86th floor to land safely on Fifth Avenue. Also, in case you're wondering, pennies thrown off the Empire State *cannot* kill passersby walking below, but they can cause severe burns.

The Empire State Building's observation decks, tel. (212) 736-3100, are open daily 9:30 a.m.-midnight. Tickets are sold until 11:30 p.m. on the concourse level, one floor below the main lobby. Admission is adults $4.50, seniors and children 5-12 $2.50, children under five free.

Also in the Empire State Building is **Skyride,** tel. (212) 279-9777, a kind of virtual-reality flight taking viewers over, under, and through New York. Introduced in 1995, the 7.5-minute journey takes place in a theater built with a hydraulic floor that rises, falls, and banks left and right to match the on-screen action. Tickets are adults $9, children and seniors $7. Open daily 10 a.m.-10 p.m.

Next door to the Skyride is **Transporter: Movies You Ride,** tel. (212) 947-4299, another big-screen flight simulator. Tickets are adults $8.50-14.50, kids $6.50-10.50; open daily 9 a.m.-11 p.m.

Koreatown

In recent years, the two blocks between Fifth Ave. and Broadway on 32nd and 33rd Sts. have become packed with Korean bars, restaurants, bookstores, and health and beauty shops. For the most part, these new enterprises cater to Koreans, not tourists, but if you want to check out a shop or restaurant, chances are you'll be welcome. Most of the signs are in Korean.

SHOPPING

Arts and Crafts

Chisholm Prats Gallery, 145 Eighth Ave., at 17th St., tel. (212) 741-1703, specializes in European travel and product posters. **Wood Artists,** 259 W. 18th St., near Eighth Ave., tel. (212) 989-3980, sells unique, handcrafted objects. Doll lovers will want to visit the **Manhattan Doll House,** 176 Ninth Ave., at 21st St., tel. (212) 989-5220, which boasts the city's largest doll collection.

Books and Music

Housed in a renovated cast-iron building along Sixth Ave. is a **Barnes & Noble** megastore, 675 Sixth Ave., bet. 21st and 22nd Sts., tel. (212) 727-1227. It features frequent readings, a cafe, and many comfortable chairs, and is open until 11 p.m. nightly. **Revolution Books,** 9 W. 19th St., tel. (212) 691-3345, the country's largest radical bookstore, harks back to Union Square's inflammatory Sacco-and-Vanzetti days.

Books of Wonder, 16 W. 18th St., tel. (212) 989-3270, is a great children's bookstore.

Around the corner is **A Different Light,** 151 W. 19th St., bet. Sixth and Seventh Aves., tel. (212) 989-4850, a top store for gay and lesbian books. Between Fifth and Sixth Aves. are the venerable **Academy Books,** 10 W. 18th St., tel. (212) 242-4848, selling used books; and **Academy Records,** 12 W. 18th St., tel. (212) 242-3000, selling used classical and jazz recordings. **Skyline Books,** 13 W. 18th St., tel. (212) 759-5463, and **Chelsea Books and Records,** 111 W. 17th St. bet. Sixth and Seventh, tel. (212) 645-4340, also specialize in used books, while J&R Music World operates the **Jazz Record Center** at 236 W. 26th St., 8th Fl., tel. (212) 675-4480.

Clothes

Loehmann's, the Bronx emporium known for its discounted designer wear, now has a branch at 101 Seventh Ave., at 16th St., tel. (212) 352-0856.

Along 34th St. between Fifth and Sixth Aves. are shops, shops, and more shops, most selling clothing and shoes. Some are branches of national stores such as **The Gap, The Limited,** and **Benetton.** Others are discount emporiums.

On Fifth Ave. is New York's largest and oldest hat store, the **J.J. Hat Center,** 310 Fifth Ave., at 32nd St., tel. (212) 239-4368. Established in 1911, J.J.'s stocks over 15,000 men's hats, including fedoras, Stetsons, homburgs, and caps.

Department Stores

Sleek, fashionable, expensive **Barney's New York,** 17th St. at Seventh Ave., tel. (212) 593-7800, once catered exclusively to men but now also boasts a sizable women's department. A second Barney's is located uptown (see "Upper East Side").

King of the department stores is **Macy's** (see "Macy's and Herald Square" under "The Garment District," above), 151 34th St., at Sixth Ave., tel. (212) 695-4400. A few blocks farther northeast is **Lord & Taylor,** Fifth Ave. at 38th St., tel. (212) 391-3344, a comfortable midsize store that may not be as glamorous as some, but still carries a first-rate selection. One of the store's most gracious touches is the free coffee, served in a silver pot, that it offers to shoppers who arrive before the place opens at 10 a.m.

Garment District Retailers
Most of the Garment District shops are wholesale only. Some of the stores that sell retail are **Margola**, 48 W. 37th St., bet. Fifth and Sixth Aves., tel. (212) 695-1115, offering glass beads, rhinestones, and trinkets; **Cinderella**, 60 W. 38th St., tel. (212) 840-0644, specializing in feathers and bridal veils; **Manny's,** 26 W. 38th St., tel. (212) 840-2235, selling hats and notions; and **M&J Trimming**, 1008 Sixth Ave., tel. (212) 391-9072, offering beads, buttons, lace, and feathers.

Flea Markets
On Sixth Ave. north of 23rd St. is New York's flea market center, open weekends only. The largest and oldest market here is the open-air **Annex Antique Fair and Flea Market,** between 24th and 27th Sts., tel. (212) 243-5343. Started over 30 years ago, the market is open 9 a.m.-5 p.m.; admission is $1.

The Annex's success has recently led to the establishment of several new markets. Run by the same people who run the Annex is the indoor **Garage,** 112 W. 25th St., a former parking garage with about 125 vendors. Next door is the 12-floor **Chelsea Antiques Building,** 110 W. 25th St., tel. (212) 929-0909 (open daily), while to the east is **Markus Antiques Gallery,** 30 W. 26th St., tel. (212) 255-7615 (open Tues.-Sun.).

ACCOMMODATIONS

Inexpensive
Once the home of *Life* magazine, the beaux arts **Herald Square Hotel,** 19 W. 31st St., bet. Fifth and Sixth Aves., tel. (212) 279-4017 or (800) 727-1888, boasts a lovely facade complete with lacy iron fretwork and a plump, gilded cherub reading the magazine. Inside, a friendly staff welcomes budget travelers from around the world. Rooms are small but adequate and come with or without private bath. The shared baths are reasonably clean; old *Life* covers line the hallways. $50-75 s, $95-105 d.

Just east of the Herald Square is another beaux arts hostelry—the **Hotel Wolcott,** 4 W. 31st St., near Fifth Ave., tel. (212) 268-2900. Its elaborate but well-worn lobby is packed with marble columns, enormous mirrors, and shiny

chandeliers—all contrasting strangely with the room's utilitarian furnishings and the harried men at the front desk. Rooms are small but adequate; a self-service laundry is on site. $90 s or d.

Moderate
One of the city's most historic hotels is the **Chelsea,** 222 W. 23rd St., bet. Seventh and Eighth Aves., tel. (212) 243-3700, once home to everyone from Dylan Thomas to Sid Vicious (see "The Chelsea Hotel," under "Chelsea West," above). Nowadays, the Chelsea is neither particularly clean nor particularly cheap, but it does have atmosphere. Offbeat, bohemian, and chic in its own faded way, it offers thick walls, many rooms with kitchenettes, a friendly staff, and excellent people-watching. Next door is El Quixote, a neighborhood institution that's one part Spanish-American restaurant, one part kitsch-filled shrine to the Cervantes hero. $125 s, $135-190 d.

Down the block from the Chelsea is the brand new **Chelsea Savoy Hotel,** 204 W. 23rd St., at Seventh Ave., tel. (212) 929-9353, offering 90 moderately sized rooms done up in dark floral greens and woods. The decor is nothing special, but everything's very clean and reasonably priced. This is also one of the only hotels in Chelsea. $99 s, $125 d.

The new **Best Western Manhattan Hotel,** 17 W. 32nd St., bet. Fifth and Sixth Aves., tel. (212) 736-1600 or (800) 551-2303, is more imaginatively designed than its name might imply. In the busy lobby, find neo-art deco decor in black and white; upstairs, find well-kept rooms designed in "airy Central Park," "sophisticated Fifth Avenue," and "trendy SoHo" themes. Adjoining the lobby is a Korean restaurant—in keeping with surrounding Koreatown. $119-169 s, $129-179 d.

An excellent new addition to Midtown is the spiffy, neo-art deco **Metro,** 45 W. 35th St., bet. Fifth and Sixth Aves., tel. (212) 947-2500. Built in 1901, the recently renovated hotel features 175 comfortable guest rooms and a large sitting room, where complimentary coffee is served throughout the day. Photos from the 1930s adorn the walls; on the top floor is an exercise room and rooftop terrace, where drinks are served in summer. $145-165 s or d; includes continental breakfast.

YMCA

Offering adequate accommodations for around $50 is the **McBurney YMCA**, 215 W. 24th St., near Seventh Ave., tel. (212) 741-9226.

FOOD

American

Inexpensive-to-Moderate: Though somewhat overpriced, the **Empire Diner**, 210 Tenth Ave., at 22nd St., tel. (212) 243-2736, is a stylish, art deco original well worth visiting; open 24 hours. **Chelsea Commons**, 242 Tenth Ave., near 24th St., tel. (212) 929-9424, is a creaky tavern with good bar food, a splendid old-fashioned bar, and a small outdoor garden.

Moderate: A tiny gem of a hideaway, serving just five entrees, is **Alley's End**, 311 W. 17th St., bet. Eighth and Ninth Aves., tel. (212) 627-8899. **Keens Chop House**, 72 W. 36th St., bet. Fifth and Sixth Aves., tel. (212) 947-3636, is an old-time pub with a crackling fireplace in winter.

French

Expensive: The charming **Gascogne**, 158 Eighth Ave., near 18th St., tel. (212) 675-6564, specializes in the foods of Southern France.

Italian

Moderate: The low-key **Intermezzo**, 202 Eighth Ave., bet. 20th and 21st Sts., tel. (212) 929-3433, serves basic pastas and entrees.

Expensive: **Da Umberto**, 107 W. 17th St., near Sixth Ave., tel. (212) 989-0303, is a classy spot acclaimed for its Northern Italian fare.

Korean

Moderate: The spotless **Gam Mee Ok**, 43 W. 32nd St., bet. Fifth and Sixth Aves., tel. (212) 695-4113, filled with artwork, is one of Koreatown's top restaurants. **Han Bat**, 53 W. 35th St., bet. Fifth and Sixth Aves., tel. (212) 629-5588, specializes in the country dishes of southern Korea.

Latin/Caribbean

Inexpensive: La Taza De Oro, 96 Eighth Ave., bet. 14th and 15th Sts., tel. (212) 243-9946, is a tiny luncheonette serving Puerto Rican food. For hearty Cuban-Chinese fare, try hole-in-the-wall **La Chinita Linda,** 166 Eighth Ave., bet. 18th and 19th Sts., tel. (212) 633-1791.

Moderate: Mary Ann's, 116 Eighth Ave., at 16th St., tel. (212) 633-0877, is one of a popular chain of three Mexican restaurants known for homemade touches. Mexican cuisine is also featured at **Blue Moon,** 150 Eighth Ave., bet. 17th and 18th Sts., tel. (212) 463-0560 (try the fajitas); and **Rocking Horse Mexican Cafe,** 182 Eighth Ave., bet. 19th and 20th Sts., tel. (212) 463-9511.

Other Ethnic

Inexpensive: Ngone, 823 Sixth Ave., bet. 28th and 29th Sts., tel. (212) 967-7899, is a homey Senegalese restaurant. The tiny **Bright Food Shop,** 216 Eighth Ave., tel. (212) 243-4433, offers unusual Mexican-Asian cuisine.

Moderate: Negril, 362 W. 23rd St. bet. Eighth and Ninth Aves., tel. (212) 807-6411, serves spicy Caribbean fare in a lively setting. **Pad Thai,** 114 Eighth Ave. bet. 15th and 16th Sts., tel. (212) 691-6226 is a friendly, popular spot.

Watering Holes and Lounges

Merchant's N.Y., 112 Seventh Ave., at 17th St., tel. (212) 366-7267, is a stylish bar with a sidewalk cafe in summer and a crackling fireplace in winter; on the menu are gourmet sandwiches, salads, and desserts. The well-worn **Peter McManus,** 152 Seventh Ave., at 19th St., tel. (212) 929-9691, still attracts some long-time regulars as well as young professionals. Juicy burgers are served at the big, rickety booths in back. Sleek, chic **G's,** 223 W. 19th St., bet. Seventh and Eighth Aves., tel. (212) 929-1085, is an ultra-popular gay bar/lounge centered around a steel circular bar in front and a juice bar in the back. **Chelsea Commons** (see "American," above) also has a lively bar scene.

MIDTOWN

Rush, rush, rush. Sometimes all the people in the world seem to be elbowing their way through here. Most of Manhattan's skyscrapers are in Midtown, along with most of its offices, major hotels, theaters, famous shops and restaurants, and many visitor attractions. If you only have time to visit one part of Manhattan, Midtown should probably be it.

Fifth Avenue is the heart of Midtown, the artery to which all other addresses relate. Though nothing more than a line on a map as late as 1811, Fifth Avenue was the city's most fashionable address by the time of the Civil War. The Astors, Vanderbilts, and many other wealthy families all had homes along it, leading *Leslie's Weekly,* a popular magazine of the day, to comment that Fifth Avenue "has upon it 340 residences, all of the finer class, except for a few shanties near the Park. It may safely be said that of these 340 houses, not one costs less than $20,000."

Fifth Avenue began to turn commercial in the early 1900s. Today, its Midtown stretch is almost entirely lined with shops and office buildings. In the lower 40s and upper 30s, these shops tend to be tourist traps selling discounted electronic gadgetry and junky souvenirs; in the upper 40s and 50s stand the upscale boutiques and department stores for which the avenue is famous.

As in other parts of the city, Fifth Avenue is also the dividing line between the wealthier, more established East Side, and the scruffier, more fly-by-night West Side. In Midtown on the East Side are a plethora of expensive office buildings and posh residences, along with such institutions as the Waldorf Astoria and the United Nations. Immediately west of Fifth Avenue are more of the same—including Rockefeller Center and the Plaza Hotel. But continue west past Sixth Avenue, and things get a bit more disheveled. Here, you'll find Times Square and the once notorious neighborhood of Hell's Kitchen.

To see Midtown at its frenzied best, you should tour during the week. However, most of the visitor attractions are also open on weekends. With the exception of Times Square, much of Midtown shuts up tight after business hours. First-time visitors will probably want to make stops at Grand Central Station, Times Square, the Museum of Modern Art, Rockefeller Center, and Fifth Avenue between 50th and 59th Streets.

EAST 42ND STREET AND VICINITY

Grand Central Station

Though currently hard to appreciate due to an ongoing $100-million renovation, Grand Central Station, on 42nd St. bet. Vanderbilt and Lexington, is one of New York's most glorious buildings. To step inside its vast 125-foot-high concourse—with glassed-in catwalks, a grand staircase, and a vaulted, star-studded ceiling—is to be transported back to a more romantic era when women wore hoop skirts and men wore top hats.

Completed in 1913 by the design firms of Reed & Stem, and Warren & Wetmore, Grand Central Station is a city within a city. Beaux arts eclectic on the outside, early 20th-century modern on the inside, it houses innumerable shops and newsstands, several bars and restaurants, and a library devoted to railroading (open by appointment only). Also here, but off-limits to the public, are a shooting range and a rooftop tennis court. Adjoining the station are 27 miles of track that loop and stretch beneath Park Ave. as far north as 50th St., and seven stories of tunnels containing electric power facilities, water and gas mains, sewage pipes, steam, and rats.

In its heyday, Grand Central was the terminus for two major railroads: the New York Central, and the New York, New Haven, and Hartford lines. Trains with romantic names such as the Empire State Express and Super Chief rolled in daily. A theater in the station screened newsreels, and CBS broadcast from the roof. Today, Grand Central Station is but a shadow of its former self. Only about 500 commuter trains arrive and depart daily (all long-distance trains use Pennsylvania Station), and many of the station's shops are grimy or abandoned, a situation that should be remedied by the present restoration.

To get the best view of Grand Central, take the escalators up to the balconies on the north side. From here, you can watch the foot traffic crisscrossing beneath you in seemingly choreographed style, while listening to the musicians who frequently perform by the east wall. Sometimes you can get up into the catwalks from the staircases on the west side of the terminal.

Adjoining Grand Central to the north, via the escalators, is the wide, 59-story Met Life Building, better known among many New Yorkers by its former name, the Pan Am Building. In its lobby is one of the city's best newsstands.

Fascinating one-hour tours of the terminal are conducted every Wednesday by the Municipal Art Society, tel. (212) 935-3960. Groups

© MOON PUBLICATIONS, INC.

meet at 12:30 p.m. at the Chemical Commuter Bank on the east side of the concourse level. The tour is free, but donations are appreciated.

Vanderbilt Avenue and Nathan Hale

The short street between 42nd and 47th Sts. along the west side of Grand Central is named after Commodore Cornelius Vanderbilt (1794-1877), the man responsible for building Grand Central Station. Born working class, Vanderbilt began accumulating his fortune at the age of 16 when he started ferrying passengers between his native Staten Island and Manhattan. Gradually, he transformed that simple service into a large fleet of transatlantic steamships and, later in life, switched to railroading.

On an outside wall of the Yale Club at Vanderbilt Ave. and 44th St. is a plaque honoring Nathan Hale, the Revolutionary War hero hung by the British for spying. The blond, blue-eyed, twenty-something Hale—a Yale grad—was caught in Brooklyn on Sept. 21, 1776, and was executed just east of here (see "Beekman Place," below).

Around Grand Central

Just across 42nd St. from Grand Central is the **Philip Morris Building,** 120 Park Ave., which houses an atrium and a branch of the **Whitney Museum of American Art,** tel. (212) 878-2550. The museum is open Mon.-Fri. 11 a.m.-6 p.m., Thurs. 11 a.m.-7:30 p.m. Admission is free. The exhibits are always first-rate, but sadly, the atrium often fills up with the down-and-out and can be depressing.

At 110 E. 42nd is the impressive, Romanesque **Bowery Savings Bank,** now known as Home Savings Bank. Designed by York & Sawyer in 1923, the bank boasts a vast lobby filled with mosaic floors, marble columns, and huge pendant lamps. At 122 E. 42nd is the equally handsome **Chanin Building,** a 1929 art deco treasure done up in bronze and marble. The lobby is filled with bas-reliefs depicting the "City of Opportunity," where a man of poor beginnings rises to a position of wealth and power.

Next to Grand Central is the glitzy **Grand Hyatt,** 109 E. 42nd, built on the shell of the old Commodore Hotel. In 1920, the Commodore was temporary home to Scott and Zelda Fitzgerald. Newly married, they moved in here after

Grand Central Terminal is now undergoing a $100 million restoration.

being kicked out of the nearby Biltmore Hotel for disturbing the other guests. But things didn't go well at the Commodore, either. When the Fitzgeralds spent half an hour spinning in the revolving door and generally creating a ruckus, they were asked to leave.

Free tours of historic East 42nd St. are offered by the Grand Central Partnership Business Improvement District, tel. (212) 818-1777. The tours leave from the Phillip Morris Building, Fridays at 12:30 p.m.

The Chrysler Building and East

At the northeast corner of 42nd St. and Lexington Ave. stands the stunning Chrysler Building, a 1930 art deco masterpiece. Financed by Walter Chrysler, the towering building is a tribute to the automobile age. Winged gargoyles shaped like hood ornaments, and brick designs taken from wheels and hubcaps lead the eye up to a gleaming, stainless steel spire. At night, the concentric circles of the spire light up, tripping the city with a touch of the light fantastic.

Another block east, at 220 E. 42nd St., is the **Daily News Building,** a soaring art deco skyscraper designed by Raymood Hood in 1930. The *Daily News* left for cheaper digs (at 450 W. 33rd St.) in 1995, but the huge, slowly revolving globe in the building's lobby remains. Used in the *Superman* movie remakes of the 1980s, the globe is delightfully out-of-date, depicting countries that haven't existed in years.

Down the street from the News is the **Ford Foundation** building, 320 E. 42nd St., which has a wonderful three-story indoor garden enclosed by walls and ceilings of glass. Visitors are welcome to wander along the garden's meandering paths, surrounded by lush plants and trees. The garden lacks benches, however; to rest your weary peds, you'll have to trudge another half block east to **Tudor City.** Head up the stone staircases on either side of 42nd St. near First Ave. to reach the self-contained community with its 3,000 apartments, hotel, and small park. Tudor City's buildings—brick with Gothic touches—all face inward, with limited views of the river. That's because back in the 1920s, an ugly, foul-smelling slaughterhouse was situated below.

United Nations Plaza

Extending from 42nd to 48th Sts. and from First Ave. to FDR Dr. is the windswept United Nations Plaza, where the flags of the nearly 200 member nations flap noisily in the breeze. Legally, the United Nations isn't part of New York at all but is international territory. The U.N. has its own post office, postage stamps, and uniformed security force.

Built in 1948, on 18 acres bought and donated by J.D. Rockefeller Jr., the United Nations complex is made up of three buildings. The vertical greenish glass slab is the Secretariat Building, housing many offices. The low-slung horizontal edifice is the Conference Building, and the dramatic white building with concave sides is the General Assembly.

Only the General Assembly Building is open to the public; to see it, you must join one of the

> *"I don't like the life here. There is no greenery. It would make a stone sick."*
>
> —NIKITA S. KHRUSHCHEV

scheduled 45-minute tours. English-language tours, tel. (212) 963-7713, leave daily every 30 minutes 9:15 a.m.-4:45 p.m.; for information on other languages, call (212) 963-7539. The tours take you past much wonderful art donated by member nations, and into the General Assembly Hall and Security Council Chamber. If meetings are in session, you can listen in on simultaneous interpretation in six languages.

The U.N.'s visitor entrance is at 46th St. and First Ave. Tour fees are adults $6.50, senior citizens $4.50, students $4, children in grades 1-8 $3.50, children under age five not admitted. The basement holds a gift shop selling handicrafts from around the world; the Delegates Dining Room, tel. (212) 963-7625, is sometimes open to visitors on weekends.

Just north of the General Assembly building are peaceful and surprisingly underutilized gardens filled with interesting sculptures, donated to the U.N. by member nations. The gardens have splendid views of the East River and are a good place to catch some sun on a summer's day.

Beekman Place

At the north end of the U.N. Plaza, just east of where 49th St. meets First Ave., is Beekman Place, a tony residential avenue lined with townhouses and private parks. It's named after the Beekman family, whose mansion—Mount Pleasant—once stood here. The British commandeered Mount Pleasant during the Revolutionary War, using the mansion as their headquarters. Nathan Hale was tried as a spy in the greenhouse and hung in the nearby orchard. A fresco depicting his trial and death is in the Hale House, 440 E. 51st Street.

The great American songwriter, Irving Berlin, lived at 17 Beekman Pl. for over three decades; a plaque marks the spot. Greta Garbo lived at 2 Beekman Pl. during the 1930s, Billy Rose at 33 Beekman Pl. in the 1940s.

Sparks Steak House

On Dec. 16, 1985, mob boss Paul Castellano and his driver Thomas Bilotti were gunned down outside this modern Midtown eatery at 210 E. 46th St., near Second Avenue. As they climbed out of their car, both were shot six times by a hit squad armed with walkie-talkies and semiautomatics. "Dapper Don" John Gotti—so named because of his predilection for double-breasted silk suits and floral print ties—was convicted of ordering the murders and sent to jail in 1992.

THE DRAFT RIOTS

One of the bloodiest riots in U.S. history began at the corner of Third Ave. and 46th St. during the Civil War. By the time the riots were over, nearly 100,000 people had rampaged through the streets, 18 blacks had been lynched, as many as 2,000 other people had been injured or killed, and innumerable buildings had been destroyed.

The riots began on the hot morning of July 12, 1863, when the first draft lottery in U.S. history was held at an enrollment office then located here. A large crowd looked on as names of local men were selected at random to join the Union army. Most of the unlucky "winners" were poor Irish laborers; the rich had already bought their way out of military service by paying the government $300 (the equivalent of one year's wages for the poorer men). The laborers weren't too keen on the idea of risking life and limb to free Southern slaves, who might then come north and compete for work.

As the names were being called, someone fiercely yelled out, "I ain't going!" and a few moments later an enraged crowd attacked the Union Army office, destroying it and the draft lottery wheel. From there, the crowd swarmed through the streets, gaining momentum and more followers as it went. The city's 800-man police force stood by helplessly as the mob overran the city's arsenal, burned down mansions, and looted stores. The protesters chased down the police chief and beat him unconscious; attacked the Colored Orphans Asylum on Fifth Ave. at West 43rd St., killing one child as 250 others escaped out the back door; and strung up black boys along the trees of Bleecker St., then a black residential district.

Finally, on July 15, Lincoln sent in troops—badly needed in the war itself—and the riots were quelled. Afterward, the lottery was quietly forgotten.

TIMES SQUARE AND HELL'S KITCHEN

Simultaneously New York's glitziest and seediest symbol, Times Square centers around the intersection of Broadway and Seventh Ave. bet. 42nd and 48th Streets. Not really a square at all, but rather two elongated triangles, it is named after *The New York Times,* which was once located in the white Times Tower building where Broadway, Seventh Ave., and 42nd St. meet. (The *Times* is now around the corner at 229 W. 43rd Street.) It is from Times Tower that the illuminated ball drops every Dec. 31, ushering in the New Year.

Before 1904, when *The New York Times* moved in, Times Square was known as Longacre Square. The center of the horse business in a city then largely dependent upon four-footed transportation, the square was lined with horse exchanges, carriage factories, stables, and blacksmith shops. Not until the 1910s did Times Square become a bona fide theater district; not until the 1960s did it become known for its thriving sex industry.

Times Square's biggest year for theatrical productions was 1927-28, when 257 shows were mounted at 71 theaters. The sex industry peaked here in the early 1970s with an estimated 150 sex joints and porn shops. The man most responsible for turning the area into a porno-amusement park was Martin Hodas, the "Peep Show King." Hodas first introduced the coin-operated viewing booth to Times Square about 25 years ago. At the height of his career, he was said to have been grossing $13 million annually.

Times Square has been much cleaned up in recent years, thanks largely to the efforts of the Times Square Business Improvement District—a nonprofit organization formed of the area's business and community leaders. Since 1993, Times Square's crime rate has decreased by about 42%. Many of the old porn shops have been closed down and the three-card-monte games broken up. Police and private security officers patrol the streets 24 hours a day.

All this has not come without a price. A number of fine old movie theaters were destroyed along with the porn shops, to be replaced by

TIMES SQUARE INFORMATION

The excellent Times Square Visitors Center occupies the lobby of the Embassy Theater, on Broadway between 46th and 47th Streets. It's open daily 10 am.-6 p.m., and the staff is multilingual. Free and very enjoyable walking tours of the area, led by actors, leave from the center on Fridays at noon; call (212) 869-5453 for more information.

sterile glass-sheathed office buildings and hotels. And without the denizens of the night—evicted from their traditional haunts—Times Square is rapidly losing much of its character. As of this writing, plenty of tawdriness remains, but a square sanitized for the middle class seems to be well on its way. Catch the remaining con men, pickpockets, pedophiles, junkies, perverts, pimps, hustlers, and prostitutes while you can.

Two things that could help protect Times Square from a bland future are its street performers—each one more inventive than the next —and its neon signs. The lights start to burn at dusk, hinting at the magic yet to come, and by night, the streets are ablaze with huge panels of red, green, yellow, blue, and white. Except for the Las Vegas strip, no other place in America boasts more neon lights.

The Theater District

Most of the Broadway theaters are not on Broadway at all, but on the side streets surrounding Times Square. The area is home to 37 legitimate theaters, 22 of which are city landmarks. West 44th and 45th Sts. bet. Seventh and Eighth Aves. are especially rich blocks; here you'll find the **Shubert,** the **Helen Hayes,** the **Booth,** the **Majestic,** the **Minskoff,** and several more.

Next to the Shubert, connecting 44th and 45th Sts., is **Shubert Alley,** where unemployed performers once waited, hoping for a part. Today, a souvenir shop selling theater memorabilia is located here. Across the street from the Shubert is the legendary **Sardi's** restaurant, 234 W. 44th St., its walls lined with caricatures. Once frequented by theater folks, Sardi's now attracts mostly tourists.

West 42nd Street

Big changes are afoot along 42nd St. between Seventh and Eighth Avenues. For years a center for porn movies, this most historic of theatrical streets is now being slowly returned to its turn-of-the-century grandeur.

Nine historic theaters in various stages of restoration line the block. The Victory, 207 W. 42nd St., opened by Oscar Hammerstein in 1900, is now the **New Victory,** specializing in programming for young people. The **New Amsterdam,** 214 W. 42nd, once home to the Ziegfeld Follies, is now owned by Disney. On its

For discount theater tickets, stop by the TKTS booth at Times Square.

docket are both movies and plays, while next door is the splashy **Disney Store,** 210 W. 42nd St. tel. (212) 221-0430. The **Empire,** 236 W. 42nd; **Liberty,** 234 W. 42nd; and **Harris,** 226 W. 42nd, are being transformed into a movie complex and Madame Tussaud's wax museum.

At 1457 Broadway, just off 42nd Street, is Times Square's newest attraction—the virtual-reality arcade **XS New York,** tel. (212) 398-5467. Inside the extremely noisy, three-story extravaganza, find games ranging from the educational to the violent, along with a restaurant, microbrewery, and cybercafe. Open Sun.-Thurs. 10 a.m.-midnight and Fri.-Sat. 10 a.m.-2 p.m.

Meanwhile, many of the illicit businesses once found on 42nd St. or in Times Square proper have since relocated onto Eighth Avenue. According to the police, Eighth Ave. bet. 40th and 53rd Sts. is now the city's most sex-saturated street.

Port Authority and West
Between 40th and 42nd Sts., Eighth and Ninth Aves., is the Port Authority Bus Terminal, also much cleaned up in recent years but still no place to voluntarily linger. To the rear of the terminal's second floor is the well-kept, '50s-era **Leisure Time Bowling,** tel. (212) 268-6909, one of the only bowling alleys left in Manhattan.

Across the street from the Port Authority is the 1870 **Church of the Holy Cross,** 333 W. 42nd St., studded with windows and mosaics designed by L.C. Tiffany. Father Francis Duffy, chaplain of the "Fighting Irish" 69th Division during WW I, became pastor of the church in 1921 and helped break up the area's notorious Hell's Kitchen gangs (see below). Much beloved by theater people, Duffy is honored with a statue in Times Square, across from the statue of George M. Cohan.

Down the block is the former **McGraw-Hill** building, 330 W. 42nd Street. This blue-green art deco tower was designed by Raymond Hood as a complement to his *Daily News* skyscraper at the eastern end of the street.

Between Ninth and Tenth Aves., 42nd St. is known as **Theater Row** because of the its Off-Broadway theaters. Among them are the **Harold Clurman Theatre,** 412 W. 42nd St., and **Playwrights Horizon,** 416 W. 42nd Street.

> *On any person who desires such queer prizes, New York will bestow the gift of loneliness and the gift of privacy. It is this largess that accounts for the presence within the city's wall of a considerable section of the population: for the residents of Manhattan are to a large extent strangers who have pulled up stakes somewhere and come to town, seeking sanctuary or fulfillment or some greater or lesser grail. The capacity to make such dubious gifts is a mysterious quality of New York. It can destroy an individual, or it can fulfill him, depending a good deal on luck.*
>
> —E.B. WHITE

Hell's Kitchen
Up until a few years ago, the whole area west of Eighth Ave. bet. 23rd and 59th Sts. was usually referred to as Hell's Kitchen. During the late 1800s and much of the 1900s, this seedy part of town was gangland territory, home to such rival groups as the Gophers, the Gorillas, the Hudson Dusters, and more recently, the Westies. The Westies were still in business up until 1987 when former gang member Mickey Featherstone, arrested for murder, testified against his former colleagues in exchange for immunity.

Today, many civic-improvement types prefer to call the northern part of Hell's Kitchen "Clinton," in recognition of the extensive cleanup efforts made here in recent years. Though still home to plenty of crumbling tenements and shady characters, "Clinton," especially around Ninth Ave., is slowly becoming gentrified.

For foodies, Ninth Ave. bet. 37th and 54th Sts. is nirvana. One tiny, often disheveled, ethnic food shop or restaurant follows another in an update of the old pushcart market that flourished here around the turn of the century. Every May, the whole avenue celebrates with a gigantic two-day **Ninth Avenue Food Festival** that draws thousands of people from all over the city.

Intrepid Sea-Air-Space Museum

Docked at Pier 86, on the far western edge of Manhattan, is the Intrepid, W. 46th St. at 12 Ave., tel. (212) 245-0072. A former WWII aircraft carrier now devoted to military history, the museum houses lots of audio visuals and hands-on exhibits, most designed to appeal to kids. The decks are strewn with small aircraft and space capsules; permanent exhibits explore the mysteries of satellite communication and ship design; special exhibits focus on such subjects as women pilots and Charles Lindbergh. Open May 1-Sept. 30, Mon.-Sat. 10 a.m.-5 p.m., Sunday 10 a.m.-6 p.m.; Oct. 1-April 30, Wed.-Sun. 10 a.m.-5 p.m. Admission is adults $10; veterans, senior citizens, and students 12-17 $7.50; children 6-11 $5, children under 6 $1.

BRYANT PARK TO THE DIAMOND DISTRICT

New York Public Library

Filling two blocks of Fifth Ave. bet. 40th and 42nd Sts., this lavish beaux arts building, houses one of the world's top five research libraries. The library's vast collection of over nine million books and 21 million other objects occupies some 88 miles of shelves above ground and 84 miles below.

Designed by Carrere & Hastings, and completed in 1911, the library occupies the former site of Croton Reservoir, a huge 150-million-gallon granite water tank that stood here from 1842 to 1900. The promenade that once encircled the top of the reservoir was a popular place from which to take in the local sights.

Libraries aren't usually worth touring, but the New York Public Library is an exception. On the main floor is an elaborate entrance hall with a vaulted ceiling and wide sweeping staircases. Behind the entrance hall is **Gottesman Hall,** where unusual exhibits on such subjects as illustrator Charles Addams or photographer Berenice Abbott are displayed.

Big as a football field, the Main Reading Room on the third floor is the library's highlight. Books are ordered via a pneumatic tube system that sucks call slips down into the bowels of the stacks. Also on the third floor is the Map Room—where the U.S. Army planned the invasion of

Patience, or is it Fortitude? outside the New York Public Library

North Africa during WW II—and the Science and Technology Room, where Chester Carlson invented Xerox and Edwin Land invented the Polaroid camera.

The stone lions lounging on the library's front steps were originally named "Leo Astor" and "Leo Lenox," after the library's founders John Jacob Astor and James Lenox. Later, in the 1930s, Mayor La Guardia dubbed the felines "Patience" and "Fortitude"—qualities he felt New York would need to survive the Depression. A popular saying of that time had it that the lions roared whenever a virgin passed by, but no one's mentioned that bit of folklore in years.

Free tours of the library are given Mon.-Sat. at 12:30 and 2:30 p.m. For exhibit information, call (212) 869-8089.

Bryant Park

Just behind the library is the recently restored Bryant Park, filled with pretty flower beds, gravel paths, a stylish indoor-outdoor restaurant, and lots of benches that are usually packed with office workers at lunchtime. The park is named after poet and journalist William Cullen Bryant, a great proponent of parks and one of the people most responsible for the creation of Central Park.

ICP Midtown

Heading north one block, you'll find the largely subterranean Midtown branch of the International Center of Photography at 1133 Sixth Ave., at 43rd St., tel. (212) 768-4680. Like its parent institution on E. 94th St., the spacious center presents some of the city's most important photography exhibits. Hours are Tues. 11 a.m.-8 p.m., Wed.-Sun. 11 a.m.-6 p.m. Admission is adults $4, students and seniors $2.50, children under 12 $1; free Tues. 6-8 p.m.

The Algonquin and Vicinity

At the famed old Algonquin Hotel, 59 W. 44th St., bet. Fifth and Sixth Aves., Dorothy Parker and friends assembled in the 1920s at a round table in the Rose Room. Notable residents have included editor H.L. Mencken, who stayed here in 1914 while starting up the magazine *The Smart Set* with George Nathan; writer James Thurber, who lived here for long periods in the 1930s and 1950s; and actor Douglas Fairbanks who, while living here from 1907 to 1915, did gymnastics on the roof. Today the venerable Algonquin remains cozy and old-fashioned.

Across the street from the Algonquin are *The New Yorker* editorial offices, 5 W. 45th St.; and the 1898 **Royalton Hotel,** 44 W. 44th St., transformed by Ian Schrager of Studio 54 fame into a sleek, artsy, and very expensive hostelry. Next door to the Algonquin is the **Iroquois Hotel,** 49 W. 44th St., where James Dean lived as a young actor in 1951. The first thing friends saw upon entering Dean's apartment was the shadow of a hangman's noose, created by a small model of a gallows that Dean had backlit.

The Diamond District

Continuing north, you'll come to the Diamond District, W. 47th St. bet. Fifth and Sixth Aves., where an estimated $400 million in gems is exchanged daily. Many of the dealers and cutters are Hasidic Jews, with their long beards and sidelocks, and somber black frock coats. As has long been their tradition, the Hasidim often negotiate their biggest deals in back rooms or out on the sidewalks. Their shops cater primarily to the tourist trade.

ROCKEFELLER CENTER AND VICINITY

The area between 48th and 51st Sts., and Fifth and Sixth Aves., was once a notorious red-light district. Today it's occupied by New York's most famous city within a city, Rockefeller Center. Built by John D. Rockefeller during the height of the Depression, the magnificent art deco complex is comprised of 19 buildings, connected by plazas and underground passageways. Throughout the year, thousands of tourists and New Yorkers, street performers and the homeless, congregate here daily.

Rockefeller called upon his international contacts to sponsor the center, which helps account for its international feel. On the Fifth Ave. side, bet. 49th and 50th Sts., the wryly named **Channel Gardens** separate the **British Empire Building** to the north from **La Maison Française** to the south. Lovely friezes adorn both buildings' facades, while their ground floors are filled with international shops and tourism offices.

The Channel Gardens lead to the sunken **Lower Plaza** at the heart of the complex. This plaza offers an outdoor restaurant in summer, an ice-skating rink in winter, and great people-watching year-round. All around the plaza are towering flagpoles bearing brightly colored banners flapping in the wind, while at one end lounges an ungainly gilded Prometheus. At Christmastime, the famous Rockefeller tree is erected directly behind him.

Just west of Lower Plaza is **30 Rockefeller Plaza,** a wonderful, 70-story art deco skyscraper designed by Raymond Hood. Still known as the RCA building—though its correct name these days is the GE building—it features a bearded bas-relief of *Genius* above its door. Inside the lobby is a rather bland mural, *American Progress,* painted by Jose Maria Sert to replace a much more controversial one by Diego Rivera. Commissioned by Rockefeller to create the original artwork, Rivera chose to depict Lenin and the proletariat taking over industry while important plutocrats were being eaten away by syphilis. Not surprisingly, that was too much for Rockefeller, and he had it replaced. At the top of the RCA building is the famed **Rainbow Room,** featuring a revolving dance floor, big bands, and magnificent views.

Also in 30 Rockefeller Plaza are the **NBC Studios,** tel. (212) 664-4000, where you can take a tour, or—if you're lucky—pick up free standby tickets for *Late Night With Conan O'Brian.* Call for more information regarding these tickets, or tickets to *Saturday Night Live,* which are granted by lottery in advance. The NBC Studio Tours last one hour, and leave every 15 minutes 9:15 a.m.-4:30 p.m. daily, with extended hours in spring and summer. Tickets cost $10 per person and are distributed on a first-come, first-served basis beginning at 9 a.m. Come early, as they go fast. Children under six are not admitted.

For walking tour maps and general information on Rockefeller Center, stop by the **Visitors' Bureau** in the lobby of 30 Rockefeller Plaza; tel. (212) 632-3975. The bureau is open Mon.-Fri. 8:30 a.m.-5 p.m.

Radio City Music Hall

Despite, or perhaps because of, its dated feel, this art deco landmark at the corner of Sixth Ave. and 50th St. has been bringing them back for generations. An over-the-top creation with a stage as wide as a city block, it's the world's largest indoor theater.

Part of Rockefeller Center, the Music Hall was largely created by impresario Samuel Lionel Rothafel, nicknamed Roxy. Born in a Lower East Side tenement, Roxy began his career by showing movies in the back room of a bar. From that humble beginning, he soon rose to become a major power in show business, producing radio shows and plays, and managing a string of theaters including the sumptuous Roxy which once stood in Times Square.

Roxy had a hand in designing the Music Hall; the magnificent, egg-shaped, 6,200-seat auditorium is said to be based on an idea he had while sailing on an ocean liner at dawn. The proscenium arch, painted with multicolored rays, represents the sun, while the carpet adorned with art deco fish represents the sea. Roxy also equipped his theater with all the latest technology of the day, including four elevators for the raising and lowering of scenery, machines capable of creating rain and steam, and the "Mighty Wurlitzer," an organ loud enough to be heard in the subway below.

Though the Music Hall has hosted many unusual performers over the years—including elephants and horses—its most famous are the Rockettes. Chorus girls all between five feet four inches and five feet seven inches in height, the Rockettes once appeared nightly. Now they kick and strut their stuff only during the Music Hall's two-month-long Christmas show.

One-hour backstage tours of the Music Hall are offered Mon.-Sat. 10 a.m.-5 p.m. and Sun. 11 a.m.-5 p.m. The tour costs adults $13.75, children under 12 $9; call (212) 247-4777 for more information.

Two Fifth Avenue Churches

On Fifth Ave. bet. 50th and 51st Sts. is **St. Patrick's Cathedral,** the largest Roman Catholic cathedral in the United States. Designed by James Renwick, this elaborate Gothic creation with its soaring towers and lovely rose window took 21 years to build, replacing the old St. Pat's in Little Italy in 1879. Its grandeur attests to the success of New York's Irish Catholic immigrants who, at the time the church was being built, were largely shunned by the city's predominantly Protestant upper classes. Back then, some snooty upper crusts even went out of their way not to cross in front of the cathedral.

Kitty-corner to St. Pat's, at the corner of 53rd St., is another famous New York church, the Protestant Episcopal **St. Thomas Church,** completed in 1914. A French Gothic gem known for its lovely stonework and stained glass, the church has long been a favorite site for society weddings. St. Thomas has a wonderful choir that can be heard on Sunday mornings or daily at evensong. Call (212) 757-7013 for more information.

52nd Street

Back in the 1930s and '40s, more great musicians congregated on 52nd St. bet. Fifth and Sixth Aves. than anyplace else in the world, before or since. Art Tatum, Billie Holiday, Cole-

statuary at St. Thomas Church

man Hawkins, Oran "Hot Lips" Page, Roy Eldridge, Teddy Wilson, Fats Waller, Erroll Garner, Mary Lou Williams, Dizzy Gillespie, Charlie Parker, Miles Davis, Sarah Vaughan, Count Basie, Woody Herman, Buddy Rich, Dave Tough, George Shearing—all were here.

The magic began just after Prohibition when New York's jazz epicenter began shifting from Harlem to downtown. "The Street" at that time was lined with dark and smoky speakeasies, all housed in dilapidated brownstones with tiny vestibules, long bars, pressed-tin ceilings, and water-stained walls.

The first music club to open on 52nd St. was the Onyx, later dubbed the "Cradle of Swing." Then came the Famous Door, named for the door inscribed with autographs that sat on a small platform near the bar; the Downbeat, where Dizzy Gillespie often played; and the Three Deuces, a regular gig for Erroll Garner. The Street's most famous club, Birdland—named after Charlie Parker—was not actually on 52nd St. at all, but around the corner at 1674 Broadway, in a building that still stands.

The Street began to decline after WW II, and today all but one of the brownstones have been torn down, replaced by modern skyscrapers. The only reminders of the past are the street signs reading "Swing Street," and the sidewalk plaques embedded near Sixth Ave. that honor some of the jazz greats.

The one brownstone that *does* remain is the upscale **"21" Club,** 21 W. 52nd St., tel. (212) 582-7200. The restaurant is marked by a line of miniature cast-iron jockeys out front.

Museum of Television and Radio

This shiny museum at 25 W. 52nd St., bet. Fifth and Sixth Aves., tel. (212) 621-6800, was founded by William Paley and designed by Philip Johnson. Here you can watch your favorite old TV show, listen to a classic radio broadcast, or research pop-culture subjects such as '50s sitcoms or beer commercials. In the museum for your listening and viewing pleasure are 96 semi-private radio and television consoles, two large theaters, and two screening rooms.The museum also offers more traditional exhibits on such topics as animation and costume design.

The museum is open Tues.-Wed. and Fri.-Sun. noon-6 p.m., Thurs. noon-8 p.m. If you're interested in using one of the consoles on the weekend, it's advisable to come early. Admission is adults $6, students $4, senior citizens and children under 13 $3.

The Museum of Modern Art (MoMA)

MoMA, 11 W. 53rd St., bet. Fifth and Sixth Aves., tel. (212) 708-9480, is one of the world's foremost museums of modern art. Opened in 1929, shortly after the crash of the stock market, the museum's collection includes over 100,000 paintings, sculptures, drawings, prints, and photographs, and some 10,000 films and four million film stills.

MoMA's interior is awash in light. At the building's center is a huge glass atrium filled with crisscrossing escalators, while just outside is a lovely sculpture garden with works by Picasso, Rodin, Matisse, and others.

Most of MoMA's temporary exhibits are hung on its ground floor and basement level, while the permanent painting and sculpture collections are on the second and third floors. Nearly every work here is a masterpiece; among the many highlights are Cezanne's *The Bather,* Van Gogh's *Starry Night,* Rousseau's *The Sleeping Gypsy,* Magritte's *The Empire of Light,* Hopper's *Gas,* Rothko's *Red, Brown and Black,* de Chirico's *The Song of Love,* and Picasso's *Les Demoiselles d'Avignon.* One whole room is devoted to Monet's *Water Lilies;* other whole rooms to Mondrian, Pollock, and Matisse.

Also on the museum's second floor are superb photography and drawing collections, while on the third floor are prints and illustrated books. The small fourth floor, which feels a bit like an afterthought, is devoted to architecture and design. In the basement is a comfortable auditorium where classic, foreign, and experimental films are screened.

The museum's biggest drawback is that it's often very crowded, especially on weekends. Ditto the adjacent **MoMA Book Store,** which sells an excellent collection of cards and art books, and the **MoMA Design Store** across the street, selling everything from art nouveau furniture to wristwatches.

MoMA is open Sat.-Tues. 11 a.m.-6 p.m., and Thurs.-Fri. noon-8:30 p.m. Admission is adults $8.50, students and senior citizens $5.50, children under 16 free, except Thurs.-Fri. 5:30-8:30 p.m., when you may pay what you wish. Films are included in the admission price, but tickets must be picked up at the entrance.

American Craft Museum

Directly across the street from MoMA, this museum, 40 W. 53rd St., tel. (212) 956-3535, is engaged in an ambitious decade-long exhibit series tracing the history of American crafts. Exquisite textiles, ceramics, glasswork, and other crafts are on display, but unfortunately, the exhibits often seem to be more geared toward experts than the general public. Still, if you've any interest in crafts, the museum and its unique, albeit pricey, gift shop are well worth a look.

Hours are Tues. 10 a.m.-8 p.m., Wed.-Sun. 10 a.m.-5 p.m. In addition, the gift shop is open Mon. 10 a.m.-5 p.m. Admission is adults $5, students and seniors $2.50, children under 12 free.

Rock's Demise

Poor Nelson Rockefeller met his inopportune death in the gorgeous family townhouse at 13 W. 54th St. at 11:15 p.m. on Jan. 26, 1979. At first, an official spokesperson tried to claim that the 71-year-old former New York governor had died an hour earlier in his nearby office. But as the truth emerged, it turned out that Rocky had not only died at home, but had also suffered his fatal heart attack while in the company of his attractive, 25-year-old assistant, Megan Marshack. Marshack had been dressed in a black evening gown.

Happy Rockefeller had her husband's body cremated the day after his death; Marshack has never spoken publicly about her last night with Rocky.

THE EAST 50s

Villard Houses/Helmsley Palace Hotel

On Madison Ave. bet. 49th and 50th Sts. are the Villard Houses, a group of six Italianate brownstones now incorporated into the Helmsley Palace Hotel. Built for railroad magnate Henry Villard in 1886 by McKim, Mead & White, the houses center around a courtyard, with the glitzy glass hotel tower rising behind. It's incongruous, but the old houses have been well restored. Especially wonderful are two sweeping staircases and the Gold Room, built to resemble the music room of an Italian Renaissance palace.

Leona Helmsley—wife of real estate kingpin and Helmsley Palace Hotel developer Harry Helmsley—was convicted of tax evasion in 1989 and sentenced to four years in prison. New York had a field day with her trial, with the tabloids dubbing her the "Queen of Mean," the TV stations gleefully reporting her every indiscretion, and the public rubbing their hands over her downfall. There's no doubt that Leona did deserve her nickname—this is a woman who once said, "I don't pay taxes. The little people pay taxes." But the ferocity of the attack upon her was hardly New York's finest hour.

Appropriately, the north wing of the Villard Houses serves as the **Urban Center,** of the **Municipal Art Society,** 457 Madison Ave., tel. (212) 935-3960, an organization dedicated to historic preservation and urban planning. The center holds an excellent bookstore and exhibition halls where temporary shows on the city's history and architecture are mounted. Hours are Mon.-Wed. and Fri.-Sat. 11 a.m.-5 p.m. Admission is free.

Waldorf-Astoria

At 301 Park Ave., bet. 49th and 50th Sts., is the extravagant Waldorf-Astoria Hotel. When rebuilt on this location in 1931 (the original stood at 34th St. and Fifth Ave.), it was the world's tallest, most lavish hotel, with 2,200 rooms, 2,700 telephones, and 16 elevators, one of which was big enough to take a limousine up to the ballroom for the annual automobile exhibition.

Now a Hilton hotel catering to a largely business clientele, the Waldorf has lost its exclusive edge but is still well worth a look. Recently restored, it features a lobby filled with marble, bronze, and wood, and a giant 1893 clock built for the Chicago Columbian Exposition.

Looking south from the Waldorf, you'll see Park Ave. swerve to both sides around a white beaux arts building with a splendid gold roof. Also now owned by the Helmsleys, the 1929 **Helmsley Building** is especially lovely at night, when its lit roof serves as a beacon for the Upper East Side.

All of this section of Park Ave. was once an open railroad yard, and the tracks leading to Grand Central still run beneath it. The avenue itself is actually just a thin skin of metal and pavement, held up and together with planks, while the buildings on either side stand on stilts wedged between the tracks. Sometimes, as the cars whisk past, you can hear the avenue clanking.

St. Bartholomew's

On Park Ave. bet. 50th and 51st Sts. is the romantic Romanesque dome of St. Bartholomew's Church, looking oddly dwarfish compared to the towering General Electric Building behind it. The church was designed by architect Stanford White. Inside, an elaborate mosaicked ceiling depicts the story of Creation.

Two Architectural Landmarks

The **Seagram's Building,** on the east side of Park Ave. bet. 52nd and 53rd Sts., was designed in 1958 by Ludwig Mies van Der Rohe and Philip Johnson. It was unusual at the time for its spare, streamlined construction, and its wide, wide plaza. Still considered one of New York's finest skyscrapers, it's home to the famed **Four Seasons Restaurant.**

On the west side of Park Ave. bet. 53rd and 54th Sts. is the **Lever House,** designed by Skidmore, Owings & Merrill in 1952. It was the city's first glass-encased office tower and was used as a model by dozens of other architects. Today, the Lever House doesn't look all that unusual, but back in the 1950s, surrounded by heavy stone apartment buildings, it was as alien as a spaceship.

Citicorp Building and Vicinity

The gleaming skyscraper with the strange sloping roof at the corner of Lexington Ave. and 54th St. is the Citicorp Building, built in 1978. On its lower level is an indoor courtyard filled with tables and chairs, and surrounded by stores and gourmet takeout eateries.

BIG APPLE ATRIUMS

Scattered throughout Midtown are numerous hidden atriums and courtyards that offer a welcome respite from the madding crowds. Some of these free public spaces are landscaped with plants and waterfalls, while others hold restaurants and shops.

The atriums of the **Ford Foundation,** 320 E. 42nd St.; the **Sony Building,** Madison Ave. at 55th St.; and **Citicorp Center,** Lexington Ave. at 53rd St., are covered elsewhere in this chapter. Also noteworthy are the atriums at **Olympic Tower,** Fifth Ave. and 51st St., filled with inviting benches, a waterfall, and a first-class Japanese restaurant called **Shinwa,** tel. (212) 644-7400; the **IBM Garden Plaza,** Madison Ave. at 56th St., equipped with tables and chairs, towering bamboo trees, and a refreshment kiosk; and **Equitable Center,** 787 Seventh Ave., bet. 51st and 52nd Sts., which features many shops and restaurants, along with stunning artwork by Roy Lichtenstein, Thomas Hart Benton, and others.

Also in the Citicorp Building is **St. Peter's Lutheran Church,** tel. (212) 935-3300, a big, modern sanctuary with towering ceilings. Nicknamed the "jazz church" because of its ministrations to the jazz community, St. Peter's hosts frequent jazz events, including Sunday afternoon jazz vespers, Sunday evening jazz concerts, and free Wednesday noontime concerts.

Kitty-corner to St. Peter's, at Lexington Ave. and 55th St., is **Central Synagogue.** Designed in 1872 by Henry Fernbach, the first Jewish architect in New York, it's the oldest synagogue in continual use in the state.

Meanwhile, on a more frivolous note, it was at the northwest corner of Lexington Ave. and E. 52nd St. that a draft from a subway vent blew up Marilyn Monroe's skirt in *The Seven Year Itch.* The now-famed scene took place in front of the since demolished Trans Lux theater, but the subway vent is still there.

Sony Wonder Lab
On Madison Ave. bet. 55th and 56th Sts. is the Sony Building, whose soaring atrium houses several gourmet takeout shops and something called the Sony Wonder Technology Lab. Part giant advertisement, part electronics amuse-ment park, the four-story "lab" is packed with dozens of high-tech video games, along with a sound board and editing console where you can play at producing CDs and videos of Sony recording artists. The lab, tel. (212) 833-8830, is open Tues.-Sat. 10 a.m.-6 p.m., Sunday noon-6 p.m. Admission is free.

Trump Tower
At Fifth Ave. and 56th St. stands the notorious Trump Tower, tel. (212) 832-2000, a glittering rose-and-gilt edifice with its own nexus of shops. Open daily 8 a.m.-10 p.m. (the building, not the shops, whose hours vary), Trump Tower boasts a skinny cascading waterfall, far too much brass, and a multitude of glitzy escalators. On the top level is **Trump Gifts,** where you can buy T-shirts and coffee mugs with the Trump Tower logo, along with your very own recorded edition of Donald Trump's personal manifesto, *Trump, The Art of the Deal.*

57TH STREET AND THE PLAZA

57th Street
Like 42nd St., 57th St. is one of the city's major

THE GYPSY TEA KETTLE WHISTLES FORTUNES

"Mrs. Crystal will read your entire life without asking a single question." "Mrs. Lisa tells—past—present—future." "Thousands of people who have been CROSSED, HAVE SPELLS, CAN'T HOLD MONEY, WANT LUCK, WANT THEIR LOVED ONES BACK, WANT TO STOP NATURE PROBLEMS or WANT TO GET RID OF STRANGE SICKNESS . . . are amazed at the results gotten by MRS. STELLA."

Walk the streets of Manhattan for any length of time and chances are good a silent dark-haired man will hand you a flyer printed with promises similar to these. Follow the flyer's advice, and you'll probably find yourself in a small storefront where a woman dressed in long flowing garments sits next to a crystal ball. In the back, children and cats hover.

Though not as plentiful as they were just a few years ago, dozens of unlicensed and unregulated fortune-tellers dot the streets of Manhattan. Many are Gypsies—or Roma, as they preferred to be called —who've immigrated here from Eastern Eu-rope. Others are "professional" astrologers, psychics, and New Age spiritualists. The former usually charge around $10 to read your palm or the tarot cards; the latter charge $20-50 and up, and advertise in the Yellow Pages.

One creaky and highly regarded mecca for those seeking a glimpse into the future is the **Gypsy Tea Kettle,** located on the second floor of 137 E. 56th St., at Lexington, tel. (212) 752-5890. "Tea Leaves Read Gratis" states a sign in the window, while inside sit eight readers ready to predict your future through the tarot cards. A 15-minute reading costs $10; tips are strongly encouraged.

The Tearoom, as it is more popularly known, was first established back in 1930, when its restaurateur founder added fortune-telling to his menu to attract more customers. The idea took off and soon the food was dropped in favor of full-time soothsaying. In the 1940s, the Tearoom stopped reading tea leaves and began reading tarot cards instead.

east-west thoroughfares and one that changes character as it heads crosstown. To the east, 57th is the poshest of areas, with some of the city's most expensive boutiques and art galleries. To the west, the street becomes sort of an outdoor theme park for adults.

Among the most famous galleries on 57th St. are **PaceWildenstein,** 32 E. 57th St., tel. (212) 421-3292, which represents such heavyweights as Picasso, Louise Nevelson, and Julian Schnabel; and **Andre Emmerich,** 41 E. 57th St., tel. (212) 752-0124, where work by David Hockney and Helen Frankenthaler is frequently shown. **Robert Miller,** also at 41 E. 57th St., tel. (212) 980-5454, exhibited the late Robert Mapplethorpe's controversial photographs, and the **Marlborough,** 40 W. 57th, tel. (212) 541-4900, represents such artists as Larry Rivers and Francis Bacon. **Sidney Janis,** 110 W. 57th, tel. (212) 586-0110, exhibits everyone from Piet Mondrian to Annie Liebowitz. The **Mary Boone Gallery,** once a fixture on the SoHo scene, is now located at 745 Fifth Ave., bet. 57th and 58th Sts., tel. (212) 752-2929. Come here to view the works of David Salle and Eric Fischl, Barbara Kruger, and Bryan Hunt, to name but a few.

To find out about other galleries, or about who's exhibiting where, pick up a copy of the *Art Now Gallery Guide,* available at many bookstores and galleries. Or check magazine or Sunday newspaper listings.

As for that theme park, the fun begins at Sixth Avenue. On Sixth Ave. one block south of 57th St. is the glitzy **Harley Davidson Cafe,** tel. (212) 245-6000, adorned with motorbikes and leather jackets. On 57th St. just north of Sixth Ave. is the **Jekyll and Hyde Club,** tel. (212) 541-9505, decked out with sinking bar stools and talking corpses. On 57th St. proper are the **Motown Cafe,** 104 W. 57th St., tel. (212) 581-8030, featuring ersatz Motown performers in an art deco setting; **Planet Hollywood,** 140 W. 57th St., bet. Sixth and Seventh Aves., tel. (212) 333-7827, jam-packed with stuff once worn by the stars; and the **Hard Rock Cafe,** 221 W. 57th St., bet. Broadway and Seventh Ave., tel. (212) 459-9320, bejewelled with shiny guitars and gold records.

Tourists line up by the thousands to get into these joints, which are marked by obsequious service and a profusion of souvenirs for sale;

an essential part of each visit seems to be purchasing the de rigueur T-shirt. The whole scene is a complete mystery to most New Yorkers, but hey, as your cab driver will tell you, who are they to judge?

Other addresses to watch out for on W. 57th St. include the famed **Russian Tea Room,** 150 W. 57th, tel. (212) 265-0947, now under renovation; and **Carnegie Hall,** W. 57th St. at Seventh Ave., tel. (212) 247-7800. The dean of concert halls since its completion in 1891, Carnegie Hall was originally built by Andrew Carnegie as a home for the Oratorio Society, of which he was then president.

The Plaza

Just west of Fifth Ave. bet. 58th and 59th Sts. stands the famed Plaza Hotel, still one of New York's loveliest buildings. Designed by Henry Hardenbergh in 1907, it's built in a French Renaissance style, with lots of dormers, high roofs, and rounded corners. In 1988, the hotel was

the Plaza Hotel, a French Renaissance gem

bought and extensively renovated by real-estate mogul Donald Trump and his then-wife Ivana.

The **Palm Court,** in the hotel's lobby, is decorated with white marble columns, small tea tables, and fresh flowers. In the back is the comfortable **Oak Bar,** paneled in heavy wood. Both are ridiculously expensive and frequented by hordes of people, but are nevertheless excellent spots in which to get a taste of old New York.

The hotel stands on the edge of Grand Army Plaza, home of the ornate Pulitzer Memorial Fountain. To the north is Central Park, and a gathering place for the horse-drawn hansoms that clip-clop their way throughout this part of town. No New Yorker ever rides these things, but many tourists love them; rates are $20 for the first half-hour, $5 for each additional half-hour.

SHOPPING

Books, Newspapers, Maps

Tucked in between the glittering jewelry stores in the Diamond District is one of the city's most historic bookstores, the **Gotham Book Mart,** 41 W. 47th St., bet. Fifth and Sixth Aves., tel. (212) 719-4448. The store was established in 1920 by Frances Steloff, who was an early supporter of such writers as James Joyce, Henry Miller, and T.S. Eliot.

In Rockefeller Center is the one-of-a-kind **New York Bound Bookshop,** 50 Rockefeller Pl., off Fifth Ave. and 50th St., tel. (212) 245-8503, specializing in books about the city; and **Traveller's Bookstore,** 22 W. 52nd St., near Fifth Ave., tel. (212) 664-0995, carrying both guidebooks and travel literature. Nearby is **Urban Center Books,** 457 Madison Ave., bet. 50th and 51st Sts., tel. (212) 935-3595, specializing in books on architecture and urban design.

Major chains on Fifth Ave. are **B. Dalton's,** 666 Fifth Ave., at 52nd St., tel. (212) 247-1740; **Doubleday's,** 724 Fifth Ave., bet. 56th and 57th Sts., tel. (212) 397-0550 (open until midnight, Mon.-Sat.); and **Barnes & Noble,** 600 Fifth Ave., at 48th St., tel. (212) 765-0590. The classy, wood-paneled **Rizzoli,** 31 W. 57th St., tel. (212) 759-2424, stocks an especially fine collection of art and photography books.

Coliseum Books, 1771 Broadway, at 57th St., tel. (212) 757-8381, is the city's largest independent bookstore, carrying a superb selection. It's open until 11 p.m. daily except Sunday. **Mysterious Book Shop,** 129 W. 56th St., bet. Sixth and Seventh Aves., tel. (212) 765-0900, sells hardcover, paperback, new, and used. The **Argosy,** 116 E. 59th St., bet. Park and Lexington Aves., tel. (212) 753-4455, carries an excellent selection of used books.

Hotalings Foreign News Depot, 142 W. 42nd St., at Broadway, tel. (212) 840-1868, is New York's best store for out-of-town newspapers. **Hagstrom Map and Travel Center,** 57 W. 43rd St., bet. Fifth and Sixth Aves., tel. (212) 398-1222, stocks an impossible number of maps. The **Rand McNally Map & Travel Store,** 150 E. 52nd St., bet. Lexington and Third Aves., tel. (212) 758-7488, also stocks a good selection of maps, along with travel guides and travel accessories.

Department Stores

Lots of fun for both shopping aand browsing is **Saks Fifth Avenue,** 611 Fifth Ave., bet. 49th and 50th Sts., tel. (212) 753-4000, a wonderfully plush store with high-quality merchandise. **Henri Bendel,** 712 Fifth Ave., bet. 55th and 56th Sts., tel. (212) 247-1100, is frequented by the very rich and the very thin. **Bergdorf Goodman,** 754 Fifth Ave., tel. (212) 753-7300, bet. 57th and 58th Sts., is a favorite among wealthy socialites. New to Fifth Ave. as of the early 1990s is the Japanese department store, **Takashimaya,** 693 Fifth Ave., near 53rd St., tel. (212) 350-0100. An elegant mansionlike place with a soaring atrium, it feels more like a museum than a store, and does indeed present frequent art exhibits.

Food Shops

At the lower end of the Ninth Ave. food-shopping stretch, around 40th St., are **Manganaro's,** 488 Ninth Ave., tel. (212) 563-5331, an 1893 Italian grocery store that also sells six-foot-long hero sandwiches; **Esposito & Sons Meat Shop,** 500 Ninth Ave., tel. (212) 279-3298, selling pork chops, pork knuckles, pork brain, pigs' feet, and the like; and **Ninth Avenue Cheese Market,** 615 Ninth Ave. tel. (212) 397-4700. selling dozens of varieties. The twin **International Groceries,** 529 Ninth Ave., tel. (212) 279-5514, and

International Foods, 543 Ninth Ave., tel. (212) 279-1000, are spic-and-span markets run by two Greek brothers.

Around 45th St. are the 1908 **Empire Coffee & Tea Company,** 592 Ninth Ave., tel. (212) 596-1717, one of the oldest gourmet coffee shops in town; and **Poseidon Bakery,** 629 Ninth Ave., tel. (212) 757-6173, a Greek shop that has been hand-rolling phyllo dough for about 75 years. Everything at **Amy's Bread,** 672 Ninth Ave., near 50th St., tel. (212) 977-3856, is homemade.

Health and Beauty
Two of the city's oldest and most respected salons are **Elizabeth Arden,** 691 Fifth Ave., bet. 54th and 55th Sts., tel. (212) 546-0200; and **Georgette Klinger,** 501 Madison Ave., bet. 52nd and 53rd Sts., tel. (212) 838-3200.

At **Osaka Health Center,** 50 W. 56th St., bet. Fifth and Sixth Aves., tel. (212) 682-1778, masseurs can knead your knots or walk on your back. **Caswell-Massey,** 518 Lexington Ave., at 48th St., tel. (212) 755-2254, is Manhattan's oldest apothecary. The wood-paneled den dates back to 1752, and claims to have sold George Washington his shaving cream.

Jewelry and Glass
The well-known **Cartier's** is at 653 Fifth Ave., bet. 52nd and 53rd Sts., tel. (212) 753-0111, but if you're in the market for jewelry, you'll probably be much happier just up the street at **Tiffany's,** 727 Fifth Ave., bet. 56th and 57th Sts., tel. (212) 755-8000. In Truman Capote's *Breakfast at Tiffany's,* character Holly Golightly opines, "Nothing bad can ever happen to you at Tiffany's," and she may be right. The store is as classy as Cartier's, but much friendlier. Another exclusive store that nonetheless welcomes the hoi polloi is **Steuben's Glass,** 717 Fifth Ave., tel. (212) 424-4240 or (800) 424-4240, which is filled with darkened halls spotlighted with works of glass.

Music and Musical Instruments
Just east of Broadway on W. 48th St. is a row of top-notch musical-instrument stores, including **Sam Ash,** 160 W. 48th St., tel. (212) 719-2299; **Manny's,** 156 W. 48th St., tel. (212) 819-0576; and the **International Woodwind & Brass Cen-**ter, 174 W. 48th St., tel. (212) 575-1508. **Colony Records,** 1619 Broadway, at 49th St., tel. (212) 265-2050, is the largest provider of sheet music in New York City. **Steinway & Sons,** 109 W. 57th St., bet. Sixth and Seventh Aves., tel. (212) 246-1100, is a lovely, old-fashioned piano showroom.

The three-tiered **Virgin Megastore,** 1540 Broadway, bet. 45th and 46th Sts., tel. (212) 921-1020, bills itself as "the largest music and entertainment store in the world." Inside find more than a million CDs, 7,400 film titles on laserdisc, and 20,000 video tapes. Also on site are a bookstore and a cafe.

Souvenirs and Sneakers
Near 56th St. is a strange new addition to Fifth Avenue—the **Coca-Cola Company,** 711 Fifth Ave., tel. (212) 355-5475. Always packed with tourists, this seems to be the place to go to get those essential Coca-Cola bottles, mugs, postcards, and socks. Along the same lines is the new **Warner Brothers Studio Store** at Fifth Ave. and 57th St., tel. (212) 754-0300, a three-story extravaganza filled with video screens, life-size cartoon characters, and kitschy souvenirs.

Homage to the almighty sneaker is paid at **Niketown,** 6 E. 57th St., at Fifth Ave., tel. (212) 891-6453, a sleek gray emporium built in neo-art deco style. As many as 30,000 people a day are said to pass through this five-story shrine, which sits on prime Manhattan real estate. Inside, you'll find not only Nike sneakers and clothing, but also multiple aquariums, a recreated "Town Square," a short film, and museum-style cases displaying Nike sneakers once worn by such stars as Michael Jordan.

Toys and Games
Across the street from the Plaza Hotel is **F.A.O. Schwarz,** 767 Fifth Ave., at 58th St., tel. (212) 644-9400, a vast, highly imaginative, and super-expensive toy emporium that's as much fun for adults as it is for kids.

Other Shops
Kaufman Surplus, 319 W. 42nd St., near Eighth Ave., tel. (212) 757-5670, is an excellent military surplus store that often sells uniforms and military paraphernalia to Broadway shows.

Manhattan Art & Antiques Center, 1050 Second Ave., just south of 57th St., tel. (212) 355-4400, houses about 100 small antique shops. At **How-to Video Source,** 953 Third Ave, at 57th St., tel. (212) 486-8155, you can pick up videos on everything from "How to Draw Comics the Marvel Way" to "How to Butcher Wild Game." **Hammacher Schlemmer,** 147 E. 57th St., near Lexington, tel. (212) 421-9000, and at other Midtown locations, features the world's most imaginative and expensive high-tech gadgets. The **Uncle Sam Umbrella Shop,** 161 W. 57th St., bet. Sixth and Seventh Aves., tel. (212) 582-1976, is a genteel establishment that has been selling handmade umbrellas and canes for over 130 years.

ACCOMMODATIONS

Inexpensive
East Side: One of the better deals in the city is **Pickwick Arms,** 230 E. 51st St., bet. Third and Second Aves., tel. (212) 355-0300 or (800) PICKWIK, on a quiet block that's nonetheless near everything. The Pickwick's rooms are small but comfortable, and there's a sundeck on the roof. The cheapest single rooms share bathrooms. $55-75 s, $105 d.

The **Allerton House for Women,** 130 E. 57th St., at Lexington Ave., tel. (212) 753-8841, is a for-women-only hotel with tiny, spartan rooms and a worn, spacious lobby that's almost devoid of furniture. Book as far ahead as possible, as the hotel is largely residential, and be prepared to assist with doors and elevators—many of the residents are in their 70s and 80s. On the roof is a sundeck. $58 s, $75 d.

West Side: A theater hotel since 1904, the small **Portland Square Hotel,** 132 W. 47th St., bet. Sixth and Seventh Aves., tel. (212) 382-0600 or (800) 388-8988, is a good choice for budget travelers. The rooms are spartan but adequate and clean. Photographs of Broadway in the '20s and '30s line the utilitarian lobby and hallways; James Cagney was once a resident here. $50-75 s, $89-99 d; cheaper single rooms share baths.

Moderate
East Side: The homey, old-fashioned **Beverly,** 125 E. 50th St., at Lexington Ave., tel. (212) 753-2700 or (800) 223-0945, feels as if it should be filled with visiting maiden aunts. The service is down-home friendly, and the rooms are good-sized floral affairs filled with plump sofas, big beds, and old-fashioned writing tables. Among the hotel's services are hair stylists and a 24-hour prescription service. $159 s, $169 d.

West Side: Two of the best deals in the Theater District are the **Broadway Inn,** 264 W. 46 St., at Eighth Ave., tel. (212) 997-9200 or (800) 826-6300, and **The Mayfair,** 242 W. 49th St., bet. Broadway and Eighth Ave., tel. (212) 586-0300 or (800) 55-MAYFAIR. Both are extremely attractive, spanking clean, friendly, and priced around $90-130.

The Broadway Inn offers 45 spacious rooms appointed in greens and greys and an airy, second-floor lobby filled with potted plants and inviting chairs. The rooms are well furnished with comfortable beds, modern bureaus and tables, and good reading lamps. $85 s, $95-140 d; continental breakfast included.

The Mayfair offers a classy lobby lined with warm woods and rare historic photographs from the Museum of the City of New York. The 78 rooms vary widely in size, but all are equipped with mahogany furnishings, cheery pink bedspreads, hair dryers, and thick Irish towels. Some also have marble baths. $80-120 s, $90-150 d.

Also offering good value for money is the friendly **Hotel Iroquois,** 49 W. 44th St., bet. Fifth and Sixth Aves., tel. (212) 840-3080 or (800) 332-7220, once home to James Dean (see "The Algonquin and Vicinity," above). Don't be put off by the hotel's worn, utilitarian lobby; the rooms themselves are considerably more attractive, with homey poster beds, dark wood furnishings, and tiled bathrooms. No two rooms are exactly alike. $99 s, $125 d.

Similar in price to the Hotel Iroquois but not as nice is the **Hotel Remington,** 129 W. 46th St., bet. Sixth Ave. and Broadway, tel. (212) 221-2600. The rooms are outfitted in maroon and beige, while the lobby is lined with mirrors galore. Adjoining the entranceway is an old-fashioned barber shop. $119 s, $129 d.

One of the largest hotels in New York is the 1,000-room **Edison,** 228 W. 47th St., near Eighth Ave., tel. (212) 840-5000 or (800) 637-

7070. Most notable for its striking art deco lobby lined with murals of the 1920s Yankees, the Cotton Club, construction workers, and much more, the hotel also offers clean, good-sized rooms. Adjoining the lobby is a hair salon, two restaurants, and a cafe popular among young actors. $105 s, $115 d.

Farther north is the clean and comfortable **Westpark,** 308 W. 58th St., near Columbus Circle, tel. (212) 246-6440 or (800) 248-6440. Rooms are small but well kept; those overlooking Central Park cost extra. $95-110 s, $110-140 d.

Similar in style, albeit more loudly floral in its decor, is the **Park Savoy,** 158 W. 58th St., bet. Sixth and Seventh Aves., tel. (212) 245-5755. Again, rooms are small but well kept. Cheaper single rooms share baths. $55-85 s, $110-149 d.

Across from the famed Plaza Hotel is the **Wyndham,** 42 W. 58th St., near Fifth Ave., tel. (212) 753-3500 or (800) 257-1111, a spacious old hostelry with a cozy, low-ceilinged lobby and rooms airily decorated with lots of flowered wallpaper, upholstery, and chintz. The owners designed the place themselves and live on the premises, which helps account for the hotel's easygoing, old-fashioned feel. Many of the guests are actors in town for Broadway runs. $120-135 s, $135-150 d; reserve well in advance.

Moderate-to-Expensive
East Side: The tranquil **Hotel Lexington,** 511 Lexington Ave., at 48th St., tel. (212) 755-4400 or (800) 458-8825, is owned by the Taj Group, which is headquartered in India. The polished lobby gleams with marble floors and warm wood pillars, while upstairs are large guest rooms done up in pale beiges and whites. $165-205 s or d.

West Side: Filled with eclectic touches, the sleek **Paramount,** 235 W. 46th St., near Eighth Ave., tel. (212) 764-5500 or (800) 225-7474, is a fun place to stay. Created by the Schrager-Rubell team of Studio 54 fame, it features a darkened lobby filled with lollipop-colored chairs and a big-checked rug, and, in the rooms, beds slung close to the floor and stainless steel sinks shaped like ice cream cones. A second-story restaurant wraps around the lobby, and the hotel's Whiskey Bar is a late-night hot spot. $99-195 s, $165-215 d.

Expensive
East Side: With only 120 rooms, the stylish **Gorham,** 136 W. 55th St., bet. Sixth and Seventh Aves., tel., (212) 245-1800 or (800) 735-0701, offers a personalized European ambience. Downstairs, find a warm lobby paneled in bird's-eye maple; upstairs find contemporary Italian-design-style rooms complete with kitchenettes. A cheery breakfast room overlooks the historic City Center across the street. $180-320 s or d.

Also European in flavor is the unusual **Hotel Elysee,** 60 E. 54th St., bet. Madison and Park Aves., tel. (212) 753-1066 or (800) 535-9733, furnished in dark woods, plush carpets, and Oriental antiques. Most of the rooms have Italian marble bathrooms, and adjoining the lobby is the classy Monkey Bar, its walls covered with murals. Among the famous residents who once lived in the Elysee were Joe Dimaggio, Tallulah Bankhead, and Tennessee Williams. $245-265 s or d; continental breakfast included.

Manhattan East Suite Hotels, tel. (212) 465-3600 or (800) ME-SUITE, is a group of nine fine suite hotels, most on the east side of Midtown. The hotels offer custom-priced extended-stay programs and are good places for families— their suites are large and competitively priced on the weekends. One of the snazziest of the group is the **Beekman Tower Hotel,** 3 Mitchell Pl., off First Ave at 49th St., tel. (212) 355-7300, equipped with a 26th-floor art deco lounge offering dazzling views of the city. A one-bedroom suite here, complete with a kitchenette and sleeping accommodations for four, is $229 weekdays, $189 weekends.

No two rooms are alike at the **Roger Smith,** 501 Lexington Ave., at 47th St., tel. (212) 755-1400 or (800) 445-0277. The atmosphere-infused hotel was once a worn haven for graying businessmen but is now a jazzy retreat complete with several art galleries, a gift shop selling arts and crafts, and a long, narrow restaurant painted with a floor-to-ceiling mural. The rooms are tastefully furnished; live jazz is sometimes presented on weekends. $195-210 s, $210-225 d.

West Side: Still deliciously old-fashioned, with lots of wood paneling and brocaded chairs, is the 1902 **Algonquin,** 59 W. 44th St., bet. Fifth and Sixth Aves., tel. (212) 840-6800 or (800) 548-0345. Each floor has a different color scheme, and the inviting rooms offer plump beds, comfy armchairs, and bathrooms equipped with plenty of amenities. Downstairs, where Dorothy Parker and friends once met (see "The Algonquin and Vicinity," above), are several snug lounges perfect for afternoon tea, cocktails, or aperitifs. $255 s, $275 d.

The **Mansfield,** 12 W. 44th St., bet. Fifth and Sixth Aves., tel. (212) 944-6050, was built in 1904 as a residence for well-to-do bachelors. Now a gleaming 123-room hotel, it features gorgeous woodwork, a 12-story oval staircase, and rooms equipped with everything from Victorian sleigh beds to etched glass French doors. Complimentary cappuccino is offered throughout the day, and a complimentary after-theater dessert buffet is served every evening, accompanied by a piano/harp recital. $195-305 s or d; includes continental breakfast.

The sleek, art deco **Millenium Broadway,** 145 W. 44th St., bet. Sixth and Seventh Aves., tel. (212) 768-4400 or (800) 622-5569, sits on the edge of Times Square. A 52-story hotel, it offers superb views, 638 tasteful rooms styled in gray and black, and a block-long lobby lined with murals by the Italian artist Carlo Maria Mariani. $185-225 s or d.

The big and bustling **Marriott Marquis,** 1535 Broadway, at 45th St., tel. (212) 398-1900 or (800) 228-9290, is all chrome and glass, business people and conventioneers. Inside, find 1,874 rooms, a *37-story* atrium, 12 glass-enclosed elevators, umpteen conference rooms, and the city's only revolving restaurant. For the individual traveler, the hotel's main attraction are its weekend packages—as much as 30% off the regular $179-230 rates.

Luxury
East Side: The **Drake Swissotel,** 440 Park Ave., at 56th St., tel. (212) 421-0900 or (800) 372-5369, is a lovely hostelry, managed to perfection in impeccable Swiss style. The lobby gleams with marble and polished glass; the rooms are spacious and airy, with separate sitting areas and oversized desks. In back of the lobby is the Drake Bar and Cafe, serving Swiss, European, and American specialties. $225-255 s, $245-295 d.

Now owned by Hilton and catering primarily to a business clientele, the famed **Waldorf-Asto-**ria, 301 Park Ave., bet. 49th and 50th Sts., tel. (212) 355-3000 or (800) WALDORF, nonetheless continues to beckon with opulence and romance. Surrounding the darkened, maroon-carpeted lobby are glittering stores selling jewelry, antiques, and rare books. Downstairs is Peacock Alley, an elegant cafe with a piano that once belonged to Cole Porter. Upstairs are 1,120 rooms in varying shapes and sizes, and numerous conference rooms. $250-350 s, $290-410 d.

Step into the lobby of the minimalist I.M. Pei-designed **Four Seasons New York,** 57 E. 57th St., bet. Madison and Park Aves., tel. (212) 758-5700 or (800) 332-3442, and you feel as if you're about to request an audience with the king. The reception desk is just so big and far away—up two flights of stairs—and you're so small. Once you get used to it, however, the place feels grand. Designed with earth tones, a muted skylight, and octagonal columns, it offers an understated restaurant to one side, a lounge to the other. The guest rooms are the largest in New York (600 square feet), and come equipped with all things state-of-the-art, including bathtubs that fill in 60 seconds. Alas, all this futuristic luxury does not come cheap. $440-625 s, $490-675 d.

One of the city's most opulent hostelries is the **St. Regis,** 2 E. 55th St., at Fifth Ave., tel. (212) 753-4500 or (800) 759-7550, built by John Jacob Astor in 1904. Filled with marble, crystal, and gold leaf, the St. Regis underwent a $100-million restoration several years ago and now offers every conceivable amenity—as well it should, given the prices. $455-565 s or d.

West Side: The **Royalton,** 44 W. 44th St., near Fifth Ave., tel. (212) 869-4400, is another hip Schrager-Rubell creation. Its long, tunnel-like lobby is lined with shiny black elevators to one side, a step-down sitting area to the other. Chairs are draped in white cloth; a posh restaurant caters to media types in the back. All is not as well kept as it should be, however. Some of the lobby chairs are worn, and dead goldfish float in bowls. $265-330 s, $295-360 d.

Across from the St. Regis is another ultra-elegant hostelry—the **Peninsula,** 700 Fifth Ave., at 55th St., tel. (212) 247-2000 or (800) 262-9467, run by the Hong Kong-based Peninsula Group. Housed in a landmark beaux arts building, the hotel features a grand double staircase, luscious art nouveau antiques, deluxe-sized rooms, and superb service. On the 23rd floor are a luxurious spa and an inviting roof terrace bar that's open in summer only. $365-475 s or d; weekend packages available.

The **Plaza,** 768 Fifth Ave., at 59th St., tel. (212) 759-3000 or (800) 759-3000, one of New York's best-known hotels, was nicely restored by the Trumps in the late 1980s. The rooms come in all shapes and sizes and are furnished with both period antiques and reproductions. Some rooms offer grand four-poster beds, others marble fireplaces and crystal chandeliers. $275-625 s or d.

YWCA

The centrally located **Vanderbilt YWCA,** 224 E. 47th St., bet. Third and Second Aves., tel. (212) 756-9600, is a good bet for budget travelers. Open to both men and women, it offers small, clean rooms with shared baths. $53 s, $66 d.

FOOD

Note: If you're planning to eat in the Theater District before a show, make reservations or give yourself plenty of time. Many restaurants are packed between 6:30 and 8 p.m.

American
Inexpensive: The **Carnegie Deli,** 854 Seventh Ave., near 54th St., tel. (212) 757-2245, is a New York City landmark, famous for enormous overstuffed deli sandwiches. Similar in style is **Stage Deli,** 834 Seventh Ave., bet. 53rd and 54th Sts., tel. (212) 245-7850, the Carnegie's major competitor.

Moderate: In the Theater District, you'll find the **West Bank Cafe,** 407 W. 42nd St., near Ninth Ave., tel. (212) 695-6909, a friendly, saloonlike spot; and the cozy **Hourglass Tavern,** 373 W. 46th St., near Ninth Ave., tel. (212) 265-2060, serving simple, home-cooked fare. **Joe Allen,** 326 W. 46th St., near Eighth Ave., tel. (212) 581-6464, is a well-known restaurant/bar that attracts many celebrities, but the service can be rude.

Moderate-to-Expensive: The **American Festival Cafe,** 20 W. 50th St., tel. (212) 332-7620, is a Rockefeller Center institution, overlooking the skating rink. Be sure to make reservations for lunch. Behind the New York Public Library, overlooking Bryant Park, are the **Bryant Park Grill** and the **Bryant Park Cafe,** 25 W. 42nd St., tel. (212) 840-6500. Both serve imaginative American fare in a handsome, airy setting, but the grill is somewhat more expensive and more formal. In summer, a rooftop terrace opens up.

Expensive: For steak, try **Smith & Wollensky,** 797 Third Ave., at 49th St., tel. (212) 753-1530, sporting a wood-and-brass decor; or the classy **Sparks Steak House,** 210 E. 46th St., near Third Ave., tel. (212) 687-4855. In the Mil-

Overstuffed sandwiches are a Carnegie Deli tradition.

lenium Broadway Hotel is the **Restaurant Charlotte,** 145 W. 44th St., bet. Fifth and Sixth Aves., tel. (212) 768-4400, under the direction of a Cherokee-Texan-Mexican chef.

Asian

Inexpensive: Bustling **Ollie's Noodle Shop,** 200 W. 44th St., near Broadway, tel. (212) 921-5988, offers a wide variety of noodle and dumpling dishes. **Take-Sushi,** 71 Vanderbilt Ave., bet. 45th and 46th Sts., tel. (212) 867-5120, is a popular lunch spot. **Dosanko,** 423 Madison Ave., bet. 48th and 49th Sts., tel. (212) 688-8575, and other Midtown locations, serves steaming bowls of noodles.

Moderate: Zen Palate, 663 Ninth Ave., at 46th St., tel. (212) 582-1669, is known for its imaginative Asian-vegetarian fare.

Expensive: Vong, 200 E. 54th St., at Third Ave., tel. (212) 486-9592, theatrically designed by David Rockefeller, offers an unusual array of French/Thai dishes. Two superb Japanese restaurants are **Hatsuhana,** 17 E. 48th St., bet. Fifth and Madison Aves., tel. (212) 355-3345; and **Sushisay,** 38 E. 51st St., near Madison Ave., tel. (212) 755-1780.

Eclectic

Very Expensive: Still New York's best-known spot for power dining is the minimalist **Four Seasons,** 99 E. 52nd St., near Park Ave., tel. (212) 754-9494, in the landmark Seagram building designed by Mies van der Rohe.

French/Continental

Inexpensive: A budget traveler's lifesaver, **La Bonne Soup,** 48 W. 55th St., bet. Fifth and Sixth Aves., tel. (212) 596-7650, serves hearty soups with bread, salad, dessert, and wine for about $10. Across the street, **La Fondue,** 43 W. 55th St., tel. (212) 581-0820, is also very reasonably priced.

Moderate: Tout Va Bien, 311 W. 51st St., near Eighth Ave., tel. (212) 265-0190, is a homey and reliable place, one of the last of the old-style French bistros in the Theater District.

Moderate-to-Expensive: The friendly, upscale **Brasserie,** 100 E. 53rd St., near Park Ave., tel. (212) 751-4840, is a neighborhood institution. It's open 24 hours and serves imaginative fare. **Chez Josephine,** 414 W. 42nd St.,

near Ninth Ave., tel. (212) 594-1925, is a charming French/Southern bistro run by one of Josephine Baker's adopted French children. The food at **Cafe Un, Deux, Trois,** 123 W. 44th St., bet. Sixth and Seventh Aves., tel. (212) 354-4148, is nothing special, but the restaurant's towering columns, gilt-edge mirrors, and lively clientele make it great fun nonetheless.

Very Expensive: Though now under new ownership, **Lutece,** 249 E. 50th St., near Second Ave., tel. (212) 752-2225, is still New York's top classic French restaurant. The recently relocated **La Côte Basque,** 60 W. 55th St., bet. Fifth and Sixth Aves., tel. (212) 688-6525, immortalized in Truman Capote's unfinished *Unanswered Prayers,* is another bastion of French haute cuisine. The legendary, over-the-top **Rainbow Room,** 30 Rockefeller Pl., bet. 49th and 50th Sts., 65th Fl., tel. (212) 632-5100, features a revolving inlaid dance floor and big bands outfitted in bright, flamboyant costumes. The plush and highly acclaimed **Le Bernardin,** 155 W. 51st St., bet. Sixth and Seventh Aves., tel. (212) 489-1515, specializes in fresh seafood.

Indian

Moderate: For good and reasonably priced Indian cuisine, try **Darbar,** 44 W. 56th St., bet. Fifth and Sixth Aves., tel. (212) 432-7227.

Expensive: The sophisticated **Dawat,** 210 E. 58th St., near Third Ave., tel. (212) 355-7555, is considered to be one of the city's best Indian restaurants. **Nirvana,** 30 Central Park S, bet. Fifth and Sixth Aves., tel. (212) 486-5700, may be a touristy spot, but you can't beat its spectacular views of Central Park.

Italian

Inexpensive-to-Moderate: Just north of Grand Central in the MetLife Building, 200 Park Ave., is **Cucina & Co.,** tel. (212) 682-2700, an Italian-accented eatery serving gourmet sandwiches, salads, pastas, and baked goods.

Moderate: Borsalino, 255 W. 55th St., bet. Broadway and Eighth Ave., tel. (212) 246-0710, is friendly, unpretentious, and reliably good. The sprawling, noisy **Carmine's,** 200 W. 44th St., bet. Broadway and Eighth Ave., tel. (212) 221-3800, serves huge portions of Southern Italian food.

Expensive: Near Carnegie Hall is the stylish **Trattoria dell'Arte,** 900 Seventh Ave., bet.

56th and 57th Sts., tel. (212) 245-9800, featuring tasty pastas and pizzas. The recently revamped **Barbetta's,** 321 W. 46th St., bet. Eighth and Ninth Aves., tel. (212) 246-9171, is a classy spot housed in a townhouse with a romantic garden out back.

Very Expensive: Palio, 151 W. 51st St., bet. Sixth and Seventh Aves., tel. (212) 245-4850, with its stunning mural by Sandro Chia, specializes in Northern Italian cuisine.

Latin

Moderate: Several Brazilian restaurants are found on West 45th and 46th Sts. bet. Fifth and Seventh Avenues. The two-story **Cabana Carioca,** 123 W. 45th St., near Seventh Ave., tel. (212) 581-8088, painted with vibrant tropical scenes, is tops for decor and generous portions, but the service can be rude. The decor at **Brazilia Restaurant,** 7 W. 45th St., bet. Fifth and Sixth Aves., tel. (212) 869-9200, is considerably more sedate, but the food is excellent and the service first-rate. **Ipanema,** 13 W. 46th St., bet. Fifth and Sixth Aves., tel. (212) 730-5848, is also very good.

Russian

Inexpensive: Uncle Vanya's Cafe, 315 W. 54th St., bet. Eighth and Ninth Aves., tel. (212) 262-0542, is a cheery and inexpensive spot serving traditional Russian fare.

Expensive: The legendary **Russian Tea Room,** 150 W. 57th St., near Seventh Ave., tel. (212) 265-0947, has been under renovation for the last two years; it is tentatively scheduled to reopen in spring 1998. In the meantime, try the splendid new **Firebird,** 365 W. 46th St., bet. Eighth and Ninth Aves., tel. (212) 586-0244. Housed in two brownstones, the posh eatery resembles a prerevolutionary St. Petersburg mansion, complete with paintings, objets d'art, antiques, crystal, and authentic cuisine.

Seafood

Inexpensive and Expensive: For a classic New York lunch, eat at Grand Central Station's **Oyster Bar,** 42nd St. and Park Ave., lower level, tel. (212) 490-6650, complete with red-checked tablecloths and a vaulted ceiling. On the menu is a wide variety of fish; adjoining the main restaurant is a much cheaper counter area. Closed

weekends. Also acclaimed for seafood is **Manhattan Ocean Club,** 57 W. 58th St., near Sixth Ave., tel. (212) 371-7777.

Southern/Soul/Creole

Moderate-to-Expensive: The sophisticated, streamlined **B. Smith's,** 771 Eighth Ave., at 47th St., tel. (212) 247-2222, serves first-rate Southern-accented food. Its host is supermodel Barbara Smith.

Expensive: The elegant **Jezebel,** 630 Ninth Ave., at 45th St., tel. (212) 582-1045, serves gourmet-style soul food in a lush, elegant New Orleans setting complete with lace curtains, antiques, and fresh flowers.

Other Ethnic

Inexpensive-Moderate: The **Afghan Kebab House,** 764 Ninth Ave., bet. 51st and 52nd Sts., tel. (212) 307-1612, serves succulent kebabs in exotic surroundings. **Uncle Nick's,** 747 Ninth Ave., bet. 50th and 51st Sts. tel. (212) 245-7992, is one of Manhattan's best—and only—Greek restaurants.

Moderate: The charming **Taprobane,** 234 W. 56th St., near Broadway, tel. (212) 333-4203, is one of the city's only Sri Lankan restaurants.

Expensive: Solera, 216 E. 53rd St., bet. Second and Third Aves., tel. (212) 644-1166, is a handsome establishment specializing in tapas. The South Beach-inspired **Bistro Latino,** 1711 Broadway, at 54th St., tel. (212) 956-1000, offers nouveau Latin American fare *and* tango lessons.

Light Bites

During warm weather, both Bryant Park (between 40th and 42nd Sts., Fifth and Sixth Aves.) and the steps of the New York Public Library are good spots for lunch. Nearby vendors sell everything from hot dogs to gourmet fare. Grazers might want to head over to Ninth Ave. and nibble their way through its many food shops (see "Shopping," above). Be sure to include a dessert stop at **Cupcake Cafe,** 522 Ninth Ave., tel. (212) 465-1530, known for its baked goods. **Rumpelmayer's** in the St. Moritz Hotel, 50 Central Park S, tel. (212) 755-5800, is a sumptuous old-fashioned ice cream parlor. And don't forget the pretzel and chestnut vendors along Fifth Avenue—they're as New York as it gets.

Watering Holes and Lounges
For a bird's-eye view of New York at night, Midtown is the neighborhood. The cozy **Top of the Tower** at the Beekman Hotel, 3 Mitchell Pl., off First Ave. at 49th St., tel. (212) 355-7300, offers an art deco lounge and an outdoor terrace open in summer. The posh **Peninsula,** hotel, 700 Fifth Ave., at 55th St., tel. (212) 247-2200, features a rooftop bar and garden open in summer. The Promenade Bar at the **Rainbow Room,** 30 Rockefeller Pl., off Fifth Ave. and 50th St., 65th Fl., tel. (212) 632-5100, is a glamorous, art deco icon that gets extremely crowded on the weekends. For a drink in the city's only revolving bar, overlooking Times Square, take an elevator to the top of the glitzy **Marriott Marquis,** 1535 Broadway, at 45th St., tel. (212) 398-1900.

Back on ground level, near the Theater District is the elegant, wood-paneled **Algonquin Hotel,** 59 W. 44th St., bet. Fifth and Sixth Aves., tel. (212) 840-6800, offering several bars and lounges. The stylish **Whiskey Bar,** in the Paramount Hotel, 235 W. 46th St., near Eighth Ave., tel. (212) 819-0404, attracts a lively international crowd. Ditto the bar at the swank and considerably more expensive **Royalton Hotel,** 44 W. 44th St., bet. Fifth and Sixth Aves., tel. (212) 869-4400. The **Bryant Park Cafe,** 25 W. 42nd St., tel. (212) 840-6500, is at its liveliest at cocktail hour.

Farther north, in the post-modern Four Seasons Hotel, is the **Fifty Seven Fifty Seven Bar,** 57 E. 57th St., bet. Madison and Park, tel. (212) 758-5700, serving 15 different kinds of oversized martinis. Drinks at the posh St. Regis Hotel's **King Cole Bar and Lounge,** 2 E. 55th St., at Fifth Ave., tel. (212) 753-4500, don't come cheap, but the room's beautifully restored mural makes it all worthwhile. In the Plaza Hotel is the famed **Oak Bar,** Fifth Ave. and 59th St., tel. (212) 759-3000, a plush but pricey spot, always filled with tourists. Nearby, find **Mickey Mantle's,** 42 Central Park S, bet. Fifth and Sixth Aves., tel. (212) 688-7777, the city's best-known sports bar. **P.J. Clarke's,** 915 Third Ave., at 55th St., tel. (212) 759-1650, is an out-of-time saloon sporting brass railings, worn wood, and sawdust on the floor. Featured in the 1945 movie *The Lost Weekend,* P.J.'s also serves overpriced burgers and sandwiches.

Rapidly gentrifying Ninth Avenue is home to a number of SoHo-esque lounges complete with exposed brick walls, overstuffed sofas, and stamped tin ceilings. Among them are **Otis,** 754 Ninth Ave., bet. 50th and 51st Sts., tel. (212) 246-4471, and **Bar Nine,** 807 Ninth Ave., bet. 53rd and 54th Sts., tel. (212) 399-9336.

On Second Ave., you'll find two solid Irish singles' bars: **Murphy's,** 977 Second, near 52nd St., tel. (212) 751-5400; and the **Green Derby,** 994 Second, near 53rd St., tel. (212) 688-1250. **Billy's,** 948 First Ave., near 52nd St., tel. (212) 753-1870, is an old-style, family-run joint serving stout and good pub grub.

DOVER PUBLICATIONS, INC.

THE UPPER EAST SIDE

Since the turn of the century, the Upper East Side has been associated with wealth. Everyone from Andrew Carnegie to Gloria Vanderbilt, from Henry Clay Frick to Franklin Delano Roosevelt has resided in this hushed, exclusive neighborhood. Here you'll find so many mansions and brownstones, clubs and penthouses, that at times the neighborhood resembles an open-air museum.

The wealthy began arriving on the Upper East Side in the late 1800s as an ever-encroaching business tide forced them off the Midtown stretches of Fifth Avenue. But the real turning point came in 1905, when steel magnate Andrew Carnegie built his mansion on Fifth Ave. at 91st Street. Soon thereafter, one industrialist after another followed suit, until the stretch of Fifth Ave. facing Central Park became known as "Millionaires Row." Many of these mansions have since been converted into museums and cultural institutions.

But the Upper East Side is not only about the wealthy. It's also about more ordinary folk, who —as elsewhere in Manhattan—settled closer to the river. At one time, Madison, Park, and Lexington Aves. were basically middle-class, while the area east of Lexington was working-class and home to recent immigrants. Yorkville, a hamlet established in the 1790s between what are now 83rd and 88th Sts., had an especially large German population.

Today, these sections of the Upper East Side are slowly becoming gentrified, but many remnants of their earlier days still exist, especially east of Lexington Ave. and north of 86th Street. Here, the streets can get as funky and eclectic as anywhere else in town.

Stretching roughly from 59th to 100th Sts., Fifth Ave. to the East River, the Upper East Side's long residential blocks are pleasant for strolling. Most of the sights and shops are along the north-south avenues rather than the east-west side streets. Madison Avenue is known all over the world for its upscale shops. Many are designer boutiques, astronomically priced, but a few more moderate establishments are found here and there.

First-time visitors will probably want to walk up Fifth Ave. to the Metropolitan, and then perhaps visit Central Park or stroll back downtown along Madison Avenue.

UP FIFTH AND MADISON AVENUES

The Pierre
One of the most famous and elegant hostelries in New York is the Pierre, at the northeast corner of Fifth Ave. and 61st Street. A favorite among monarchs and presidents, the Pierre has also been home to heiress Barbara Hutton, writer John O'Hara, then-married actors Robert Taylor

and Barbara Stanwyck, and writer Dashiell Hammett. Hammett began his book *The Thin Man* here in 1932, but that same year—having run up a tab he couldn't pay—he disguised himself and left the hotel without settling his bill.

The Pierre was also the site of one of the greatest jewel heists ever. On Jan. 2, 1972, at 4 a.m., four thieves dressed in tuxedos arrived at the hotel in a chauffeur-driven limousine. The security guard, suspecting nothing, let them in. Once inside, the thieves whipped out guns, tied up 21 hotel employees and guests, and made off with $8 million in jewelry, cash, and securities.

The only evidence the thieves left behind were the rubber noses they'd dropped on the lobby floor. Nevertheless, within a week, with the help of an informant, the police tracked the robbers down. All were arrested and sentenced, but according to Paul Schwartzman and Rob Polner, writing in *New York Notorious,* it's believed that several million dollars' worth of jewels were never recovered.

Al Smith's Residence

Former New York governor and 1928 Democratic presidential candidate Al Smith lived at 820 Fifth Ave., bet. 63rd and 64th Sts., from the early 1930s until his death in 1944. A great animal lover, Smith often spent his afternoons across the street at the Central Park Zoo.

City Parks Commissioner Robert Moses was a close friend and political ally of Al Smith's. In 1934, with great fanfare, Moses had the old city zoo renovated, largely as a favor to his friend. Moses also arranged for Smith to be appointed the zoo's night superintendent, which meant that he was given a key. As Robert Caro describes it in *The Power Broker,* the doormen at No. 820 became accustomed to seeing Smith—a paunchy figure often wearing a big brown derby—walk out the front door in the evenings, cross Fifth Ave., and disappear down the steps of the darkened zoo, not to reappear for hours.

Temple Emanu-El

The world's largest Reform synagogue is the imposing Temple Emanu-El at 1 E. 65th Street. It's built in a mix of Moorish and Romanesque styles to symbolize the joining of Eastern and Western cultures. Inside, the temple is overwhelmingly large and dark, with a bronze-grilled

ark containing the Torah, and blue-and-gold mosaics by artist Hildreth Meiere. The temple is open Sun.-Thurs. 10 a.m.-5 p.m., Sat. noon-5 p.m. Organ recitals are presented Fridays at 5 p.m.

Frick Collection

Now a museum, the former home of industrialist Henry Clay Frick, 1 E. 70th St., is one of the city's most beautiful residences. It's a classic 1914 mansion built around a courtyard and an exquisite European art collection. Every room is hung with masterpieces—by Breughel, El Greco, Hogarth, Vermeer, Rembrandt, Turner, and others—yet the place maintains a private, homey feel.

The Frick's most famous room is the Fragonard Room, where all four walls are covered with *The Progress of Love,* painted by French artist Jean-Honoré Fragonard. The panels were orginally commissioned by Louis XV for his lover, Mme. du Barry.

Despite his impeccable taste, Frick was reputedly one of the nastiest of the early American capitalists. A pioneer in the coke and steel industries, he repeatedly used violence to break up labor unions, at one time sending in 300 thugs who provoked a riot in which 14 people were killed. It was shortly after this incident that young anarchist Alexander Berkman—Emma Goldman's lover—tried to assassinate Frick in his office. Frick was badly wounded but survived. Berkman was sentenced to 14 years in jail.

The Frick, tel. (212) 288-0700, is open Tues.-Sat. 10 a.m.-6 p.m., Sun. 1-6 p.m. Admission is adults $5, students and seniors $3, children under 10 not admitted.

Famous Area Residents

In the late 1950s, actress **Joan Crawford** lived with her husband, Pepsi-Cola tycoon Al Steele, in a penthouse apartment at 2 E. 70th St., directly across the street from the Frick. The couple spent over $1 million redoing their apartment, but when it was finished, according to Crawford's adopted daughter Christina, writing in *Mommie Dearest,* "There was something barren about it . . . Everything was new and modern and plastic. Even the flowers and plants were plastic . . . There were plastic covers on all the

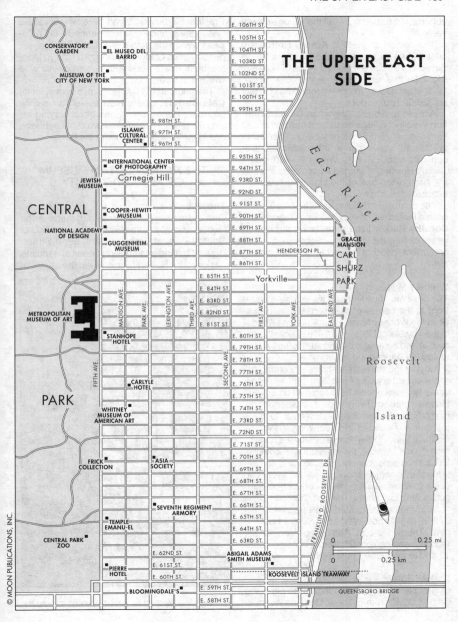

upholstered furniture . . . All the windows were sealed."

The notorious gambler **Arnold Rothstein,** best known as the man who fixed the World Series of 1919, spent the last years of his life at 912 Fifth Avenue. He was living here in Nov. 1928 when he was murdered for refusing to pay a $320,000 poker debt.

Actress and businesswoman **Gloria Swanson** lived in the large apartment building at 920 Fifth Ave., at 73rd St., from 1938 until her death in 1983. While living here, she made a magnificent comeback in Billy Wilder's 1950 movie *Sunset Boulevard,* started a cosmetics company, and hosted one of the world's first weekly television talk shows.

The apartment building at 23 E. 74th St. was once a residential hotel called the Volney. Writer **Dorothy Parker** lived here during the last 15 years of her life; she was discovered in her apartment, dead of a heart attack, on June 7, 1967.

Whitney Museum
The boxy gray building with the wedge-shaped front at the corner of Madison Ave. and 75th St. is the Whitney Museum of American Art, designed by Marcel Breuer in 1966. Recently renovated and enlarged, the museum offers plenty to see but not enough to overwhelm.

Most of the museum's shows are temporary and feature the work of one 20th-century American artist. Past shows have focused on Edward Hopper, Maurice Prendergast, Jasper Johns, Isamu Noguchi, and Jacques Basquiat, to name just a few. Founded in Greenwich Village by Gertrude Vanderbilt Whitney in 1930 (see "Greenwich Village," above), the museum is also known for its superb permanent collection and its controversial "Biennial" show, presented every two years to showcase the latest works of contemporary American artists. The next show is in 1999.

The Whitney, 945 Madison Ave., tel. (212) 570-3676, is open Wed., Fri.-Sun. 11 a.m.-6 p.m., Thurs. 1-8 p.m. Admission is adults $8, students and seniors $6; free to children under 12 and to everyone Thurs. 6-8 p.m.

Carlyle Hotel
One of New York's most elegant hotels is the Carlyle, 35 E. 76th St. near Madison Avenue.

President Truman stayed here whenever he was in town, and President Kennedy had a duplex suite on the hotel's 34th floor. Kennedy reportedly often brought an incognito Marilyn Monroe back to the hotel with him when his wife was not in town.

The understated Carlyle is also known for its **Cafe Carlyle,** where high society's favorite jazzman, Bobby Short, has been playing for over 25 years. He performs two stints annually, one in the spring, the other in the fall.

THE METROPOLITAN MUSEUM OF ART AND VICINITY

The Met
One of the world's greatest museums is the Metropolitan Museum of Art, on the east side of Central Park at Fifth Ave. and 82nd Street. Housed behind an imposing beaux arts facade designed by Robert Morris Hunt, the museum

the peerless Met—to be visited time and time again

boasts collections of almost everything from Egyptian sarcophagi to modern American paintings.

Equally important, the museum's exhibitions are well edited and well viewed. This is not an elite or stuffy institution. On weekends, the place takes on a carnival air as jugglers, acrobats, vendors, and mimes hawk their talents and wares on the museum's wide staircase out front. And even early on weekday mornings, the museum's grand marble halls echo with excited whispers.

Founded in 1870, the Met centers around the Great Hall, a vast entrance room with an imposing staircase leading to the second floor. From the hall, the Met spreads out over about 1.5 million square feet. Other impressive statistics: the Met houses over two million works of art; has 19 curatorial departments; is visited by more than four million people a year; has an annual operating budget of about $80 million; and employs over 2,000 paid workers and 600 volunteers.

To do the Met justice takes a number of visits, so the best approach is to study the floor plan and decide what interests you most. Free orientation tours leave from the information booth in the Great Hall every half-hour or so.

The Met's European Paintings galleries—some 20 rooms' worth—house a whole roomful of Rembrandts, five of the fewer than 40 known Vermeers, a rich collection of Hals and Van Dyck, and works by Breughel, Rubens, Botticelli, El Greco, Goya, and others. The best way to view these galleries is to go through them in numerical order; otherwise, it's easy to get disoriented.

Right next door to the European Paintings galleries are two new (1993) galleries holding 19th-century European paintings and sculpture. Here, painters such as Corot, Courbet, Manet, Monet, and Cézanne all have entire rooms devoted to them, while van Gogh, Gauguin, Seurat, Pissarro, and Renoir are also well represented.

Three sides of the Met's original building are flanked by modern glass wings that contrast beautifully with the old limestone edifice. At the back is the arrowhead-shaped Robert Lehman Collection, which houses an impressive collection of Old Masters and 19th-century French painters. On the south side are the Rockefeller and Acheson Wings. The Rockefeller Wing is named after Michael C. Rockefeller, the son of the late vice president who disappeared while on a research expedition in New Guinea. Many of the items on display were collected during Rockefeller's earlier expeditions, and they're mind-boggling works ranging from intricately carved 100-foot-long canoes to towering musical instruments made of hollowed logs. The Lila Acheson Wing is devoted to 20th-century art. This wing includes a number of masterpieces, but for modern art, the Met is not the place. (Try the Modern, the Guggenheim, or the Whitney instead.) Don't miss the sculpture garden on the Acheson roof, however. The views from here are terrific.

On the north side are the Sackler and American Wings. The Sackler Wing houses the low-lit, 15th-century-B.C. Temple of Dendur, carved in faded hieroglyphics. The American Wing has its own private courtyard, framed by Tiffany windows; exhaustive galleries of decorative arts; and many fine paintings by the likes of Gilbert Stuart, Thomas Eakins, John Singer Sargent, Mary Cassatt, and James Whistler.

Other important stops in the Met include the Egyptian department, housing the largest collection of Egyptian art outside Egypt; the Islamic art collection, one of the world's finest; the new South and Southeast Asian art collection; and, of course, the museum's many superb temporary exhibits. Finally, too, if you have the time or are weary of concentrated viewing, it's well worth just roaming around the museum to see what treasures you might stumble across. One of the most winsome is the 16th-century Spanish patio, a small and peaceful inner courtyard near the grand staircase.

The Met has one of the city's best gift shops, but the same cannot be said for its noisy cafeteria and separate sit-down restaurant. Be prepared for long waits and high prices.

If possible, avoid the Met on weekends, when it can get exceedingly crowded. Come on a weekday morning instead, or on a Friday or Saturday evening when the candlelit Great Hall Balcony Bar is open and a jazz or classical quintet performs.

The Met, tel. (212) 535-7710, is open Tues.-Thurs., Sun. 9:30 a.m.-5:15 p.m., Fri.-Sat. 9:30 a.m.-8:45 p.m. Suggested admission is adults

$8, students and seniors $4, children under 12 free, but you can pay what you wish.

Stanhope Hotel

Directly across from the Met, at the southeast corner of 81st St. and Fifth Ave., is the Stanhope, an ornate luxury hotel filled with Louis XVI furnishings and Baccarat chandeliers. In summer, the hotel's restaurant spills out into a sidewalk cafe that's expensive but perfect for peoplewatching.

Jazz musician Charlie Parker died in the hotel apartment of Baroness "Nica" de Koenigswarter on March 12, 1955, while watching jugglers on the "Tommy Dorsey Show." The eccentric baroness, who was a friend and patron of many jazz musicians, had called a doctor upon Bird's arrival three days earlier, and he had warned her that the musician could die at any time.

Parker was only 34 when he died, but his death certificate estimated his age to be 53. Drugs and alcohol had so ravaged his body that he seemed much older.

Frank E. Campbell Funeral Home

The small building at 1076 Madison Ave., at 81st St., is the funeral home of the rich and famous. Rudolph Valentino started the trend in 1926, followed by Montgomery Clift, James Cagney, Joan Crawford, John Garfield, and Tommy Dorsey.

Judy Garland's funeral was also held at the Campbell Home. Her daughter Liza Minnelli, wanting to keep things upbeat, insisted that the rooms be decorated in yellow—Judy's favorite color—and that the mourners wear "anything but black." Before the funeral, about 22,000 fans filed past the glass-topped blue-velvet-lined casket, many clutching portable record and tape players that played Judy's greatest hits.

THE FINE ART OF JAYWALKING

Jaywalking has long been a favorite sport among New Yorkers, and out-of-towners are welcome to join in. As Sig Spaeth wrote in a 1926 article entitled "The Advantages of Jay Walking":

"Visitors to New York will find that both exercise and excitement may be had at a minimum of expense through the simple practice of jaywalking. With only a little experience, they may actually compete on even terms with the native New Yorker . . .

One of the first things to be learned is the proper time to start across the street. It is not considered sporting to do this while traffic is standing still. Wait for the policeman's whistle, which is the signal that the cross-current is about to begin. But if you are a stickler for etiquette, take the first step only after the sound of shifting gears has been heard on both sides of the street.

If you get across after that, without having to stop in the middle, you are credited with a perfect score."

Nowadays, the game is played not with policemen's whistles but with "Don't Walk" signs. These usually blink between 10 and 14 times before the traffic starts, and it's perfectly safe to saunter across during the first five blinks. Much more sporting, however, as Spaeth would agree, is to hurry over during the last two or three, or, even better, dash across in those few seconds just after the blinking has stopped and before the traffic has begun. Note: Several signs on Fifth Ave. blink only five times.

CARNEGIE HILL AND VICINITY

The area bounded roughly by 86th and 98th Sts. and by Fifth and Park Aves. is known as Carnegie Hill, one of the city's wealthiest districts. Several important museums line Fifth Ave. here, while the side streets hold a treasure trove of sights.

Guggenheim Museum

The Solomon R. Guggenheim Museum, 1071 Fifth Ave., at 88th St., tel. (212) 423-3500, first opened its doors in 1959, and immediately met with considerable controversy. The city's only Frank Lloyd Wright-designed building, it was compared to everything from a snail to a toilet bowl. Nowadays it's hard to see what the fuss was about. From the outside, the circular building seems as permanent a part of Fifth Ave. as the neoclassic buildings that surround it, while from the inside, the multileveled spirals of the

The once-controversial Guggenheim Museum is now the city's youngest architectural landmark.

main galleries seem almost staid. To show how times have changed, the museum was even declared a New York City landmark in 1989—the youngest building ever to be so honored.

The main galleries of the Guggenheim are usually devoted to a temporary exhibition of a major modern artist or group of artists. Most of the exhibits start at the top, then curve their way slowly downward through a series of bays linked by a circular ramp.

Abutting the main galleries to the north is a small rotunda housing the Justin K. Thannhauser Collection. Works by Picasso, Rousseau, van Gogh, Cézanne, Modigliani, and Seurat, to name but a few, are on permanent display, and they're a stunning group, not to be missed.

Also abutting the main galleries is a glistening 10-story tower, which, upon its completion in 1992, doubled the museum's exhibition space. Lit by skylights, the tower looks out over the Central Park reservoir and boasts an outdoor sculpture garden open in fair weather.

The Guggenheim is open Sun.-Wed. 10 a.m.-6 p.m., Fri.-Sat. 10 a.m.-8 p.m. Admission is adults $8, students and seniors $5, children under 12 free, voluntary donation Fri. 6-8 p.m.

National Academy of Design

The musty National Academy, 1083 Fifth Ave., bet. 89th and 90th Sts., tel. (212) 369-4880, is one of the country's oldest art institutions. It was founded in 1825 by artists Thomas Cole, Rembrandt Peale, Samuel Morse, and others. Today,

425 contemporary artists, elected by their peers, are members of the Academy, which also owns a large collection of 19th- and 20th-century American art.

A selection of work from the permanent collection is always on display, along with loan exhibitions. The museum itself is also an eyeful; it's housed in an stately turn-of-the-century mansion donated to the Academy by sculptor Anna Hyatt Huntington.

Hours are Wed.-Thurs. and Sat.-Sun. noon-5 p.m., Fri. noon-8 p.m. Admission is adults $5, students and senior citizens $3.50, free to children under 12; voluntary donation Fri. 6-8 p.m.

Cooper-Hewitt Museum

A branch of the Smithsonian Institution dedicated to design and the decorative arts, the Cooper-Hewitt, 2 E. 91st St., tel. (212) 860-6898, concentrates on such subjects as textiles, metalwork, wallpaper, ceramics, furniture, and architectural design. But half the story is the building itself; the museum occupies a 64-room mansion built by industrialist Andrew Carnegie after his marriage at the ripe old age of 51.

Carnegie was a Scottish immigrant who began his career as a bobbin boy in a cotton factory. By the time he built this mansion, he was one of the world's richest men, head of an empire that included steamship and railroad lines, and iron, coal, and steel companies.

The magnificent 1901 building is a delight to wander through. Built by Babb, Cook & Willard in a heavy Georgian style, the mansion incorporated all the advanced technologies of its day, including air-conditioning, central heating, and the first passenger elevator in a private home. The plush interior boasts dark wood paneling, an imposing carved staircase, and chandeliers. Out back is a romantic garden, where concerts are sometimes presented, while on the ground floor is an unusual gift shop where you can buy such things as handmade bird houses and reproduction Victorian toys.

The museum is open Tues. 10 a.m.-9 p.m., Wed.-Sat. 10 a.m.-5 p.m., and Sun. noon-5 p.m. Admission is adults $3, students and seniors $1.50, free to children under 12, and free to everyone Tues. 5-9 p.m.

Jewish Museum
Housed in a magnificent French Gothic mansion once belonging to businessman Felix Warburg, the newly restored Jewish Museum, 1109 Fifth Ave., at 92nd St., tel. (212) 423-3200, is the nation's largest Jewish-culture museum. Spread over three floors and a basement are top-notch, changing exhibits on such subjects as "The Dreyfus Affair," or "Jews and African Americans," as well as an outstanding permanent collection of ceremonial objects and cultural artifacts. Among the latter are an ancient Israelite altar; part of a 16th-century Persian synagogue wall; and a collection of Torah cases.

The museum is open Sun.-Thurs. 11 a.m.-5:45 p.m., Tues. 5:45-8 p.m. Admission is adults $7, students and seniors $5, free to children under 12, and free to everyone Tues. 5-8 p.m.

Exploring the Side Streets
On Park Ave. at 92nd St. is a towering Louise Nevelson sculpture called *Night Presence.* The views from here are splendid, stretching all the way down to the gold-topped Helmsley Building at 46th Street.

At 56 E. 93rd St. stands a gorgeous white limestone mansion with a curving facade. Erected in 1932, the 45-room edifice was once home to theatrical producer Billy Rose, who lived here until his death in 1965. Today, the building houses one of the city's most chic and expensive rehab centers, the **Smithers Alcohol and Drug Treatment Center.** Among those who've sought treatment here have been Truman Capote, John

Cheever, Joan Kennedy, Dwight "Doc" Gooden, and Darryl Strawberry.

At 75 E. 93rd St. is the **Russian Orthodox Church Outside Russia,** housed in the former mansion of banker George Baker. In Baker's day, a private railroad line ran directly beneath the house to Grand Central.

Just a few blocks farther north is a second Russian sanctuary—the **Russian Orthodox Cathedral of St. Nicholas,** 15 E. 97th Street. With its five onion domes, gold crosses, and red, yellow, and blue tiles, it's a strange and exotic interloper in this conservative neighborhood.

International Center of Photography
Housed in a red-brick, neo-Georgian mansion is the International Center of Photography (ICP), 1130 Fifth Ave., at 94th St., tel. (212) 860-1777. Cornell Capa founded the center in 1974 to preserve the work of photographers that he felt was being lost (including that of his brother Robert Capa, a photojournalist killed in Vietnam). Today ICP is the city's top exhibitor of photography. Several temporary exhibits, often focusing on the work of one artist, are usually on display at any one time, and they're always first-rate. On the ground floor is a well-stocked gift shop filled with photography books, postcards, and posters.

ICP is open Tues. 11 a.m.-8 p.m., Wed.-Sun. 11 a.m.-6 p.m. Admission is adults $4, students and seniors $2.50, voluntary donation Tues. 6-8 p.m.

Museum of the City of New York
The newly renovated, neo-Georgian building on Fifth Avenue bet. 103rd and 104th Streets houses the one-of-a-kind Museum of the City of New York, tel. (212) 534-1672. Inside this eclectic establishment, find a vast collection of paintings and photographs, maps and prints, furniture and clothing, Broadway memorabilia and old model ships—all telling the story of New York City.

The museum also features imaginative temporary exhibits. Recent examples include exhibitions on Duke Ellington, New York City mayors, photographer Jessie Tarbox Beals, and stickball. On the museum's ground floor is a delightful gift shop.

Hours are Wed.-Sat. 10 a.m.-5 p.m. and Sun. 1-5 p.m. Suggested donation is adults $5; students, seniors and children $3; families $8. The museum also sponsors occasional walking tours.

"You know, the more they knock New York, the bigger it gets."
—WILL ROGERS

El Museo del Barrio

A community museum dedicated to the art and culture of Puerto Rico and Latin America, El Museo del Barrio, 1230 Fifth Ave., bet. 104th and 105th Sts., tel. (212) 831-7272, presents both contemporary and historical exhibits. Just a few blocks from Spanish Harlem, it was founded in an elementary school classroom over 25 years ago, and continues to work closely with local residents. Most of its exhibits are temporary; on permanent display is a superb collection of *santos de palo,* or carved wooden saints.

The museum is open Wed. and Fri.-Sun. 11 a.m-5 p.m., Thurs. noon-7 p.m. Suggested admission is adults $4, seniors $2, children under 12 free.

Note: One block north of *El Museo* at 105th St. is the lovely **Conservatory Garden,** a sometimes overlooked nook of Central Park most easily entered from Fifth Ave.; see "Central Park and the Upper West Side," below.

Islamic Cultural Center

At the corner of 96th St. and Third Ave. is a surprising sight—a modern, gold-domed mosque, built off the axis, facing Mecca. Beside it is a tall skinny minaret from which taped calls-to-prayer are broadcast five times a day.

Largely subsidized by the government of Kuwait, the $17-million mosque was designed in 1988 by an Islamic architect working for the very American company of Skidmore, Owens, & Merrill. Inside, the mosque is a tranquil oasis—all pale greens and blues, with an enormous carpet covered with geometric shapes. About 1,000 men can be accommodated here; the women worship upstairs on the mezzanine level, where they're out of sight.

On Fridays, the mosque is surrounded by a sea of cabs, as Indo-Pakistani, Moroccan, Egyptian, and Arab drivers come from all over the city for the most important service of the week. Smaller services are held on Sundays.

Visitors are welcome to visit the mosque, tel. (212) 722-5234, or to attend the Sunday service, but it's best to call in advance.

Marx Brothers' Residence

Groucho (Julius), Harpo (Adolf), and Chico (Leonard) Marx grew up in a small apartment at 179 E. 93rd St., bet. Lexington and Third Aves., where they lived with seven other family members from 1895 to 1910. In those days, this block was part of a poor Jewish neighborhood sandwiched between an Irish neighborhood to the north and a German one to the south.

The Marxes moved out in 1910 because Minnie Marx, the brothers' mother, decided that the family vaudeville act would do better in Chicago than it had in New York. The Marxes didn't return to live permanently in New York until the 1920s. By then they were famous.

PARK AND LEXINGTON AVENUES

The sights below are arranged from north to south.

The Asia Society

First-rate exhibits, concerts, films, and lectures on various aspects of Asian culture and history are always on tap at the Asia Society, 725 Park Ave., at 70th St., tel. (212) 517-NEWS. Inside the modern red-granite building, you'll also find an extensive book and gift shop. On weekends April-Nov., a bus runs from here to the Isamu Noguchi Garden Museum in Long Island City (see "Queens" in the chapter on The Boroughs); a roundtrip ticket costs $5.

The Asia Society galleries are open Tues.-Sat. 11 a.m.-6 p.m., Thurs. 6-8 p.m., Sun. noon-5 p.m. Admission is adults $3, students and seniors $1; free Thurs. 6-8 p.m.

Seventh Regiment Armory

Between Park and Lexington Aves., 66th and 67th Sts., is an odd sight—an enormous castle-like armory with crenellated towers and iron-studded wooden doors. Inside are long dark corridors, a drill hall, and ornate rooms designed by Louis Tiffany. Large-scale events such as a winter antiques show and a spring crafts show are held here, but otherwise the armory is seldom open.

Jimmy Walker's Uptown Abode

Jimmy Walker, the flamboyant gentleman mayor of New York from 1925 to 1932, lived in a suite at the charming **Mayfair Hotel,** 610 Park Ave., at 65th St., during the last four years of his term. By then he had already left his wife for showgirl Betty Compton. While living here, Walker was forced to resign from office, largely because he was unable to explain how $1 million had mysteriously appeared in his bank account. Immediately thereafter, under a cloud of suspicion, he left for Europe, where he married Compton and lived for the next three years. When he returned to New York, however, his loyal public welcomed him back with open arms, and he was appointed chairman of the garment industry by his old political foe, Fiorella La Guardia. When Walker died on Nov. 18, 1946, hundreds of people tried to see him at the hospital, while thousands more jammed the hospital's telephone lines.

CARL SCHURZ PARK AND VICINITY

This small, idyllic park with meandering walkways and wonderful views stretches between 84th and 90th Sts., East End Ave. and the East River. The park is named for a German-American politician and soldier who campaigned for Abraham Lincoln, served as a brigadier general in the Civil War, and was appointed secretary of the interior under Rutherford Hayes.

From the park southward extends **John H. Finley Walk,** a pleasant pedestrian walkway built above FDR Drive. The brainchild of City Parks Commissioner Robert Moses, the walk was named after a *New York Times* editor who enjoyed walking around Manhattan Island, a distance of 32 miles.

Gracie Mansion

At the north end of the park, at East End Ave. and 88th St., is New York City's mayoral mansion, tel. (212) 570-4751, a pretty wooden house sitting on a small rise. It was built in 1799 as the country home of merchant Archibald Gracie, who once entertained such luminaries as Alexander Hamilton and Washington Irving here. The City of New York appropriated the mansion in 1896 for back taxes, but it wasn't until 1942 that it became the official mayoral residence. New York is one of the nation's only cities with a mayor's mansion.

The house is filled with lovely period pieces, and the guides are brimming with interesting anecdotes. The tour also gives you a good sense of mayoral life; the Giulianis' personal effects are strewn here and there, and it's not unusual to see their children playing on the front lawn.

From Gracie Mansion you have a good view of choppy **Hell Gate,** a treacherous stretch of the East River. Hundreds of wrecks are believed to lie beneath its waters, including a Revolutionary War frigate that went down in 1780 carrying an estimated $500 million in gold and silver coins. The money was meant to be payroll for the British troops stationed in America. Spanning Hell Gate is the Triborough Bridge and, north of that, Hell Gate Arch, which carries railroad tracks.

Tours of Gracie Mansion take place on Wednesdays only, mid-March to mid-November. Reservations must be made two to three weeks in advance. Tour cost is adults $4, seniors $3, children under 12 free.

Henderson Place

On the north side of 86th St. between East End and York Aves. is a small residential alley lined with 24 quaint Queen Anne-style townhouses. The houses were developed by John Jacob Astor, and were once part of his country estate.

In 1944, literary critic Edmund Wilson, his wife novelist Mary McCarthy, and their young son lived at 14 Henderson Place. In the 1950s, actors Lynn Fontanne and Alfred Lunt were Henderson Pl. residents.

Yorkville

Once home to a large German and Hungarian population, Yorkville is now an eclectic neighborhood filled with everything from tacky shops to luxury apartment buildings. The ethnic communities have disappeared, save for a few leftover businesses still in operation here and there.

Most of the German shops and restaurants are on or just off 86th St., a wide and scruffy thoroughfare also known for discount stores. Between Third and Second Aves. are **Kleine Konditorie,** 234 86th St., tel. (212) 737-7130, featuring a bakery up front and traditional German food in back; and **Elk Candy Company,** 240 86th St., tel. (212) 650-1177, known for its old-fashioned marzipan. Just around the corner are **Schaller & Weber,** 1654 Second Ave., tel. (212) 879-3047, a 1937 butcher shop that will mail sausages anywhere in the world; and **Kramer's Pastries,** 1643 Second Ave., tel. (212) 535-5955, often filled with older German women in kerchiefs. Also nearby is **Glaser's Bake Shop,** 1670 First Ave., bet. 87th and 88th Sts., tel. (212) 289-2562, where the *linzer torte* is a local favorite.

What's left of the Hungarian shops is centered around Second Ave. bet. 78th and 84th Streets. **Tibor Meat Specialties,** 1508 Second Ave., at 78th St., tel. (212) 744-8292, sells traditional veal and pork sausage made with plenty of paprika. Ditto the more upscale **Yorkville Packing House,** 1560 Second Ave., at 81st St., tel. (212) 628-5147. Among Hungarian restaurants, **Mocca Restaurant,** 1588 Second Ave., bet. 81st and 82nd Sts., tel. (212) 734-6470, is said to be the best, although the rustic **Red Tulip,** 439 E. 75th St., near First Ave., tel. (212) 734-4893, also draws a big crowd.

LOWER YORK AVENUE AND ROOSEVELT ISLAND

Dead Ringers
The twin gynecologists upon whose life story David Cronenberg's movie *Dead Ringers* was based once lived in an apartment building at 450 E. 63rd St., bet. York Ave. and FDR Drive. Born two minutes apart, Stewart and Cyril Marcus did everything together. They attended the same college and medical school, were captains in the army, held prestigious jobs at New York Hospital, and ran a very successful joint practice on East 72nd Street. Women came from all over the courtry to consult them about fertility problems, and sometimes the doctors switched patients without telling anyone.

The Drs. Marcus also shared an addiction to barbiturates. In 1975, their decomposed bod-ies were found in this building, surrounded by half-eaten sandwiches and empty bottles of pills. The city's medical examiner determined that they were killed by withdrawal from the drugs they'd been taking.

Abigail Adams Smith Museum
The sixth-oldest building in Manhattan now houses the tranquil Abigail Adams Smith Museum, 421 E. 61st St., bet. First and York Aves., tel. (212) 838-6878. The 1799 building sits apart from hurly-burly city life, on a small hill behind a stone wall not far from the East River. It was originally intended to be the carriage house for the country estate of Pres. John Adams's daughter, but due to financial difficulties, she never moved in.

The carriage house then became part of the Mt. Vernon Hotel, which catered to New Yorkers who wanted a day in the country; back then, Uptown was predominantly rural. "Come bathe and sail in the East River," ran the early advertisements.

Today, the nine-room museum is full of period furnishings and paintings, including one that shows E. 61st St. as it once was, complete with meadows, sailboats, and a bathing dock. The museum is run by the Colonial Dames of America, and enthusiastic volunteer guides escort visitors through the rooms.

The museum is open Tues.-Sun. 11 a.m.-4 p.m. Admission is adults $3, students and seniors $2, children under 12 free.

Roosevelt Island
Swinging high above the east end of 60th St. is one of Manhattan's more incongruous sights—the Roosevelt Island cable car. The ride lasts four minutes, costs $1.40, offers great views of the Upper East Side and the East River, and sets you down in one of New York's stranger neighborhoods, Roosevelt Island.

Eerily quiet and empty after the hubbub of Manhattan, Roosevelt Island is a planned residential community where no private cars are allowed. Designed by Philip Johnson and John Burgee, it was built in the 1970s as an "Instant City." In addition to about 3,200 units of mixed-income housing, the community has its own schools and stores, several hospitals, and a promenade with good views of Manhattan.

The best way to get to Roosevelt Island is via cable car.

Roosevelt Island was once known as Blackwell's Island, named after its original owner, Robert Blackwell. Blackwell built the farmhouse that still stands today just north of the tram station. In 1828, the city bought the island and turned it into a penal institution for petty criminals. A grim and nasty place, it was notorious for frequent riots and innovative tortures, including "cooler" rooms and the "water drop cure." Politician Boss Tweed served time there in 1873, and actress Mae West spent 10 days behind bars in 1927 for her notorious play *Sex*. Others incarcerated on the island included anarchist Emma Goldman and birth control advocate Ethel Byrne.

During the 1800s, a poorhouse, a pavilion for the insane, and several hospitals were added to the island, which in 1921 was renamed Welfare Island. These institutions were also notorious for their inhumane conditions, and were

eventually exposed by Charles Dickens and Nellie Bly. Today, the remains of the insane pavilion—a haunting octagonal structure of gray stone—still stand near the island's north end. Also at the north end is a 50-foot-high stone lighthouse, designed by James Renwick, who also designed St. Patrick's Cathedral on Fifth Avenue.

The Roosevelt Island tram station is at the corner of Second Ave. and 60th Street. Maps of the island are available at the ticket booth for 25 cents.

SHOPPING

Books
The enormous **Barnes & Noble** megastore at 1280 Lexington Ave., at 86th St., tel. (212) 423-9900, features endless aisles of books along with comfortable armchairs and an upscale cafe. It's open until 11 p.m. weeknights, 7 p.m. on Sunday.

Kitchen Arts & Letters, 1435 Lexington Ave., near 93rd St., tel. (212) 876-5550, stocks an astonishing array of cookbooks.

Clothing
Among the many upscale clothing stores you'll find on Madison Ave. are **Yves St. Laurent,** 855 Madison, near 71st St., tel. (212) 988-3821; **Polo Ralph Lauren,** 867 Madison, at 72nd St., tel. (212) 606-2100; and **Issey Miyake,** 992 Madison, near 78th St., tel. (212) 439-7822.

Across from Bloomingdale's are many moderately priced clothing shops, including the **Levi Store,** 750 Lexington Ave., at 60th St., tel. (212) 826-5957, a huge warehouse selling jeans in all colors, sizes, and styles. For $65, the store will custom tailor a pair of women's jeans in their 512 cut. **Second Chance Consignment Shop,** 1133 Lexington Ave., bet. 78th and 79th Sts., 2nd fl., tel. (212) 744-6041, is the place to go for secondhand couture. **Tracey Tooker Hats,** 1211 Lexington Ave., near 83rd St., tel. (212) 472-9603, sells an imaginative array of handmade hats.

Department Stores
Once a bargain basement, **Bloomingdale's,** Lexington Ave. at 60th St., tel. (212) 705-2000,

is now one of New York's most glamorous department stores. It's well worth a browse, even if you're not planning to buy. The uptown branch of **Barney's New York,** 660 Madison Ave., at 61st St., tel. (212) 826-8900, headquartered in Chelsea, opened in 1994. It carries fashionable and expensive clothing for men and women.

Gourmet Goodies
Godiva Chocolates sells its luscious confections at 793 Madison Ave., at 67th St., tel. (212) 249-9444. The **Elk Candy Company,** 240 86th St., bet. Second and Third Aves., tel. (212) 650-1177, is known for old-fashioned marzipan. **Schaller & Weber,** 1654 Second Ave., tel. (212) 879-3047, is a 1937 German butcher shop that will mail sausages anywhere in the world.

Gifts
Tenzing & Pena, 956 Madison Ave., near 76th St., tel. (212) 288-8780, offers much in the way of unusual gifts. **Star Magic,** 1256 Lexington Ave., bet. 84th and 85th Sts., tel. (212) 988-0300, is known for "space-age gifts."

Music
The **Metropolitan Opera Shop,** 835 Madison Ave., near 69th St., tel. (212) 734-8406, stocks hundreds of recordings and opera souvenirs. **HMV,** 1280 Lexington Ave. at 86th St., tel. (212) 348-0800, is a vast music supermarket open until 10 p.m. during the week, midnight on Fridays and Saturdays.

Toys and Games
A Bear's Place, 789 Lexington Ave., at 61st St., tel. (212) 826-6465, sells a whole menagerie of stuffed animals. **Big City Kite Company,** 1210 Lexington Ave., at 82nd St., tel. (212) 472-2623, offers kites in all shapes and sizes. **Game Show,** 1240 Lexington Ave., bet. 83rd and 84th Sts., tel. (212) 472-8011, carries games galore; and **Dollhouse Antics,** 1343 Madison Ave. at 94th St., tel. (212) 876-2288, is known for miniatures.

Other Stores
Over a half-dozen **antique stores** are on 60th St. bet. Third and Second Avenues. Nearby is **Things Japanese,** 127 E. 60th St., 2nd Fl., bet.

Lexington and Park Aves., tel. (212) 371-4661, offering antiques, kimonos, and folk art in a variety of price ranges. **Handblock,** 860 Lexington Ave., at 65th St., tel. (212) 570-1816, carries lovely hand-printed fabrics; while **Lalique,** 680 Madison Ave., near 62nd St., tel. (212) 355-6550, is renowned for its crystal and glass. **Dialogica,** 1070 Madison Ave., near 81st St., tel. (212) 737-7811, sells gorgeous art deco furniture.

ACCOMMODATIONS

Moderate
One of the more unusual hotels in this category is the small and stylish **Franklin,** 164 E. 87th St., bet. Lexington and Third Aves., tel. (212) 369-1000. Downstairs is a tiny streamlined lobby done up in black and burnished steel with mirrors and fresh flowers. Upstairs are 53 cozy guest rooms featuring beds with billowing canopies, cherrywood furnishings, and a fresh rose at each bedside. $169-189 s or d; includes continental breakfast and after-theater dessert buffet.

A few blocks north of the Franklin is its Victorian sister hotel, the **Hotel Wales,** 1295 Madison Ave., bet. 92nd and 93rd Sts., tel. (212) 876-6000. Small and old-fashioned in flavor, the Wales centers around a dark green lobby hung with illustrations from the story of Puss and Boots. A worn marble staircase in back leads to 92 attractive guest rooms; next door is Sarabeth's Kitchen, known for its baked goods. $175-185 s or d; includes continental breakfast and after-theater dessert buffet.

The sturdy, red brick **Barbizon Hotel,** 140 E. 63rd St., at Lexington Ave., tel. (212) 838-5700 or (800) 223-1020, was once an old-fashioned hostelry catering exclusively to women; men were only allowed in the public rooms downstairs. In the late '80s, however, the hotel was completely revamped and now caters to both sexes. The low-ceilinged lobby sports vaguely Oriental decor; the guest rooms are newly renovated, with lots of blond wood. $165-200 s, $185-220 d.

Expensive
The friendly **Surrey Hotel,** 20 E. 76th St., bet. Fifth and Madison Aves., tel. (212) 289-3700

or (800) ME-SUITE, is one of the Manhattan Suites properties (see "Midtown," above). Features include a marble-lined lobby furnished in 18th-century style, wood-paneled elevators, and 133 spacious suites accented with molded ceilings and beveled glass. Some of the suites have kitchenettes, others full-sized kitchens. $250-270 s, $270-335 d.

Luxury

First-class service and unerring good taste have made the **Carlyle,** 35 E. 76th St., at Madison Ave., tel. (212) 744-1600 or (800) 227-5737, one of the city's top hotels ever since it opened, in 1930 (see "Up Fifth and Madison Avenues," above). The airy, spacious rooms are equipped with every conceivable amenity, while downstairs, the Cafe Carlyle is home to Bobby Short and other superb jazz musicians. $310-410 s, $340-470 d.

The **Mark,** 25 E. 77th St., near Madison Ave., tel. (212) 744-4300 or (800) 843-6275, is small, stylish, and very elegant, with a neoclassical Italian look. In the lobby, gleaming marble floors reflect sumptuous vases overflowing with fresh flowers. The Mark's Bar offers plenty of cozy nooks and crannies; the guest rooms are large and comfortably furnished. $330-370 s, $355-395 d; weekend rates start at $260 s or d, continental breakfast included.

A magnificent slice of the Old World can be found at the **Pierre,** Fifth Ave. at 61st St., tel. (212) 830-3000 or (800) 332-3442 (see "Up Fifth and Madison Avenues," above). The stunning lobby is adorned with chandeliers, fresh flowers, silks, and damasks, while the guest rooms are lavishly furnished with antiques. A good way to sample the Pierre, even if you can't afford to stay, is to stop in at the baroque-styled Rotunda for an elegant afternoon tea. $375-540 s, $415-580 d.

YMCA

If you're staying a week or more, the **De Hirsch Residence at the 92nd Street Y,** 1395 Lexington Ave., bet. 91st and 92nd Sts., tel. (212) 415-5650 or (800) 858-4692, is a good choice. The newly renovated rooms are spanking clean, and you can attend the Y's many cultural events —including concerts and literary readings—at discounted rates.

FOOD

American

Inexpensive: Open for breakfast, lunch, and dinner is the **Barking Dog Luncheonette,** 1678 Third Ave., at 94th St., tel. (212) 831-1800, a cheery place with good soups, sandwiches, and simple entrees. **Soup Burg,** 1150 Lexington Ave., bet. 79th and 80th Sts., tel. (212) 737-0095, or 1347 Third Ave., at 71st St., tel. (212) 879-4814, is open for lunch and dinner. It's a reliable old standby for hearty soups and salads.

Moderate-to-Expensive: Adjoining the Hotel Wales is **Sarabeth's,** 1295 Madison Ave., bet. 92nd and 93rd Sts., tel. (212) 410-7335, serving homemade American food in a lace and floral setting. The colorful **Arizona 206,** 206 E. 60th St., bet. Third and Second Aves., tel. (212) 838-0440, specializes in creative Southwestern fare; adjacent to the main restaurant is the more moderately priced **Arizona Cafe.**

Asian

Inexpensive: Good Thai restaurants include the friendly **Siam Cuisine,** 1411 Second Ave., at 74th St., tel. (212) 988-5348; and **Sala Thai,** 1718 Second Ave., bet. 89th and 90th Sts., tel. (212) 410-5557.

French

Inexpensive-to-Moderate: Dimly lit **L'Ardoise,** 1207 First Ave., bet. 65th and 66th Sts., tel. (212) 744-4752, is a casual bistro featuring an imaginative menu.

Expensive: Chic **Le Bilboquet,** 25 E. 63rd St., bet. Madison and Park Aves., tel. (212) 751-3036, is a bit snooty, but the food is fine.

Very Expensive: Sign of the Dove, 1110 Third Ave., at 65th St., tel. (212) 861-8080, is a romantic spot, complete with fresh flowers, dark wood, and excellent French-American cuisine; adjacent to the main restaurant is a chic bar and more moderately priced cafe.

Italian

Inexpensive-Moderate: Caffe Grazie, 26 E. 84th St., bet. Fifth and Madison Aves., tel. (212) 717-4407, and **Caffee Buon Gusto,** 236 E. 77th St., bet. Third and Second Aves., tel. (212) 535-6884, are good choices for tasty pasta and other basic entrees.

Expensive: The chic bistro **Paper Moon Milano,** 39 E. 58th St., bet. Madison and Park Aves., tel. (212) 758-8600, may be pricey, but it's also very satisfying, with beautifully presented food. At the intimate **Paola's,** 343 E. 85th St., bet. Second and First Aves., tel. (212) 794-1890, the service is impeccable and the food, first rate.

Latin
Inexpensive: Peruvian **El Pollo,** 1746 First Ave., bet. 90th and 91st Sts., tel. (212) 996-7810, featuring innovative chicken dishes, has proved so popular that it's now opening other branches around the city.

Moderate-to-Expensive: Rosa Mexicano, 1063 First Ave., at 58th St., tel. (212) 753-7407, is a sort of haute-Mexican restaurant popular among East Siders. The pretty and sometimes frenetic bistro **Island,** 1305 Madison Ave., bet. 92nd and 93rd Sts., tel. (212) 996-1200, features eclectic Caribbean cuisine.

Other Ethnic
Moderate: Several German and Hungarian restaurants can still be found in Yorkville; see "Yorkville" under "Carl Schurz Park and Vicinity," above. The **Afghan Kebab House,** 1345 Second Ave., bet. 70th and 71st Sts., tel. (212) 517-2776, serves savory kebabs in a colorful setting. Good Persian food can be found at the cheerful **Persepolis,** 1423 Second Ave., bet. 74th and 75th Sts., tel. (212) 535-1100.

Light Bites
Near the Metropolitan is **Nectar,** 1090 Madison Ave., near 81st St., tel. (212) 772-0916, a standard but reliable coffee shop. **E.A.T.,** 1064 Madison Ave., bet. 80th and 81st Sts., tel. (212) 772-0022, is a pricey gourmet-food shop and cafe.

Lexington Candy Shop, 1226 Lexington Ave., at 83rd St., tel. (212) 288-0057, is an old-fashioned luncheonette founded in 1925. For German bakeshops, see "Yorkville," under "Carl Schurz Park and Vicinity," above.

The funky, standing-room-only **Papaya King,** E. 59th St., at Third Ave. and E. 86th St. at Third Ave., sells luscious papaya juice and succulent franks. Greenwich Village's first-rate **John's Pizzeria** has an uptown location at 408 E. 64th St., near First Ave., tel. (212) 935-2895.

Watering Holes and Lounges
The institutions in this part of town are **J.G. Melon,** 1291 Third Ave., at 74th St., tel. (212) 744-0585, a friendly joint also serving great burgers; and **Jim McMullen's,** 1341 Third Ave., bet. 76th and 77th Sts., tel. (212) 861-4700, especially popular among ex-football players, models, and business execs. The famed **Elaine's,** the celebrity hangout and Italian restaurant, is at 1703 Second Ave., bet. 88th and 89th Sts., tel. (212) 534-8103, and sports a crowded bar that's especially worth a visit if you've just got to spot SOMEONE. For class, stop into the dark and gracious **Bemelmans Bar,** in the posh Hotel Carlyle, 35 E. 76th St., at Madison Ave., tel. (212) 744-1600.

The Upper East Side is also home to a number of singles bars that come and go with the seasons. Among them is the **Big Cat Cafe,** 1374 First Ave., bet. 73rd and 74th Sts., tel. (212) 717-2288, which takes its name very seriously, with paw prints on the floor and drawings of cats on the rough, brown walls. **Rudy's Tap House,** 1754 Second Ave., bet. 91st and 92nd Sts., tel. (212) 348-2328, is a lively joint with a twenty-something crowd. **Merchants NY,** 1125 First Ave., at 62st St., tel. (212) 832-1551, is sleek and stylish, with a polished semicircular bar, lots of small tables, and flickering candles.

Among neighborhood hangouts, **Rathbones,** 1702 Second Ave., near 88th St., tel. (212) 369-7361, is a large, creaky tavern with heavy wooden tables and sawdust-covered floors. The laid-back **Kinsale Tavern,** 1672 Third Ave., at 94th St., tel. (212) 348-4370, an Irish pub, attracts everyone from clerical workers to politicians. Beer buffs can boogie into the new **Yorkville Brewery,** 1359 First Ave., at 73rd St., tel. (212) 517-2739.

DOVER PUBLICATIONS, INC.

CENTRAL PARK AND THE UPPER WEST SIDE

A mix of ornate 19th-century landmarks, solid pre-WW II apartment buildings, and well-worn tenements, the Upper West Side is primarily a residential district. Unlike the Upper East Side with its upper-crust traditions, the Upper West Side is known for its feisty liberal politics, love of culture, and upper-middle class, including an especially large quotient of doctors, lawyers, writers, actors, musicians, dancers, and intellectuals.

Up until the late 19th century, the Upper West Side was called the Bloomingdale district, named after the Dutch word for "vale of flowers." Washington Irving once described the area as "a sweet rural valley, beautiful with many a bright flower, refreshed by many a pure streamlet, and enlived here and there by a delectable little Dutch cottage."

The district began developing in the late 1800s with the building of the Dakota, a grand apartment house. Prior to the Dakota, most middle-class and wealthy Americans regarded the apartment-house concept as too "French"—i.e., risqué and common. All those strangers rubbing shoulders together in communal hallways. The lavish appointments of the Dakota quickly changed that attitude.

The Upper West Side received its second seismic shift in the late 1960s when Lincoln Center displaced the sprawling, largely poor neighborhood of San Juan Hill. As the poorer people were forced out, the wealthier ones moved in, and the area became more and more fashionable—a process that is continuing today throughout the Upper West Side.

The best streets for wandering are Broadway and Columbus Ave., both lined with a multitude of shops. In comparison, the streets running from east to west tend to be quiet and almost exclusively residential.

Central Park lies between Fifth and Eighth Aves., 59th and 110th Streets. The two gracious avenues lining it to the south and west are called Central Park South (a continuation of 59th St.) and Central Park West (a continuation of Eighth Ave.), respectively.

Weekends are the best time to visit Central Park; any time is a good time to tour the Upper West Side. First-time visitors will probably want to check out the southern end of Central Park, Lincoln Center, and the American Museum of Natural History, and take a stroll along Columbus or Broadway.

CENTRAL PARK

Between the Upper East and the Upper West Sides lies that most glorious of New York institutions, Central Park. Without this vast, rolling estate of green—the lungs of the city—life in New York would become unbearable. Despite the highly publicized crimes that occasionally occur here, Central Park is where New Yorkers go to escape cramped apartments, roaring traffic, and an endless cityscape of concrete and steel.

The Central Park, as it was once known, was the brainchild of poet turned newspaper editor William Cullen Bryant. Worried that the city was being smothered by block after block of relentless building, Bryant first called for the park's creation in the July 3, 1844, edition of his *Evening Post.* Landscape architect Andrew Jackson Downing and a number of politicians soon added their voices to Bryant's plea. Together, they hammered away at city government for 12 years until finally, in 1856, the city bought most of what is now the park for $5 million. The land at that time was ugly and desolate, filled with scrawny trees and rocky outcroppings, but it was also home to several small villages, established by groups of squatters. Among them was Seneca Village, an early African-American settlement whose existence was only rediscovered in 1996; it and all other villages were destroyed in the building of the park.

Frederick Law Olmsted and Calvert Vaux were the visionary landscape architects who turned Bryant's Central Park dream into reality. As Olmsted saw it, the park had two functions. One was to provide a place for the contemplation of nature. The other was to create a social mixing bowl where the haves and have-nots could pass each other every day, providing an opportunity for the poor to become inspired by the rich.

Entirely manmade—with every bush, tree, and rock planned—the park took 20 years to complete. By the time it was finished, workers had shifted 10 million cartloads of dirt, imported a half-million cubic yards of topsoil, and planted four- to five-million trees. Central Park was such an immediate and overwhelming success that it led to a park movement across the U.S. and the world.

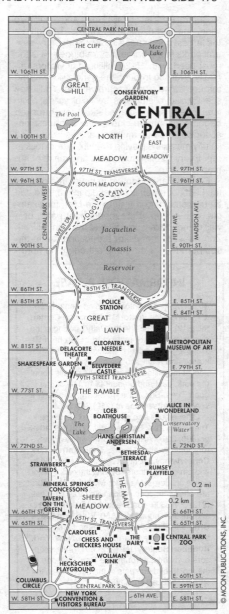

Central Park is 2.5 miles long and a half mile wide, and covers about 843 acres. Though not the largest open space in New York City—several parks in the boroughs are bigger—it is the most used, with 15-20 million day visitors annually. Walking through the park is like walking through some gigantic carnival site. You'll see scantily clad rollerbladers, svelte bicyclists, oblivious lovers, sports-crazed kids, cough-racked beggars, cashmere-clad matrons, professional dogwalkers with multiple canines in tow, and scruffy musicians playing everything from rock to rap. Every size, shape, color, and make of humanity is here.

Central Park is too big to cover in a day, so the best approach is to just dip into it here and there, combining a visit to the Met, for example, with a stop at the model-boat pond, or a visit to the Plaza with a stop at the Central Park Zoo. Most of the visitor attractions are in the southern half of the park, although the north-ern reaches are currently being restored and rediscovered. On the weekends, most of the park is safe (though keep your eyes open when visiting the Ramble and some northern areas), but during the week, it's best to stick to well-populated areas. Avoid the park completely at night. If you get lost during your visit, just find a lamppost—each is marked with the number of the nearest street.

South of 65th Street

Entering Central Park at Fifth Ave. and 59th St., through what is known as **Scholar's Gate,** you'll soon come to the delightful **Central Park Zoo,** tel. (212) 861-6030. Completely overhauled in 1988, this small state-of-the-art gem groups its animals by climatic zones; especially fun is Polar Circle, where polar bears prowl and penguins promenade in a snowy clime behind thick glass. The zoo is open daily 10 a.m.-4:30 p.m., with longer hours in summer. Admission is adults $2.50, seniors $1.25, children 3-12 fifty cents, under three free.

Above the arch at the zoo's northeast end is **Delacorte Clock,** where every hour a parade of bronze animals marches around playing nursery tunes. The clock was a gift to the city from philanthropist George Delacorte, who also gave the park the Alice in Wonderland statue at Conservatory Water and the open-air Delacorte Theater at the Great Lawn. Ironically, Mr. Delacorte and his wife, then ages 92 and 66, respectively, were mugged in the park one morning in 1985. The thieves got away with Mr. Delacorte's wallet and Mrs. Delacorte's $5500 mink coat. That incident might have discouraged a lesser man, but Delacorte simply said, "I've walked five miles in the park every day of my life. This will not stop me." He kept walking in the park until his death in 1991 at age 98.

Just across East Dr. from the zoo is **Wollman Rink,** tel. (212) 396-1010, packed in winter with exuberant ice skaters of all ages. In summer, Wollman becomes a roller rink and miniature golf course. Admission is adults $6, children under 13 $3.

North of the rink is the octagonal **Chess and Checkers House,** complete with 24 concrete game boards outside and 10 tables inside. Free playing pieces for the boards can be picked up with a photo ID in the nearby **Dairy** building,

INFORMATION, PLEASE

For up-to-date information on Central Park, stop by the **Visitors' Information Center,** tel. (212) 794-6564, in the Dairy building in the center of the park just south of the 65th St. Transverse. The center features a small exhibit area and a gift shop, where you can buy a pocket map filled with wonderful details about the park, past and present ($4). The center is open Tues.-Sun. 11 a.m.-5 p.m., and runs a special events hotline at (212) 360-3456.

Other groups also sponsor events in the park. The **Urban Park Rangers,** tel. (212) 427-4040 or (800) 201-PARK, offers free weekend environmental walking tours. The **Central Park Conservancy,** tel. (212) 360-2727, offers hour-and-a-half trolley tours covering the park's major points of interest May-Oct. Mon.-Fri. The tours are offered in conjunction with Gray Line, tel. (212) 397-3809; cost is adults $15, seniors $13, and children under 12 $7.50. **Wild Man Steve Brill,** tel. (718) 291-6825, leads fascinating botany and foraging tours. The **New York Audubon Society,** tel. (212) 691-7483, sponsors bird walks through the Ramble—one of the top 10 birding spots in the country—in the spring, summer, and fall.

the perennial Central Park chess game, this one circa 1946

NATIONAL ARCHIVES

which also houses the **Visitors' Information Center.** Dating back to the park's earliest days, the Dairy was once an actual working dairy selling glasses of fresh milk. The cows were kept in a pasture where the Wollman Rink is now.

Directly west of the Dairy are the gay colors and the 58 beautifully carved horses of the **Carousel,** tel. (212) 879-0244, built in 1908. The carousel operates daily 10:30 a.m-5 p.m., weather permitting. Just south of the Carousel is **Heckscher Playground,** with five softball diamonds, handball courts, horseshoes, and a puppet theater.

The sunken transverse road running from E. 65th St. to W. 66th St. is one of four such roads in the park (the others are at 79th, 85th, and 97th Streets). These roads were one of Olmsted's most brilliant innovations. Dynamited out of bedrock, they allow cars and buses to pass below the level of the park, while pedestrians pass on bridges above. This makes it possible, in Olmsted's words, for even "the most timid and nervous to go on foot to any district of the park."

65th Street to 72nd Street
Heading a bit farther north and west, you'll come to **Tavern-on-the-Green,** tel. (212) 873-3200, a glittering extravaganza of a restaurant on the edge of the park near 67th St. and Central Park West. Built to resemble a deluxe Victorian cottage, the over-the-top Tavern is packed to the bursting point with brass, glass, mirrors, chandeliers, thousands upon thousands of tiny lights, and, of course, tourists. It's all very festive, especially in the late afternoons when it takes on a fairy-tale air.

The Tavern-on-the-Green borders **Sheep Meadow,** a huge expanse of lawn covered with thousands of semiclad sun-worshippers in warm weather. Real sheep grazed here until 1934 when Parks Commissioner Robert Moses got rid of them. By then, the sheep were so inbred that many were malformed.

East of Sheep's Meadow is the **Mall,** a promenade lined with trees and busts of famous men. This quarter-mile avenue was once a parade ground for the elite, who cruised up and down in the late afternoons, courting and showing off their fancy carriages. Today, the Mall is frequented by rollerbladers, especially on the weekends when an impromptu blading party regularly takes place. Then, seemingly hundreds of lithe, muscular skaters dressed in tight, bright spandex, twist and turn, jump and flex, 'round and 'round as a deejay blasts out music from a big black box.

North of the Mall is the bandshell at **Rumsey Playfield,** where a first-rate series of free outdoor concerts is presented every summer by **SummerStage,** tel. (212) 360-CPSS (-2777). Past performers have ranged from blueswoman Ruth Brown to the Erick Hawkins Dance Company.

72nd Street to 79th Street
Bethesda Terrace, just north of the bandshell

and the 72nd St. Transverse, is one of the park's grandest sights. The wide, brick-paved plaza centers around an ornate fountain featuring a statue called *Angel of the Waters* by Emma Stebbins. Surrounding the plaza is a semicircle of tiered steps where you can sit and listen to the street musicians who perform here in warm weather. Lapping at the north end of the terrace is **The Lake,** a peaceful spot usually crowded with splish-splashing rowboats. These boats can be rented at the nearby **Loeb Boathouse,** tel. (212) 517-4723, daily 10 a.m.-dusk. The cost is $10 per hour, with a $30 deposit. Also at the boathouse is a bike-rental shop.

West of Bethesda Terrace is **Strawberry Fields,** which Yoko Ono had landscaped into a Garden of Peace as a memorial to her husband John Lennon (see "The Dakota" under "Central Park West," below). Just inside the garden's wall at 72nd St. is a circular Italian-marble mosaic spelling out the word *Imagine.* Fans gather here in especially large numbers every Oct. 9 and Dec. 8 to commemorate Lennon's birth and death, and a few regulars can almost always be found here. One of those regulars is Poet O., a burly man with wiry white hair who sits in front of a basket with a bell and calls out, "Ring the bell. Make a wish." If you stop, Poet O. will tell you to concentrate, make a wish, ring the bell, and donate something to his dinner fund. Yet Poet O. is also a genuine wordsmith. When asked, he'll recite part of his poem "Grief," written during the all-night vigil following Lennon's assassination.

East of Bethesda Terrace is the **Conservatory Water,** better known to New Yorkers as the model-boat pond. The pond is often dotted with miniature boats, most radio-controlled. During warm weather, a model-boat regatta is held on Saturday mornings.

Near the model-boat pond are two of the park's most famous statues: *Alice in Wonderland,* by Jose de Creefts, perches on a mushroom to the north, while *Hans Christian Andersen,* by Georg Lober, sits with his Ugly Duckling to the west. Both statues are usually covered with adoring children, playing, climbing, and posing for photographs. Storytellers often perform at the Hans Christian Andersen statue on Saturday mornings.

West of the model-boat pond and north of The Lake is the 38-acre **Ramble,** a near wild place crisscrossed with meandering footpaths. Far removed from city life, the Ramble is a favorite spot among birdwatchers; on a typical morning, about 15 kinds of warblers and 35 other species can be seen. It's also a prime haunt for gay men on the make, and condoms litter the woods. It's best not to visit the Ramble alone.

79th Street to 97th Street

North of the Ramble is the Gothic Revival **Belvedere Castle,** designed in 1858 by Calvert Vaux. Situated atop Vista Rock, one of the park's highest spots, the castle offers bird's-eye views from its top floor. Downstairs is the **Central Park Learning Center.** The castle is open during daylight hours; admission is free.

Near the castle are the bedraggled **Shakespeare Garden,** filled with plants and flowers mentioned in the playwright's work, and the **Delacorte Theater,** where a free **Shakespeare-in-the-Park** festival, tel. (212) 861-7277 or 539-6500, is presented every summer. Two plays are usually featured, each running about a month. The free tickets for each day's show are handed out beginning at 6:15 p.m. the same day, and people start lining up for the tickets in the early afternoon.

Abutting the Delacorte Theater is the dry and often dusty **Great Lawn,** where yet more free events are held in summer. Tens of thousands of New Yorkers spread out their blankets and picnic baskets on the lawn when the New York Philharmonic and the Metropolitan Opera Company perform here. At other times, the Great Lawn hosts innumerable softball, soccer, football, field hockey, and Frisbee games.

At the southeastern edge of the Great Lawn, just behind the Metropolitan Museum of Art, is **Cleopatra's Needle.** The 200-ton granite obelisk was rolled here on cannonballs in 1880. It was once engraved with hieroglyphics, but those have been almost completely worn away by pollution and the elements.

North of the Great Lawn is Central Park Reservoir, now known as **Jacqueline Onassis Reservoir** because the former first lady used to jog around its 1.58-mile perimeter. This is the city's most popular jogging course; Dustin Hoffman even jogged here in *Marathon Man.* The reservoir holds about a billion gallons of water, most of which comes via aqueduct from the Catskills.

North of 97th Street

The northernmost section of Central Park, between 97th and 110th Sts., is often overlooked by locals and out-of-towners alike, but holds a number of unusual gems. As Frederick Law Olmsted originally intended, the park here becomes rugged and wild, filled with secret waterfalls, craggy cliffs, and—at 105th St. near Fifth Ave.—the lovely, formal **Conservatory Garden.** Actually three gardens in one, the Conservatory was restored in the mid-1980s and now blooms from late spring through early fall. Its most popular spot is the Secret Garden, named after Frances Hodgson Burnett's classic book. A statue of the book's two central characters—Mary and Dickon—stands at the garden's center.

Just above the Conservatory is 11-acre **Meer Lake,** surrounded by bald cypress trees, flowering shrubs, and wetlands. Up until recently, this lake—like much of the park above 97th St. —was avoided by New Yorkers fearful of crime. But since the early 1990s, the Central Park Conservancy has been pouring millions of dollars into the area and it's been vastly improved. Meer Lake is now stocked with some 50,000 bluegill, largemouth bass, and catfish, and has become a favorite fishing grounds for youngsters who are given free poles and told to go fish.

Also new to Meer Lake is the **Charles A. Dana Discovery Center.** The center houses natural history exhibits, and offers free hands-on science programs.

LINCOLN CENTER AND VICINITY

Columbus Circle

This gray, windswept circle is marked by a constant rush of traffic and a tiny statue of Columbus perched atop an 80-foot column. On the south side stands a white, vaguely Islamic-style building originally designed by Edward Durrell Stone to house the art collection of A&P heir Huntington Hartford. Considered an architectural fiasco when it opened in 1965, the building is now just another New York anomaly.

It was at Columbus Circle that Mafia boss Joe Colombo was gunned down on June 28, 1971. Colombo, who always claimed to be just a simple real estate salesman from South Brooklyn, had formed the Italian American Civil Rights League earlier in the year. On that June day, he sponsored an Italian Unity Day at Columbus Circle. Thousands showed up for the antidiscrimination rally, but before things could get properly underway, a young man wearing press credentials shot Colombo in the face and head. Colombo was rushed to the hospital, but ended up permanently and almost totally paralyzed. He died of a stroke seven years later. Investigators believe that Joe Gallo, Colombo's arch rival, was responsible for the hit; Gallo didn't last too much longer himself (see "Umberto's Clam House" under "Little Italy" in "Chinatown, Little Italy, and the Lower East Side," above).

Lincoln Center

On the west side of Broadway between 62nd and 66th Sts. is the famed Lincoln Center for the Performing Arts, which presents about 3,000 performances each year. Centering around a circular fountain and a wide marble plaza, the 14-acre complex always seems to be filled with well-dressed concertgoers scurrying to get to their seats on time, and pastel-clad sightseers swinging their legs as they sit on the fountain's rim.

Completed in 1969, Lincoln Center was another Robert Moses project. The center aroused much controversy when it was built, due to its displacement of San Juan Hill—a neighborhood named in honor of the black veterans of the Spanish-American War who once lived there. When construction began, over 7,000 families were thrown out of their apartments and, despite city government assurances to the contrary, received little or no relocation assistance. Most resettled in Harlem and the Bronx.

Lincoln Center consists of three major theaters and an assortment of related buildings. **Avery Fisher Hall,** tel. (212) 875-5030, on the plaza's north side, is where the New York Philharmonic performs, and where most of the larger classical-music and jazz concerts are presented. The **Metropolitan Opera House,** tel. (212) 362-6000, on the plaza's west side, is the center's most ornate building, graced with sparkling multistoried windows and two vivid murals by Marc Chagall. The **New York State**

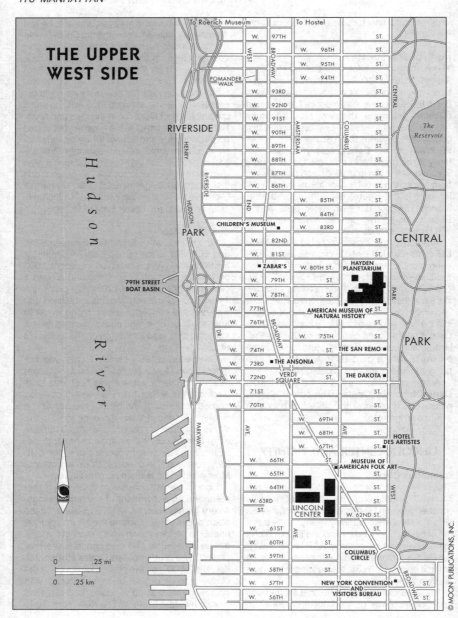

THE UPPER WEST SIDE

To Roerich Museum

To Hostel

W. 97TH
W. 96TH
W. 95TH
W. 94TH
W. 93RD
W. 92ND
W. 91ST
W. 90TH
W. 89TH
W. 88TH
W. 87TH
W. 86TH
W. 85TH
W. 84TH
W. 83RD
W. 82ND
W. 81ST
W. 80TH ST.
W. 79TH ST.
W. 78TH ST.
W. 77TH
W. 76TH
W. 75TH
W. 74TH
W. 73RD
W. 72ND
W. 71ST
W. 70TH
W. 69TH
W. 68TH
W. 67TH
W. 66TH
W. 65TH
W. 64TH
W. 63RD ST.
W. 62ND ST.
W. 61ST
W. 60TH
W. 59TH
W. 58TH
W. 57TH
W. 56TH

POMANDER WALK

WEST
BROADWAY
AMSTERDAM
COLUMBUS
CENTRAL

RIVERSIDE

HENRY HUDSON

RIVERSIDE END

PARK

Hudson River

CENTRAL

The Reservoir

PARK

CHILDREN'S MUSEUM

ZABAR'S

79TH STREET BOAT BASIN

HAYDEN PLANETARIUM

AMERICAN MUSEUM OF NATURAL HISTORY

THE SAN REMO

THE ANSONIA

VERDI SQUARE

THE DAKOTA

BROADWAY

DR.

PARKWAY

AVE.

HOTEL DES ARTISTES

MUSEUM OF AMERICAN FOLK ART

WEST

LINCOLN CENTER

AVE.

COLUMBUS CIRCLE

NEW YORK CONVENTION AND VISITORS BUREAU

BROADWAY

0   .25 mi
0   .25 km

MOON

© MOON PUBLICATIONS, INC.

Theater, tel. (212) 870-5570, on the plaza's south side, is home to the New York City Opera and the New York City Ballet.

Lincoln Center extends to the northwest just beyond Avery Fisher Hall. Here are located the **Vivian Beaumont Theater,** tel. (212) 362-7600, which stages Broadway plays and musicals; and the **Lincoln Center Library for the Performing Arts,** tel. (212) 870-1630, which stores a vast collection of sheet music and recordings, and presents frequent exhibits on the performing arts.

Ho-hum tours of Lincoln Center leave daily from the concourse level; call (212) 875-5350 for information. More interesting tours of the Metropolitan Opera House, tel. (212) 769-7020, are also offered. The Lincoln Center hotline for upcoming events is (212) 875-5400. In late July and early August, **Midsummer Night Swing,** tel. (212) 875-5102, offers dancing to live bands on the plaza beneath the stars.

Miss Liberty

Looking east from Lincoln Center, you'll see a miniature Statue of Liberty perched atop the former Liberty Warehouse at 43 W. 64th Street. The 55-foot replica of the original lady was commissioned by the warehouse owner in the late 1800s. It was sent to New York by rail from an Ohio foundry, and had to be sliced in half to fit through the railroad tunnels.

Museum of American Folk Art

Directly across from Lincoln Center is the small but delightful Museum of American Folk Art, 2 Lincoln Center, Broadway bet. 65th and 66th Sts., tel. (212) 595-9533. The museum is housed in an airy complex of rooms containing plenty of inviting benches. The temporary exhibits focus on quilts, toys, weather vanes, samplers, paintings, handmade furniture, and the like.

Hours are Tues.-Sun. 11:30 a.m.-7:30 p.m. Admission is by donation. Next door is an eclectic gift shop filled with imaginative items, many of them handmade.

Columbus Avenue

Actually an extension of Ninth Ave., Columbus Ave. begins just north of the Museum of American Folk Art, at 66th St., and is packed cheek-by-jowl with shops and restaurants. Some of these establishments have been around for decades, but most started up in the late 1980s or '90s, and this is usually the strip people are referring to when they complain about the "yuppie-ization" of the Upper West Side.

Just north of Lincoln Center are numerous coffee bars, ice cream shops, and restaurants. Then around 71st St. begin the clothing and specialty stores.

Hotel des Artistes

At 1 W. 67th St. stands the renowned Hotel des Artistes, its elaborate interior bursting with plush furnishings, dark wooden beams, and mildly erotic murals by Howard Chandler Christy. Originally built to accommodate artists, the 1915 hotel was soon too expensive for anyone but the well-to-do. Famous residents have included Rudoph Valentino, Noel Coward, Norman Rockwell, Isadora Duncan, and former New York mayor John Lindsay. On the building's ground floor is the romantic and pricey **Cafe des Artistes,** tel. (212) 877-3500, featured in Louis Malle's 1981 film, *My Dinner with Andre.*

James Dean's Apartment

After leaving the Hotel Iroquois (see "Bryant Park to the Diamond District" under "Midtown," above), Dean settled into a tiny room with a bathroom down the hall at 19 W. 68th Street. He was living here when he left for Hollywood in 1954 to shoot his first major film, *East of Eden,* and he returned here in 1955 for what would prove to be an unhappy visit home. According to friends, he was cranky and ill at ease, and blew up at his former girlfriend when she refused to take any money out of his suitcase full of cash. Dean left New York soon thereafter, and died in a car crash nine months later.

CENTRAL PARK WEST

Many of the Upper West Side's most impressive buildings stand sentinel along Central Park West (CPW). Just south of the Hotel des Artistes are the splendid art deco **Century Apartments,** 25 CPW, bet. 62nd and 63rd Sts.; and **55 CPW,** at 65th Street. Ethel Merman lived in the Century Apartments in the 1930s; Sigourney Weaver's character lived at 55 CPW in *Ghostbusters.*

At the southwest corner of 70th St. is the synagogue of the **Congregation Shearith Israel,** 99 CPW. The nation's oldest Jewish congregation, the Shearith Israel, or "remnant of Israel," dates to 1654 when the first Jewish refugees arrived in the New World after escaping the Spanish Inquisition. Their graveyard near Chinatown is New York City's oldest artifact.

On the southwest corner of 72nd St. and CPW is the twin-towered art deco **Majestic,** one of the city's most luxurious apartment houses. Movie director Elia Kazan and entertainer Milton Berle once lived here, along with gangsters Frank Costello, Meyer Lansky, and Lucky Luciano. Costello was shot in the Majestic's lobby on May 2, 1957, but survived the attack and continued to peacefully reside in his penthouse apartment with his wife, their poodle, and Doberman pinscher until he died of natural causes in 1973.

The Dakota

On the northwest corner of 72nd St. and Central Park West is the avenue's most famous apartment building—the Dakota. Built in 1884, the Dakota was financed by Edward Clark, heir to the Singer Sewing Machine fortune. At the time of its construction, the building stood so far north of the rest of Manhattan that it was said to be as remote as Dakota. Clark liked that idea, and had the architect, Henry Hardenburgh, add ears of corn and an Indian's head above the entrance.

Built of light-colored brick, the Dakota resembles a European chateau. A dry moat topped with a cast-iron fence surrounds the building, and a porter in a sentry box guards the front door.

The Dakota's roster of famous tenants may be the most impressive in the city. Among those who've lived here are Lauren Bacall, Judy Holliday, Jack Palance, Roberta Flack, Fannie Hurst, Jose Ferrer, Rosemary Clooney, John Lennon, Yoko Ono, Gilda Radner, and William Henry Pratt, a.k.a. Boris Karloff. Legend has it that on Halloween, the kids in the building were too afraid of Karloff to take any of the trick-or-treat candy he left outside his door.

John Lennon was murdered outside the Dakota on Dec. 8, 1980. His assassin, Mark David Chapman (whose *Double Fantasy* album

John Lennon was murdered outside the grand Dakota in 1980.

Lennon had autographed only six hours earlier), jumped out of the shadows as the star returned home and shot him four times in the back and chest. By the time the cops arrived, Chapman was leaning against the side of the Dakota reading *Catcher in the Rye*. "Please don't hurt me," he said as he was arrested.

Directly across from the Dakota in Central Park is **Strawberry Fields,** the teardrop-shaped acre of land that Yoko Ono had landscaped in her husband's memory.

San Remo

Two blocks north of the Dakota at 74th St. is another famous Upper West Side residence, the mammoth twin-towered **San Remo Apartments,** 145-146 CPW. Home at various times to Dustin Hoffman, Mary Tyler Moore, Raquel Welch, Donald Sutherland, Paul Simon, Tony Randall, and Diane Keaton, the San Remo is also where the legendary actress Rita Hayworth lived at the sad end of her life. A victim of Alzheimer's disease, Hayworth needed nurses round the clock. Up until her death in 1987, a single rose arrived for her daily, sent by her old friend, Glenn Ford.

American Museum of Natural History

Though long one of the city's greatest museums, justifiably famous for its breathtaking dioramas, the American Museum of Natural History, CPW at 79th St., tel. (212) 769-5100, has traditionally been a rather chaotic and musty affair. Recently, however, the museum—always crowded with hundreds of shouting, shoving, enthusiastic kids—has been quietly entering the modern era, refurbishing old galleries and introducing new, state-of-the-art exhibitions.

At the heart of the museum's collections are its approximately 100 dinosaur specimens, nearly 85% of which are real fossils. Housed beneath soaring windows and ceilings in the newly renovated Theodore Roosevelt Memorial Hall, the dinosaurs are mounted in dramatic poses, just as they must have appeared millions of years ago while hunting, climbing trees, rearing up, or running. The most amazing skeleton of all is that of a skinny, 50-foot-high barosaurus arching its angry neck high into the dome as it protects its young from the much smaller allosaurus. The collection's smallest artifact is a tiny, fossilized dinosaur embryo, unearthed in the Gobi Desert in 1993.

Other highlights of the museum—which owns about 37 million specimens—include the African Mammals wing, featuring seven furious stampeding elephants; the recently expanded Hall of Human Biology and Evolution, where a holographic "Visible Woman" struts her circulatory stuff; and the brand-new Hall of Primitive Vertebrates, which traces the evolution of the first animals with backbones. Also, be sure to visit at least one of the museum's several gift shops, which are packed with unusual items from around the world.

The Hayden Planetarium, which adjoined the museum for decades, is now closed. An ambitious new state-of-the-art planetarium is scheduled to open as part of the museum's Center for Earth and Science in the year 2000.

The museum is open Sun.-Thurs. 10 a.m.-5:45 p.m. and Fri.-Sat. 10 a.m.-8:45 p.m. Suggested admission is adults $7, students and seniors $5, children under 12 $4.

72ND STREET AND BROADWAY

At the busy intersection of 72nd St. and Broadway is **Verdi Square**, complete with a statue of composer Giuseppe Verdi, erected in 1906. Though much cleaned up in recent years, this small triangle of green was once known as Needle Park. At one point, 25% of New York's heroin addicts were believed to live within a few blocks of here; the 1971 movie *Panic in Needle Park* was filmed here. Immediately across from Verdi Square is one of the only original subway kiosks still left in the city. Built to look like a Dutch cottage, the structure dates back to 1904, when the IRT reached the Upper West Side.

Of Murder and Madams

At 250 W. 72nd St., bet. Broadway and West End, once stood Tweed's, the tavern where schoolteacher Roseanne Quinn met psychopath John Wayne Williams on New Year's Eve, 1973. The pair were strangers when they met, but they danced and partied for hours and then crossed the street to Quinn's apartment at 253 W. 72nd St., where Williams stabbed Quinn to death. That killing became the inspiration for Judith Rossner's book, *Looking for Mr. Goodbar,* later made into a movie starring Diane Keaton and Richard Gere. Williams was eventually arrested; he killed himself in jail. Tweed's is now the All-State Cafe.

Yet another infamous New York address is two blocks north at 307 W. 74th St., bet. West End and Riverside. This solid, innocuous-looking brownstone is where the Mayflower Madam, Sydney Biddle Barrows, conducted her $1-million-a-year prostitution ring from 1979 to 1984. The daughter of blue bloods listed in the Social Register, Barrows never served time for running her 300-woman service; instead she copped a plea and paid a mere $5,000 fine. That light sentencing probably had something to do with her "black book" listing the names of her rich and famous clients, who were *very* interested in keeping the case from going to trial. Barrow has since gone on to write several best-selling books, and runs seminars teaching women "call girl secrets that work."

The Ansonia

From 72nd St. north, Broadway is a mix of ornate old apartment buildings, specialty food stores, and dingy, hole-in-the-wall shops. At the northwest corner of Broadway and 73rd St. is the extraordinary, though now somewhat worn, beaux arts Ansonia. Covered with towers, mansard roofs, balconies, and gargoyles, this opulent building had all the state-of-the-art amenities of its day when it opened in 1903, including electric stoves, air-conditioning, freezers, a pneumatic tube system for delivering messages, two swimming pools, a lobby fountain complete with playful seals, and a roof garden inhabited by a bear.

The building also had incredibly thick walls, which meant that its rooms were among the most soundproof in the city. This feature attracted many famous musicians to take up residence, including Enrico Caruso, Igor Stravinsky, Arturo Toscanini, Ezio Pinza, and Lily Pons. Theatrical impresario Florenz Ziegfeld moved into the building as well, living with his wife on one floor and keeping a mistress on another.

Members of the 1919 Chicago White Sox were staying at the Ansonia when they conspired to fix the World Series that year. Babe Ruth moved into the building in 1920 when he joined the New York Yankees, and stayed until 1929. Entertainer Bette Midler got her start in a gay spa that occupied the Ansonia's basement in the early 1960s. Some of this history is chronicled in an informal exhibit in the Ansonia's lobby.

Children's Museum of Manhattan

The bright and cheery Children's Museum, 212 W. 83rd St., bet. Broadway and Amsterdam Ave., tel. (212) 721-1223, is full of hands-on exhibits for kids ages 2-10. Here, children can draw and paint, learn crafts, play at being newscasters, listen to stories, or just explore one of the ever-changing play areas. The museum is open Wed.-Thurs. 10 a.m.-5 p.m. and Fri.-Sun. 10 a.m.-5 p.m. Admission is $5, free to children up to age one.

Amsterdam Avenue

Though it lacks the foot traffic of Broadway and the cachet of Columbus, Amsterdam Ave.— running parallel between the two—has a scruffy appeal. Home to a mix of neighborhood stores and Spanish bodegas, boisterous bars and trendy restaurants, it attracts a multicultural crowd, especially at night when the avenue comes alive.

WEST END AND RIVERSIDE

Heading west of Broadway anywhere between 72nd and 106th Sts., you'll come first to West End Ave. and then to Riverside Dr., two peaceful residential thoroughfares. West End Ave. is straight and very wide, filled with one big boxy red-brick apartment building after another. Riverside Dr. is more exclusive and curvaceous, lined with a mix of mansions, townhouses, and smart apartment buildings.

Many well-known people have lived on or just off these two streets. Marlon Brando was living with his mother and two sisters at 270 West End Ave., at 73rd St., when he was a young actor appearing in the Broadway play *I Remember Mama*. George Gershwin was living at 33 Riverside Dr., at 75th St., when he finished writing *Porgy and Bess.* Babe Ruth lived at 100 Riverside Dr., at 83rd St., from 1942 until 1948, when he died of throat cancer at age 53. Spencer Tracy resided at 790 West End Ave., bet. 98th and 99th Sts., while studying at the American Academy of Dramatic Arts.

Miles Davis bought the handsome red townhouse—once a Russian Orthodox church—at 312 W. 77th St., bet. West End and Riverside, in the early 1960s. He had a gym and music room installed in the basement, and recorded many important albums while living here, including *In a Silent Way* and *Bitches Brew.* Davis sold the place in the early 1980s, when he and Cicely Tyson started living together.

In 1918, William Randolph Hearst bought the multimillion-dollar home at 331 Riverside Dr., at 105th St., for his mistress, musical comedy star Marion Davies. He then spent another cool million redecorating it for her. Ironically, the lovely beaux arts building today houses the Buddhist Academy of the Jodo Shinshu sect.

Pomander Walk

Tucked between Broadway and West End Ave. on 94th St. is Pomander Walk, a tiny Tudor street blocked off by iron gates. Built in 1921 to resemble the set of a hit play of that same name, the street has been home to a number of celebrities over the years, including Humphrey Bogart, Rosalind Russell, and Lillian and Dorothy Gish. In 1986, Woody Allen set several scenes from *Hannah and Her Sisters* here.

Humphrey Bogart was born not far away from Pomander Walk at 245 W. 103rd St., just east of West End Ave., in 1899. The son of a surgeon and a magazine illustrator, Bogart—unlike the tough-guy characters he would later play—grew up in an upper middle-class world. He attended fashionable private schools, including Phillips Academy in Andover, Massachusetts (from which he was expelled for "excessive high spirits"), then joined the Navy. He took up acting in his mid-20s.

Riverside Park and the Boat Basin

Riverside Dr. abuts Riverside Park, a long and narrow sloping slice of green that stretches from 72nd to 153rd Sts. along the Hudson River. Designed in the 1870s by Frederick Law Olmsted and Calvert Vaux, the park is a pleasant, though well worn, place with glorious views of the Hudson.

Near the south end of the park is the low-key, somewhat neglected **79th Street Boat Basin,** where a number of houseboats are docked. Go by here on a weekday morning and you'll see Federal Express making deliveries just as if this were any other street.

Nicholas Roerich Museum

This odd little museum at 319 W. 107th St., near Riverside Dr., tel. (212) 864-7752, is dedicated to Nicholas Roerich—artist, philosopher, scientist, and humanitarian. Born in Russia in 1874, Roerich painted over 6,000 paintings, wrote over 30 books, conducted extensive archaeological research in Russia and Central Asia, and authored the Roerich Pact, an agreement for international protection that was signed by the heads of 21 nations, including Pres. Franklin D. Roosevelt.

Visiting the Roerich Museum is a bit like visiting the home of a family friend. Upon ringing a buzzer, you enter a cozy house complete with a piano, fireplaces, Oriental vases, and dozens upon dozens of bright paintings hung willy-nilly along the walls and staircase well. No one grunts much more than a hello, and you are free to wander about as you please.

The museum is open Tues.-Sun. 2-5 p.m. Admission is free, but contributions are welcome.

SHOPPING

Arts and Crafts

La Belle Epoque, 282 Columbus Ave., near 73rd St., tel. (212) 362-1770, specializes in French posters of the 1890s and 1900s. Next door, **Exotiqa II,** 284 Columbus Ave., tel. (212) 721-4394, is filled with carved, colorful things. **Objects of Bright Pride,** 455A Columbus Ave., at 81st St., tel. (212) 721-4579, sells a nice collection of handcrafted items from Central and South America.

Books and Music

Applause Theatre Books, 211 W. 71st St., just west of Broadway, tel. (212) 496-7511, specializes in drama. **Gryphon Bookshop,** 2246 Broadway, at 80th St., tel. (212) 362-0706, is a good shop for secondhand books and records. The **Barnes & Noble** megastore at 2289 Broadway, bet. 82nd and 83rd Sts., tel. (212) 362-8835, features a cafe and frequent readings.

Murder Ink, 2486 Broadway, bet. 92nd and 93rd Sts., tel. (212) 362-8905, sells mysteries new and old. **Black Books Plus,** 702 Amsterdam Ave., at 94th St., tel. (212) 749-9632, carries new and used books by and about African Americans, including a large collection of children's books.

Tower Records, 1961 Broadway, at 66th St., tel. (212) 799-2500, stocks a huge inventory of recordings, and features a music-video computer that lets you preview songs before buying. The store is open until midnight daily. **Gryphon Records,** 251 W. 72nd St., 2nd Fl., bet. Broadway and West End, tel. (212) 874-1588, is a collector's paradise selling many rare recordings.

Clothing

Designer **Betsey Johnson** has a store at 248 Columbus Ave., near 72nd St., tel. (212) 362-3364, while **Laura Ashley** is at 398 Columbus Ave., at 79th St., tel. (212) 496-5110. **Alice Underground,** 380 Columbus Ave., near 78th St., tel. (212) 724-6682, is one of the city's best vintage clothing stores, while **Off Broadway,** 139 W. 72nd St., off Broadway, tel. (212) 724-6713, sells secondhand clothes once worn by stars.

Food Shops

Zabar's, 2245 Broadway, at 80th St., tel. (212) 787-2000, is the city's most beloved food store. Dating back to the 1930s, when it moved to Broadway from Brooklyn, Zabar's sells over 10,000 pounds of coffee, 10 tons of cheese, and 1,000 pounds of salmon a week, not to mention pots and pans, microwave ovens, vacuum cleaners, and the like. Some 10,000 customers are said to pass through its friendly portals on a Saturday afternoon. The best time to come is weekdays before 5 p.m.

Across the street from Zabar's is **H&H Bagels,** 2239 Broadway, tel. (212) 595-8000, the city's largest bagel manufacturer, selling about 70,000 bagels a day. Incongruously, H&H is owned and run by a Puerto Rican baker who learned his craft as a child, working after school in a bakery.

Citarella's, 2135 Broadway, at 75th St., tel. (212) 874-0383, is a fish market known for its window displays.

Other Shops

The **Ballet Company,** 1887 Broadway, at 62nd St., tel. (212) 246-6893, is a mecca for ballet fans. **Dapy's,** 230 Columbus Ave., near 71st St., tel. (212) 877-4710, stocks oddball pop-culture gifts. **Uncle Futz,** 408 Amsterdam Ave. near 80th St., tel. (212) 799-6723, is an eclectic toy store. **Maxilla & Mandible,** 451 Columbus Ave., near 81st St., tel. (212) 724-6173, offers a most unusual assortment of skulls, skeletons, bones, teeth, beetles, butterflies, seashells, and fossils.

Among the Latino businesses on Amsterdam Ave. above 96th St. are a few botanicas selling herbs and incense, crystal balls, and carved saints. The largest and best stocked is **Botanica Altagracia,** 852 Amsterdam, near 103rd St., tel. (212) 316-6270.

Flea Markets

An indoor/outdoor flea market is held every Sun. 10 a.m.-5:30 p.m. at P.S. 44, on Columbus Ave. bet. 76th and 77th Streets.

ACCOMMODATIONS

Cheap

Entering the cheerful **Malibu Studios Hotel,** 2688 Broadway, at 103rd St., tel. (212) 222-2954 or (800) 647-2227, is like entering a giant swimming pool. The hallways are painted a bright aqua blue with a bubble and wave motif, while stenciled palm trees adorn the lobby. Rooms are basic but clean, and most share bathrooms. $45 s, $59 d.

Inexpensive

The stark, red brick **Riverside Tower Hotel,** 80 Riverside Drive, at 80th St., tel. (212) 877-5200 or (800) 724-3136, is not much to look at, but its rooms are serviceable and clean. Many feature great views of the Hudson River; downstairs is a sunny lobby furnished in rattan. $65 s, $70-80 d.

Straining against the upper end of the "Inexpensive" category is the well-worn but friendly **Hotel Olcott,** 27 W. 72nd St., bet. CPW and Columbus Ave., tel. (212) 877-4200. Rooms are remarkably large, and many are equipped with kitchenettes. The old-fashioned elevators come complete with elaborate brass doors. $90 s, $100 d.

Moderate

One of the best hotels in this category is the **Milburn,** 242 W. 76th St., bet. Broadway and West End Ave., tel. (212) 362-1006 or (800) 833-9622. In its classy, old-fashioned lobby, find marble columns, tapestries, and original artwork; upstairs, spacious, well-kept guest rooms boast spic-and-span bathrooms and modern kitchenettes. $99-140 s, $109-150 d; $159-199 for a one-bedroom suite.

The **Hotel Beacon,** 2130 Broadway, at 75th St., tel. (212) 787-1100 or (800) 572-4969, also offers excellent value for the money. Its rooms are large and attractive and equipped with two double beds and kitchenettes. The lobby gleams with marble and brass. $115-125 s, $135-145 d.

The well-maintained **Excelsior,** 45 W. 81st St., bet. CPW and Columbus Ave., tel. (212) 362-9200 or (800) 368-4575, has been a favorite among budget travelers for decades. Its handsome, step-down lobby is adorned with dark woods, mirrors, and wrought iron; next door is an attractive, lace-curtained coffee shop. $99-149 s or d.

Moderate-to-Expensive
The comfortable, 365-room **Mayflower,** 15 Central Park West, at 61st St., tel. (212) 265-0060 or (800) 223-4164, is an Upper West Side institution, known for both its Old World charm and great views of Central Park. It's especially popular among musicians, opera singers, and ballet dancers, all in town to perform at Lincoln Center. $155-195 s, $170-210 d. Rooms with park views cost extra.

Hostel, YMCA
One of the cheapest places to stay in New York is the **New York International American Youth Hostel,** 891 Amsterdam Ave., bet. 103rd and 104th Sts., tel. (212) 932-2300. Occupying a block-long landmark building designed by Richard Morris Hunt, this hostel is the nation's largest, with 90 spanking-clean, dorm-style rooms each sleeping four to eight in bunk beds, as well as some family rooms. Also on the premises are kitchens, lounges, coin-operated laundry machines, and a garden. The hostel's only real drawback is its off-the-beaten-track location.

Hostel reservations should be made two to three months in advance; rates are $22-25 per person, $70 for the family rooms. AYH membership is open to students and nonstudents alike. Annual membership fees are adults $25, seniors $15, youth under 18 $10, and families $35; call for more information.

West Side YMCA, 5 W. 63rd St., near CPW, tel. (212) 787-4400, offers small rooms for $52s, 62 d. The rooms themselves are reasonably clean, but the shared bathrooms and halls are a little grungy.

FOOD

American
Inexpensive: Tasty homemade soups and breads are the specialties at **Popover Cafe,** 551 Amsterdam Ave., bet. 86th and 87th Sts., tel. (212) 595-8555. **Good Enough to Eat,** 483 Amsterdam Ave., near 80th St., tel. (212) 496-0163, serves hearty brunches. The long-time neighborhood institution **Barney Greengrass,** 541 Amsterdam Ave., bet. 86th and 87th Sts., tel. (212) 724-4707, offers traditional bagels and lox.

Moderate: The **Saloon,** 1920 Broadway, at 64th St. across from Lincoln Center, tel. (212) 874-1500, is an enormous restaurant with an enormous menu and outdoor tables perfectly suited for people-watching. In Central Park, the **Boathouse Cafe,** on East Dr., near 72nd St., tel. (212) 517-2233, serves grilled meats and fish, salads, and sandwiches on a patio overlooking the lake.

Expensive: A traditional New York favorite for celebrating graduations and the like is the festive **Tavern-on-the-Green,** Central Park West and 67th St., tel. (212) 873-3200, ablaze with mirrors, chandeliers, and 350,000 lightbulbs. The menu features imaginative American and continental cuisine.

Asian
Inexpensive: Broadway Cottage, 2492 Broadway, bet. 92nd and 93rd Sts., tel. (212) 873-0211, is one of a chain serving excellent MSG-free fare. The popular **Empire Szechuan Gourmet,** 2574 Broadway, at 97th St., tel. (212) 663-6004, is also one of a reliable chain. The friendly **Mingala West,** 325 Amsterdam Ave., near 75th St., tel. (212) 873-0787, serves exotic Burmese fare. For delicately flavored Vietnamese cuisine, try **Miss Saigon,** 473 Columbus Ave., bet. 82nd and 83rd Sts., tel. (212) 595-8919.

Moderate: Sakura, 2298 Broadway, at 83rd St., tel. (212) 769-1003, is a good choice for sushi. **Jo-An,** 2707 Broadway, bet. 103rd and 104th Sts., tel. (212) 678-2103, is a homey family-run restaurant with a menu ranging from teriyaki to sushi.

French
Moderate: Cafe St. John, 1018 Amsterdam Ave., at 110th St., tel. (212) 932-8420, is a handsome wood-and-tile bistro featuring an eclectic, French-accented menu.

Expensive: Housed in the turn-of-the-century Hotel des Artistes is **Cafe des Artistes,** 1 W. 67th St., at CPW, tel. (212) 877-3500, a plush and romantic belle epoque spot known for its superb French food and naked nymphs cavorting on the walls. **Cafe Luxembourg,** 200 W. 70th St., near Amsterdam Ave., tel. (212) 873-7411, is sister restaurant to the Odeon downtown. An art deco hot spot, it features a zinc bar, rattan chairs, and a lively bar scene.

Italian
Moderate: The streamlined **Isola,** 485 Columbus Ave., bet. 83rd and 84th Sts., tel. (212) 362-7400, serves tasty Northern Italian fare cooked in a wood-burning oven. **Meridiana,** 2756 Broadway, bet. 105th and 106th Sts., tel. (212) 222-4453, is a friendly place with good food, slow service, and a relaxing outdoor garden.

Latin/Caribbean
Inexpensive: The hole-in-the-wall **La Caridad,** 2199 Broadway, at 78th St., tel. (212) 874-2780, is the best of the Cuban-Chinese restaurants in this part of town. The big Dominican luncheonette **La Rosita,** 2809 Broadway, bet. 108th and 109th Sts., tel. (212) 663-7804, serves lots of savory black beans, fried fish, and flan. **Harry's Burrito Junction,** 241 Columbus Ave., at 71st St., tel. (212) 580-9494, features tasty nachos, burritos, and the like. **Cafe con Leche,** 424 Amsterdam Ave., at 80th St., tel. (212) 595-7000, is a modern Latin diner.

Moderate: Gabriela's, 685 Amsterdam Ave., at 93rd St., tel. (212) 961-0574, offers authentic Mexican cooking in an inviting spot accented with desert murals. The cheese- and spinach-stuffed eggplant and *posole* (traditional Mexican stew) are especially good.

Other Ethnic
Moderate: Featuring tasty Middle Eastern fare, along with live jazz and a classy circular bar, is **Cleopatra's Needle,** 2485 Broadway, bet. 92nd and 93rd Sts., tel. (212) 769-6969. The **Blue Nile,** 103 W. 77th St., bet. Columbus and Amsterdam, tel. (212) 580-3232, serves savory Ethiopian cuisine that's eaten with a spongy pancake, not silverware. The **World Cafe,** 201 Columbus Ave., at 69th St., tel. (212) 799-8090, offers an eclectic mix of dishes from around the world.

Seafood
Moderate: The small, often packed **Fish Restaurant,** 2799 Broadway, at 108th St., tel. (212) 864-5000, serves fresh, innovative seafood dishes.

Soul/Southern
Moderate: Mo' Better, 570 Amsterdam Ave., bet. 89th and 90th Sts., tel. (212) 580-7755, serves soul food in a colorful and comfortable setting. The stylish **Shark Bar,** 307 Amsterdam Ave., bet. 74th and 75th Sts., tel. (212) 874-8500, is part soul-food restaurant, part hip late-night hangout.

Light Bites
In Central Park, food vendors set up shop in various locations, including near Central Park Zoo and Bethesda Terrace, and in the Mineral Springs Pavilion just north of Sheep Meadow. An outdoor cafe and snack bar abut the model-boat pond.

cheap eats at Gray's Papaya

A number of outdoor/indoor cafes are near Lincoln Center. Most are crowded and over-priced, but they're all excellent for people-watching. Among them is the tiny **Opera Expresso Cafe,** 1928 Broadway, near 64th St., tel. (212) 799-3050. During warm weather, a pricey outdoor cafe operates near Lincoln Center's fountain.

Among the coffee bars lining Columbus Ave. are **Coopers Coffee,** 159 Columbus Ave., near 68th St., tel. (212) 362-0100; and **Seattle Coffee,** 188 Columbus Ave., near 69th St., tel. (212) 877-6699. Nearby is **Cafe Mozart,** 154 W. 70th St., near Broadway, tel. (212) 595-9797, serving especially good desserts.

Also serving excellent desserts is **Eclair,** 141 W. 72nd St., off Broadway, tel. (212) 873-7700, one of the last of the many kosher restaurants that once dotted 72nd Street. Funky **Gray's Papaya,** 2090 Broadway, at 72nd St., tel. (212) 799-0243, sells some of the city's best cheap hot dogs—to be eaten standing up.

Watering Holes and Lounges
Streamlined **KCOU,** 430 Amsterdam Ave., near 81st St., tel. (212) 580-0556, resembles its sister bar, WCOU, in the East Village. Down the street is trendy, '50s-ish **Hi-Life Bar and Grill,** 477 Amsterdam Ave., at 83rd St., tel. (212) 787-7199, sporting aluminum walls, pink flamingos, and an outdoor terrace. The uptown version of the **Raccoon Lodge,** 480 Amsterdam Ave., at 83rd St., tel. (212) 874-9984, tries to re-create the laid-back pleasures of the original but is considerably more studied and not as much fun.

The sleek, dark **420 Bar & Lounge,** 420 Amsterdam Ave., at 80th St., tel. (212) 579-8450, offers high ceilings, flickering candles, and a good-looking crowd; upstairs, a DJ spins. A triumvirate of friendly **Dive Bars,** all decked out in an aquatic theme, are located at 95th St. and Amsterdam Ave., tel. (212) 749-4358 (the original); Broadway and 101st St., tel. (212) 865-2662 (Broadway Dive Bar); and 75th St. and Columbus Ave. (Dive 75).

Two popular Irish pubs are the rowdy **Dublin House,** 225 W. 79th St., bet. Broadway and Amsterdam Ave., tel. (212) 874-9528, which boasts a good jukebox; and the more low-key **Emerald Tavern,** 205 Columbus Ave., near 70th St., tel. (212) 874-8840.

Among the restaurants mentioned above, Cafe Luxembourg and the Shark Bar both have late-night bar scenes.

DOVER PUBLICATIONS, INC.

HARLEM AND UPPER MANHATTAN

Stretching roughly from 110th to 168th Sts., between the Harlem and Hudson Rivers, Harlem is one of the city's most historic and least understood neighborhoods. Often written off as a crime-infested no-man's-land, it's actually a diverse place, with many streets that are well-worn rather than raw, and a landscape studded with an impressive number of elegant brownstones and churches. Harlem has more than its share of crime and poverty, but it also has more than its share of attractions.

The neighborhood is divided into West/Central Harlem-comprised mostly of African Americans—and East Harlem, home to many Latinos and a smaller number of Italians. West of Morningside Park between 110th and 125th Sts. is **Morningside Heights,** where Columbia University is located; to the north of 155th St. is **Washington Heights,** home to the Cloisters. Harlem and the Heights are considerably hillier than the rest of Manhattan; here you'll find steep streets, gentle valleys, and magnificent bluffs overlooking the Hudson.

History

Established as Niew Haarlem in 1658, Harlem remained a quiet farming community until 1837. Then the Harlem Railroad arrived, bringing with it hundreds of new settlers. In 1873, the village was annexed to the city, and by the early 1900s, it was an affluent white suburb.

In 1901, the IRT subway was extended along Lenox Ave. and wealthy speculators, seeing the chance to make millions, built row after row of attractive townhouses. But they overextended themselves, and sales were slow. When a black realtor offered to fill the empty buildings with black tenants, the developers jumped at the chance. Fearing racial changes, the neighborhood's white residents fled.

During the 1920s and '30s, Harlem was the country's African American cultural center. The Harlem Renaissance bloomed, attracting writers and intellectuals such as Langston Hughes and W.E.B. DuBois, while the streets were jammed with jazz clubs, theaters, dance halls, and speakeasies. Duke Ellington played at the Cotton Club, Chick Webb at the Savoy.

Harlem lost much of this vibrancy during and after the Depression, when poverty began taking a stronger hold. In the '60s, however, civil rights leaders Malcolm X, Stokely Carmichael, and others turned the neighborhood into a mecca for black consciousness.

Today, Harlem, for all its continuing problems with poverty and drugs, is in the midst of a small renaissance. Some middle-class residents have moved back in, and there's a growing citywide awareness of the need to preserve the neighborhood's historic and cultural landmarks. Blocks are being rehabilitated, and more small businesses are opening up, especially around

HARLEM AND UPPER MANHATTAN

Bronx

To the Cloisters and Yeshiva University

W. 160TH ST.
W. 159TH ST.
W. 158TH ST.
W. 157TH ST.
W. 156TH ST.

MORRIS JUMEL MANSION

SYLVAN TERRACE

EDGECOMBE PARK

AUDUBON TERRACE

CHURCH OF THE INTERCESSION

TRINITY CEMETERY

W. 155TH ST.
W. 154TH ST.
153RD ST.
W. 152ND ST.
W. 151ST ST.
W. 150TH ST.
W. 149TH ST.
W. 148TH ST.
W. 147TH ST.
W. 146TH ST.
W. 145TH ST.
W. 144TH ST.

JACKIE ROBINSON PARK

Sugar Hill

Harlem River

9A

HENRY HUDSON PARKWAY

RIVERSIDE DR

BROADWAY

AMSTERDAM AVE.

HAMILTON PL.

ST. NICHOLAS AVE.

ST. NICHOLAS PL.

EDGECOMBE

Hamilton Heights

HAMILTON GRANGE

CITY UNIVERSITY OF NEW YORK

W. 143RD ST.
W. 142ND ST.
W. 141TH ST.
W. 140TH ST.

STRIVER'S ROW 139TH ST.

W. 138TH ST.
W. 137TH ST.
W. 136TH ST.
W. 135TH ST.
W. 134TH ST.
W. 133RD ST.
132ND ST.

ABYSSINIAN BAPTIST CHURCH

MOTHER A.M.E. ZION CHURCH

SCHOMBURG CENTER

22 WEST RESTAURANT

SIXTH AVE.

FIFTH AVE.

W. 131ST ST.

CONVENT AVE.

ST. NICHOLAS TER.

EIGHTH AVE.

SEVENTH AVE.

TREE OF HOPE SCULPTURE

W. 130TH ST.
W. 129TH ST.
W. 128TH ST.
127TH ST.

LIBERATION BOOKSHOP

E. 131ST ST.
E. 130TH ST.
E. 129TH ST.

LANGSTON HUGHES RESIDENCE

Hudson River

GRANT'S TOMB

RIVERSIDE CHURCH

UNION THEOLOGICAL SEMINARY

MORNINGSIDE DR.

PARK

MORNINGSIDE

ST. NICHOLAS AVE.

CLAYTON POWELL JR. BLVD.

FREDERICK DOUGLASS BLVD.

ADAM

LENOX AVE.

MADISON AVE.

PARK AVE.

LEXINGTON AVE.

STATE OFFICE BUILDING

BLACK FASHION MUSEUM

APOLLO THEATER

STUDIO MUSEUM

W. 126TH ST.
W. 125TH ST.
W. 124TH ST.
123RD ST.
122ND ST.
121ST ST.
120TH ST.
119TH ST.

E. 126TH ST.
E. 125TH ST.
E. 124TH ST.
E. 123RD ST.
E. 122ND ST.
E. 121ST ST.
E. 120TH ST.
E. 119TH ST.

EPHESUS SEVENTH DAY ADVENTIST CHURCH

MARCUS GARVEY PARK

HALE HOUSE

MT. OLIVET BAPTIST CHURCH

BARNARD COLLEGE

COLUMBIA UNIVERSITY

MINTON'S PLAYHOUSE

FIRST CORINTHIAN BAPTIST CHURCH

AFRICAN AMERICAN WAX MUSEUM

W. 118TH ST.
W. 117TH ST.
W. 116TH ST.
W. 115TH ST.
W. 114TH ST.
W. 113TH ST.
W. 112TH ST.
W. 111TH ST.
W. 110TH ST.

CANAAN BAPTIST CHURCH OF CHRIST

116TH ST. MARKET

MALCOLM SHABAZZ MOSQUE

OTTO CHICAS RENDON

LA MARQUETA

E. 118TH ST.
E. 117TH ST.
E. 116TH ST.
E. 115TH ST.
E. 112TH ST.
E. 111TH ST.
E. 110TH ST.

ST. JOHN THE DIVINE

CENTRAL PARK

0   0.2 mi
0   0.2 km

© MOON PUBLICATIONS, INC.

125th Street. The Disney Company and Cineplex Odeon have even announced plans to build an entertainment complex on the block bounded by 124th and 125th Sts., Frederick Douglass Blvd., and St. Nicholas Avenue.

Orientation

Though Harlem has a notorious reputation for crime, much of it can safely be explored on foot. The areas around 116th St., 125th St., and the Schomburg Center, especially, are always crowded with people. Stick to the main and populated streets, however, and avoid the parks completely. If you're white, you may encounter some hostility, but then, too, you'll also encounter much friendliness.

The following list of sights begins near Columbia University, then heads east (cross on 110th or 125th Sts.; don't go through Morningside Park) to the Lenox Ave.-116th St. area. Next comes a foray into *El Barrio,* or Spanish Harlem; followed by an exploration of 125th St., and a zigzagging route uptown. Subway directions are included to the more distant sights.

In Harlem, many of the numbered avenues take on proper names. Sixth Ave. becomes Lenox Ave. or Malcolm X Blvd.; Seventh Ave. becomes Adam Clayton Powell Jr. Blvd. (ACP Blvd.); and Eighth Ave. becomes Frederick Douglass Boulevard.

First-time visitors should be sure to visit the Cathedral of St. John the Divine, 116th St., 125th St., the Studio Museum in Harlem, and the Morris-Jumel Mansion. Organized tours are also a good way to see Harlem the first time around; see "Tours," in the New York City introduction.

COLUMBIA UNIVERSITY AREA

Cathedral of St. John the Divine

The world's largest Gothic cathedral is on Amsterdam Ave. at W. 112th St., tel. (212) 316-7540. Supposedly large enough to fit both Notre Dame and Chartres inside, it accommodates some 10,000 people, and is still under construction. Scheduled completion date, *if* enough money becomes available: 2050.

Begun in 1892, the cathedral's imposing but still towerless facade is covered with stone carvings and bronze sculptures. Inside, it's a vast

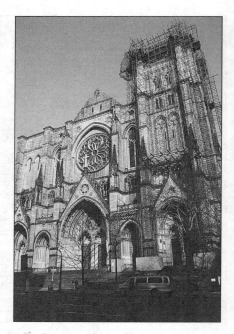

The Cathedral of St. John the Divine will not be completed until at least the year 2050.

and cavernous space with endless rows of seats, many floor inscriptions ("Live all you can; it's a mistake not to"—Henry James; "Out of space—out of time"—Edgar Allan Poe), and several chapels housing changing exhibits. To the rear is an excellent gift shop filled with oddities, while out back is a workshop where you can see stonemasons at work.

In addition to its regular services, the cathedral stages concerts and special events. One of the most wonderful is the Blessing of the Animals, held every October on Saint Francis of Assisi's feast day. The event draws thousands of New Yorkers into the church with a hodgepodge of animals in tow.

The cathedral is open daily 9 a.m.-5 p.m.; tours are given Sun. at 1 p.m. Immediately south of the cathedral is its Peace Fountain, lined with an odd and whimsical mix of figures and animals, many of them sculpted by schoolchildren.

Columbia University and Vicinity

The campus of Columbia University stretches from W. 114th St. to W. 120th St., between Amsterdam Ave. and Broadway. Founded as King's College in 1754, it educated some of the country's earliest leaders, including Alexander Hamilton—the first secretary of the treasury—and John Jay, first chief justice of the U.S. Supreme Court. Free tours are given year-round; call (212) 854-4900 for more information.

Across Broadway from Columbia is **Barnard College,** founded in 1899 by Frederick A.P. Barnard, a former president of Columbia and a champion of higher education for women. The college is especially well known for its anthropology department; among its alumni are Margaret Mead and Zora Neale Hurston.

North of Columbia are three more prestigious educational institutions. **Teachers College,** where John Dewey once taught, is on the east side of Broadway bet. 120th and 121st Sts.; **Union Theological Seminary,** known for its liberal thought and social activism, is on the west side bet. 120th and 122nd Sts.; and the **Jewish Theological Seminary**—with a light burning in its tower in remembrance of the Holocaust victims—is at the northeast corner of 122nd St. and Broadway.

Grant's Tomb

High on a bluff overlooking the Hudson is Grant's Tomb, 122nd St. and Riverside Dr., tel. (212) 666-1640, an imposing mausoleum where the former president and his wife are buried. The site is run by the National Park Service, but had been neglected in recent years. The tomb's deteriorating condition was the subject of a 1994 lawsuit filed by the Civil War hero's admirers and descendants. The primary mover behind the suit was a Columbia undergraduate. Thanks largely to his efforts, the tomb's operating budget has been tripled. That's not enough to fully restore the monument, but the graffiti has been removed and round-the-clock security posted.

Hours are daily 9 a.m.-5 p.m. Admission is free.

Riverside Church

Next door to Grant's Tomb is the Gothic-inspired Riverside Church, 490 Riverside Dr., bet. 120th and 122nd Sts., tel. (212) 870-6700. Built in the 1920s, the church is home to an impressive 74-bell carillon, donated to the church by the Rockefeller family. The carillon's 20-ton bell is the world's largest; the carillon's smallest bell weighs only 10 pounds. The carillon tower, offering grand views of upper Manhattan, is open to visitors Mon.-Fri. 9 a.m.-5 p.m. and Sunday 12:30-4 p.m. Admission is $1.

RANDOLPH SQUARE AREA

Minton's Playhouse

One of the greatest revolutions in jazz was spawned in a neighborhood club run by one-time bandleader Teddy Hill in the Cecil Hotel, 210 W. 118th St., just west of St. Nicholas Avenue. Hill hired a house band that included pianist Thelonious Monk and drummer Kenny Clarke, and soon the small, dark place was packed every night with talent eager to jam. Dizzy Gillespie, Charlie Parker, Charlie Christian, and Max Roach were among the regulars who came here to experiment with a brand-new style of jazz that came to be called bebop.

Minton's—now on the National Register of Historic Places—is being restored. It's slated to reopen in late 1997 as a restaurant and jazz club, and promises to be a beautiful place. Still hanging in the back of the club is a striking mural depicting four musicians, two of whom have been identified as Tony Scott and Charlie Christian.

Today, the renovated Cecil Hotel houses apartments for the elderly. It sits on the edge of **A. Phillip Randolph Square,** at the intersection of ACP Blvd., St. Nicholas Ave., and 117th Street. Randolph organized the Brotherhood of Sleeping Car Porters, and in 1941 persuaded President Roosevelt to establish the Fair Employment Practices Commission which made it possible for blacks to work in defense jobs.

African American Wax Museum

Slightly to the south and west of the old Minton's is the African American Wax Museum, 318 W. 115th St., tel. (212) 678-7818. It's a delightfully quirky private museum created and run by artist Raven Chanticleer. A Haitian-born sculptor and painter who grew up in New York and studied at the University of Ghana, Chanticleer has turned the bottom floor of his home into a museum filled with wax figures of famous African Americans. Among these lifelike figures, casually standing about here and there, are Adam Clayton Powell Jr., Nelson Mandela, Josephine Baker, Mother Clara Hale, Magic Johnson, Martin Luther King Jr., Malcolm X, and a self-portrait of the artist.

Also in the museum are dozens of Chanticleer's paintings and sculptures, depicting everything from cotton pickers in Mississippi to the Savoy Ballroom in New York. Many of the sculptures have an interesting African feel, as does the garden out back.

The museum's polished parquet floors are made of ebony imported from Ghana, and visitors must don paper slippers before entering. Up front is a small gift shop, selling everything from T-shirts with the museum's logo to Malcolm X wristwatches.

The museum is open Tues.-Sun. 1-6 p.m., but it's advisable to call in advance. Because Chanticleer accepts no outside financing, admission is a suggested adults $10, children under 12 $5; consider it a donation to a worthy cause.

Two Baptist Churches

At the corner of Adam Clayton Powell Jr. Blvd. and 116th St. is **First Corinthian Baptist Church,** a playful building covered with a multitude of colored tiles. The building was once the Regent Theater, completed in 1913 as the city's first deluxe movie palace. Before that, movies had been shown in storefronts or tiny vaudeville theaters. In its heyday, the Regent had its own eight-piece orchestra, pipe organ, uniformed ushers, and printed programs.

Just east of the First Corinthian is **Canaan Baptist Church of Christ,** 132 W. 116th St., tel. (212) 866-0301, known for its high-spirited gospel choirs—some of the city's most exuberant. Sunday services begin at 10:45 a.m.

Malcolm Shabazz Mosque

The silver-domed mosque topped with a star and a crescent at 102 W. 116th St., at Lenox Ave., tel. (212) 662-2200, is named after civil-rights leader Malcolm X, who taught here in the 1960s just

before his break with the Black Muslims. After his death, the mosque was firebombed.

On the busy block surrounding the mosque are the 116th St. Market (see "Shopping," below) and a hodgepodge of small Muslim-run businesses, such as bookstores, barber shops, and the **Shabazz Restaurant.** Established by Malcolm X, the restaurant was once famous for its bean pies and health food. Today, it's under different ownership, and a sign reads, "Shabazz Fried Chicken—The Name You Can Trust."

EL BARRIO

Heading farther east on 116th St., you'll come to the heart of Spanish Harlem, a lively area filled with discount clothing stores, toy shops, beauty and wig salons, storefront churches, bakeries selling towering wedding cakes, pet stores selling homing pigeons, botanicas, ice cream vendors, and the sounds of salsa. Despite all its activity, however, this is one of Manhattan's poorest sections, with an unemployment rate of about 40%.

Composed of a motley array of buildings— you'll find few fine churches or brownstones here—East Harlem has been a slum since the late 1800s, when it was settled by Germans, Scandinavians, Italians, and Irish. The Hispanics, most of whom are Puerto Rican, Cuban, and Dominican, began moving here in the 1920s, with the largest influx arriving just after WW II.

At Park Ave. bet. 116th and 111th Sts. is **La Marqueta,** a large indoor market selling fruits and vegetables, meats and poultry. Here you can pick up Puerto Rican specialties such as beef tripe, conches, plantains, and papayas. Though recently in a period of decline, La Marqueta is now being renovated.

LENOX AVENUE CHURCHES AND HALE HOUSE

Heading north on Lenox from the Malcolm Shabazz Mosque, you'll pass one enormous church after another, along with a number of grand old funeral homes. At W. 120th St. is the 1907 **Mt. Olivet Baptist Church,** originally one of New York's most elegant synagogues. At W. 122nd St. is the 1888 **St. Martin's,** a Romanesque church known for its carillon and stained-glass windows. At W. 123rd St. is the 1887 **Ephesus Seventh Day Adventist Church,** notable for its lofty spire.

At 152 W. 122nd St., bet. Lenox Ave. and ACP Blvd., is the **Hale House,** tel. (212) 663-0700, founded by Mother Clara Hale in 1969 to help babies born to drug-addicted mothers. Mother Hale passed away in 1993, but during her lifetime she took in nearly 1,000 infants. Many of these babies were suffering withdrawal pains after becoming addicted to drugs in the womb. Mother Hale started her work out of her own home; in the early days, the babies slept in cribs next to her bed. Later she was aided by a staff and volunteers, and won international recognition for her efforts. Today, her work is being carried on by her daughter, Lorraine.

125TH STREET

The heart of Harlem is 125th St., always alive with vibrant colors, sights, and sounds. As the neighborhood's main commercial drag for decades, 125th St. has had many ups and downs. It's currently riding an optimistic wave, with more small businesses in operation here today than at any other time in recent history. The street is also home to three major Harlem landmarks—the **Studio Museum in Harlem,** the **Theresa,** and the **Apollo.**

At the corner of 125th St. and Fifth Ave., outside a shop selling tapes and records, linger the neat, well-dressed disciples of Nation of Islam leader Louis Farrakhan. "Stop the Killing," "Salaam Salaam," read the signs in the shop's windows, as an amplified tape broadcasts the teachings of Muhammad. Across the street from the Farrakhan headquarters is a **Ben & Jerry's** and a **Body Shop**—two mainstream indicators of Harlem's increasing viability as a commercial district.

On the corner of 125th St. and Adam Clayton Powell Jr. Blvd. is the ugly 1973 **Harlem State Office Building,** 163 W. 125th Street. The tallest building in Harlem, the tower houses government offices and the **Adam Clayton Powell Jr. Gallery,** showcasing community artwork. The

second-floor gallery, run by the Studio Museum, is open Mon.-Fri. noon-3 p.m.

Studio Museum in Harlem
The Studio Museum, 144 W. 125th St., bet. Lenox Ave. and ACP Blvd., tel. (212) 864-4500, was founded in 1968 in a small factory loft. Today, it's a first-class institution spread over several well-lit floors of a turn-of-the-century building. The "principal center for the study of Black art in America," its permanent display features works by such masters as Romare Bearden, James VanDerZee, and Jacob Lawrence.

The Studio is also known for excellent temporary exhibits, showcasing both world-renowned and emerging artists, and its lively lecture, concert, and performance series. A tempting gift shop is on the ground floor.

Hours are Wed.-Fri. 10 a.m.-5 p.m., Sat.-Sun. 1-6 p.m. Admission is adults $5, students and seniors $3, children under 12 $1. Free first Saturday of each month.

Theresa Hotel
The glistening white-brick Theresa, 2090 ACP Blvd., at 125th St., was once Harlem's largest and most famous hotel. Among the notables who stayed here were musicians Lena Horne, Jimi Hendrix, Dizzy Gillespie, Lester Young, Milt Hinton, and Andy Kirk (who managed the place in the late 1950s). Boxer Joe Louis stayed here as well.

In 1960, Cuban leader Fidel Castro and his 85-member entourage checked into the Theresa after checking out of a downtown hotel due to what Castro considered to be poor treatment. Castro was in town to deliver an address to the United Nations, and while he was staying at the Theresa, thousands of demonstrators and Soviet leader Nikita Khrushchev stopped by to show their support.

The Theresa is now an office building. In 1990, Nelson Mandela, then the leader of the South African antiapartheid movement, held a huge rally outside the hotel's doors to celebrate his release from prison.

The Apollo
Perhaps the single most important landmark in the history of African American music, the Apollo, 253 W. 125th St., near Frederick Douglass

The Apollo has hosted nearly every major jazz, blues, R&B, and soul artist to come along.

Blvd., tel. (212) 749-5838, has hosted nearly every major jazz, blues, R&B, and soul artist to come along. Bessie Smith, Ella Fitzgerald, Billie Holiday, Duke Ellington, Louis Armstrong, Count Basie, Fats Waller, Ray Charles, James Brown, The Ink Spots, Mahalia Jackson, Aretha Franklin, Diana Ross, Al Green, Gladys Knight, and Michael Jackson all played the Apollo, and the list could go on and on. It is said that when a teenage Elvis Presley first came to New York, the one place he wanted to see was the Apollo. The same was later said of the Beatles.

Originally built in 1913, the Apollo was once Hurtig & Seamon's New Burlesque Theatre, known for presenting vaudeville to a Harlem that was then predominantly white. Back in those days, the best seats in the house cost a whopping $1.65.

By 1935, the neighborhood's racial mix had shifted, and the two-balconied theater, capable of seating 2,000, became famous for its Amateur

Nights. Lena Horne was one of the unfortunate ones—the audience booed and threw pennies at her, driving her off the stage.

The Apollo was closed down in the late 1970s. In the early 1980s, Percy Sutton—an NAACP official and cofounder of the Inner City Broadcasting Corp.—bought the abandoned building, which at that time was flooded and full of rats. After a several-million-dollar renovation, the theater—now a nonprofit enterprise—once again presents a variety of entertainment, including a Wednesday amateur night. In the lobby is a small exhibit on the theater's early history.

NORTH TO 135TH STREET

Black Fashion Museum
Another small and unusual Harlem museum, the Black Fashion Museum is behind the reinforced metal door at 155 W. 126th St., bet. Lenox Ave. and ACP Blvd., tel. (212) 666-1320. Here in a brownstone adjoining the nonprofit Harlem Institute of Fashion is a stunning collection of clothes designed, sewn, or worn by African Americans. Included in the collection are over 3,000 items dating from the mid-1800s to the present.

Highlights of the museum include a reproduction of the purple inaugural dress sewn by black dressmaker Elizabeth Keckley for Mrs. Mary Todd Lincoln (the original is in the Smithsonian); the yellow print dress that Rosa Parks was sewing on that day in 1955 when she refused to give up her seat on the bus; two authentic slave dresses; and costumes from the Broadway productions of *The Wiz, Bubbling Brown Sugar, Eubie,* and others. One showcase is devoted to black milliners—almost all of whom were men—and another to Ann Lowe, the dressmaker who designed Jacqueline Kennedy's wedding gown.

The museum is open by appointment only, noon-8 p.m. Admission is by donation; $2 is suggested.

Langston Hughes Residence
The famed Harlem Renaissance author and poet lived in the three-story, Italianate brownstone at 20 E. 127th St., bet. Lenox and Fifth

AFRICAN AMERICAN HISTORIC SITES

It goes without saying that you'll find innumerable important African American historic sites in New York City. Sections of Harlem in particular are lined with one landmark after another. Here are only a few of the highlights.

HARLEM

Studio Museum in Harlem. A world-class institution with changing exhibits by such masters as Romare Bearden and Jacob Lawrence.

The Apollo. Perhaps the single most important landmark in the history of African American music.

Malcolm Shabazz Mosque. Where civil rights leader Malcolm X taught in the 1960s.

African American Wax Museum. Tributes to such greats as Nelson Mandela, Josephine Baker, Magic Johnson, and Mother Hale.

Black Fashion Museum. A stunning collection of clothes designed by African Americans from the mid-1800s to the present.

Schomberg Center. A renowned institution for research in black culture. Includes a spacious art gallery and gift shop.

Abyssinian Baptist Church. The former church of Adam Clayton Powell; one of largest black congregations in the U.S.

Striver's Row. Designed by architects McKim, Mead & White; once home to W.C. Handy and Eubie Blake, among numerous others.

ELSEWHERE IN MANHATTAN

Fraunces Tavern, Lower Manhattan. Many historians believe the original Revolutionary War–era Fraunces Tavern, of which this is a replica, was owned by a black French West-Indian.

Former slave market, Lower Manhattan. One of the busiest slave markets of the 1700s once stood on Wall Street.

African Burial Grounds, Lower Manhattan. Only rediscovered in 1991, this graveyard may once have covered nearly six acres and held the remains of 20,000 African Americans.

Charlie Parker Place, East Village. The former abode of the jazz great.

THE OUTER BOROUGHS

Weeksville, Crown Heights, Brooklyn. Four wooden houses, once part of a free black community established in the 1840s.

Plymouth Church of the Pilgrims, Brooklyn Heights. The former pulpit of minister Henry Ward Beecher, whose rousing, antislavery sermons helped galvanize the North during the Civil War.

Louis Armstrong house, Corona, Queens. The legendary trumpeter's home from the early 1940s until his death in 1971.

Sandy Ground, Staten Island. One of the oldest free black communities in the U.S.; settled by African American oystermen.

Aves., for the last 20 years of his life. This is the only residence that Hughes, who died in 1967, occupied for any length of time. The block is now called Langston Hughes Place.

Tree of Hope Sculpture

The rusting steel sculpture of purple, black, and green standing in the middle of Adam Clayton Powell Jr. Blvd. at 131st St. marks the spot where the Tree of Hope once grew. The Tree—whose bark passersby rubbed for good luck—had originally stood on the side of the street, but when the avenue was widened, Bill "Bojangles" Robinson had it moved and replanted in the street's midway. His nearby plaque reads: "You wanted a tree of hope and here it is. Best Wishes."

You'd never know it now, but this intersection was once one of the hottest spots in Harlem. Known as "The Corner," it was home to numerous jazz clubs and dance halls, including Connie's Inn, the Band Box, the Barbeque, and the Hoofers' Club. "This wasn't just one more of them busy street crossings, with a poolroom for a hangout. Uh, uh," writes Mezz Mezzrow in *Really the Blues.* "On The Corner in Harlem you stood with your jaws swinging wide open while all there is to this crazy world, the whole frantic works, strutted by."

Liberation Book Shop
This most famed of Harlem bookstores, once a 125th St. landmark, is now at 421 Lenox Ave., at 131st St., tel. (212) 281-4615. Founded by Lewis Michaux, the store has been a favorite gathering spot for decades, and has one of the largest selections of African American, African, and Caribbean books in New York. Malcolm X once bought much of his reading matter here.

22 West Restaurant
Another favorite Malcolm X hangout was the informal 22 West Restaurant, 22 W. 135th St., near Fifth Ave., tel. (212) 862-7770. Today a red-cushioned booth in the back, where he usually sat, bears a plaque reading: "El Hajj Malek El Shabazz (Malcolm X) . . . Always face the door—Watching my back!"

The Schomburg Center
The Schomburg Center for Research in Black Culture, 515 Lenox Ave., at 135th St., tel. (212) 491-2200, is a world-renowned institution founded by Arthur A. Schomburg, a Puerto Rican of African descent who as a child was told that the Negro had no history. Scholars come from all over the world to consult the extensive collections of this branch of the New York Public Library, housed in a modern brick and glass building.

For the sightseer, however, the center's most interesting attraction is its adjacent exhibition area, where a wide array of changing exhibits is presented. In the back, too, is an excellent book and gift shop.

The Schomburg's galleries and shop are open Mon.-Wed. noon-8 p.m., Thurs.-Sat. 10 a.m.-6 p.m., and Sun. 1-5 p.m. Admission is free.

Directly across the street from the Schomburg is **Harlem Hospital,** where two exquisite Depression-era murals by African American artists can be found. In the 136th St. lobby is

Charles Alston's *Magic of Medicine,* while in the 135th St. lobby is Vertis Hayes's eight-paneled panorama of black history. The murals were originally rejected by the hospital's white administrator because they contained "too much Negro subject matter."

Harlem YMCA
The Harlem YMCA, 180 W. 135th St., bet. Lenox and ACP Blvd., was an important gathering spot for artists, writers, and entertainers during the Harlem Renaissance. Writers Langston Hughes and Ralph Ellison lived here temporarily, and Paul Robeson began his acting career here.

CENTRAL AND UPPER HARLEM

Mother A.M.E. Zion Church
The impressive neo-Gothic Mother A.M.E. Zion Church, 140 W. 137th St., bet. Lenox and ACP Blvd., was New York City's first church organized by and for blacks. It was founded in 1796 —originally downtown at 156 Church St.—with money donated by a former slave. The current church was designed by the noted African American architect George Washington Foster Jr.

Also known as the "Freedom Church" because of its connection to the Underground Railroad, the church has had many famous members, including Harriet Tubman, Frederick Douglass, Paul Robeson, and a woman named Isabella. One Sunday morning, Isabella, already highly respected by her community, announced during the service that she wanted to be called Sojourner Truth—"Sojourner because I am a wanderer, Truth because God is truth."

Abyssinian Baptist Church
One of Harlem's most famous addresses is the impressive Abyssinian Baptist Church, 132 W. 138th St., near ACP Blvd., tel. (212) 862-7474. It was founded in 1801 when a few members of the First Baptist Church refused to accept that church's racially segregated seating policy. The Abyssinian now has one of the country's largest black congregations.

Two of the church's most famous leaders were the Adam Clayton Powells—Sr. and Jr. The flamboyant Powell Jr. was also the first black U.S. congressman from an Eastern state, and he did much to empower the black community before being charged with misconduct and failing to win reelection. The church houses a small memorial room honoring both Powells.

The Reverend Dr. Calvin Butts is the Abyssinian's current pastor, and he continues the church's activist tradition. Services, complete with gospel music, are held Sunday at 9 a.m. and 11 a.m. Visitors are welcome; arrive early to get a seat.

Striver's Row

Just down the street from the Abyssinian church are two famous blocks, located on 138th and 139th Sts. bet. ACP and Frederick Douglass Boulevards. Built in 1891 by developer David King, the blocks—lined with 158 four-story buildings—were designed by three sets of architects, with McKim, Mead & White designing the most impressive, northernmost row. The blocks acquired their nickname when they became the preferred address of early ambitious blacks. They continue to be immaculately kept, with service alleys running behind and flower boxes out front. Among the rich and famous who've lived here are W.C. Handy, Eubie Blake, and Stepin Fetchit.

Currently in the works is the **Striver's Center Development Project,** which will be centered just south of Striver's Row, along 134th, 135th, and 136th Sts., bet. ACP Blvd. and St. Nicholas Avenue. The development will eventually include restaurants, boutiques, jazz clubs, and art galleries. As of this writing, many of the buildings along 135th St. have already been restored.

Hamilton Heights

A few blocks northwest of Striver's Row is **Hamilton Grange,** 287 Convent Ave., bet. 141st and 142nd Sts., a Federal-style mansion where Alexander Hamilton lived before being killed in a duel by Aaron Burr. In 1889, the Grange was moved to this site, where it sits—looking uncomfortably squeezed—on a narrow plot between two other buildings.

The Grange, now managed by the National Park Service, is closed due to structural problems and isn't scheduled to reopen any time soon. There's talk it may be moved again, this time to a park or other more accessible site.

Above Hamilton Grange is Hamilton Heights,

stretching from 142nd to 145th Sts. bet. Amsterdam and St. Nicholas Avenues. Once part of Hamilton's estate, this historic district is filled with grand mansions and elegant brownstones.

Looking south from the Grange, you can see the impressive, neo-Gothic spires of the **City University of New York,** centering around Convent Ave. bet. 130th and 135th Streets. The college was founded as a free academy for qualified city students in 1849. Though no longer free, it still offers relatively inexpensive tuition (about $2,500 a year).

Sugar Hill

Just north of Hamilton Heights is Sugar Hill, stretching from 143rd to 156th Sts. bet. St. Nicholas and Edgecombe Avenues. Built on a steep incline, Sugar Hill is another affluent residential area that's long been known for its "sweet life."

The great jazz artist Duke Ellington lived at 935 St. Nicholas Ave., near 156th St., from 1939 to 1961, and the handsome building has since been named a National Historic Landmark in his honor. While living here, Ellington performed at the Cotton Club, wrote many of his most famous compositions, and premiered his controversial "Black, Brown, and Beige"—which he called a "tone parallel to the history of the American Negro"—at Carnegie Hall.

Future Supreme Court justice Thurgood Marshall, scholar W.E.B. Du Bois, and civil rights leader Roy Wilkins all once lived at 409 Edgecombe Ave., at 155th St., a worn-looking apartment house with a commanding view of the valley below. Declared a city landmark in 1993, the 13-story building was also home to many other members of the black elite from the 1930s through the 1950s.

Morris-Jumel Mansion

This big white gem of a mansion on W. 160th St. and Edgecombe Ave., tel. (212) 923-8008, sits in a small, lush park. Manhattan's last remaining Colonial residence, it was built in 1765 as a country home for British colonel Roger Morris. The house once offered excellent views of both the Hudson and East Rivers (now obstructed by other buildings), and served as a temporary headquarters for George Washington during the Revolutionary War.

Several decades following the war, the house was purchased by Stephen Jumel, a wealthy French wine merchant. His wife, Mme. Jumel, was said to have been a manipulative, scheming ex-prostitute from Providence, Rhode Island, who let her husband die of neglect after he was seriously wounded in a carriage accident. His death made her one of America's richest women, and she then married Aaron Burr, with whom she had a tempestuous relationship. She continued to live in the mansion until her death in 1865 at the age of 93, and her ghost is said to haunt the place.

Some of the furnishings in the house are original, others are period pieces. The handsome octagonal dining room to the rear is where Washington hosted a famous dinner, attended by Hamilton, Madison, and Jefferson.

Immediately west of Morris-Jumel is **Sylvan Terrace.** Once the carriage drive to the mansion, this short cobblestone street is now lined with historic wooden row houses, and is one of the city's most idyllic spots.

Theoretically, the mansion is open Wed.-Sun 10 a.m.-4 p.m., but it's not as well run as it should be, and you must knock on the door *hard* if you want to get inside. Admission is adults $3, students and seniors $2.

Audubon Terrace

This monumental marble terrace is often dishearteningly empty, especially since its most famous one-time resident, the Museum of the American Indian, moved to the former U.S. Custom House (see "Battery Park and the Statue of Liberty" under "Lower Manhattan," above). Still here are the **Hispanic Society of America,** the **American Numismatic Society,** and the **American Academy of Arts and Letters,** but they're seldom visited thanks to the terrace's off-the-beaten-track location on Broadway bet. 155th and 156th Streets.

Visitors who do venture up this far, however, will find themselves in an historic spot, with an impressive array of beaux arts buildings to the south, and a plaza filled with friezes and statuary to the north. All of this land was once part of ornithologist John James Audubon's estate; the terrace was built later, in 1904.

Easternmost of the plaza's three museums is the dark and somber Hispanic Society. Mansionlike in feel, it houses a number of paintings by Goya, Velasquez, and El Greco, along with heavy Spanish furnishings, porcelain, and mosaics. The Hispanic Society, tel. (212) 926-2234, is open Tues.-Sat. 10 a.m.-4:30 p.m. and Sun. 1-4 p.m. Admission is by donation.

Next door in the Numismatic Society, you'll find coins dating back to Greek, Roman, Renaissance, and Colonial times,

ONLY IN NEW YORK!

It's one of the oddest sites in the city: a gorgeous, 23-acre park built on top of a sewage treatment plant. To the north is the glistening expanse of the George Washington Bridge; to the south, the skyline of Manhattan; down below, a cluster of sludge storage, settling, and aeration tanks.

Located on the Hudson River between 137th and 145th Sts., Riverbank State Park is one of the best equipped parks in the city, attracting residents from all over New York. Within its spic-and-span confines—blanketed with an emerald-green synthetic turf—are baseball and football fields, a 400-meter track, three swimming pools (one Olympic size), four tennis courts, four basketball courts, four handball courts, four playgrounds, an ice-skating rink, picnic areas, a cultural center, a bike path, a community garden, and 700 trees. On a busy weekend day, as many as 15,000 to 20,000 people come here to relax.

The park was conceived in 1968, when the sewage treatment plant originally planned for West 72nd St. was bumped up to Harlem, due to influential Upper West Side residents. Harlem's rage was so great that the city promised it a park in return. The $1.3-billion North River Water Pollution Control Plant was completed in 1986; the $129-million park, in 1994.

When the sewage-treatment plant first opened, residents complained bitterly about its smell. Since then, about $20 million has been spent on odor control. While the problem has not been eradicated, at least it's rarely noticeable within the confines of the park itself.

and pick up all sorts of odd tidbits, such as the fact that Marco Polo was the first to tell the Western World about the Chinese invention of paper money. The Numismatic Society, tel. (212) 234-3130, is open Tues.-Sat. 9 a.m.-4:30 p.m. Admission is free.

The American Academy of Arts and Letters is only open when presenting exhibits, of which there are about three a year. Call (212) 368-5900 for schedule information.

To reach Audubon Terrace, take either the No. 1 train to 157th St. and Broadway, or take the B train to 155th St. near Amsterdam and walk two blocks west.

Church of the Intercession
Just south of Audubon Terrace is the enormous, Gothic Revival Church of the Intercession, surrounded by idyllic **Trinity Cemetery.** Both look as if they belong more in the English countryside than they do in Harlem.

Trinity Cemetery is owned by Trinity Church (see "Wall Street" under "Lower Manhattan," above), and is the final resting place of numerous famous New Yorkers, including John James Audubon (whose gravestone is covered with carved animals and birds). The cemetery is open daily 9 a.m.-4:30 p.m.; long-robed priests can sometimes be seen strolling the grounds. The gate to the eastern section is near the church; the gate to the western section is on 155th St. near Riverside Drive.

MANHATTAN'S NORTHERN TIP

Yeshiva University and Museum
Founded in 1886 and enrolling more than 7,000 students, this is the oldest and largest Jewish university in the Western Hemisphere. The main building is constructed in a Moorish-Byzantine style with numerous tiles, turrets, minarets, domes, and arches. Of primary interest to visitors is the Yeshiva University Museum, which houses both changing exhibits and an impressive permanent collection of art and religious objects. A highlight of the museum is its display of detailed models of 10 historic synagogues from around the world, including the 1763 Touro Synagogue of Newport, Rhode Island, which is the nation's oldest synagogue.

The university is on Amsterdam Ave. bet. 183rd and 187th Sts.; take the No. 1 train to 181st or 191st Street. The museum is in the Yeshiva University Library, 2520 Amsterdam Ave., at 185th St., tel. (212) 960-5390. Hours are Tues.-Thurs. 10:30 a.m.-5 p.m., Sun. noon-6 p.m. Admission is adults $3, seniors and children $2.

The Cloisters and Fort Tyron Park
High on a hill at the northern tip of Manhattan is the Cloisters, tel. (212) 923-3700, a magical "medieval monastery" with wonderful views of the Hudson. Financed in 1938 by John D. Rock-

serenity at the Cloisters

efeller, the Cloisters house the Metropolitan Museum of Art's medieval collections. Incorporated into the building are the actual remains of four medieval cloisters—transported here from Europe—along with a reconstructed chapter house and exhibition galleries.

The museum's most prized possessions are its 16th-century Unicorn Tapestries, hung in a darkened room all their own. Six of the seven priceless tapestries are complete, and they tell the story of the "Hunt of the Unicorn" in rich, astonishing detail. The series begins with the "Start of the Hunt" and ends with the "Unicorn in Captivity"—that famous image of the mythical creature in a round, wooden corral with a tree in the center.

Surrounding the museum are the flowering plants and trees, walkways and benches of Fort Tyron Park, designed by Frederick Law Olmsted Jr., son of the man who designed Central Park. Near the park's south end is a plaque marking the site of the fort where the Americans were defeated on Nov. 16, 1776. After that defeat, the British renamed the site Fort Tyron in honor of the last British governor of New York.

A visit to the Cloisters takes the better part of the day. It's best to go in warm weather so you can wander the grounds, which offer wonderful views of the Hudson. Hours are March-Oct., Tues.-Sun. 9:30 a.m.-5:15 p.m.; Nov.-Feb., Tues.-Sun. 9:30 a.m-4:45 p.m. Suggested admission is adults $8, students and seniors $4, children under 12 free, but you may pay what you wish. To reach the Cloisters, take the A train to 190th St.-Overlook Terrace. Exit by elevator, then catch the M4 bus or walk 15 minutes through Fort Tyron park to the museum.

SHOPPING

Bookstores

The famous **Liberation Book Shop,** 421 Lenox Ave., at 131st St., tel. (212) 281-4615 (see "North to 135th Street," above) is a Harlem landmark. Many other bookstores and book vendors are just south of Columbia University and Barnard College. Of these, **Barnard Book Forum,** 2955 Broadway, at 116th St., tel. (212) 749-5535, has an especially good selection.

Botanicas

Otto Chicas Rendon, 60 E. 116th St., bet. Madison and Park Aves., tel. (212) 289-0378, is the city's oldest and best-known botanica, selling everything from crystal balls to herbs and love potions. Founded in 1945, the store has been so successful that it now sells wholesale to botanicas around the country, and manufactures Catholic saints, *orishas* (Cuban Santeria gods), and perfumes with names such as "Chinese Floor Wash" and "Run Devil Run."

Other smaller botanicas near 116th St. are **El Congo,** 1787 Lexington Ave., bet. 110th and 111th Sts., tel. (212) 860-3961, carrying a good selection of books, miracle beads, and dried herbs; and **Paco's Botanica,** 1864 Lexington Ave., at 115th St., tel. (212) 427-0820, a spic-and-span shop with lots of religious statues wrapped in plastic.

Music

La Marketa Records, 100 116th St., no phone, is a good spot for discount salsa records, CDs, and cassettes. **Rainbow Music Shop,** 102 W. 125th St., just west of Lenox Ave., tel. (212) 864-5262, is an old neighborhood favorite selling a terrific selection of R&B and gospel, along with some jazz and blues.

Outdoor Markets

Across the street from the Malcolm Shabazz Mosque (102 W. 116th St. at Lenox Ave.) is an outdoor market where dozens of vendors sell T-shirts, Kente cloth, African art, wool skullcaps, Gambian drums, women's hair twists, down coats, and CDs. Prices range from about $5 for the skullcaps to about $100 for the down coats, and many of the shoppers are European.

Up until 1994, this outdoor market was located along the sidewalks and empty lots of 125th Street. Moved here by the Giuliani administration, intent upon enforcing a law prohibiting unlicensed street vendors, the new market caused considerable division within the Harlem community. Some felt the move was warranted because the vendors were hurting 125th Street's legitimate businesses; others believed this more out-of-the-way location would destroy the outdoor market's vitality.

But the new market has proven to be a resounding success, attracting many West

Africans to open more shops and stalls along 116th St. bet. Lenox Ave. and Frederick Douglass Boulevard. You'll also find outdoor stalls, primarily Latino-operated, on the south side of 116th St. bet. Park and Lexington Avenues. For sale here is everything from salsa recordings to bouffant wigs.

Other Shops

Mart 125, 260 W. 125th St., tel. (212) 316-3340, bet. Adam Clayton Powell Jr. and Frederick Douglass Blvds., is a massive indoor shopping center where over 50 specialty shops sell African art, jewelry, clothing, food, music, and books. Shop hours vary, but the Mart itself is open Mon.-Sat. 10 a.m.-10 p.m. and Sunday noon-5 p.m.

ACCOMMODATIONS

Hostels and Dorms

The small **Sugar Hill International House,** 722 St. Nicholas Ave., at 146th St., tel. (212) 926-7030, and its larger sister, the **Blue Rabbit International House,** 730 St. Nicholas Ave., tel. (212) 491-3892, offer both dorm-style and private rooms. Rates per person are $16-18; a passport is required of all guests, including U.S. citizens. At the **New York Uptown International Hostel,** 239 Lenox Ave., at 122nd St., tel. (212) 666-0559, beds are available in small, clean dorm rooms sleeping 4-6 for $12 a night. Affiliated with the Uptown Hostel is the **New York Bed and Breakfast,** 134 W. 119th St., near Lenox Ave., tel. (212) 666-0559, offering small private rooms for $20 per person, double occupancy.

The **International House of New York,** 500 Riverside Drive, at W. 122nd St., tel. (212) 316-8400, is primarily in the business of renting rooms to Columbia University graduate students and visiting scholars. In the summer, however, when occupancy rates are low, single student rooms are available to the general public for $35-40 s, with a $5 breakfast voucher included. Guest suites are also available; $90-125 a night. **Columbia University,** 1230 Amsterdam Ave., at 120th St., tel. (212) 678-3224, also offers single dorm rooms ($45 a night) and doubles with baths and kitchens ($75 a night) during the summer months.

FOOD

Southern/Soul

Inexpensive: M&G Diner, 383 W. 125th St., bet. St. Nicholas and Morningside Aves., tel. (212) 864-7326, is an excellent spot for fried chicken. **Wilson's Bakery & Restaurant,** 1980 Amsterdam Ave., at 158th St., tel. (212) 923-9821, is a lively neighborhood joint serving Southern-style food.

Moderate: The legendary **Sylvia's,** 328 Lenox Ave., bet. 126th and 127th Sts., tel. (212) 996-0660, has been expanding in recent years, and attracting tourists by the busload. The food's still fine but the atmosphere is not what it once was. **Copeland's,** 549 W. 145th St., bet. Broadway and Amsterdam, tel. (212) 234-2357, is the soul food restaurant of choice among politicians and businesspeople. The upscale **Emily's,** 1325 Fifth Ave., at 111th St., tel. (212) 996-1212, draws an eclectic crowd with its especially good ribs and fried chicken.

Caribbean and African

Inexpensive: The **Jamaican Hot Pot,** 2260 Seventh Ave., at 133rd St., tel. (212) 491-5270, offers mouthwatering curried goat stews, oxtail soups, and the like. The informal **Tropix,** 354 W. 125th St., bet. Frederick Douglass Blvd. and St. Nicholas Aves., tel. (212) 864-6192, serves tasty West Indian fare. **Obaa Koryoe,** 3143 Broadway, near 125th St., tel. (212) 316-2950, serves West African *fufu* and other mash-based foods—to be eaten with fingers only, please. **Zula Cafe,** 1260 Amsterdam Ave., at 122nd St., tel. (212) 663-1670, is a vibrant East African eatery.

Italian

Inexpensive: Patsy's Pizza, 2287 First Ave., bet. 117th and 118th Sts., tel. (212) 534-9783, was the country's first coal-stoked brick-oven pizzeria. A Frank Sinatra favorite, it was established in 1932.

Expensive: To get into tiny **Rao's,** 455 E. 114th St., near Pleasant, tel. (212) 722-6709, you have to book about three months in advance. The Rao family has been serving fine home cooking in this former Dutch saloon since 1896.

Latin

Inexpensive: Only Spanish is spoken at the bustling **La Hacienda,** 219 E. 116th St., bet. Second and Third Aves., tel. (212) 987-1617. On the menu is authentic fare ranging from mole poblano to grilled pork chops.

Light Bites

Near Columbia University, the sprawling **West End,** 2911 Broadway, bet. 113th and 114th Sts., tel. (212) 662-8830, was once a favorite haunt of Jack Kerouac and Allen Ginsberg. It still offers cheap pitchers of beer and a standard bar menu. **Tom's,** 2880 Broadway, near 112th St., tel. (212) 864-6137, is best known for its milk shakes. The traditional **Hungarian Pastry Shop,** 1030 Amsterdam Ave., near 111th St., tel. (212) 866-4230, sells mouthwatering strudel and other sweet treats.

Several excellent bakeries are located along 125th Street. **Peacemaker Fingerlicking Bakery,** 251 W. 125th, near ACP Blvd., tel. (212) 749-6298, is a West Indian place selling spicy meat patties. **Georgie's Pastry Shop,** 50 W. 125th, bet. Fifth and Lenox Aves., tel. (212) 831-0722, is a tiny joint known for tasty donuts and sweet-potato pies. **Wimp's Bakery,** 29 W. 125th, bet. Fifth and Lenox Aves., tel. (212) 410-2296, is a modern spot also serving excellent sweet-potato pies, banana puddings, and the like.

In East Harlem, **La Nueva Bakery,** 2129 Third Ave., bet. 116th and 117th Sts., tel. (212) 876-2990, offers fresh breads and Cuban sandwiches.

Watering Holes and Lounges

The casual, low-ceilinged **West End,** 2911 Broadway, bet. 113th and 114th Sts., tel. (212) 662-8830, has long been a favorite watering hole among Columbia University students and professors. The vintage art deco **Lenox Lounge,** 288 Lenox Ave., bet. 124th and 125th St., tel. (212) 427-0253, beckons with shiny steel bar fixtures, comfy semicircular banquettes, and gorgeous light fixtures shaped like fins. First-class musicians present live jazz on weekends. Around the corner is the '50s-era **Club Lido,** 35 W. 125th St., near Lenox Ave., tel. (212) 722-3250, adorned with white chandeliers and wrought-iron railings. You must ring the buzzer to get in; in back, find a great jukebox filled with soul classics.

DOVER PUBLICATIONS, INC.

THE OUTER BOROUGHS

Manhattan offers so much to see and do that few visitors—or Manhattanites, for that matter—ever make it to the outer boroughs, where most New Yorkers actually live. Those who do venture outside Manhattan, however, will find in the other boroughs a number of one-of-a-kind sights and an astounding ethnic stew, made up of enormous communities of Italians, Poles, Russians, Chinese, Japanese, Koreans, Thais, Indians, West Indians, West Africans, Latin Americans, Greeks, Orthodox Jews, and African Americans. Most of these neighborhoods don't have "visitor attractions" in the usual sense of the term, but they do have excellent restaurants and food shops, and are an easy way to experience another culture, if only for an afternoon.

The boroughs also offer great views of Manhattan—Brooklyn Heights and Long Island City are two especially good spots—and wide-open outdoor spaces. Prospect Park and Coney Island in Brooklyn, Flushing Meadows-Corona Park in Queens, the Bronx Zoo and Botanical Gardens in the Bronx, and the Staten Island Greenbelt are all unique places offering a welcome respite from the frenzy of Manhattan.

Orientation
Because the boroughs are so vast and geographically confusing, the sections below are divided into manageable chunks—all easily accessible by subway from Manhattan. First-time visitors might want to ride the Staten Island ferry, or visit Brooklyn Heights or Coney Island in Brooklyn, Astoria or Jackson Heights in Queens, or the Bronx Zoo in the Bronx.

BROOKLYN

Up until 1898, Brooklyn was a city in its own right, separate from New York. It had its own city hall, central park, downtown shops, museums, theaters, beaches, botanical garden, and zoo—all of which helps account for its fierce sense of identity and pride. Of all the boroughs, Brooklyn is the most individualistic, the most mythic, and the most complex.

Brooklyn is: Walt Whitman, Coney Island, the Brooklyn Dodgers, the Brooklyn Bridge, Mae West, Nathan's Famous, Bazooka bubble gum, Lena Horne, John Travolta, Jackie Gleason, the Brooklyn Navy Yards, Mickey Rooney, Topps baseball cards, Pete Hamill, Barbra Streisand, Prospect Park, Chock Full o' Nuts, Junior's cheesecake, Spike Lee. Brooklyn is also "the borough of churches," and the borough of ethnic neighborhoods. In total, 93 ethnic groups call Brooklyn home, among them Hasidic Jews, West Indians, Latin Americans, Russians, Poles, Scandinavians, Asians, Italians, Middle Easterners, and Irish.

History

The largest borough in population (2.5 million) and the second largest in area (78.5 square miles), Brooklyn was first inhabited by the Carnarsie Indians. In 1607, Henry Hudson landed briefly on Coney Island, and a few years later, the Dutch began establishing farms. The first battle after the Declaration of Independence-the Battle of Long Island—was fought in Brooklyn. The colonists lost, but Washington and his troops retreated with enough strength to continue the fight.

After the Revolution, Brooklyn began to boom.

Its deep waters were developed into a major shipping port, and in 1814, Robert Fulton's ferry service connected the borough to Manhattan, strengthening its ties of commerce even more. By the end of the 19th century, Brooklyn was plump and prosperous, home to one million residents and countless flourishing industries.

That's when the borough made what journalist Pete Hamill calls the "Big Mistake," signing an 1898 agreement that annexed it to New York City. The annexation was probably inevitable, however, as the Brooklyn Bridge had opened up 16 years before, and the two cities' economies were becoming more and more entwined.

After WW II, Brooklyn's fortunes began to go downhill. The Brooklyn Navy Yards—for nearly a century one of the borough's largest employers—closed down, and the borough's famed newspaper, the *Brooklyn Eagle,* went out of business. Some neighborhoods lost their middle

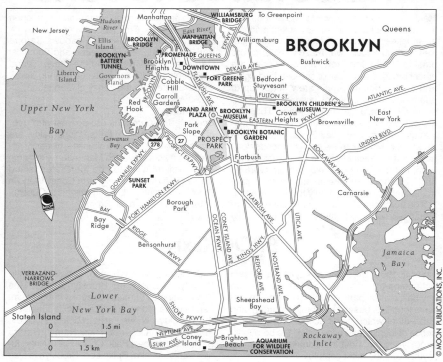

hoofing it across the Brooklyn Bridge

class to the suburbs, and—worst of all—the Brooklyn Dodgers moved to Los Angeles, just two years after winning the World Series for the first time in 1955. Large sections of the borough began to have a bombed-out, abandoned look.

Today, Brooklyn is on the rebound. Although poverty is still a major problem in some areas, neighborhoods such as Park Slope and Fort Greene—which as recently as the 1970s were considered marginal—are now home to large numbers of professionals, attracted by the areas' brownstones and relatively low rents. Other neighborhoods such as Greenpoint and Brighton Beach have witnessed the influx of thousands of energetic new immigrants.

Neighborhoods

The sheer number of neighborhoods in Brooklyn is dizzying. Immediately south of Manhattan are Brooklyn Heights, Cobble Hill, Carroll Gardens, Boerum Hill, and Fort Greene, while directly east are Williamsburg and Greenpoint. Farther

out, to the south, are Red Hook, Sunset Park, Borough Park, Bay Ridge, Bensonhurst, Coney Island, and Brighton Beach, while to the southeast are Park Slope, Crown Heights, Bedford-Stuyvesant, Bushwick, Flatbush, Brownsville, East New York, Carnarsie, and Sheepshead Bay.

BROOKLYN HEIGHTS AND VICINITY

From Manhattan: By far the best way to go is to walk over the Brooklyn Bridge, then cross through Cadman Plaza Park to the Heights. By subway, take the A train to High St., or the No. 2 or 3 to Clark Street. You can also take the No. 4 to Borough Hall and walk west.

Quiet, tree-lined streets; dignified, perfectly preserved brownstones; well-dressed parents out playing with their apple-cheeked kids—such is the refined genteel atmosphere of Brooklyn Heights, one of New York City's prettiest neighborhoods. Manhattanites even deign to visit here, largely because of the **Promenade** that runs along the district's western edge, offering magnificent, bluff-high views of the skyline, the harbor, and the Brooklyn Bridge.

Used as a refuge by General Washington and his troops after an early defeat in the Revolutionary War, Brooklyn Heights became the country's first suburb when Robert Fulton started up his ferry service in the early 1800s. Soon thereafter, wealthy Brooklyn Heights landowners—many of them bankers commuting to Wall Street—divided their property into standard building lots, and the neighborhood filled up with brownstones and churches.

Much of the pleasure of visiting Brooklyn Heights lies in simply wandering its idyllic streets. Orange, Pineapple, Clark, Pierrepont, and Montague Sts. will all take you down to the Promenade, which blooms profusely with flowers during warm weather. Washington Roebling, builder of the Brooklyn Bridge, once lived at the north end of the Promenade, where he could watch the project's progress by telescope from his invalid's bed. Montague St. is Brooklyn Heights' main commercial thoroughfare, where you'll find most of the neighborhood's restaurants, bars, and shops. During warm weather, many of these establishments set up tables on the street, giving it a vaguely European air.

Historic Buildings

At the corner of Clark and Henry Sts. is the 1885 **St. George Hotel.** (If you take the 2 or 3 train to Brooklyn Heights, you'll arrive in the hotel's basement and take a strangely quiet ride on a big freight elevator to street level.) A neighborhood landmark, the St. George was once New York City's largest hotel, with 2,632 rooms and a fabled swimming pool lined with mirrors. The building fell on hard times in the 1970s and 1980s but is now being transformed into student housing.

Two blocks from the St. George, on Orange St. bet. Henry and Hicks Sts., is the red-brick **Plymouth Church of the Pilgrims.** In the Civil War era, this church was famous all over America, thanks to minister Henry Ward Beecher's rousing antislavery sermons. A statue honoring Beecher—brother of Harriet Beecher Stowe—stands in the church's garden; inside is a marker indicating the pew at which Abraham Lincoln sat when he visited.

The Reverend Henry Beecher lived around the corner from his church at 22 Willow St., where he was accused of having an adulterous affair with a Mrs. Tilton, who sang in the church choir. Beecher was tried and acquitted, but his authority was never the same thereafter.

At 57 Willow St. is a fine 1824 house, crafted with dormers, steeply pitched roofs, and carved stone lintels. Farther south, the basement apartment of 70 Willow St. was once home to Truman Capote, who wrote *In Cold Blood* while living here. At 108-112 Willow St. are excellent examples of the elaborate Queen Anne architectural style, while superb red-brick Federal-style houses, complete with black doors and window frames, can be found at 155, 157, and 159 Willow.

Pierrepont Street is lined with some of the biggest and most playful residences in Brooklyn Heights. At 82 Pierrepont is a giant, turreted affair initially built as a private mansion and later used as a hotel, whorehouse, residence hall for Franciscan brothers, and, finally, an apartment building.

Historical Museum

The pretty, terra cotta building at 128 Pierrepont St. is home to the **Brooklyn Historical Society,** tel. (718) 624-0890. Though now closed for extensive renovations, the society promises to reopen in the fall of 1998 with an enlarged, state-of-the-art exhibit space. The society also sponsors unusual walking tours of the borough.

Jehovah's Witnesses

Brooklyn Heights is dotted with a number of large, institutional-looking buildings painted a pale mustard yellow—a sign that they're owned by the Jehovah's Witnesses. The fundamentalist religious sect bases its world headquarters here, publishing its tract, the *Watchtower,* out of the former Squibb factory just north of the Brooklyn Bridge. The Jehovah's Witnesses Residence Hall is at 124 Columbia Heights; the Jehovah's Witnesses Library is at 119 Columbia Heights.

Fulton Ferry Historic District

At the extreme northern end of Brooklyn Heights, almost beneath the Brooklyn Bridge, is the Fulton Ferry Historic District, which centers around Old Fulton St. and a clutch of historic buildings. One of these, the medieval-looking **Eagle Warehouse,** 28 Old Fulton St., is now a co-op building. Near the entrance is a plaque honoring Walt Whitman and the *Brooklyn Eagle,* which was published on this site from 1841 to 1892. Whitman served as the newspaper's editor until he was fired for his stand against slavery.

Atlantic Avenue

Brooklyn Heights ends at Atlantic Ave., a wide, gray boulevard known for its Arab restaurants and shops. The Middle Eastern community began settling here back in the days when Brooklyn was a bustling seaport. While the thoroughfare is not as lively as it once was, the block between Court and Clinton Sts. is still lined with Arab-run businesses. Atlantic Ave. is also known for its quirky antique shops. See "Shopping," below.

Cobble Hill and Carroll Gardens

South of Atlantic Ave., bet. Henry and Hoyt Sts., is Cobble Hill. Though not as classy as Brooklyn

Heights, Cobble Hill has its share of pretty brownstones and red-brick family homes, most dating from the 19th century. Particularly interesting here are **Clinton Street,** great for strolling; and **Verandah Place,** just off Clinton south of Congress, a peaceful mews filled with renovated carriage houses. Architect Robert Upjohn once lived at 296 Clinton, while Thomas Wolfe once resided at 40 Verandah Place.

Below DeGraw St., Cobble Hill turns into Carroll Gardens, an older Italian neighborhood. **Court Street,** flanked with food shops, is the main thoroughfare here, while the side streets are home to neat brownstones and gardens, many dotted with religious statues.

Entertainment

Bargemusic, foot of Fulton St., at Water St., tel. (718) 624-4061, is a converted barge now serving as a wood-paneled concert venue for chamber music and jazz. The barge also offers great views of Manhattan.

Shopping

Food shops on Atlantic Ave. include the tiny **Damascus Bakery,** 195 Atlantic, tel. (718) 625-7070, selling freshly baked pita bread; and the large, well-stocked **Sahadi Importing Company,** 187-189 Atlantic, tel. (718) 624-4550, offering dried fruits and grains, olives, feta cheese, stuffed grape leaves, and the like.

Horseman Antiques, 351 Atlantic Ave., tel. (718) 596-1048, is a four-floor emporium specializing in furniture from the early 1900s. **In the Days of Old, Limited,** 357 Atlantic Ave., tel. (718) 858-4233, specializes in late Victorian furnishings.

In the Cobble Hill area is **Bookcourt,** 163 Court St., tel. (718) 875-3677, Brooklyn's best bookstore. Among Carroll Gardens' food shops are **Esposito's,** 357 Court St., tel. (718) 875-6863, known for its fresh sausage; and **Caputo's Bakery,** 329 Court St., tel. (718) 875-6871, selling crusty semolina breads and Italian pastries.

Food

Cheerful **Slade's,** 107 Montague St., tel. (718) 858-1200, is a favorite lunch spot. Nearby is **Henry's End,** 44 Henry St., tel. (718) 834-1776,

a cozy hideaway said to be the neighborhood's best restaurant.

In the Fulton St. Historic District you'll find **Patsy's Pizza,** 19 Fulton St., tel. (718) 858-4300, the Brooklyn branch of a well-known East Harlem joint. Down at the waterfront is the famed **River Cafe,** 1 Water St., tel. (718) 522-5200, an upscale and expensive eatery offering imaginative American cuisine and marvelous views of Manhattan.

For Middle Eastern cuisine, moderately priced, try **Tripoli,** 154 Atlantic Ave., tel. (718) 596-5800, with a three-masted sailing ship painted on its huge windows; or the more casual **Moroccan Star,** 205 Atlantic Ave., tel. (718) 643-0800. Down the block is **La Bouillabaisse,** 145 Atlantic Ave., tel. (718) 522-8275, a first-rate fish bistro, and the **Waterfront Ale House,** 136 Atlantic Ave., tel. (718) 522-3794, a favorite local watering hole.

DOWNTOWN AND FORT GREENE

From Manhattan: Take the No. 2, 3, or 4 train to Borough Hall.

Adjacent to genteel Brooklyn Heights is scrappy downtown Brooklyn, home to a number of imposing government buildings that hark back to the days when Brooklyn was a city in its own right. The Greek Revival **Borough Hall,** at the intersection of Joralemon, Fulton, and Court Sts., was once Brooklyn's City Hall, and still houses government offices. The Romanesque Revival **Brooklyn General Post Office,** 271 Cadman Pl. E, once handled all of the city's mail.

New York Transit Museum

Two blocks southwest of Borough Hall is the New York Transit Museum, downstairs at the northwest corner of Schermerhorn St. and Boerum Pl., tel. (718) 243-3060. Appropriately housed in a former subway station, the museum sports well-lit tiled walls that seem to stretch out forever into the darkness. Some wonderful old restored subway cars are housed here, along with a scale model of the subway system, early turnstiles, vintage mosaics from abandoned subway stations, and an unusual gift store. The museum is open Tues.-Fri. 10 a.m.-4 p.m., Sat.-Sun. noon-5 p.m. Admission is adults $3, seniors and students under 17 $1.50.

Fulton Mall

Just east of Borough Hall along Fulton St. is the pedestrians-only Fulton Mall. Built in the 1960s to help revive a dying downtown, the mall is a lively place crowded with mainstream and discount stores, street vendors, and multiethnic crowds.

Fort Greene

Immediately east of downtown Brooklyn lies Fort Greene, named after Nathanael Greene, an American general in the Revolutionary War. Filled with rows of renovated brownstones, Fort Greene is one of the city's most racially integrated middle-class communities, as well as one of its more artistic. Many jazz musicians, including Terence Blanchard and Cassandra Wilson, call this district home, along with many artists, writers, filmmakers, and directors. The neighborhood's most famous resident is probably Spike Lee, whose production company, 40 Acres and a Mule, is headquartered in renovated Firehouse No. 256 on Dekalb Avenue. Lee's store, **Spike's Joint** is at 1 South Elliot Pl., at DeKalb.

Across from Spike's Joint, on DeKalb bet. St. Edwards St. and Washington Park, is hilly **Fort Greene Park,** designed by Frederick Law Olmsted. In the center of the park is the towering granite **Prison Ship Martyrs Monument.** The monument pays tribute to the thousands of American men who lost their lives in the British prison ships anchored nearby during the Revolutionary War. Though a little-known chapter in American history, more men perished in those horrific vessels than in all the war's battles and campaigns combined; enough bones washed up after the war to indicate that as many as 11,000 may have died. Their bones are now buried in a crypt beneath the monument.

Fort Greene is also home to the **Brooklyn Academy of Music,** 30 Lafayette Ave., at Atlantic and Flatbush, tel. (718) 636-4100, a world-famous institution known for avant garde productions; and **Williamsburg Savings Bank,** 1 Hanson Pl., at Flatbush, the tallest building in Brooklyn. Take the elevator to the 45th floor of this 1929 landmark for sweeping views of the borough.

Shopping

A number of young African American fashion designers have shops at or near the intersection of Fulton and S. Oxford Streets. **Spike's Joint,** 1 South Elliott Pl., at DeKalb, tel. (718) 802-1000, is filmmaker Spike Lee's store, selling souvenirs and an exclusive line of jeans and jackets.

Food

Two of Brooklyn's best-known eateries are on or just off the Fulton Mall. **Gage & Tollner,** 372 Fulton St., at Jay St., near the mall's center, tel. (718) 875-5181, is a classic turn-of-the-century restaurant—perhaps the oldest in the city—filled with dark woods, gilt-edged mirrors, and gaslight fixtures. The Southern-accented cuisine is first-rate, but it doesn't come cheap; reservations are required. **Junior's,** 386 Flatbush Ave., at DeKalb, tel. (718) 852-5257, is a sprawling, well-lit place, famed all over the city and beyond for its smooth, rich cheesecake.

Near the Transit Museum is **Queen,** 84 Court St., near Livingston, tel. (718) 596-5955, a first-rate Italian restaurant favored by the courthouse crowd.

A Fort Greene landmark, serving first-rate soul food since 1974, is **Ms. Ann's Southern Style Cooking,** 86 S. Portland St., near Fulton, tel. (718) 858-6997, open Wed.-Saturday. Ms. Ann cooks everything herself on an old Vulcan stove.

Near the Brooklyn Academy of Music is the romantic **New City Cafe,** 246 DeKalb Ave., bet. Vanderbilt and Clermont Aves., tel. (718) 622-5607, serving unusual variations on grilled vegetable, chicken, and fish dishes. In summer, a backyard garden opens up. Prices are moderate to expensive.

WILLIAMSBURG

From Manhattan: Take the J train to Marcy Ave. and walk south to Lee Avenue.

North of Fort Greene lies Williamsburg, home to a community of about 40,000 Satmarer Hasidim, a strict orthodox Jewish sect originally from Hungary. Men dress in long black coats with wide-brimmed hats, and sport full beards and sidelocks, while women wear long skirts and sleeves, and if married, cover their heads with wigs and scarves. Although first settled by middle-class Irish and Germans, Williamsburg became predominantly Jewish in the early 1900s after the Williamsburg Bridge was completed. The bridge connected Brooklyn to Manhattan's then-hugely-overpopulated Lower East Side, and working-class Jews fled to Williamsburg by the thousands. Though most have since moved on to more suburban pastures, the Satmar remain.

The Hasidim are centered along **Lee Avenue,** which is lined with shops selling everything from religious articles to timers that will automatically operate electrical appliances on the Sabbath. On **Bedford Avenue,** paralleling Lee, are many sturdy turn-of-the-century mansions; check out 505 Bedford, once a casino, and 559 Bedford, covered with turrets and elaborate friezes.

Also in Williamsburg are sizeable Italian and Puerto Rican communities, and an enclave of ex-Manhattanite artists, attracted to the area by its low rents and abandoned industrial spaces. Most of the artists live about 15 blocks north of Lee Avenue near **Bedford Avenue.** Here you'll find a clutch of inexpensive restaurants, shops, bars, and galleries. To reach the area directly from Manhattan, take the L train to the Bedford Avenue stop.

Italian Festival
Every July, Williamsburg is the site of a 12-day Italian festival centering around Our Lady of Mount Carmel Church, 275 N. 8th St., near Havemeyer, tel. (718) 384-0223. The highlight of the festival is the Dance of the Giglio, when a towering metallic structure weighing thousands of pounds is "danced" through the streets on the shoulders of about 120 men.

Shopping
Flaum Appetizing, 40 Lee Ave., near Wilson, tel. (718) 387-7934, sells smoked salmon, herring, and the like, at half the prices they go for in Manhattan. Shop for fresh-baked challah bread at the **Lee Ave. Kosher Bakery,** 73 Lee Ave., tel. (718) 387-4736, on Fridays before 4 p.m.

One of the biggest secondhand clothing shops in the city is **Domsey Warehouse,** 431 Kent Ave., foot of S. 9th St., tel. (718) 384-6000. Some of the clothes here are vintage, most are not, but no one leaves without at least two shopping bags full. Many articles of clothing cost less than $15.

Farther north, you'll find **Earwax Records,** 204 Bedford Ave., at N. 5th St., tel. (718) 218-9608, selling a good selection of new and used CDs and LPs. Nearby is **Max + Roebling,** 189 Bedford Ave., tel. (718) 387-0045, a pricey clothing shop stocked by local designers. The **Three Marias,** 76 Havemeyer St., near N. 5th St., tel. (718) 599-0417, offers up love potions, herbal remedies, and incense. Area galleries include **Momenta Art,** 72 Berry St., at N. 10th St., tel. (718) 218-8058, and **Pierogi 2000,** 167 N. Ninth St., near Bedford, tel. (718) 599-2144.

Food
The famed 1887 **Peter Luger Steak House,** 178 Broadway, near Driggs, tel. (718) 387-7400, is an expensive, no-frills, century-old steak house featuring enormous cuts of meat and crusty waiters who seem as old as time. It's just a short cab ride from Manhattan across the Williamsburg Bridge. **Landau's Glatt Kosher Deli,** 65 Lee Ave., near Wilson, tel. (718) 782-3700, features fat deli sandwiches. **Sabrina's Place,** 85 Broadway, at Berry St., tel. (718) 218-8580, is an authentic Spanish and American diner.

Farther north, near Bedford Avenue, rocks **Teddy's Bar and Grill,** 96 Berry St., near N. 8th St., tel. (718) 384-9787, a favorite local bar with live music on weekends. Try **Bean,** 172 N. Eighth St., at Bedford, tel. (718) 387-8222, or **Vera Cruz,** 195 Bedford Ave., near N. 6th St., tel. (718) 599-7914, for cheap and tasty Mexican food, and **Plan Eat Thailand,** 184 Bedford Ave., near N. 6th St., tel. (718) 599-5758, for cheap and tasty Thai.

GREENPOINT

From Manhattan: Take the L train to Lorimer St. and transfer to the G train heading north. Get off at Greenpoint Avenue.

The birthplace of Mae West, Greenpoint was

once a prime industrial center. Shipbuilding plants and oil refineries were located along its shoreline, while publishing, porcelain, and glass manufacturing companies were farther inland. Today, most of Greenpoint's industries have been abandoned, but the scruffy neighborhood is still very much alive, thanks mostly to its Polish community—the largest in New York. The Poles first came to Greenpoint in the late 19th century to work in the factories, and are continuing to arrive today, post-Cold War. Many Italians and Irish also live in the area.

Polish Greenpoint's commercial center is **Manhattan Avenue.** Here, you'll find a smattering of Polish butcher shops, bakeries, and grocery stores, along with standard American shops. Numerous Polish shops are also found along **Nassau Street.**

Historic Buildings

Largely residential, Greenpoint is filled with historic brick row houses interspersed with modern aluminum-sided ones. Many of the prettiest brick buildings are between Manhattan and Franklin Aves., Java and Calyer Streets. On Kent St. bet. Manhattan and Franklin is the Gothic **Elias Greek Rite Church,** along with several pretty Italianate houses. On the corner of Manhattan and Calyer is the 1908 **Greenpoint Savings Bank,** which began here and now has branches citywide.

Two other interesting churches in Greenpoint are the ornate **St. Stanislaus Kostka Church,** 607 Humboldt St., at Driggs, where Polish masses are held daily; and the stunning, onion-domed **Russian Orthodox Cathedral of the Transfiguration,** 228 N. 12th St., at Driggs, which boasts a wooden screen with icons painted by the Kiev Orthodox Monastery of the Caves. The churches are open Sunday mornings only.

Shopping

Try **W. Nassau Meat Market,** 915 Manhattan Ave., bet. Greenpoint and Kent, tel. (718) 389-6149, for kielbasa and stuffed cabbage; **Zakopane,** 714 Manhattan Ave., bet. Norman and Meserolle, tel. (718) 389-3487, for woodcarvings and peasant embroidery.

Food

One of the best Polish restaurants in Greenpoint is **Polska Restaurant,** 136 Greenpoint Ave., near Manhattan, tel. (718) 389-8368. The more fashionable **Continental Restaurant,** 11 Nevel Ave., at Driggs, tel. (718) 389-2207, is the place to polka on weekends.

PROSPECT PARK AND VICINITY

From Manhattan: Take the No. 2 or 3 train to Eastern Parkway.

Three of Brooklyn's finest attractions—the Brooklyn Museum of Art, the Brooklyn Botanic Garden, and Prospect Park—are all within a few minutes' walk of each other here, while next door is one of the borough's most historic residential districts, Park Slope. After Brooklyn Heights, Park Slope is the neighborhood of choice among ex-Manhattanites. Here you'll find many young professionals strolling about with dogs and kids, along with a decreasing number of older families who've lived in the area for generations.

Brooklyn Museum of Art

The lovely beaux arts Brooklyn Museum, 200 Eastern Pkwy., at Washington, tel. (718) 638-5000, was designed by McKim, Mead & White in 1897. Though one of the world's largest museums, it's always lived in the shadow of its mighty cousin across the river—the Metropolitan Museum of Art. But the Brooklyn Museum is very different from the Met or any other Manhattan art museum. It's usually quieter and less crowded. And more importantly, it stages some of the more unusual shows in town, among them major retrospectives by African American artists such as Romare Bearden and Jacob Lawrence, and women artists such as Elizabeth Murray and Louise Bourgeois.

Like the Metropolitan, the Brooklyn Museum's collections span virtually the entire history of art. Highlights include extensive Egyptian holdings, an excellent Native American collection, and a major permanent collection of contemporary art. Most of these contemporary pieces are housed in the light and airy West Wing, only recently renovated and reopened to the public after a 60-year hiatus. The museum also sponsors a lively jazz and blues concert series, and has one of the city's most eclectic gift shops, filled with reasonably priced handicrafts from around the world.

The museum is open Wed.-Sun. 10 a.m.-5 p.m. Suggested admission is adults $4, students $2, seniors $1.50, children under 12 free.

Brooklyn Botanic Garden
Next door to the Brooklyn Museum is the Brooklyn Botanic Garden, 1000 Washington Ave., tel. (718) 622-4433, another unusual and much beloved Brooklyn institution. Though considerably smaller than the world-famous botanical gardens in the Bronx, the Brooklyn gardens are in many ways more conducive to visit. Spread out over 50 carefully designed acres are a rose garden, a children's garden, a Japanese scholar's garden, and a garden for the blind, complete with Braille signs. The Steinhardt Conservatory houses tropical and desert plants, along with the country's largest collection of bonsais. The best time to visit is May, when the cherry blossoms burst forth, all pink and white froth.

Hours are April-Sept., Tues.-Fri. 8 a.m.-6 p.m., Sat.-Sun. 10 a.m.-6 p.m.; Oct.-March, Tues.-Fri. 8 a.m.-4:30 p.m., Sat.-Sun. 10 a.m.-4:30 p.m. Admission is adults $3, students and seniors $1.50, children 6-16 50 cents. Free to kids under 6, and to all on Tuesday.

Prospect Park
Behind the Brooklyn Museum and the Brooklyn Botanic Garden is enormous Prospect Park—525 acres of forests and meadows, lakes and streams. Now undergoing a major restoration, Prospect Park was designed by Frederick Law Olmsted and Calvert Vaux, who also designed Central Park. The two men considered this to be their masterpiece. Considerably wilder than Central Park, Prospect Park creates the illusion of being in the country.

The main entrance is at **Grand Army Plaza,** just up from the Brooklyn Museum at the intersection of Eastern Pkwy., Flatbush Ave., and Prospect Park West. In the center of the plaza, surrounded by an everpresent rush of traffic, is a towering triumphal arch honoring the Union soldiers of the Civil War.

Immediately inside the main entrance is the park's most glorious sight—Long Meadow. Stretching over a mile, this gently rolling lawn is lined on both sides with lush trees that com-

Grand Army Plaza guards the main entrance to Prospect Park.

pletely hide the cityscape. During warm weather, the meadow attracts West Indian cricket players; in winter, the cross-country skiers come out.

East of Long Meadow are an 18th-century **carousel;** a wooden Dutch farmhouse known as **Lefferts Homestead;** and the **Prospect Park Wildlife Center.** Once one of the nation's most deplorable animal parks, this zoo reopened in 1994 after a four-year $36-million restoration. It now houses about 45 species in enclosures resembling their natural habitats. The zoo, tel. (718) 399-7339, is open April-Oct., Mon.-Fri. 10 a.m.-5 p.m., Sat.-Sun. 10 a.m.-5:30 p.m.; Nov.-March, daily 10 a.m-4:30 p.m. Admission is adults $2.50, seniors $1.25, children 3-12 fifty cents, children under three free.

Other attractions in the park include the odd, usually locked **Friends' Cemetery,** where Montgomery Clift and his mother are buried; **Wollman Rink,** open for skating in winter; and

Prospect Lake, a shimmering expanse of blue at the park's south end. On the lake is the **Boathouse,** where pedalboats can be rented for $7 an hour.

Like Central Park, Prospect Park is generally safe but has its share of crime. It's not advisable to explore isolated areas alone or to enter the park after dark.

The **Urban Park Rangers,** tel. (718) 287-3474 or (718) 438-0100, conduct frequent free environmental walks through the park. For maps and special events information, stop by **Litchfield Villa,** on the park's west edge at 95 Prospect Park W, tel. (718) 965-8900; open Mon.-Fri. 9 a.m.-5 p.m.

Park Slope

West of Prospect Park and south of Grand Army Plaza is Park Slope. Once known as the "Gold Coast," the area is home to one of the country's largest concentrations of Victorian brownstones. Park Slope fell on hard times after WW II, but has been on the upswing since the 1970s.

The main commercial thoroughfares are **Seventh and Fifth Avenues,** while most of the neighborhood's prettiest brownstones are on the side streets between Prospect Park and Sixth Avenue. **Carroll Street** and **Montgomery Place** are especially worth a gander. The **Montauk Club,** 25 Eighth Ave., at Lincoln, is one of Park Slope's finest old buildings. It's an eclectic Venetian palace lined with a frieze depicting the history of Long Island's Montauk Indians.

Mobster **Al Capone** grew up in a two-story brick house at 38 Garfield Place. He moved here with his family in 1907, when he was eight years old, and used to hang out at a pool hall down the block at 20 Garfield Place. As a teenager, Capone ran with a group of mobsters-in-training known as the James Street gang. He fled to Chicago in 1919 when he became a suspect in a murder case.

Food

Cousin John's, 70 Seventh Ave., bet. Berkeley and Lincoln, tel. (718) 622-7333, offers light fare and wonderful baked goods. **Cucina,** 256 Fifth Ave., near Garfield, tel. (718) 230-0711, serves first-rate Tuscan fare in a sophisticated setting. **Aunt Suzie's,** 247 Fifth Ave., bet. Carroll and

Garfield, tel. (718) 788-3377, offers simple, inexpensive Italian dishes. **Raintree's,** 142 Prospect Park W, at 9th St., tel. (718) 768-3723, is an upscale, tile-floored spot across the street from the Prospect Park bandshell.

CROWN HEIGHTS

From Manhattan: Take the No. 3 train to Kingston Avenue.

The name Crown Heights was invented by real estate agents in the 1920s to attract residents to what was supposed to be a brand new residential area. In reality, Crown Heights is made up of bits and pieces of five older Brooklyn neighborhoods—Bedford, Stuyvesant (now known as one district, Bedford-Stuyvesant), Brownsville, East New York, and Prospect Heights.

Today, Crown Heights is best known for its two very distinct ethnic communities: the West Indians—mostly Haitians and Jamaicans—and the Lubavitch Hasidim, who comprise about nine percent of the neighborhood's population. Crown Heights also holds a sizeable African American population and a small Asian one.

The neighborhood has made the headlines in recent years due to racial tensions between the Lubavitch and the neighborhood's black populations. In 1991, a young black boy was killed by a careening car driven by a Hasidic man, touching off racial riots and the slaying of a Hasidic scholar, Yankel Rosenbaum. Reverberations from those riots are still being felt today.

The Lubavitch Hasidim

Like the Hasidim of Williamsburg (see above), the Lubavitch trace their roots to Eastern Europe. The men dress in dark suits and hats, while the women keep their collarbones, elbows, and knees covered. Unlike some Hasidim, however, the Lubavitch make use of modern technology. Until his death in 1994, the Rebbe Menachen Schneerson, the community's spiritual leader, used e-mail to send his sermons to the approximately 1,600 other Lubavitch communities worldwide.

The center of the Lubavitch community is

Kingston Ave., bet. Eastern Pkwy. and Empire Boulevard. It's lined with food shops and stores selling religious articles such as prayer shawls and yarmulkes. **Chassidic Art Institute,** 375 Kingston, tel. (718) 774-9149, showcases contemporary religious folk art. President St. is a pretty residential thoroughfare flanked with huge columned homes.

At the corner of Kingston Ave. and Eastern Pkwy. is the **Lubavitch synagogue,** where members of the community pray, meditate, and chant the liturgy at all times of day. Women sit upstairs behind a glassed-off partition, while men sit downstairs on long, plain wooden benches. Many wear black-and-white prayer shawls.

Visitors are welcome at the synagogue and in the stores, but the best way to visit is to take one of the tours offered Sundays at noon by the Chassidic Discovery Center, 305 Kingston Ave., tel. (800) 838-TOUR (-8687); the cost is $10. The tours include a short talk on the history and beliefs of the Lubavitch, followed by visits to the synagogue, the World Headquarters where religious artifacts are on display, the *mikvah* (a spiritual bathhouse), and the Smura Matzoh Bakery.

The West Indians

The West Indians first began arriving in Crown Heights in the 1920s, attracted by the neighborhood's many solid one- and two-family homes. Many were members of an aspiring middle class and were soon opening up small businesses. This influx dwindled in the 1950s due to strict immigration quotas, but soared again after 1965 when the laws were loosened up.

Today, the West Indian community is centered along Nostrand and Utica Aves. north of Eastern Parkway. Nostrand is three blocks west of Kingston Ave.; Utica is four blocks east. On both streets, you'll find a smattering of restaurants and bakeries, grocery stores and hair-braiding shops, storefront churches, and music, music, music. Bearded Rastas in brightly colored caps sell tapes of everything from reggae to country, while schoolchildren dressed in plaid skirts and jackets saunter by with armloads of books.

Brooklyn Children's Museum

Founded in 1899, this cheery place at 145 Brooklyn Ave., at St. Marks Ave., tel. (718) 735-4432, was the world's first children's museum, and still attracts families from all over the city. Most of the exhibits are hands-on and interactive, and highlights include a liquid light show, a working windmill, a greenhouse, and an artificial set of lungs and larynx that can be made to "sing." The museum is open Wed.-Fri. 2-5 p.m. and Sat.-Sun. 10 a.m.-5 p.m. Suggested admission is $3 per person.

Weeksville

On a small knoll not far from Utica Ave. stand the Weeksville Houses, 1698-1708 Bergen St., tel. (718) 756-5250. Also known as the Hunterfly Road Houses, these four proud wooden-frame structures are all that's left of Weeksville, a free black community established here in the 1840s. Weeksville was forgotten by the world until 1968, when historian James Hurley, knowing that the community had existed here someplace, flew over the site by helicopter and noticed an oddly placed lane that didn't quite jibe with the modern grid system.

Today, the restored Weeksville houses tell their story through photographs, maps, artifacts, and videos. Some of the community's earliest residents included Dr. Susan Smith McKinney-Steward, who was the nation's third black female physician; and Maj. Martin Delaney, the grandson of an enslaved West African prince, who was active in the Underground Railroad. The community was named after James Weeks, who purchased the land in 1838 from the Lefferts family. Suggested admission to the Weeksville Houses is adults $3, children $1. Usual hours are Mon.-Fri. 10 a.m.-4 p.m. and weekends by appointment, but it's best to call in advance.

Shopping and Food

Oneg Bake Shop, 425 Kingston Ave., near President, tel. (718) 797-0971, sells delicious challah and honey cakes. **Straker's Calypso Record World,** 242 Utica Ave., near St. John's, tel. (718) 756-0040, is the place to buy hard-to-find Caribbean records and tapes. **Dewar's,** 807 Nostrand Ave., near President, tel. (718) 773-8403, is a favorite family restaurant serving traditional West Indian fare.

FROM CONEY ISLAND TO SHEEPSHEAD BAY

From Manhattan: Take the B, D or F train to Coney Island/Stillwell Avenue.

If you've only got time to make one stop in Brooklyn, Coney Island/Brighton Beach should be it. Though no longer the amusement center it once was, there's something about this windy, run-down place—with its magnificent boardwalk, rusting rides, tawdry snack stands, bouyant Russian community, and hordes of summertime sunbathers—that's quintessential New York. Which is not to say that Coney Island isn't also a poor and often desperate place—it is, especially in winter when most of the pleasure seekers are gone.

If you take the long subway ride out, you'll land on the elevated tracks above scrappy Surf Avenue. One block west are the beach and boardwalk —crowded to the bursting point on hot summer days, pleasantly empty the rest of the time. Old Russian women sit gossiping beneath big black umbrellas, young boys run fishing lines off the piers, joggers kick up sand on the wide expanse of beach.

History

Named *Konijn Eiland* ("Rabbit Island") by the Dutch, Coney

Coney Island roller coaster, 1886

Island remained uninhabited until the early 1800s, when several resorts for the rich were built. After the Civil War, the railroad opened the area to the masses, and the honky-tonk days and nights began. Saloons, gambling dens, boxing rings, and racetracks soon packed the place, to be followed by three enclosed parks, or "small cities of pleasure," called Steeplechase, Luna Park, and Dreamland.

But it was the building of the subway in 1920 that really transformed Coney Island; for just a five-cent fare, almost everyone could escape the oppression of the city for a day, and Coney Island grew and grew. New technologies led to the invention of the Ferris wheel and the roller coaster, and in 1923, the 80-foot-wide boardwalk was built.

Coney Island was magical. It seemed nothing could dull its shine. But Dreamland burned down in 1911, and Luna Park went up in flames in the 1940s. Next came the rise of the automobile, the flight to the suburbs, and the invention of a new kind of midway—a tamed, sanitized place known as Disneyland. Steeplechase Park closed in 1966, leaving only a remnant of itself behind.

Astroland

That remnant is today called **Astroland-Coney Island Amusement Park.** It's on the boardwalk around W. 13th St., tel. (718) 372-0275. Inside are two rides dating back to the 1920s: the **Wonder Wheel** is a regal Ferris wheel offering fairy-tale views of Manhattan; the **Cyclone** is a terrifying roller coaster built on an old wooden frame that shakes and clatters as the cars shoot by. Enthusiasts consider the 60-mile-an-hour Cyclone —declared a city landmark in 1988—to be one of the country's best roller coasters. Also in the park are about 20 modern rides and plenty of honky-tonk video arcades and game booths. The park is open weekends in spring and daily in summer noon to midnight.

Nathan's Famous

On the island side of the amusement park, at the corner of Surf and Stillwell Aves., is Nathan's Famous, tel. (718) 946-2202. Nathan's was

DOVER PUBLICATIONS, INC.

started in 1916 by Nathan Handwerker, a some-
time employee of Charles Feltman. Feltman is
said to have "invented" the hot dog by his simple
act of putting a wiener inside a bun. Handwerker undersold his boss's fare by a nickel, and so
secured his place in entrepreneurial history.
Nowadays, on a busy summer weekend, the
stand-up eatery sells as many as 50,000 hot
dogs, 20,000 orders of French fries, and 500
gallons of lemonade.

Half Moon Hotel
Though torn down in 1996, the legendary Half
Moon Hotel once stood on the boardwalk at
29th Street. Here, mobster and star witness for
the prosecution Abe "Kid Twist" Reles jumped,
fell, or was pushed out of a sixth-floor window
while supposedly under police protection. Reles
was to have testified against his boss, Albert
Anastasia of Murder, Inc., but, despite the half-
dozen cops guarding him day and night, he was
found dead in the alleyway on the morning of
Nov. 12, 1941. The cops claimed to have found
a white sheet attached to a wire hanging out of
the Kid's window, but the fact that his body landed 20 feet from the wall made the suicide theo-
ry unlikely.

Across Surf Ave. north of the old Half Moon
site, stand Coney Island's bleak housing projects. Located about as far away from jobs as it's
possible to get, the soulless brick buildings, with
their familiar problems of poverty, drugs, and
violence, are among the city's worst examples of
urban planning.

Sideshows by the Sea
Heading east on the boardwalk from the amusement park, you'll soon come to W. 12th St. and
the brightly painted storefront of "Sideshows By
The Sea," tel. (718) 372-5159. A fierce-looking
tattooed man lounges by the door, while inside
is a madcap scene crowded with Snake Ladies,
the Fire Eater, Human Blockheads, the Elastic
Lady, Escape Artists, and the Torture King. It's
all a sort of shrine to the way Coney Island used
to be, run by a group of actors and performance
artists, many from the East Village.

Started in 1985 by a Yale Drama School graduate named Dick Zigun, the nonprofit Sideshows
also presents a whimsical, not-to-be-missed

Mermaid Parade every June, a Tattoo Festival in
late summer, and alternative rock-and-roll bands
on Friday nights in summer.

Hours are June to Labor Day Wed.-Sun. noon
to sundown. Admission is adults $3, children
$2. Next door to the theater you'll find a small
museum of Coney Island memorabilia and a
souvenir shop.

Aquarium for Wildlife Conservation
Between the boardwalk and Surf Ave. at W. 8th
St. is the delightful Aquarium for Wildlife Conservation, tel. (718) 265-3400. The thoroughly
up-to-date place contains close to 4,000 residents, including walruses, beluga whales, sharks,
stingrays, sea otters, and electric eels. In summer, dolphin and sea lion shows are featured
daily, and an outdoor exhibit allows children to
handle horseshoe crabs, sea urchins, starfish,
and the like.

The aquarium is open daily 10 a.m.-7 pm.
June-Sept. and 10 a.m.-4 p.m. Oct.-May. Admission is adults $6.75, seniors and children
under 12 $2, children under two free.

Brighton Beach
Next door to Coney Island, and spilling over into
it, is Brighton Beach. For many years home to a
small and aging Russian Jewish community,
Brighton Beach has been exploding with new
life ever since the end of the Cold War. About
100,000 Russians have settled in New York since
1989—some with green cards, others without—
and about 75% of them have moved to Brooklyn.
Stroll the streets and boardwalk here and you'll
see old women in babushkas, middle-aged men
and women in drab socialist dress, and teenagers
courting a hipness that is half East, half West.
Many of the store signs speak of Russia—
Vladimir's Unisex, Rasputin, the Stolichny Deli—
as do the smells and the music.

With all this tremendous new life have come
new tensions. An organized Russian crime ring
has entered the drug trade, bringing with it murder and extortion. Much distrust also exists between the Russian populace—who grew up
learning to evade officialdom—and the New
York City authorities.

Not that any of this affects the visitor. Step off
the boardwalk onto **Brighton Beach Avenue,**

and you'll find many friendly Russian shops, restaurants, and nightclubs. See "Shopping," below.

Sheepshead Bay

If you continue walking 20 minutes down Brighton Beach Ave. to Brighton 11th St. to Emmons Ave. (or take the B or D train one stop), you'll come to Sheepshead Bay. A tiny New England-like port inhabited by a large number of retirees, the place is full of fishing boats and yachts, seafood restaurants, and tackle shops. Fishing boats can be rented by the half-day; expect to pay about $15 per adult, with discounts for kids under 12.

Shopping

Of the Brighton Beach food shops, **M&I International,** 249 Brighton Beach Ave., tel. (718) 615-1011, is the best. The bright and modern two-story emporium is stocked with an enormous array of cheeses, fresh breads, sausages, smoked fish, and—of course—caviar and borscht. You might also want to stick your head into the nearby **White Acacia,** 281 Brighton Beach Ave., with its display cases filled with cow tongues; or the somber **Black Sea Bookstore,** 3175 Coney Island Avenue.

Knish shops abound. Two classic spots are the 50-odd-year-old **Mrs. Stahl's,** 1001 Brighton Beach Ave., tel. (718) 648-0210; and **Hirsch's Knishes,** 3145 Brighton 4th St., tel. (718) 332-0341.

Entertainment

Brighton Beach is famous for its over-the-top, Las Vegas-style Russian nightclubs where the music is fast and loud, the vodka flows nonstop, and people dance on the tabletops. Three traditional spots are the huge, glitzy **National Restaurant,** 273 Brighton Beach Ave., tel. (718) 646-1225, which draws a large tourist as well as Russian crowd (it was featured in the movie *Moscow on the Hudson* starring Robin Williams); the more streamlined but almost equally huge **Odessa,** 1113 Brighton Beach Ave., tel. (718) 332-3223; and the more intimate **Primorski,** 282B Brighton Beach Ave., tel. (718) 891-3111, which also serves an excellent, inexpensive lunch. Evenings at these restaurants don't come cheap; plan on spending $35-50 for dinner and entertainment. Reservations are a must.

Other Restaurants

Not far from the Boardwalk in Coney Island is **Gargiulo's,** 2911 W. 15th St., bet. Mermaid and Surf Aves., tel. (718) 266-4891, a long-time neighborhood favorite serving huge portions of Italian food. Reopened in 1996 in Sheepshead Bay is the enormous **Lundy's,** 1901 Emmons Ave., at Ocean Ave., tel. (718) 743-0022, a legendary seafood restaurant that had been closed for 17 years; thus far, the new has not measured up to the old. Down the block is **Randazzo's,** 2023 Emmons Ave., tel. (718) 615-0010, a big family-style Italian seafood joint.

QUEENS

Until recently, Queens was widely regarded as a snore. This was where the complacent everyman lived, in a row house exactly like his neighbor's. Queens was home to Archie Bunker and hundreds of thousands of others like him. Queens was mediocrity. Queens was suburbia. Queens was boring, boring, boring.

Whether or not this was ever really true, it certainly isn't so today. New York's largest borough now boasts some of the city's biggest and most vibrant ethnic neighborhoods, as well as some architectural and cultural gems that are just beginning to be appreciated. Queens is also where Louis Armstrong, Will Rogers, Jackie Robinson, and Jack Kerouac all once lived; where the early movie industry was headquartered; and where the wealthy once summered, on grand estates in Bayside or on the then-pristine beaches of the Rockaways.

Named for Queen Catherine of Braganza, the wife of England's Charles II, Queens was first settled in the 17th century. An important agricultural center supplying Manhattan, it was annexed to New York City in 1898. Western Queens began developing in the mid-1800s, but it wasn't until the building of the Long Island Railroad in 1910 that the borough really boomed. Then, apartment houses and private homes sprang up all over, and thousands of New Yorkers moved out into the "country."

Neighborhoods

Like Brooklyn, Queens is composed of many distinct neighborhoods. Nearest Manhattan are Long Island City and Astoria, while scattered throughout the borough are seven planned neighborhoods built around parks. Noteworthy among these "Seven Sisters," as they're known, are Richmond Hill, filled with shingled Victorian homes and the dense Forest Park; Kew Gardens, a 1910s neo-Tudor community; Forest Hills Gardens, splendidly landscaped by Frederick Law Olmsted; and Sunnyside Gardens, a 1920s utopian community still studied today as a model of middle-income housing.

Elsewhere in Queens, Forest Hills has a large Bukharan Jewish population, while many middle-class African Americans reside in Jamaica, St. Alban's, and Corona. Flushing is nicknamed "Little Asia"; Jackson Heights has large Latin American and Indian communities; and Elmhurst is home to many Thais. Thousands of new Irish immigrants have settled in Woodside.

At the southern end of Queens is Howard Beach, now associated in many New Yorkers' minds with racism and violence. In 1986, at 12:30 a.m., 23-year-old Michael Griffith's Buick broke down on an isolated stretch of Cross Bay Boulevard. He and his two companions walked into predominantly Italian Howard Beach to get help, and stopped in a pizza parlor looking for a pay phone. They were told there was none, but because they were hungry, they ordered slices and sat down. A few moments later, two cops stopped by to check out an anonymous 911 complaint about "three suspicious black males." When the threesome left the restaurant, they were attacked by a dozen white men wielding baseball bats. Griffith and his cousin ran to escape, but as Griffith crossed the Belt Parkway, he was struck by a car and killed. One year later, three members of the Howard Beach gang were sentenced to 15-30 years in prison.

South of Howard Beach stretches **Jamaica Bay** and the 10-mile-long **Rockaway peninsula.** Once a playground for the rich and then for the middle class, the Rockaways are now sadly abandoned, a dumping ground for the city's poor.

A Note on Addresses

Theoretically, Queens is laid out according to a grid system. The streets run north-south, from 1st St., paralleling the East River, to 250th St., at the borough's eastern end. Similarly, the avenues run east-west, with the lowest numbered addresses to the north and the highest numbered to the south. Addresses are supposedly coded with their nearest cross-street or avenue: 28-13 23rd Ave., for example, should mean that the building is at No. 13 23rd Avenue near 28th Street. But things don't always work out that neatly. When in doubt, it's best to call ahead.

Addresses below are listed with their closest cross-street when it's different from the one stated in the address.

LONG ISLAND CITY

From Manhattan: To reach the Noguchi Museum, take the N train to the Broadway station in Queens or the cable car from E. 60th St. and Second Ave. to Roosevelt Island, where a shuttle bus operates. The Asia Society, 725 Park Ave., at 70th St., tel. (212) 288-6400, also offers twice-weekly shuttle bus service. To reach P.S. 1, take the No. 7 train to 45th Rd./Court House Square, or the E or F train to 23rd Street.

Directly east of the Queensboro Bridge lies Long Island City. Though largely a dreary industrial area filled with windowless factories and smoke-

stacks, Long Island City has in recent years become home to a cutting-edge artistic community. Several of its museums and galleries regularly attract visitors from all over the city.

Noguchi Museum and Socrates Park

The austere Isamu Noguchi Garden Museum 32-37 Vernon Blvd., at 33rd Rd., tel. (718) 204-7088, is housed in the late sculptor's former studio. Its many rooms are filled with stone, metal, and wood sculptures, along with models of many large-scale environments designed by Noguchi. In back is a screening room showing an informative film, while a side yard holds a peaceful sculpture garden. The museum is open April-Oct., Wed.-Fri. 11 a.m.-5 p.m. and Sat.-Sun. 11 a.m-6 p.m. Suggested admission is adults $4, students and senior citizens $2.

A few blocks north of the Noguchi Museum is the delightful Socrates Sculpture Park, 31-29 Vernon Blvd., at Broadway, tel. (718) 956-1819. Dotted with huge outdoor sculptures—most of them colorful and playful, a few dark and forbidding—the park is the brainchild of artist Mark di Suvero. For 10 years, di Suvero and other area artists worked to turn the once-garbage-strewn lot into a bona fide park. The city officially recognized their efforts in 1994, and the site is now part of New York's park system. The park offers great views of Manhattan and is open daily during summer, weekends only in winter.

P.S. 1

Also in Long Island City is P.S. 1, 46-01 21st St., at Jackson, tel. (718) 784-2084, an important, cutting-edge venue for the visual and, to a lesser extent, performance arts. Housed in a former school, P.S. 1 operates an unusual studio program whereby different recognized artists are awarded working space in the building each year. Visitors can drop by and spot some of these artists at work, or attend the official openings which take place several times a year. P.S. 1 is closed in summer.

Food

The romantic and expensive **Water's Edge,** East River at 44th Dr., tel. (718) 482-0033, offers imaginative American fare and great views of the skyline. Complimentary water shuttle ser-

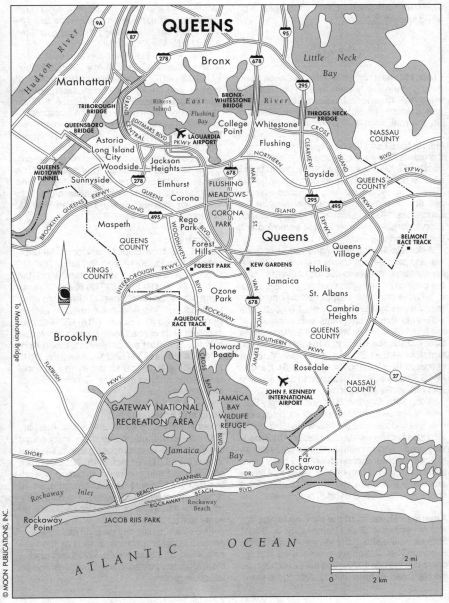

QUEENS

vice from Manhattan's East 34th St. pier is offered starting at 6 p.m.

ASTORIA

From Manhattan: To reach the Greek community, take the N train to 30th Avenue. To reach the American Museum of the Moving Image directly, take the R or G train to Steinway St. and walk south to 35th Avenue.

Not far from Long Island City is Astoria, one of the oldest settlements in Queens. It was developed in 1839 by John Jacob Astor, who built it up into a thriving shipping port. Later, in the 1920s and 1930s, the neighborhood was the center of the movie-making business on the East Coast; Astoria Movie Studios produced such legendary stars as Rudolf Valentino and Gloria Swanson.

Astoria today is a stable and well-kept working- and middle-class community with the largest concentration of Greeks outside of Greece. After the easing of immigration quotas in 1965, Astoria's Greek population expanded exponentially; today it's estimated to be about 80,000. The earliest of these immigrants began arriving in the late 1920s and promptly built **St. Demetrios Greek Orthodox Church,** a magnificent domed structure at 31st St. and 30th Drive. Another gorgeous Greek Orthodox church is **St. Irene's,** 36-25 23rd Ave., which features an altar adorned with red-and-gold peacocks.

Along **30th Ave.** bet. 31st and Steinway Sts., several wonderful food shops sell imported olive oils, feta cheese, and the like, while Greek pastry shops beckon with outdoor tables. On **Broadway,** you'll find numerous Greek bakeries, as well as butcher shops advertising baby pigs, baby lambs, and baby goats. Also in Astoria are many Pakistani, Italian, and Latino food shops, restaurants, and retail businesses.

American Museum of the Moving Image

Not far from the Greek community, at 34-12 36th St., is the site of the former Astoria Movie Studios. The studios were renovated and reopened in the late 1970s, and are now known as the **Kaufman-Astoria** Studios. Among the many movies and television shows that have been completely or partially produced here are *The Wiz, The Verdict, The World According to Garp,* and *The Cosby Show.*

Also here is the American Museum of the Moving Image, 36-01 35th Ave., at 36th St., tel. (718) 784-0077, which traces the history of movies and television. The museum houses over 70,000 artifacts covering all aspects of the film industry—from make-up to fan magazines—and features hands-on exhibits in which visitors can create their own animated films, design soundtracks, and the like. The museum also boasts an excellent screening program; call in advance to find out what's playing. The museum is open Tues.-Fri. noon-5 p.m. and Sat.-Sun. 11 a.m.-6 p.m. Admission is adults $8, seniors $5, students and children 5-18 $4, children under four free.

Shopping

Some Greek food shops to look for are **Mediterranean Foods,** 30-12 34th St., tel. (718) 728-6166, in business for over 20 years; and **Titan Foods,** 25-56 31st St., tel. (718) 626-7771, a supermarket lined with barrels of olives and other pickled foodstuffs. Also in the area are **Lefkos Pyrgos,** 22-85 31st St., tel. (718) 932-4423, an excellent and very traditional pastry shop whose clientele is almost exclusively male; and **Kentrikon Astorias,** 31-12 23rd Ave., tel. (718) 721-9190, a fancy gift shop selling traditional hand-embroidered items for Greek weddings and christenings.

Food and Entertainment

Informal **Telly's Taverna,** 28-13 23rd Ave., tel. (718) 728-9194, offers especially tasty grilled lamb dishes and an outdoor garden. **Taverna Vraka,** 23-15 31st St., tel. (718) 721-3007, is a glitzier place that has been attracting celebrities for over 20 years. **Uncle George's,** 33-19 Broadway, tel. (718) 626-0593, is a bright, 24-hour spot that's one of the neighborhood's favorite restaurants.

Live Greek music and dancing are often featured at upscale restaurants such as the Taverna Vraka on the weekends. Flyers announcing the events are posted in shop windows and on telephone poles.

JACKSON HEIGHTS

From Manhattan: Take the No. 7 train to 82nd St. and exit onto Roosevelt Avenue.

Nicknamed the "cornfield of Queens" in the early 1900s, Jackson Heights began developing in the 1910s and 1920s. Large blocks of attractive apartment houses were constructed, many featuring pretty courtyards and gardens, fireplaces, and high ceilings. Ironically, given Jackson Heights' multicultural make-up today, developers advertised it as a "restricted garden residential section," meaning Jews, blacks, and even Catholics need not apply.

Jackson Heights began turning from gardens to concrete around the time of WW II, when nearby **La Guardia Airport** was constructed. In the 1940s and 1950s, the Irish and Italians moved in, and in the 1960s, the first Latinos began arriving. Most of the latter were Argentinians fleeing an unstable government, and Cubans fleeing Castro.

Ethnic Jackson Heights
Today, Jackson Heights is still home to a few Irish, Italians, Argentinians, and Cubans, but its largest ethnic group is Colombian. Walk north or south on Roosevelt Ave. and you'll see newsstands selling Colombian newspapers, bakeries selling Colombian cakes and coffees, and stores selling Colombian videos. Residents even call the area "Chapinero" after the Bogota suburb. Jackson Heights is also home to a sizeable Indian population, centered around 74th St., and to smaller Peruvian, Uruguayan, Filipino, and Thai communities.

Historic Jackson Heights
To get a sense of what life was like in Jackson Heights when it was a "restricted garden residential district," head northwest of Roosevelt Ave. to 37th or 35th Ave. bet. 78th and 88th Streets. This area was declared a historic district in 1994 and holds many fine apartment buildings adorned with griffins, columns, and arches. Many share lush communal gardens.

Food
Two excellent Colombian restaurants are **La Pequeña Colombia,** 85-08 Roosevelt Ave., tel. (718) 478-6528; and **Tierras Colombianas,** 82-18 Roosevelt Ave., tel. (718) 426-8868, both casual spots serving heaping platters of food. **Crazy Chicken,** 78-09 Roosevelt Ave., tel. (718) 779-6711, and other locations, barbecues some of the juiciest chickens in town. For Peruvian food, try **Inti Raymi,** 86-14 37th Ave., tel. (718) 424-1938.

Jackson Diner, 37-03 74th St., tel. (718) 672-1232, is a favorite Indian eatery among New Yorkers in the know. Other popular Indian spots are **Shaheen Sweets,** 72-09 Broadway, tel. (718) 639-4791; and **Delhi Palace,** 37-33 74th St., tel. (718) 507-0666.

Manila Thai, 69-11 Roosevelt Ave., tel. (718) 779-9893, serves both Filipino and Thai cuisine and doubles as a disco on weekends. **Golden Oven,** 69-11 Roosevelt Ave., tel. (718) 429-3914, is a small, homey spot serving Filipino fare.

FLUSHING MEADOWS~ CORONA PARK

From Manhattan: Take the No. 7 train to Willets Point/Shea Stadium and follow the signs. A visit to the park can easily be combined with a visit to Jackson Heights (above) or Flushing (below), as all are located along Roosevelt Avenue.

Today, Flushing Meadows is a peaceful green oasis attracting families, couples, and kids. But back in the early 1900s, it was a towering, reeking garbage dump that smoldered by day and glowed at night. One hundred ten railroad carloads of Brooklyn's refuse were dumped here daily, providing succulent meals for hordes of rats "big enough to wear saddles," as one observer put it. F. Scott Fitzgerald, writing in *The Great Gatsby,* described the place as "a valley of ashes—a fantastic farm where ashes grow like wheat into ridges and hills and grotesque gardens . . ."

Enter Robert Moses, city parks commissioner. Moses, looking at the noxious heap, saw not an irredeemable wasteland but a potential park. In 1934, he directed the removal of some 50 million cubic tons of garbage. Thereafter began the construction of the 1939 World's Fair, followed 25 years later by the construction of

The Unisphere at Flushing Meadows–Corona Park dates back to the 1964 World's Fair.

the 1964 World's Fair. Both extravaganzas were largely created through Moses's sheer force of will, and both ended up costing the city and its backers millions of dollars.

Remains of the fairs still dot the 1,225-acre park. Most conspicuous is the 1964 **Unisphere,** a shining 140-foot-high, 380-ton hollow globe sitting in the middle of a pretty fountain. All around the fountain circle rollerbladers, kids on tricycles, and couples out for a stroll.

Flushing Meadows-Corona Park is also known for its U.S.T.A. National Tennis Center, where the U.S. Open Tennis Tournament is held each year. Other park attractions include a miniature golf course, several playgrounds, a botanical garden, two lakes, a marina, and a turn-of-the-century carousel. Signs are posted at intersections throughout the park pointing the way to attractions, and free tours are frequently offered by the Urban Park Rangers, tel. (718) 699-4204. Across the street is the huge, 55,000-

seat **Shea Stadium,** home to the New York Mets.

Queens Museum of Art
Next to the Unisphere is the Queens Museum of Art, tel. (718) 592-2405, housed in what was the New York City pavilion at both the 1939 and the 1964 World's Fairs. Recently renovated to the tune of $15 million, the museum presents first-rate temporary exhibitions and houses an unusual permanent exhibit—the New York Panorama. First showcased at the 1964 fair, the panorama is a scale model of the city, showing every single building and house in the five boroughs—some 895,000 of them, built of plastic and wood. One of Moses's pet projects, the panorama was originally intended to be a serious tool for urban planners but now feels more like a nostalgic work of art. The model was completely updated in 1994.

The museum is open Wed.-Fri. 10 a.m.-5 p.m., Sat.-Sun. noon-5 p.m. Suggested admission is adults $3, seniors and students $2, children under five free.

Queens Wildlife Center
About a five-minute walk north of the Queens Museum, over the Grand Central Parkway (take the bridge just west of the museum, next to the ice rink) is the Queens Wildlife Center, 53-51 111th St., tel. (718) 271-7761. Renovated in 1992 by the Wildlife Conservation Society (which also runs the Central Park and Prospect Park zoos), the state-of-the-art center is now devoted to North American wildlife, including mountain lions, bison, bobcats, coyotes, bears, and Roosevelt elk. Hours are Nov.-March, daily 10 a.m-4:30 p.m.; April-Oct., Mon.-Fri. 10 a.m.-5 p.m. and Sat.-Sun. 10 a.m.-5:30 p.m. Admission is adults $2.50, senior citizens $1.25, children 3-12 50 cents, and children under three free.

New York Hall of Science
West of the zoo is the New York Hall of Science, 47-01 111th St., tel. (718) 699-0005, ranked as one of the country's top 10 science museums. Housed in a dramatic, undulating building—another odd leftover from the 1964 World's Fair—the museum is packed with hands-on exhibits. Among them are a distorted room that makes people appear to shrink or grow, and an en-

larged drop of water showing microscopic organisms going about their daily lives. The museum is open Wed.-Sun. 10 a.m.-5 p.m. Admission is adults $4.50, seniors and children under 12 $3; free Wed.-Thurs. 2-5 p.m.

Corona

A few minutes south of the Hall of Science, in the small community of Corona, is the **Lemon Ice King,** 52-02 108th St., tel. (718) 699-5133, known throughout the city for selling the best Italian ices *anywhere.* The Ice King, Ben Faremo, has been making his sweets from real fruit since 1944, and flavors range from cantaloupe to peanut butter. The shop is open daily 10 a.m.-7 p.m. from Memorial Day to Labor Day; call for hours the rest of the year. To reach the Ice King from the Hall of Science, walk south on 111th St. to 51st Ave. and turn right. Continue to 108th Street.

Corona was once home to **Louis Armstrong,** who lived in a red-brick building at 34-56 107th St. from the early 1940s until his death in 1971. Tales are often told of how the jazz giant used to sit on his front steps with his trumpet and entertain the neighborhood kids, some of whom came by with horns of their own. The Armstrong home is now on the National Register of Historic Places. It's owned by Queens College, which hopes to turn it into a museum. Armstrong is buried in **Flushing Cemetery,** 163-06 46th Ave., tel. (718) 359-0100; on his tombstone is a sculpture of a trumpet draped in cloth.

FLUSHING

From Manhattan: Take the No. 7 train to Main St., the end of the line.

Asian Flushing

Once a Dutch town known as "Vlissingen," and later a popular resort for the wealthy, Flushing is now home to one of the city's largest Asian communities. Before their arrival in the late 1970s, the middle-class area was beginning to go downhill. Today, however, Flushing is a vibrant place packed with a hodgepodge of Asian billboards, shops, and restaurants.

Asian Flushing is roughly bordered by Northern Blvd. to the north, Sanford Ave. to the south, College Point Blvd. to the west, and Union St. to the east. **Main and Union Streets** are the most active thoroughfares, with the Korean community centering on Union, and the Chinese and Indian ones on the northern and southern stretches of Main, respectively.

Historic Flushing

Buildings dating back to Dutch and Colonial times still stand in Flushing. At the corner of 37th Ave. and Bowne St. is the **Bowne House,** 37-01 Bowne St., tel. (718) 359-0528, a small wooden building used for illegal Quaker meetings in the 1660s. Upon learning of these meetings, Dutch governor Peter Stuyvesant—who had banned the Quaker sect—had John Bowne put in prison and whipped. Bowne appealed his case before the more tolerant Dutch West India Company in Amsterdam and was acquitted. The company's ruling became a precedent for America's Bill of Rights.

Inside, the Bowne house is a static and somewhat musty affair, filled with furnishings belonging to many generations of Bownes, the only family who ever lived here. The house was deeded to the Bowne House Historical Society in 1945; tours are offered Tuesday and Sat.-Sun. at 2:30 p.m. Cost is adults $2, children $1.

Around the corner from the Bowne house is the **Friends Meeting House,** 137-16 Northern Blvd., bet. Main and Union Sts., where the Quak-

---

WHERE THE WILD THINGS ARE

At the far southern end of Queens is the Jamaica Bay Wildlife Refuge, in whose marshlands live over 300 species of birds, 80 types of fish, and dozens of kinds of reptiles and amphibians. It seems amazing that wildlife can flourish here. JFK Airport is directly across the bay, and all around the refuge, traffic—both ground and air—drones on incessantly. Still, the refuge is on the Atlantic flyway, and well worth a visit during the autumn and spring. The refuge is open daily 8:30 a.m.-5 p.m.; call (718) 318-4340 for more information and directions by either car or public transportation. Or write Gateway National Recreation Area, Floyd Bennett Field, Bldg. 69, Brooklyn, NY 11234.

ers met in the centuries following the Bowne decision. This dark shingled building has been in continuous use since 1719, making it New York City's oldest house of worship. Tours of the meeting house are offered on the first Sunday of every month, 2-4 p.m.; call (718) 358-9636 for more information.

Also nearby is the **Kingsland House,** 143-35 37th Ave., tel. (718) 939-0647. Built in 1785 in the English shingle style, the building is now home to the Queens Historical Society, which presents frequent exhibits and offers walking tours of various Queens neighborhoods. Hours are Tues., Sat.-Sun. 2:30-4:30 p.m. Admission is adults $2, seniors and students $1.

Hindu Temple of New York

A good 15-minute walk from the Main St. subway station is one of the more unusual sights in Flushing—the pale blue Hindu Temple of New York, 45-57 Bowne St., at Holly Ave., tel. (718) 460-8484. Tucked between two simple residences, the ornate temple was built in 1977 at a cost of nearly a million dollars. Crafts specialists were flown in from India to create the temple's rich detail.

Food

Two good Chinese bakeries to keep an eye out for are **Maria's Bakery,** 41-42 Main St, tel. (718) 358-8878, and **Tai Pan Bakery,** 135-20 Roosevelt Ave., tel. (718) 461-8668. Try a chestnut tart or an egg custard.

Everyone orders the special at the informal **Joe's Shanghai,** 136-21 37th Ave., near Main. tel. (718) 539-3838—dome-shaped "soup" dumplings filled with a rich crab or pork broth. **Szechuan Capital,** 135-28 Roosevelt Ave., tel. (718) 762-0950, is a simple storefront serving first-rate spicy fare.

For Malaysian food in an exotic setting, try **Penang Cuisine Malaysia,** 38-04 Prince St., one block from Main, tel. (718) 321-2078. For Korean food, try the tiny **Cosy House,** 36-26A Union St., tel. (718) 762-0167; or the posh **South River,** 42-05 Main St., tel. (718) 762-7214, frequented by wealthy Koreans.

THE BRONX

The Bronx is a borough of extremes. Home to such great New York institutions as the Bronx Zoo, the New York Botanical Garden, and Yankee Stadium, it has also long stood as a symbol of urban decay. In 1981, the movie *Fort Apache, The Bronx* was filmed here; in 1987, Tom Wolfe set his novel *Bonfire of the Vanities* here. Horrific stories involving murders, arson, drug warlords, and children killing children come out of here daily, while images of the borough's burnt-out walk-ups and rubble-strewn lots have been seared into the national consciousness.

But the biggest story in the Bronx in the last few years is that things are actually looking up. Since 1986, more than $1 billion in public funds has been spent on the South Bronx—where most of the decay has taken place. About 20,000 apartments have been refurbished and more than 3,000 new houses built. Charlotte Street, whose devastation Pres. Jimmy Carter drew attention to in 1977, is now lined with single-family homes surrounded by white picket fences—a strangely surreal sight in an otherwise still-blighted neighborhood. Big retail stores such as Bradlees and Pathmark are moving back in, while the borough recently opened its first new mall in decades. Though drugs, arson, and murder continue to plague the Bronx, the place is in better shape now than it's been in for years.

Of course, even at its worst, the Bronx was never as bad as its reputation. The urban devastation has been confined largely to the South Bronx, and even there, safe and stable pockets have always existed. Meanwhile, elsewhere in the borough flourish many large and pleasant residential neighborhoods, most working- and middle-class (City Island, Co-Op City, Norwood), a few quite exclusive (Riverdale, Fieldston). Most notably of all, the Bronx also boasts over 5,800 acres of parks.

History

The Bronx is New York City's second smallest borough both in size and population, and it's the only one attached to the mainland. Purchased from the Algonquins by the Dutch West India Company in 1639, it was first settled in 1644 by a Scandinavian named Jonas Bronck. The area soon became known as "The Broncks," and remained a peaceful rural community up until the late 1800s. Then the Third Avenue Elevated Railway arrived, bringing with it thousands of European immigrants. By 1900, the borough's population had soared to over 200,000.

Many consider the 1920s through the early 1950s to be the golden era of the Bronx. That's when the borough was filled with many tightly knit ethnic neighborhoods, each with its own vibrant community life. The arrival of the affordable automobile, however, soon allowed many of the

Bronx's more affluent residents to move to Long Island or Westchester. And in 1950, Robert Moses's six-lane Cross-Bronx Expressway was constructed, destroying a number of the borough's most stable neighborhoods.

THE BRONX ZOO AND BOTANICAL GARDEN

From Manhattan: To reach the zoo, take the No. 2 train to Pelham Pkwy., and walk west. Or, take a Liberty Lines express bus; call (718) 652-8400 for details. To reach the botanical garden, take the No. 4 or D train to Bedford Park Blvd. and walk a half-dozen or so long blocks east.

Though the zoo and botanical garden are next door to each other, to visit both in one day would require much fortitude, as both are very large. It's smarter to opt for one, and perhaps combine it with a meal or coffee and dessert on Arthur Avenue. The botanical garden is at its best in May and June.

The Bronx Zoo

One of the most beloved of New York institutions is the enormous Bronx Zoo, Fordham Rd. and Bronx River Pkwy., tel. (718) 367-1010, where New Yorkers have been spending weekends with their families for generations. It's among the world's largest and most important zoos, housing over 4,000 animals, many of whom roam relatively freely in large landscaped habitats. The Bronx Zoo was one of the world's first wildlife centers to adopt this technique.

Among the 250-acre zoo's most popular attractions is its Wild Asia Express, a monorail ride above a 38-acre savanna inhabited by elephants, antelope, Siberian tigers, rhinos, and many different kinds of deer. In the World of Birds, centered around a towering waterfall, about 100 species flit freely from tree to tree. In the World of Darkness, low lights make it possible to see nocturnal animals at their most active; included in this exhibit is the world's largest captive collection of bats.

Except in winter, the zoo is open Mon.-Fri. 10 a.m.-5 p.m., Sat.-Sun. 10 a.m.-5:30 p.m.; admission is adults $6.75, seniors and children

2-12 $3, free for children under two and for everyone on Wednesdays. In winter the zoo is open daily 10 a.m.-4:30 p.m. and admission fees are reduced.

Botanical Garden

Just north of the zoo is the 250-acre **New York Botanical Garden,** Southern Blvd. and 200th St., tel. (718) 817-8705, comprising dozens of constituent gardens (including a rose garden, a rock garden, and an herb garden), an arboretum, a hemlock forest, and—best of all—an enormous, shimmering, Victorian-style conservatory filled with over 100 varieties of palms, tropical plants, desert flora, ferns, and changing seasonal exhibits. The 1902 conservatory, with its 11 glass pavilions and many reflecting pools, was inspired by Kew Gardens in London. Recently renovated to the tune of $25 million, it is the largest building of its type in America, and one of the finest in the world.

The garden is open April-Oct., Tues.-Sun. 10 a.m.-6 p.m.; Nov.-March, Tues.-Sun. 10 a.m.-4 p.m. Admission is adults $3; seniors, students and children 6-16 $1; free for children under six; and free for everyone on Wednesdays.

Belmont

Just west of Bronx Zoo is the Italian community of Belmont, one of the city's older and more established ethnic neighborhoods. A stable and middle-class haven just north of the South Bronx, Belmont is chock-a-block with Italian restaurants, pastry shops, bakeries, butcher shops, poultry stores, and food markets, most of which are along **Arthur Avenue** or **187th Street.** This friendly neighborhood of spic-and-span streets and small backyard shrines has a warm, old-fashioned feel.

To reach Belmont from the zoo, walk west seven long blocks, or catch the Bx22 bus on E. Fordham Road. From the garden, walk south through the campus of Fordham University.

Food Shops

At the heart of Belmont is the indoor **Arthur Avenue Retail Market,** 2344 Arthur Ave., tel. (718) 367-5686, where some of the city's freshest and cheapest fruits and vegetables can be found, along with fresh mozzarella, ravioli cutters, and espresso machines. Just up the street

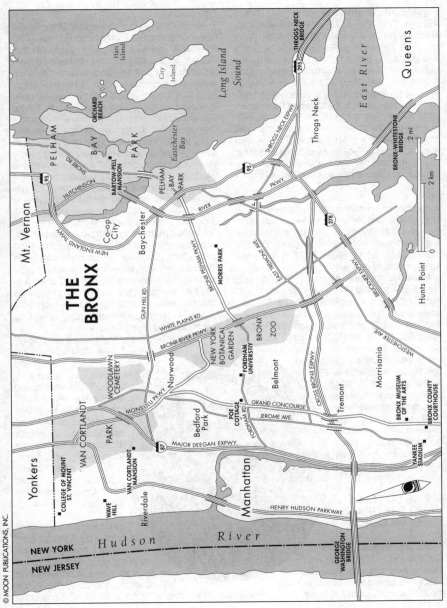

© MOON PUBLICATIONS, INC.

are **Madonia Brothers Bakery,** 2348 Arthur Ave., tel. (718) 295-5573, selling mouth-watering crusty bread; **Biancardi's,** 2350 Arthur Ave., tel. (718) 733-4058, selling whole baby lambs and goats (no place for the squeamish); and the **Arthur Avenue Poultry Market,** 2356 Arthur Ave., tel. (718) 733-4006, jam-packed with live squawking chickens, pigeons, and rabbits. Down the street is the **Calabria Pork Store,** 2338 Arthur Ave. tel. (718) 367-5145, its ceiling densely hung with meats and sausages; and **Randazzo's Fish Market,** 2327 Arthur Ave., tel. (718) 367-4139, piled high with crabs, sole, scrod, and the like. In warm weather, Randazzo's operates a raw seafood bar out front.

Food

A number of pastry shops and cafes are on 187th Street. **DeLillo's Pastry Shop,** 606 187th St., tel. (718) 367-8198, serves both pastries and homemade gelato and spumoni. **Egidio,** 622 187th St., tel. (718) 295-6077, is renowned for its miniature pastries.

Mario's, 2342 Arthur Ave., tel. (718) 584-1188, serves huge portions of Southern Italian food, and may be Belmont's best-known, though not necessarily best, restaurant; it was featured in the film *The Godfather.* Similarly, **Amici's Restaurant,** 566 187th St., tel. (718) 584-6167, which also serves Southern Italian food, is where Robert DeNiro discovered Joe Pesci. **Dominick's,** 2335 Arthur Ave., tel. (718) 733-2807, has some of the neighborhood's best food, served family style at long tables covered with red tablecloths. Good pizza joints can also be found all along Arthur Avenue.

POE COTTAGE AND THE GRAND CONCOURSE

From Manhattan: Take the No. 4 train to Kingsbridge Rd./ Jerome Ave. and walk three blocks east to the Grand Concourse, or take the D train to Kingsbridge Road.

Poe Cottage

The Poe Cottage is at the corner of the Grand Concourse and East Kingbridge Rd., tel. (718) 881-8900. Today, it seems inconceivable that this tiny white cottage surrounded by well-worn buildings and pothole-filled streets was once an isolated farmhouse. But in 1846, writer Edgar Allan Poe moved in here with his wife, Virginia, in hopes that the country air would cure her tuberculosis. When Poe wrote his famous poem "Annabel Lee," beginning "It was many and many a year ago/In a kingdom by the sea/That a maiden there lived whom you may know/By the name of Annabel Lee," it was his wife and the Bronx that he was talking about.

The cottage is a simple place with a large kitchen and sitting room downstairs and Poe's old cramped office and bedroom upstairs. A short video covers the highlights of Poe's life, leaving out many of the more controversial aspects (such as his serious drinking problem) and focusing on what the couple's lives were like while they were here. At that time, they were suffering from extreme poverty and often survived by foraging in the fields for dandelions and other edible plants. They had no money for fuel, and spent many winter days as well as nights bundled up in blankets.

After Virginia's death, in January 1847, Poe stayed on in the cottage for a few more years. His mental and physical health—already poor—continued to deteriorate, and in 1849, on his way to Richmond, Virginia, he disappeared in Baltimore. When he was found a few days later, he was delirious. He died shortly thereafter.

Hours are Sat. 10 a.m.-4 p.m. and Sun. 1-5 p.m.; closed in January. Suggested admission is $2.

Edgar Allan Poe

BRONX COUNTY HISTORICAL SOCIETY

The Grand Concourse

Outside Poe Cottage runs the Grand Concourse, once one of the city's most glamorous boulevards, now a windswept and run-down thoroughfare. During the late 1920s and 1930s, the avenue was known as the "Jewish Fifth Avenue." One of the country's first controlled-access parkways, it featured separate lanes for carriages, cyclists, and pedestrians, and was lined with one stunning art deco building after another.

Heading south on the Grand Concourse from Poe Cottage, you'll soon come to **Fordham Rd.,** an incredibly crowded street packed with all races and creeds of humans, hundreds of honking cars and noxious buses, and innumerable street vendors and discount stores. Two blocks farther south, at 2417 Grand Concourse, stands the former **Loew's Paradise,** designed in 1929 by John Eberson, the "Father of the Atmospheric Theater." Though not much to look at from the outside, the Paradise once featured an extravagant interior filled with baroque balconies, classical statues, a vast domed ceiling with blinking constellations, and a machine that could move clouds across the sky. In 1981, the theater was converted into a four-screen complex, and its interior painted bright green. Today it stands abandoned; preservationists are pushing to get it restored.

Other points of interest are farther south on the Grand Concourse, but since it's a long and not particular pleasant trek to some of them, you'd best catch a Bx1 bus.

Bronx Museum of the Arts
At 165th St. is Bronx Museum of the Arts, 1040 Grand Concourse, tel. (718) 681-6000, featuring changing contemporary art exhibits and a good permanent collection of works by Romare Bearden. The museum's hours are Wed. 3-9 p.m., Thurs.-Fri. 10 a.m.-5 p.m., Sat.-Sun. 1-6 p.m. Suggested admission is adults $3, students $2, seniors $1, children under 12 free.

Architectural Highlights
Art deco buildings to look out for include **888 Grand Concourse,** designed in 1937 by Emery Roth, who also designed many of the buildings along Central Park West; the **Bronx County Courthouse,** 851 Grand Concourse, whose immediate environs are not nearly as dangerous as Tom Wolfe described in *Bonfire of the Vanities;* and the **Bronx General Post Office,** 558 Grand Concourse.

NORTHWEST BRONX

Woodlawn Cemetery
From Manhattan: Take the No. 4 train to Woodlawn, the end of the line.

Filled with lush rolling hills, shady trees, meandering walkways, and a shimmering sky-blue lake, Woodlawn dates back to the 19th century. In that era, cemeteries were thought of as places to talk to God and commune with nature. Precursors to today's parks, they were also major tourist attractions, described in great detail in guidebooks, and so crowded on weekends that traffic controllers had to be stationed at the main intersections.

Few people think of Woodlawn as anything but a cemetery anymore, but it's still a fun place to explore. Many once-prominent New Yorkers are buried here.

One of the park's most ornate mausoleums, just inside the main gate, belongs to Oliver Hazard Perry Belmont, financier and horse lover. Belmont, who apparently thought very highly of himself, designed his final resting place after the St. Hubert Chapel in Amboise, France, where Leonardo da Vinci is buried. Also near the main gate is the fine Ionic temple where the unscrupulous financier Jay Gould was buried in 1892. The railroad speculator was so hated that stock in his empire *rose* more than two points on the day he died.

Herman Melville's grave is a more modest affair. The author of *Moby Dick* died poverty-stricken in 1891, near the Gansevoort meat market, where he had worked as a customs official. He's buried beside his wife under a tall oak tree. On his tombstone are carved an unrolled scroll and a quill pen.

Duke Ellington also rests beneath a large tree, less than 10 yards away from the shiny black granite tombstone of Sir Miles Davis. Cemetery officials say the proximity of the two jazz greats' graves is purely coincidental.

One of the strangest epitaphs in the cemetery can be found on the tombstone of one George Spenser, who died in 1909. It reads: "Lost life by stab in falling on ink eraser, evading six young women trying to give him birthday kisses in office of Metropolitan Life Building."

Woodlawn Cemetery, tel. (718) 920-0500, is open daily 9 a.m.-4:30 p.m. A free map with grave locations is available at the office near the main gate. The office is closed on Sunday.

Van Cortlandt Mansion and Park
From Manhattan: Take the No. 1 or 9 train to 242nd St./Van Cortlandt Park. The mansion is in the park's southern end, near Broadway.

A charming 18th-century mansion, all but untouched by the vagaries of time, sits in Van Cortlandt Park in the northernmost section of the Bronx. Still surrounded by woods and fields (now used as ball fields), the recently restored stone house was built in 1748 by wealthy landowner Frederick Van Cortlandt. It's furnished with antiques—some of which belonged to the Van Cortlandt family—and a number of interesting paintings, including a portrait of John Jacob Astor by Gilbert Stuart.

George Washington stayed in the mansion on and off during the Revolutionary War, using the West Parlor as his office. During the late 1700s and early 1800s, about 17 slaves lived here as well, most sleeping in cramped quarters on the third floor.

The Van Cortlandt house, tel. (718) 543-3344, is open Tues.-Fri. 10 a.m.-3 p.m. and Sat.-Sun. 11 a.m.-4 p.m. Admission is adults $2, students and seniors $1.50.

Surrounding the mansion is hilly Van Cortlandt Park, which at two miles square is the city's third largest park. Its serenity is marred, however, by the three major parkways (the Henry Hudson, the Major Deegan, and the Mosulu) that run through it. At the park's east end are the remains of the Croton Aqueduct, now a favorite path for runners. To the west, near the mansion, are the park's Parade Grounds, which attract cricket- and rugby-playing West Indians on weekends. For more information about the park, call (718) 549-6494 or (718) 430-1890. For more information about the free environmental walking tours offered by the Urban Park Rangers, call (718) 548-7070.

Wave Hill
From Manhattan: Take a Metro-North train, tel. (212) 532-4900, from Grand Central to the Riverdale Station at 254th St., and walk south-

east and uphill to Wave Hill's entrance at the intersection of Independence Ave. and 249th Street. Or, take the A train to 231st St., then board the Bx7 or Bx10 bus. Take it to 252nd St., walk across the parkway bridge, and head left to 249th Street. Liberty Lines, tel. (212) 652-8400, also offers express bus service from Manhattan to 252nd Street.

Wave Hill, an estate perched on bluffs high above the Hudson in the wealthy community of Riverdale, boasts many fine gardens and greenhouses, breathtaking views, and a pretty 1844 Greek Revival mansion. Theodore Roosevelt, Mark Twain, and Arturo Toscanini all once lived in this lovely oasis, now serving as a city park. In summer, frequent dance and music events are presented here—most of them outdoors.

When Mark Twain leased Wave Hill from 1901 to 1903, he set up a treehouse parlor in the branches of a chestnut tree on the lawn. Of winter at the estate he wrote, "I believe we have the noblest roaring blasts here I have ever known on land; they sing their hoarse song through the big tree-tops with a splendid energy that thrills me and stirs me and uplifts me and makes me want to live always."

Just west of the mansion is Abrons Woodland, 10 acres of woods and meadows currently being replanted with native plants. A trail meanders through the woodland, and signs along the way explain the project's progress.

Wave Hill, tel. (718) 549-3200, is open May-Oct. Tues.-Sun. 9 a.m.-5:30 p.m. and Oct.-May Tues.-Sun. 9 a.m.-4:30 p.m. Admission May-Nov. Wed.-Sun., is adults $4, students and seniors $2, children under six free; free to all on Tuesday, Saturday 9 a.m.-noon, and in winter.

Fonthill Castle
North of Wave Hill, at Riverdale Ave. and W. 261st St., is an odd landmark called Fonthill Castle. Now housing the administrative offices of the College of Mount St. Vincent, Fonthill was once home to the great 19th-century American actor Edwin Forrest, whose upstaging by a rival English actor started the Astor Place Riots (see "Bowery and Astor Place" under "East Village," above).

For a castle, Fonthill is puny—just 70 feet high with only six octagonal towers. Inside, however, it's lovely, with a vaulted ceiling, inlaid floors, a skylight, and dozens of carved gargoyles. Tours of Fonthill Castle are available by appointment; call (718) 405-3230. To reach Fonthill Castle from Wave Hill, take the Bx7 or Bx10 bus to the last stop.

Discount Clothing

One of New York City's best-known stores for discounted designer wear is **Loehmann's,** a warehouse-type affair at Broadway and 236th St., tel. (718) 543-6420.

CITY ISLAND AND PELHAM BAY PARK

From Manhattan: Take the No. 6 train to Pelham Bay Park, the last stop, and catch the Bx12 (summers only) or Bx29 bus to City Island. The trip is time-consuming, so budget a full day if possible.

City Island is one of New York City's oddest communities, a sailors' haven that fancies itself part of New England. "Welcome to New York City's Nautical Community, 1645," reads the sign arching over the bridge leading from the mainland. And then you're there, on a narrow strip of land lined with boatyards, tiny clapboard houses, and bustling seafood restaurants attracting the tourist trade.

Back in the 1700s, the inhabitants of City Island hoped to develop a port that would rival New York's. Obviously their plan failed, but the community has been home to a number of thriving industries, including a solar salt works (in the 1830s), an oystering industry (in the mid-1800s), and—most importantly—a shipbuilding industry that continues to this day. Several America's Cup yachts were built here.

City Island has only one real street—City Island Avenue. But some of its side roads, which are only a few blocks long, are pretty and worth a gander.

North Wind Undersea Museum

The wonderfully quirky North Wind Undersea Museum, 610 City Island Ave., tel. (718) 885-0701, occupies a tiny well-worn house with a rusting cannon, anchors, diving bells, and a one-person submarine littering the lawn. The museum was founded by Capt. Michael Sandlofer, who lives here as well. Inside are more strange treasures, including a nine-foot-wide whale jaw and heaps of shark's teeth. The museum is open Mon.-Fri. noon-4 p.m. and Sat.-Sun. noon-5 p.m. Admission is adults $3, seniors and children under 12 $2.

The "Tyrone" House

At 21 Tier St., on the north side of City Island Ave., is a charming shingled house with a turret, gazebo, and stone fence. The house was used as the Tyrone family's residence in the 1962 film version of Eugene O'Neill's *Long Day's Journey Into Night,* starring Katherine Hepburn.

Accommodations and Food

One of the most unusual places to stay in New York City is **Le Refuge Inn,** 620 City Island Ave., tel. (718) 885-2478, a French auberge and restaurant housed in a 19th-century Victorian house. Rooms cost $85 d with a shared bath, $142 d with a private bath. Continental breakfast included; the prix fixe dinners cost $40.

City Island restaurants run the gamut from simple diners to elaborate (and expensive) old-fashioned affairs with nautical themes and plush booths. The rambling **Johnny's Reef Restaurant,** 2 City Island Ave., tel. (718) 885-2086, at the far end of the island, is one of the best, offering huge portions of food cafeteria style, along with great views of the Sound. Also very good is the moderately priced **Crab Shanty,** 361 City Island Ave., tel. (718) 885-1810.

Orchard Beach

Just north of City Island, on the Manhattan side of the bridge, is Orchard Beach, another one of City Parks Commissioner Robert Moses's creations. Laid out in a semicircle lined with a broad walkway and colonnaded bathhouses, Orchard Beach is in dire need of renovation. But it's a pleasure to walk along nonetheless, especially in spring or fall, when it's marvelously empty.

From the beach looking east, you have good views of small Rat Island, once a shelter for yellow fever victims, later an artists' colony; and, farther east, Hart Island, the city's potter's field since 1868. From the southern end of the beach looking west, you can see some of the 35 massive towers of Co-Op City, the country's largest co-op housing project. The complex houses 15,372 apartments, seven schools, three shopping centers, five baseball diamonds, and over 55,000 mostly working- and middle-class people.

Pelham Bay Park

Orchard Beach is part of Pelham Bay Park, the largest park in New York City. Within its 2,118 acres are salt marshes, forests, lagoons, meadows, and seashore, along with ball fields, golf courses, tennis courts, and, incongruously, a police shooting range. Some parts of the park are exquisitely beautiful—reminiscent of the Maine coast—but many others are seriously neglected.

The park's foremost historical attraction is the 1836 **Bartow-Pell Mansion,** on Shore Rd. about a mile from the Pelham Bay Park subway (in summer, take the Bx12 bus), tel. (718) 885-1461. The gray stone, Greek Revival mansion is filled with carved woodwork and surrounded by formal gardens. Hours are Wed., Sat.-Sun. noon-4 p.m.; the garden is open Tues.-Sun. 8:30 a.m.-4:30 p.m. Both are closed the last three weeks of August. Admission to the house is adults $2.50, seniors $1.25, children under 12 free. Admission to the gardens is free.

Pelham Bay Park is the site where Anne Hutchinson—a Puritan religious leader expelled by the Massachusetts Bay Colony for her liberal views—settled with her children and followers in 1638. Five years later, their settlement was attacked by Indians, and everyone but Hutchinson's youngest daughter was killed. The Hutchinson River, which splits Pelham Bay Park, is named after Anne Hutchinson.

For more information on Pelham Bay Park, call (718) 430-1890.

DOVER PUBLICATIONS, INC.

STATEN ISLAND

From Manhattan: Take the ferry from Battery Park to the northern end of Staten Island, where buses fan out to cover the island. The Staten Island Rapid Transit trains (SIRT), tel. (718) 356-3214, also begin at the ferry terminal.

Staten Island is difficult to explore. Buses run much less frequently than they do elsewhere in New York City and have more ground to cover, making travel between destinations a time-consuming business. Travel by car can also be frustrating, as many of the streets are poorly marked.

One way to get an overall sense of the island is to take a SIRT train from St. George in the north to Tottenville in the south. The 14.3-mile journey passes through such typical residential communities as New Dorp, Bay Terrace, and Great Kills, before terminating in Tottenville, a well-worn town of narrow tree-lined streets and Victorian houses.

The Forgotten Borough

Sometimes dubbed "the forgotten borough," Staten Island is different from the rest of New York City. Significantly more rural and suburban than the other boroughs, it's also predominantly white, politically conservative, and working- to middle-class. As *The New York Times* put it in a recent article, "Staten Island is the land of Kiwanis Clubs and big gas guzzlers for sale on small front lawns, and guys who don't split the

checks with their dates, and girls who wear high heels to the grocery store and marry young."

All of which means that Staten Island frequently feels estranged from the rest of the city—and periodically threatens to secede. The last time was in 1993 when the issue was put to a public vote; the referendum was enthusiastically passed; but its implementation remains doubtful, as numerous legal and political obstacles have yet to be hurdled.

Yet Staten Island, pop. 380,000, is considerably more complex than these facts might imply. On the one hand, it provides Manhattan with 65,000 daily commuters, has some of the city's most polluted waters, and is home to the city's largest garbage dump—some 100,000 tons are dumped here weekly. On the other, the borough holds an annual county fair with bed races and ribbons for the best home-grown vegetables, and boasts over 1,800 acres of protected forests and seashore. Staten Island has also been the favored retreat of Mafia bosses for generations.

History

Fourteen miles long by seven miles wide, Staten Island is a hilly place made up largely of bedrock. Originally settled by Native Americans who successfully fought off the Dutch until 1661, it became a military camp for the British during the Revolutionary War. The borough remained predominantly agricultural throughout the 1800s, and was still largely undeveloped in 1964 when the Verrazano-Narrows Bridge opened. The bridge connected the island to the rest of the city for the first time, bringing with it new industry, residents, and crime. Many Staten Islanders still blame the bridge for many of the island's current problems, and divide life into "Before the Bridge" and "After the Bridge."

Before the Bridge, Staten Island was almost exclusively white, and yet it has a surprisingly interesting African American history. During the Revolutionary War, when the British controlled New York, three British soldiers attacked a black Staten Islander named Bill Richmond. A strong man with considerable boxing talent, Richmond managed to hold them off. Later, the Duke of Northumberland—who was a big boxing fan— heard of the incident, and brought Richmond to London, where he became a major sports figure. Richmond also trained Tom Molineaux, who was America's first unofficial black heavyweight boxing champion.

Then too, during and just after the Civil war, many black Southerners settled in the southwestern corner of Staten Island, where they established the community of **Sandy Ground,** one of the country's oldest free black communities. Several homes belonging to these early settlers still stand, and the town's history is being preserved by the Sandy Ground Historical Society, tel. (718) 317-5796.

NORTHERN STATEN ISLAND

The Ferry
The Staten Island Ferry is the borough's biggest attraction—3.5 million tourists ride it every year, but very few actually disembark on Staten Island. The views the ferry offers of the harbor and Manhattan are spectacular, especially in the early evening and at night. The ferry lands in the scruffy little hillside town of St. George, the oldest and most urban section of Staten Island.

Staten Island Institute of Arts & Sciences
Two blocks from the ferry terminal is Staten Island Institute of Arts & Sciences, 75 Stuyvesant Pl., tel. (718) 727-1135. Founded in 1881, the institute features small but well-done changing exhibits on the arts, natural sciences, and culture of the borough, and offers occasional walking tours. Hours are Mon.-Sat. 9 a.m.-5 p.m., Sun. 1-5 p.m. Suggested admission is adults $2.50, students and seniors $1.50.

Snug Harbor Cultural Center
About 1.5 miles east of the ferry terminal is Snug Harbor, 1000 Richmond Terrace, tel. (718) 448-2500, an odd complex of historic buildings with a decidedly institutional feel. Once a maritime hospital and home for retired sailors, Snug Harbor is now a National Historic Landmark District slowly being transformed into an arts center. Much work still needs to be done on the sprawling estate filled with Greek Revival, beaux arts, and Italianate architecture, but the place has a spooky grandeur. Its highlight is a restored 1833 building featuring a soaring gallery adorned with stained glass and ceiling murals. The building now holds the **Newhouse Center for Contemporary Art,** open Wed.-Sun. noon-5 p.m. Suggested admission is $2.

Adjoining Snug Harbor is the 80-acre **Staten Island Botanical Garden,** a historic Victorian landscape made up of woodlands, natural ponds, and formal gardens. The new Chinese Scholar's Garden, opened in 1996, was designed by China's foremost authority on classical gardens and is the only one of its kind in America.

Snug Harbor is open during daylight hours. Admission is free, and free tours are offered summer weekends at 2 p.m. Complimentary maps are available at the visitor center. From the ferry terminal, take the S40 bus; the ride takes about 15 minutes.

Staten Island Children's Museum
The third component of Snug Harbor is the Staten Island Children's Museum, tel. (718) 273-2060, which draws families from all over the city. Among the most popular of its many hands-on exhibits are its simulated radio and TV stations. The museum is open Tues.-Sun. noon-5 p.m. Admission is $4, free for kids under two.

Alice Austen House
Several miles southwest of St. George is a pretty gabled house, 2 Hylan Blvd., tel. (718) 816-4506, that was once home to photographer Alice

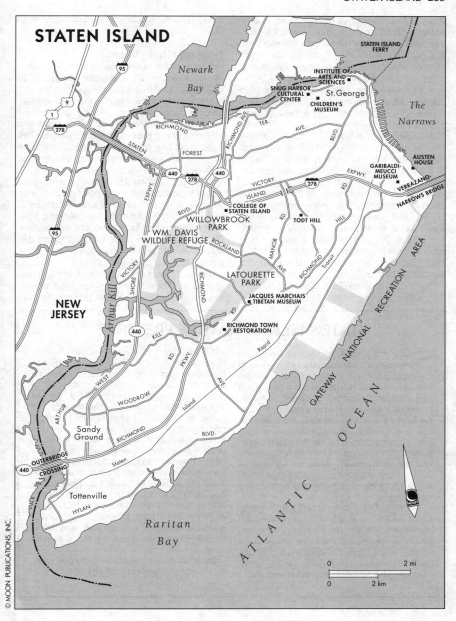

STATEN ISLAND

Newark Bay

The Narrows

STATEN ISLAND FERRY

INSTITUTE OF ARTS AND SCIENCES

SNUG HARBOR CULTURAL CENTER

St. George

CHILDREN'S MUSEUM

RICHMOND

FOREST

RICHMOND AVE.

TER.

AVE.

BLVD.

AUSTEN HOUSE

GARIBALDI-MEUCCI MUSEUM

VERRAZANO-NARROWS BRIDGE

STATEN

EXPWY.

VICTORY

ISLAND

EXPWY.

RD.

COLLEGE OF STATEN ISLAND

WILLOWBROOK PARK

WM. DAVIS WILDLIFE REFUGE

ROCKLAND

TODT HILL

MANOR AVE.

RICHMOND RD.

Transit

HILL

LATOURETTE PARK

RICHMOND RD.

JACQUES MARCHAIS TIBETAN MUSEUM

RICHMOND TOWN RESTORATION

Rapid

GATEWAY NATIONAL RECREATION AREA

NEW JERSEY

Arthur Kill

VICTORY

SHORE

RD.

KILL

PKWY.

WEST

ARTHUR

WOODROW

RICHMOND

Island

AVE.

BLVD.

Sandy Ground

OUTERBRIDGE CROSSING

Staten

Tottenville

HYLAN

Raritan Bay

ATLANTIC OCEAN

0   2 mi

0   2 km

© MOON PUBLICATIONS, INC.

Austen. A contemporary of Jacob Riis, Austen never worked professionally but took photographs just "for fun." Between 1884 and 1932 she produced more than 8,000 photos, which comprise one of the finest extant pictorial records of turn-of-the-century American life.

Austen lived in her 17th-century cottage from the age of two to the age of 70, when she was forced out due to poverty. Crippled with arthritis, she moved into the poorhouse. There she was "discovered" by an editor of *Life* magazine, who wanted to publish her work. She was then moved into a private nursing home, and lived to see her photographs published to much acclaim.

A visit to the Austen house begins with a short documentary film, narrated by Helen Hayes. The house has been restored to the way it was in Austen's day, and is full of Victoriana clutter. One room houses a gallery which mounts changing exhibits of Austen's and other photographers' work. Outside is a wonderful view of the harbor.

The house is open Thurs.-Sun. noon-5 p.m. Suggested admission is $2. From the ferry terminal, take the S51 bus; the ride takes 15 minutes.

Garibaldi-Meucci Museum

Not far from the Austen House is the Garibaldi-Meucci Museum, 470 Tompkins Ave., tel. (718) 442-1608. The museum is housed in the former home of Antonio Meucci, the Italian-American inventor who developed the first working model of the telephone in 1857. Though kudos for the invention went to Alexander Graham Bell throughout Meucci's lifetime, he was declared the first inventor of the telephone by the Supreme Court in 1886.

Meucci also offered his home as a refuge to Italian expatriate hero Giuseppe Garibaldi, who lived here in 1850 while recuperating from ill health. During that time, the two men supported themselves by hunting, fishing, and making candles in the backyard. Later, Garibaldi returned to Italy, where he and his followers succeeded in establishing Italy as a nation.

Today, Meucci's simple, white home is a low-key, special-interest kind of place, filled with letters, photos, and memorabilia documenting the

---

STATEN ISLAND NATURE PRESERVE

Smack in the middle of Staten Island is the Greenbelt, a 2,500-acre nature preserve made up of contiguous woodlands, wetlands, and open fields, along with a golf course and a few historic sites. Though surrounded by development, the Greenbelt is a favorite stop for migratory birds on the Atlantic flyway. It also supports one of the most diverse floras in the northeast, thanks to a wide variety of soils deposited by the Wisconsin glacier about 10,000 years ago. In the Greenbelt's upland hills, the soil covers an uncommon serpentinite bedrock found only a few places in the world. When exposed to the elements, the bedrock weathers to a light gray-green.

Two major hiking trails traverse the Greenbelt. One is the 8.5-mile Blue Trail (17 miles roundtrip), marked with blue dots, which runs east-west from the College of Staten Island to the William Davis Wildlife Refuge. Highlights along the way include Deer Park, which lies on the slopes of the highest point along the Atlantic coastline between Maine and Florida; Reed's Basket Willow Swamp, often filled with blooming wildflowers; and High Rock Park, where outcroppings of the serpentinite bedrock can be seen. To reach the College of Staten Island from the ferry terminal, take the S66 bus. The trail begins on Milford Dr., and is marked by a sign.

The other trail is the four-mile White Trail (eight miles roundtrip), marked with white dots, which begins at High Rock Park and runs north to Willowbrook Park. Highlights along the way include Bucks Hollow, notable for its wetlands, and the steep Egbertville Ravine. To reach the trail, take the S74 bus to the corner of Richmond Rd. and Rockland Avenue. Walk two blocks on Rockland to Nevada Ave. and turn right up the hill to the park's entrance and visitor center. Maps are available at the visitor center on weekends; on weekdays, stop by the Greenbelt's administration office at 200 Nevada Avenue.

Other, shorter trails also traverse the Greenbelt. For more information, call (718) 667-2165.

*Richmond Town
Restoration*

lives of both men. The house is open Tues.-Sun. 1-5 p.m. Admission is free. From the ferry terminal, take the S78 bus; the ride takes 15 minutes.

CENTRAL STATEN ISLAND

Todt Hill
Just off Richmond Rd. south of the Staten Island Expressway rises the rocky hump of Todt Hill, an exclusive residential neighborhood filled with rambling estates and white, columned mansions. Francis Ford Coppola turned one of them into the Corleone family estate for his film *The Godfather;* it's at 110 and 120 Longfellow Rd., at the end of a tree-lined dead-end street. Todt Hill is best reached and explored by car.

Jacques Marchais Museum of Tibetan Art
Perched on a steep hill farther south, off Richmond Hill Rd., is the Tibetan Museum, 338 Lighthouse Ave., at Windsor, tel. (718) 987-3500. The museum was created by Jacqueline Norman Klauber, who adopted the alias Jacques Marchais to promote her career as a New York art dealer. Fascinated with Tibetan figurines from childhood (her great-grandfather had brought some home from his travels), she spent her adult years collecting Asian art. In the 1940s, she built this personalized museum, which was

designed to resemble a Buddhist temple.

The Marchais Center houses the biggest collection of Tibetan art in the Western world, but is still quite small, contained in just one high-ceilinged room and a rectangular garden. Highlights include a series of brightly colored masks, and a large collection of golden *thangkas,* or religious images, lined up at a red-and-gold altar. A garden out back offers distant views of the bay, and a gift shop sells a nice selection of books and crafts.

The Marchais Center is open April-Nov., Wed.-Sun. 1-5 p.m.; Dec.-March by appointment. Admission is adults $3, students and senior citizens $2.50, children $1. From the ferry terminal, take the S74 bus; the ride takes about 35 minutes.

Historic Richmond Town
Just a few minutes' walk from the Tibetan Museum is Richmond Town, 441 Clarke Ave., tel. (718) 351-1611, a 30-acre complex filled with historic buildings. Most have been moved here from elsewhere on the island, and they line up neatly along several streets which come alive in summer with craftspeople and guides in period dress.

Richmond Town sits on the site of an early Dutch settlement and interprets three centuries of daily life. The oldest building is the 1695 Voorlezer's House (a voorlezer was a lay minister and teacher); one of the newest is the New Dorp

Railroad Station, complete with a Queen Anne-style porch and gables. Other interesting buildings include a two-story jail, tinsmith shop, general store, carriage "manufactory," gift shop, cafe, and visitor center with changing exhibitions.

Richmond Town is open July-Aug., Wed.-Fri. 10 a.m.-5 p.m. and Sat.-Sun. 1-5 p.m.; Sept.-June, Wed.-Sun. 1-5 p.m. Admission is adults $4; students, seniors, and children 6-18 $2.50; children under six free. From the ferry terminal, take the S74 bus; the ride takes about 40 minutes.

APPENDIX:
QUICK REFERENCE GUIDES
MANHATTAN ACCOMMODATIONS

The following accommodations are covered in the district sections listed.

CHEAP (UNDER $60)

From Union Square to Gramercy Park
Murray Hill Inn, Gershwin (dorm rooms)

Upper West Side and Central Park:
Malibu Studios Hotel

INEXPENSIVE ($60-100)

**Chinatown, Little Italy,
and Lower East Side:**
Off-Soho Suites (Lower East Side)

Greenwich Village
Larchmont Hotel

From Union Square to Murray Hill:
Gershwin Hotel (private rooms); Hotel 17

From Chelsea to the Garment District:
Herald Square Hotel; Hotel Wolcott

Midtown:
Allerton House for Women; Pickwick Arms;
Portland Square Hotel

Upper West Side and Central Park:
Riverside Tower; Hotel Olcott

MODERATE ($100-175)

**Chinatown, Little Italy,
and Lower East Side:**
Holiday Inn Downtown(Chinatown)

Greenwich Village:
Washington Square Hotel

From Union Square to Murray Hill:
Carlton; Gramercy Park Hotel; Quality Hotel;
Americana; Howard Johnson on Park Avenue

From Chelsea to the Garment District:
Chelsea; Hotel Metro; Chelsea Savoy; Best
Western Manhattan

Midtown:
Beverly; Edison; Lexington; Paramount; Wyndham; Broadway Inn; Mayfair; Iroquois; Remington; Westpark; Park Savoy

Upper East Side:
Barbizon; Franklin; Wales

Upper West Side and Central Park:
Milburn; Excelsior; Hotel Beacon

EXPENSIVE ($175-275)

Lower Manhattan:
Manhattan Seaport Suites; Marriott Financial
Center

SoHo and TriBeCa
Soho Grand

From Union Square to Murray Hill:
Morgans; Shelburne Murray Hill

Midtown:
Algonquin; Beekman Tower Hotel; Elysee;
Marriott Marquis; Millenium Broadway; Roger
Smith; Gorham; Mansfield

Upper East Side:
Surrey Hotel

Upper West Side:
Mayflower

LUXURY (OVER $275)

Lower Manhattan:
Millenium Hilton

Midtown:
Drake Swissotel; Four Seasons New York;
Peninsula; Plaza; Royalton; St. Regis;
Waldorf-Astoria

Upper East Side:
Carlyle; Mark; Pierre

HOSTELS, YMCA'S, DORMS

Greenwich Village:
New York University (summers only)

From Chelsea to the Garment District:
McBurney YMCA

Midtown:
Vanderbilt YWCA

Upper East Side:
De Hirsch Residence at the 92nd St. Y

Upper West Side and Central Park:
West Side YMCA

Harlem and Upper Manhattan
Columbia University (summers only); International House of New York; New York International AYH; Sugar Hill International House; Blue Rabbit International House

SELECTED NEW YORK CITY RESTAURANTS

The price categories used in this book correspond to the following dollar amounts:

Inexpensive—**$**; under $15
Moderate—**$$**; $15-30

Expensive—**$$$**; $30-50
Very Expensive—**$$$$**; over $50

AMERICAN

Lower Manhattan
$$ Bridge Cafe; Liberty Cafe
$$$ Morton's of Chicago

Soho and Tribeca
$ Bell Caffe; Moondance Diner
$$ Jerry's; SoHo Kitchen and Bar; Spring Street Natural
$$$ Cub Room; TriBeCa Grill; Zoe

East Village
$ Around the Clock; Caravan of Dreams; Life Cafe; 7A
$$ Miracle Grill

Greenwich Village
$ Corner Bistro
$-$$ Aggie's; Boxer's
$$ Anglers & Writers; Cornelia Street Cafe; Grange Hall; Old Homestead; Paris Commune
$$$ Gotham Bar and Grill

From Union Square to Murray Hill
$$ Albuquerque Eats; America; Brew's; Luna Park
$$$ An American Place; Mesa Grill; Water Club; Granville

Chelsea and the Garment District
$-$$ Chelsea Commons; Empire Diner
$$ Alley's End

Midtown
$ Carnegie Deli; Stage Deli
$$ Hourglass Tavern; Joe Allen; West Bank Cafe
$$-$$$ American Festival Cafe; Bryant Park Grill
$$$ Restaurant Charlotte; Smith & Wollensky; Sparks Steak House; 44

Upper East Side
$ Barking Dog Luncheonette; Soup Burg
$$-$$$ Arizona 206; Sarabeth's

Upper West Side and Central Park
$ Good Enough to Eat; Popover Cafe
$$ Boathouse Cafe; The Saloon
$$$ Tavern on the Green

Brooklyn
$-$$ Aunt Sonia's; Junior's; Leaf 'N Bean; Slade's
$$$ Gage & Tollner; Henry's End; Peter Luger's; River Cafe

Queens
$$$ Water's Edge

ASIAN

Chinatown, Little Italy, and Lower East Side
numerous; see Chinatown "Food" section

East Village
$ Dojo's; Mingala Burmese Restaurant
$$ Iso; Shabu Tatsu; Siam Square

SoHo and TriBeCa
$ Thai House Cafe

Greenwich Village
$$ Ginger Toon (Thai); Japonica (sushi)

From Union Square to Murray Hill
$ Galaxy; Sam's Noodles
$$ Zen Palate (vegetarian); Tatany (Japanese)

Chelsea and the Garment District
$$ Gam Mee Ok (Korean); Han Bat (Korean)

Midtown
$ Dosanko; Ollie's Noodle Shop; Take-Sushi
$$ Zen Palate (vegetarian)
$$$ Hatsuhana (Japanese); Sushisay (Japanese); Vong (French/Thai)

Upper East Side
$ Sala Thai; Siam Cuisine (Thai)

Upper West Side and Central Park
$ Broadway Cottage; Empire Szechuan Gourmet; Mingala West (Burmese); Miss Saigon (Vietnamese)
$$ Jo-An (Japanese); Sakura (sushi)

Queens
$-$$ Cosy (Korean); Golden Oven (Thai); Joe's Shanghai; Manila Thai
$$$ South River (Korean)

FRENCH/CONTINENTAL

Soho and Tribeca
$$ La Jumelle; Lucky Strike
$$$ Felix's; Le Pescadou; Odeon; Provence; Raoul's
$$$$ Bouley's; Chanterelle

East Village
$$ Jules

Greenwich Village
$$ Florent, Caffe Lure
$$-$$$ Cafe de Bruxelles; Marylou's
$$$ Cafe Loup

From Union Square to Murray Hill
$$$ Les Halles; Park Bistro

Chelsea and the Garment District
$$$ Gascogne

Midtown
$ La Bonne Soupe; La Fondue
$$ Tout Va Bien
$$-$$$ Brasserie; Cafe Un, Deux, Trois; Chez Josephine
$$$$ La Cote Basque; Le Bernardin; Lutece; Rainbow Room

Upper East Side
$-$$ L'Ardoise
$$$ Le Bilboquet
$$$$ Sign of the Dove

Upper West Side and Central Park
$$ Cafe St. John
$$$ Cafe des Artistes; Cafe Luxembourg

INDIAN

East Village
$$ Bombay; Gandhi; Haveli; Mitali; Sonali

From Union Square to Murray Hill
$ Curry in a Hurry; Joy
$$ Annapurna; Mavalli Palace; Muriya

Midtown
$$ Darbar
$$$ Dawat; Nirvana

Queens
$-$$ Delhi Place; Jackson Diner

ITALIAN

Lower Manhattan
$$-$$$ Ecco

Chinatown, Little Italy, and Lower East Side
$-$$ Benito I; DaNico
$$$ Il Cortile; Taormina

SoHo and TriBeCa
$$ Il Corallo Trattoria; Trattoria Vente
             Tre
$$-$$$ Barolo; Rosemarie's

East Village
$$ John's; Lanza; Spaghetteria

Greenwich Village
$ Arturo's; John's
$-$$ Mappamondo II
$$ Grand Ticino
$-$$$ Cent'Anni
$$$ Il Mulino

From Union Square to Murray Hill
$ Pasta Presto
$$ Trattoria Siciliana

Chelsea and the Garment District
$$ Intermezzo
$$$ Da Umberto

Midtown
$-$$ Cucina & Co.
$$ Borsalino; Carmine's
$$$ Barbetta's; Trattoria dell'Arte
$$$$ Palio

Upper East Side
$-$$ Caffee Buon Gusto; Caffe Grazie
$$$ Paola's; Paper Moon Milano

Upper West Side and Central Park
$$ Isola; Meridiana

Harlem and Upper Manhattan
$ Patsy's Pizza
$$$ Rao's

Brooklyn
$ Patsy's Pizza
$-$$ Aunt Suzie's
$$-$$$ Cucina

Bronx
$$ Amici's; Dominick's; Mario's

LATIN/CARIBBEAN

SoHo and TriBeCa
$ Lupe's Kitchen
$$ El Teddy's

East Village
$$ Boca Chica; Maryann's; Pedro
             Paramo

Greenwich Village
$ Benny's Burritos
$$ Caribe; Mi Cocina; Tapestry

From Union Square to Murray Hill
$$ Coffee Shop
$$$ Lola; Patria

Chelsea and the Garment District
$ La Chinita Linda; La Taza de Oro
$$ Blue Moon; Mary Ann's; Rocking
             Horse Mexican Cafe; Negril's

Midtown
$$ Brazilia Restaurant; Cabana Cario-
             ca; Ipanema
$$$ Bistro Latino

Upper East Side
$ El Pollo (Peruvian)
$$-$$$ Island (Caribbean); Rosa Mexicano

Upper West Side and Central Park
$ Harry's Burrito Junction; Cafe con
             Leche; La Caridad (Cuban-
             Chinese); La Rosita (Dominican)
$$ Gabriela's (Mexican)

Harlem and Upper Manhattan
$ Jamaican Hot Pot; Tropix; La Ha-
             cienda

Brooklyn
$ Caribbean Pavillion

Queens
$-$$ Inti Raymi (Peruvian); La Pequeña
             Colombia; Tierras Colombianas

RUSSIAN

SoHo and TriBeCa
$$$ Pravda

Midtown
$ Uncle Vanya's Cafe
$$$ Russian Tea Room; Firebird

Brooklyn
$$$ National Restaurant; Odessa; Primorski

SEAFOOD

Lower Manhattan
$ Jeremy's Ale House
$$ Sloppy Louie's

East Village
$ Cucina di Pesce
$$-$$$ Pisces

Midtown
$$$ Manhattan Ocean Club; Oyster Bar

Upper West Side
$$ Fish Restaurant

Brooklyn
$$ Lundy's; Randazzo's

Bronx
$-$$ Johnny's Reef
$$ Crab Shanty

SOUTHERN/SOUL/CREOLE

East Village
$-$$ Acme Bar & Grill; Great Jones Cafe; Baby Jake's

Greenwich Village
$-$$ Pink Teacup

SoHo
$-$$ Brother's Barbeque

From Union Square to Murray Hill
$-$$ Live Bait

Midtown
$$-$$$ B. Smith's
$$$ Jezebel

Upper West Side
$$ Mo' Better; Shark Bar

Harlem and Upper Manhattan
$ M&G Diner; Wilson's Bakery
$$ Sylvia's; Copeland's; Emily's

Brooklyn
$ Ms. Ann's
$$ Sheila's

OTHER

Lower Manhattan
$$-$$$ Windows on the World (eclectic)

Lower East Side
$-$$ Katz's; Ratner's (both Jewish)

SoHo and TriBeCa
$ Abyssinia (African)
$$ Cafe Noir (French-Moroccan)

East Village
$ Christine's (Polish); Kiev (Eastern European); Odessa (Ukrainian); Second Ave. Deli; Veselka (Eastern European); Yaffa Cafe (eclectic);
$$ Time Cafe (eclectic); Two Boots (eclectic)
$$-$$$ First (eclectic)

Greenwich Village
$$ El Faro (Spanish); Gus' Place (Greek/Mediterranean)

From Union Square to Murray Hill
$$ Tibetan Kitchen; Turkish Kitchen
$$$ Periyali (Greek); Union Square Cafe (eclectic)

Chelsea and the Garment District
$ Bright Food Shop (Mexican-Asian); Ngone (Senegalese)

Midtown
$-$$ Afghan Kebab House; Uncle Nick's (Greek)
$$ Taprobane (Sri Lankan)
$$$ Solera (Spanish)
$$$$ Four Seasons (eclectic)

Upper East Side
$$ Afghan Kebab House; Mocca Restaurant (Hungarian); Persepolis (Persian); Red Tulip (Hungarian)

Upper West Side and Central Park
$$ Blue Nile (Ethiopian); Cleopatra's Needle (Middle Eastern); World Cafe (eclectic)

Harlem and Upper Manhattan
$ Obaa Koryoe (West African); Zula Cafe (East African)

Brooklyn
$ Moroccan Star (Middle Eastern); Polska Restaurant (Polish)
$$ Continental (Polish); Tripoli (Middle Eastern)

Queens
$$ Penang Cuisine Malaysia; Roumeli Taverna (Greek); Telly's Taverna (Greek)
$$$ Taverna Vraka (Greek)

NEW YORK CITY MUSEUMS

New York is a city of museums. From the huge Metropolitan Museum of Art in Manhattan to the tiny Tibetan Museum in Staten Island, a person could spend weeks doing nothing but museum-hopping and still not have covered them all.

The city's most important museums are the Metropolitan Museum of Art, the Museum of Modern Art, and the American Museum of Natural History. Following not far behind, are the Whitney, the Guggenheim, the Brooklyn Museum, the Studio Museum in Harlem, the Cooper-Hewitt, the National Museum of the American Indian, and the Frick.

ART MUSEUMS

SoHo:
Alternative Museum
Guggenheim SoHo
Museum for African Art
New Museum of Contemporary Art

Union Square to Murray Hill
Pierpont Morgan Library

Midtown:
American Craft Museum
ICP Midtown
Museum of Modern Art

Upper East Side:
Cooper-Hewitt
Frick
Guggenheim
International Center of Photography
Metropolitan Museum of Art
National Academy of Design
Whitney Museum of American Art

Upper West Side:
Museum of American Folk Art

Harlem and Upper Manhattan:
Cloisters
Studio Museum in Harlem

The Bronx:
Bronx Museum of the Arts

Brooklyn:
Brooklyn Museum

Queens:
American Museum of the Moving Image
Isamu Noguchi Garden Museum
Queens Museum of Art

CHILDREN'S MUSEUMS

SoHo:
Children's Museum of the Arts

Upper West Side:
Children's Museum of Manhattan

Brooklyn:
Brooklyn Children's Museum

Staten Island:
Staten Island Children's Museum

CULTURAL MUSEUMS

Lower Manhattan:
National Museum of the America Indian

**Chinatown, Little Italy,
and the Lower East Side:**
Museum of Chinese in the Americas

East Village:
Ukrainian Museum

Upper East Side:
Asia Society
Jewish Museum
Museo del Barrio
Museum of the City of New York

Harlem and Upper Manhattan:
African American Wax Museum
Black Fashion Museum
Hispanic Society
Yeshiva University Museum

Staten Island:
Tibetan Museum

HISTORICAL MUSEUMS

Lower Manhattan:
Ellis Island Immigration Museum
South Street Seaport Museum

**Chinatown, Little Italy,
and the Lower East Side:**
Lower East Side Tenement Museum

East Village:
Old Merchant's House

Union Square to Murray Hill:
Theodore Roosevelt's Birthplace

Upper East Side:
Abigail Adams Smith Museum

Brooklyn:
Brooklyn Historical Society

SCIENCE AND TECHNOLOGY MUSEUMS

Lower Manhattan:
New York Unearthed

Midtown:
Intrepid Sea-Air-Space Museum
Museum of Television and Radio

Upper West Side:
American Museum of Natural History

Queens:
New York Hall of Science

OTHER MUSEUMS

SoHo:
New York City Fire Museum

Greenwich Village:
Forbes Magazine Galleries

Union Square to Murray Hill:
Police Academy Museum

Upper West Side:
Nicholas Roerich Museum

Harlem and Upper Manhattan:
American Numismatic Society

The Bronx:
North Wind Undersea Museum

Brooklyn:
New York Transit Museum

Staten Island:
Staten Island Institute of Arts and Sciences

MANHATTAN SHOPPING

DEPARTMENT STORES

Chelsea and the Garment District:
Barney's New York
Lord & Taylor
Macy's Herald Square

Midtown:
Bergdorf Goodman's
Henri Bendel
Saks Fifth Avenue
Takashimaya

Upper East Side:
Barney's Uptown
Bloomingdale's

ANTIQUES AND FURNISHINGS

SoHo and TriBeCa
Lost City Arts
Urban Archaeology
various, esp. Lafayette and Wooster Sts.

East Village
various, esp. Ninth St.

Greenwich Village
American Folk Gallery
Old Japan, Inc.
Susan Parrish
Uplift Lighting
various, along Broadway

Union Square to Murray Hill
ABC Carpet and Home

Chelsea and the Garment District
Chelsea Antiques Building
Markus Antiques
(see also "Flea Markets/Outdoor Markets,"
below)

Midtown
Manhattan Arts & Antiques Center

Upper East Side
Dialogica (art deco furniture)
Things Japanese (Japanese antiques)
various other antique shops, esp. Madison
Ave. above 59th St., and 60th St. bet. Third
and Second Aves.

BOOKS

SoHo and TriBeCa
A Photographer's Place
Rizzoli's
SoHo Books (used)

East Village
St. Marks Bookshop
Gem Spa (newsstand)

Greenwich Village
B. Dalton's
Biography Bookshop
East West Books (Eastern/New Age
   philosophy)
Oscar Wilde Memorial Bookshop (gay books)
Shakespeare & Co.
Three Lives & Co.
Tower Books

Chelsea and the Garment District
Academy Books (used)
A Different Light (gay and lesbian)
Barnes & Noble
Books of Wonder (children's)
Skyline Books (used)

Union Square to Murray Hill
Barnes & Noble
Complete Traveller Bookstore
Revolution Books (radical)
Strand Book Store (eight miles of used books)

Midtown
Argosy
Barnes & Noble
B. Dalton's
Coliseum Books
Doubleday's
Gotham Book Mart
Hagstrom Map and Travel Center
Hotalings Foreign News Depot
How-to Video Source (instructional videos)
MoMA Book Store
Mysterious Book Shop
New York Bound Bookshop
Rand McNally Map & Travel Store
Rizzoli
Traveller's Bookstore
Urban Center Books

Upper East Side
Barnes & Noble
Books & Co.
Kitchen Arts & Letters (cookbooks)

Upper West Side
Applause Theatre Books
Barnes & Noble
Black Books Plus
Gryphon
Murder Ink

Harlem/Upper Manhattan
Posman Books
Liberation Book Shop

CAMERAS AND ELECTRONICS

Lower Manhattan
J&R

Union Square to Murray Hill
The Wiz (branches citywide)

CLOTHES

Lower Manhattan
Century 21 (discount; esp. menswear)

Lower East Side
Forman's (discount women's designers)
various, along Orchard St.

SoHo and TriBeCa
Agnes B.
Alice Underground (vintage)
Canal Jean
French Connection
Harriet Love (vintage)
Putumayo (women's clothing, natural fabrics)
Stella Dallas ('40s-era)

East Village
Love Saves the Day (vintage)
Screaming Mimi's (vintage)
Trash and Vaudeville
Kanae + Onyx

Greenwich Village
Andy's Chee-Pees (vintage)
Antique Boutique (vintage)
Cheap Jack's (vintage)
Reminiscence (vintage)
Star Struck (vintage)
Urban Outfitters
Patricia Field

Union Square to Murray Hill
Bolton's (discount designer wear)
Daffy's (discount designer wear)
Emporio Armani
Matsuda (Japanese clothing)

Chelsea and the Garment District
J.J. Hat Center
Loehmann's
various, 34th St. bet. Fifth and Sixth Aves.

Upper East Side
Issey Miyake
Levi Store
Polo Ralph Lauren
Second Chance Consignment Shop
Tracey Tooker Hats
Yves St. Laurent

Upper West Side
Alice Underground (vintage)
Bead Dazzled (beads)
Betsey Johnson
Laura Ashley
Off Broadway (secondhand)

CRAFTS AND GIFTS

Chinatown
Quong Yuen Shing

SoHo and TriBeCa
Bazaar Sabato (Mexican handicrafts)
Boca Grande (Latin American gifts)
Keith Haring Pop Shop (pop art)

East Village
Howdy Do
Little Rickie's
Made in Detroit
various, along Ninth St.

Chelsea and the Garment District
Wood Artists

Midtown
Coca-Cola Co.
Hammacher Schlemmer
MoMA Design Store
Warner Bros. Studio Store

Upper East Side
Handblock

Upper West Side
Dapy's (pop culture)
Exotiqa II (carvings0
Objects of Bright Pride

Harlem and Upper Manhattan
Mart 125

FLEA MARKETS/OUTDOOR MARKETS

SoHo and TriBeCa
SoHo Antiques Fair and Collectibles

Greenwich Village
by Tower Records
P.S. 41

Chelsea and the Garment District
Annex Antique Fair and Flea Market
Garage

Upper West Side
P.S. 44

Harlem and Upper Manhattan
by Malcom Shabazz Mosque
116th St. bet. Park and Lexington

HEALTH AND BEAUTY

East Village
Kiehl's (natural beauty products)
Tenth Street Russian and Turkish Baths
(saunas, steam rooms, etc.)

Greenwich Village
Aphrodisia (herbs, oils)
Bigelow Chemists (pharmacy)

Union Square to Murray Hill
Carapan (New Age spa)
Gauntlet (body piercing)
La Casa de Vida Natural (Puerto Rican spa)

Midtown
Caswell-Massey (apothecary)
Elizabeth Arden (salon)
Georgette Klinger (salon)
Osaka Health Center (massage)

RECORD STORES

Lower Manhattan
J&R

East Village
Fat Beats
Final Vinyl
Footlight Records
Sounds

Greenwich Village
Bleecker Bob's
Revolver Records
Tower Records

Chelsea and the Garment District
Academy Records
Jazz Record Center

Midtown
Colony Records
Virgin Megastore

Upper East Side
HMV
Metropolitan Opera Shop

Upper West Side
Gryphon Records
Tower Records

Harlem and Upper Manhattan
La Marketa Records
Rainbow Music Shop

SHOES

Lower East Side
Lace-Up Shoe Shop (discount designers)

Greenwich Village
various, along 8th St.

Midtown
Niketown

TOYS AND GAMES

SoHo and TriBeCa
After the Rain
Enchanted Forest

Greenwich Village
Abracadabra
Chess Shop
Game Show

Union Square to Murray Hill
B. Shackman's
The Compleat Strategist
Manhattan Doll House

Midtown
F.A.O. Schwarz

Upper East Side
A Bear's Place
Big City Kite Company
Dollhouse Antics
Game Show

Upper West Side
Uncle Futz

ONE-OF-A-KIND

Art Postcards: Art Market; Untitled (both SoHo)

Art Supplies: Pearl Paint Co. (Chinatown)

Ballet Supplies: Ballet Company (Upper West Side)

Botanicas: Botanica Altagracia (Upper West Side); El Congo, Otto Chicas Rendon, Paco's (all Harlem/Upper Manhattan)

Brassware: Brass Antique Shoppe (Lower East Side)

China: Fishs Eddy (Union Square to Murray Hill)

Condoms: Condomania (Greenwich Village)

Cookware: Broadway Panhandler (SoHo and TriBeCa)

Glassware: Steuben's Glass (Midtown); Lalique (Upper East Side)

Jewelry: Cartier's, Tiffany's (both Midtown)

Military Surplus: Kaufman Surplus (Midtown)

Musical Instruments: Matt Umanov Guitar Store (Greenwich Village); Manny's, Sam Ash, Steinway & Sons (all Midtown)

Posters: Chisholm Prats Gallery (European Travel posters; Chelsea and the Garment District); La Belle Epoque (turn-of-the-century French posters; Upper West Side)

Science and Natural History: Evolution (SoHo); Dinosaur Hill (East Village); Star Magic (Greenwich Village); Maxilla & Mandible (Upper West Side)

Sporting Goods: Paragon (Union Square to Murray Hill)

Stationery: Kate's Paperie (SoHo); Jam Paper and Envelope (East Village)

Umbrellas and Canes: Uncle Sam's (Midtown)

ETHNIC GOODS

Balinese: Mostly Bali (East Village)

Chinese: Pearl River Chinese Products (and others; Chinatown)

Guatemalan: Back From Guatemala (East Village)

Italian: Rossi & Co. (and others; Little Italy)

Indian: Little India Emporium (Union Square to Murray Hill)

Jewish: various, Essex St., Rivington St. (Lower East Side)

Native American: Common Ground (Greenwich Village)

Russian: Russian Arts (Greenwich Village)

Ukrainian: Surma (East Village)

BOOKLIST

New York, city of writers, has been the subject of or setting for innumerable essays, biographies, memoirs, histories, guidebooks, poems, and novels. Here are but a few:

SPECIALTY GUIDES AND TRAVEL ESSAYS

Alleman, Richard. *The Movie Lover's Guide to New York*. New York: Harper & Row, 1988. In which hotel lobby did Douglas Fairbanks first woo Mary Pickford? Where was the movie *Ghostbusters* filmed? Alleman's well-written guide is packed with information on over 240 favorite movie sites.

Asimov, Eric. *$25 and Under*. New York: Harper-Collins Publishers, Inc., 1994. A columnist for *The New York Times* points the way to some of the city's best inexpensive eateries. Includes tips on how to eat cheaply in more expensive spots.

Barnard, Josie. *New York: The Virago Woman's Travel Guide*. Berkeley, CA: Ulysses Press, 1994. Intriguing thumbnail sketches of such New York women as Emma Goldman and the Lipstick Lesbians, along with practical advice on hotels, restaurants, bars, and more.

Biondi, Joann, and James Haskins. *Black New York*. New York: Hippocrene Books, 1994. A long-overdue guide that begins with a short introduction to African American history in New York, then runs through various points of interest, including historic buildings, restaurants, music clubs, shops, and churches.

Federal Writers' Project. *The WPA Guide to New York City*. New York: Random House, 1982. First published in 1939, the classic guidebook remains remarkably on target. It provides long and evocative descriptions of everything from Ebbetts Field to the then-new Empire State Building.

Frank, Gerry. *Gerry Frank's Where to Find It, Buy It, Eat It in New York*. Salem, OR: Gerry Frank's, 1993. A monumental 600-plus-page reference manual on where to find everything from bridal gowns to massage therapists.

Freudenheim, Ellen, with Daniel P. Wiener. *Brooklyn: Where to Go, What to Do, How to Get There*. New York: St. Martin's Press, 1991. The first popular guidebook to Brooklyn since 1940 is filled with surprises. The authors explore over a dozen historic neighborhoods; listings and maps included.

Goldberger, Paul. *The City Observed: New York. A Guide to the Architecture of Manhattan*. New York: Random House, 1979. The classic architectural guide to New York by the architecture critic for *The New York Times*. Provocative, informative, and very well written.

Leapman, Michael. *The Companion Guide to New York*. New York: HarperCollins Publishers, 1991. A first-rate, literate guide by a British writer who enjoys expounding on the New York character. The book concentrates on history and points of interest; practical listings are not provided.

Leeds, Mark. *Ethnic New York: A Complete Guide to the Many Faces & Cultures of New York*. Lincolnwood, IL: NTC Publishing Group, 1994. An absorbing and detailed look at the multitude of ethnic neighborhoods—Asian, Italian, Arab, German—that make up the five boroughs. Complete with extensive listings.

Letts, Vanessa. *Cadogan City Guides: New York*. Old Saybrook, CT: The Globe Pequot Press, 1993. A prize-winning British travel writer authors an informative and entertaining guide. Many off-the-beaten-track spots are covered.

Levine, Ed. *New York Eats*. New York: St. Martin's Press, 1992. A food shopper's delight, with separate chapters on baked goods, chocolates, cheeses, pasta, fish, meats, and more.

McDarrah, Fred, and Patrick J. McDarrah. *The Greenwich Village Guide.* Chicago: Chicago Review Press, 1992. A father and son teamed up to write this breezy, anecdotal walking guide to their neighborhood. Also included are sections on SoHo, TriBeCa, and the East Village.

Plump, Stephen. *The Streets Where They Lived: A Walking Guide to the Residences of Famous New Yorkers.* St. Paul, MN: Marlor Press, 1989. A succinct and entertaining guide to the former abodes of such celebrities as John Lennon, Edna St. Vincent Millay, Greta Garbo, James Dean, and Babe Ruth. Complete with short bios and maps.

Schwartzman, Paul, and Rob Polner. *New York Notorious.* New York: Crown Publishers, 1992. Where was mob boss Albert Anastasia assassinated? Where did the Mayflower Madam set up shop? How did Nelson Rockefeller meet his untimely end? Two tabloid reporters tell all.

Simon, Kate. *New York Places & Pleasures.* New York: Meridian Books, 1962. An idiosyncratic guidebook by the well-known travel writer who grew up in the Bronx in the 1920s and lived much of her life in Manhattan.

Time Out Magazine Limited. *Time Out New York.* New York: Penguin Books, 1994. Written by the editors of *Time Out,* a London-based listings magazine that now has a New York edition, this hip, pithy guide does an especially good job of covering restaurants, bars, cafes, and music clubs.

Tucker, Alan. *The Berlitz Travellers Guide to New York City.* New York: Berlitz Publishing Company, Inc., 1994. Written by 22 travel correspondents, each one a specialist in his or her field, this guide is divided by subject matter (art, photography, dance, fashion, etc.) and filled with authoritative information. An excellent guide for the repeat visitor.

Von Pressentin Wright, Carol. *Blue Guide New York.* New York: W.W. Norton & Company, Inc., 1991. One of the most in-depth guides around, the *Blue Guide* exhaustively covers all five boroughs, concentrating on history and architecture. Practical information is limited, and the prose is often dense and dull, but herein is buried a treasure trove of oddball facts.

White, Norval, and Elliot Willensky, eds. *AIA Guide to New York City.* New York: MacMillan, 1988. The most important and entertaining book on New York architecture, organized as a series of walking tours.

Zagat, Eugene H. Jr., and Nina S. Zagat. *Zagat Survey: New York City Restaurants.* New York: Zagat Survey, 1993. This classic, pocket-size guide bases its pithy entries on the reports of volunteer reviewers covering over 1,300 eateries. Many of the reviews are on target; others waffle to an embarrassing degree, or cater to a dull mainstream.

BIOGRAPHY, HISTORY, AND JOURNALISM

Allen, Irving Lewis. *The City in Slang: New York Life and Popular Speech.* New York: Oxford University Press, 1993. A scholarly yet highly enjoyable look at words and phrases associated with New York. Among them: hot dog, rush hour, gold digger, shyster, smart aleck, pleasure hound, straphanger.

Asbury, Herbert. *The Gangs of New York.* New York: Paragon House, 1990. A lively account of the gangsters of New York, from the Revolution to the 1920s.

Botkin, B.A., ed. *New York City Folklore.* New York: Random House, 1956. Botkin edits an entertaining collection of "Legends, Tall Tales, Anecdotes, Stories, Sagas, Heroes and Characters, Customs, Traditions and Sayings" culled from other sources, including newspapers, guidebooks, biographies, children's songs, and literature.

Broyard, Anatole. *Kafka Was the Rage: A Greenwich Village Memoir.* New York: Crown Publishing Group, 1993. Funny and perceptive, acerbic and reflective—Broyard reminisces on his youth in Greenwich Village just after WW II. Among his associates were Dwight McDonald, Delmore Schwarz, and Meyer Shapiro.

Caro, Robert A. *The Power Broker: Robert Moses and the Fall of New York.* New York: Vintage Books, 1975. Much more than a biography, this Pulitzer Prize-winning tome tells the fascinating and often scandalous story behind the shaping of 20th-century New York. Though over 1,000 pages, the book is a compelling page-turner.

Christman, Henry M., ed. *Walt Whitman's New York: From Manhattan to Montauk.* New York: New Amsterdam Books, 1989. Reprints of an engaging series of articles by Whitman that first appeared in the *Brooklyn Standard* in 1861. The poet spent the first 42 years of his life in the New York area.

Cohen, Barbara, Stephen Heller, and Seymour Chwast. *New York Observed: Artists and Writers Look at the City, 1650 to the Present.* New York: Harry N. Abrams, Inc., Publishers, 1987. Packed with excerpts and artwork ranging from Washington Irving to James Baldwin, Cecil Beaton to Diego Rivera, this oversize book offers a fine armchair view of New York.

Cohn, Nik. *The Heart of the World.* New York: Vintage Books, 1993. The writer who spawned *Saturday Night Fever* takes a wild and exuberant walk down the Great White Way. During his sojourn he meets pickpockets, transvestites, strippers, ex-politicians, and even an ordinary citizen or two.

Cole, William, ed. *Quotable New York.* New York: Penguin Books, 1992. Everyone from Charles Dickens to Malcolm X sum up the Big Apple in 100 words or less. "If you live in New York, even if you're Catholic, you're Jewish"—Lenny Bruce. "In New York it's not whether you win or lose—it's how you lay the blame"—Fran Lebowitz.

Dwyer, Jim. *Subway Lives.* New York: Crown Publishers, 1991. A *New York Newsday* columnist takes a look at one of the Big Apple's most famous institutions by following the lives of seven typical New Yorkers through one composite day on the subway. Skillfully intertwined in the narrative is subway history, legend, and lore.

Friedman, Josh Alan. *Tales of Times Square.* Portland, OR: Feral Press, 1993. A startling look at the seamy side of a now all-but-vanished Times Square. Strippers, porn brokers, pimps, hookers, and cops tell their stories; as one reviewer put it, "This book made me want to shower."

Hamill, Pete. *A Drinking Life: A Memoir.* New York: Little, Brown and Company, 1994. The well-known New York journalist writes about a drinking life that began in immigrant Brooklyn during WW II—when drinking was essential to being a man—and ended on a New Year's Eve 20 years ago. Along the way unfolds a bittersweet portrayal of a bygone New York.

Jackson, Kenneth T., ed. *The Great Metropolis: Poverty and Progress in New York City.* New York: American Heritage Custom Publishing Group, 1993. A lively, fun-to-read introduction to New York City history, compiled of articles first published in *American Heritage* magazine.

Jacobs, Jane. *The Death and Life of Great American Cities.* New York: Vintage Books, 1992. The classic and enormously influential 1961 study. Jacobs often disagreed with the influential urban planners of her day, and loved many of the things that make New York New York (teeming streets, small blocks, aging buildings).

Johnson, James Weldon. *Black Manhattan.* New York: Da Capo Press, 1991. First published in 1930, this classic work paints one of the earliest portraits of the lives of African Americans in New York City. Much more than a history, the book also illuminates the Harlem Renaissance, of which Johnson was a part.

Johnson, Joyce. *Minor Characters*. New York: Pocket Books, 1983. A tender, lyrical account of Greenwich Village and the Beat Generation, written by an on-and-off lover of Jack Kerouac.

Kazin, Alfred. *A Walker in the City*. New York: Harcourt, Brace, 1951. The perambulatory memoir of a distinguished literary critic who grew up in immigrant Brownsville. Kazin's sojourns into other neighborhoods and boroughs exposed him to new worlds.

Lewis, David Levering. *When Harlem Was in Vogue*. New York: Oxford University Press, 1981. A brilliant, authoritative study of Harlem in the 1920s.

Liebling, A.J. *Back Where I Came From*. New York: North Point Press, 1989. *The New Yorker* writer of the '30s and '40s pens a "love letter to the City of New York." Liebling reveled in the sights, sounds, smells, and—above all—speech and people of his hometown.

Lobas, Vladimir. *Taxi From Hell: Confessions of a Russian Hack*. New York: SoHo Press Inc., 1991. He doesn't know how to drive, he doesn't speak English, and he doesn't know the city. Nonetheless, he lands a job as a New York City cab driver. The true story of an émigré Russian intellectual's first years in New York.

Mitchell, Joseph. *Up in the Old Hotel*. New York: Pantheon, 1992. A reprint of four classics penned by the deadpan *The New Yorker* chronicler of city life. "McSorley's Wonderful Saloon," "Old Mr. Flood," "The Bottom of the Harbor," and "Joe Gould's Secret" are included.

Morris, Jan. *Manhattan '45*. New York: Oxford University Press, 1987. The well-known travel writer imagines what Manhattan was like immediately after WW II.

Moscow, Henry. *The Street Book: An Encyclopedia Of Manhattan's Street Names and Their Origins*. New York: Fordham University Press, 1978. A meticulous street-by-street examination of the city, filled with odd surprises and delightful tidbits of history.

Sante, Luc. *Low Life*. New York: Vintage Departures, 1991. A highly original and literate book that delves into the underbelly—opium dens, brothels, sweatshops—of old New York.

Simon, Kate. *Bronx Primitive: Portraits in a Childhood*. New York: Harper & Row Publishers, 1982. A rich, evocative, and startlingly frank coming-of-age story set in an immigrant Jewish neighborhood just after WW I.

Thomas, Piri. *Down These Mean Streets*. New York: Alfred Knopf, 1967. The edgy yet lyrical autobiographical account of a young Puerto Rican's search for identity in crime-ridden East Harlem.

Wakefield, Dan. *New York in the Fifties*. Boston: Houghton Mifflin, 1992. An evocative memoir of life in Greenwich Village in the pre-1960s bohemian heyday of Dorothy Day, Jack Kerouac, James Baldwin, Allen Ginsberg, Gay Talese, and Norman Mailer.

Wang, Harvey. *Harvey Wang's New York*. New York: W.W. Norton & Company, 1990. For a first-rate introduction to New York's extraordinary cast of characters, pick up this slim volume of portraits. Among those photographed are a pillow maker, mannequin maker, gravedigger, kosher butcher, and bowling alley mechanic.

White, E.B. *Essays of E.B. White*. New York: Harper & Row, 1977. The great *The New Yorker* essayist, poet, and storyteller writes of New York and Florida, snow and pigs, railroads and Will Strunk. Included is "Here Is New York," one of the most insightful essays on the city ever written.

FICTION

Baldwin, James. *Another Country*. New York: Vintage Books, 1993. One of Baldwin's best and most disturbing novels, set largely in Greenwich Village and Harlem in the 1960s.

Another Baldwin work that takes place in the city is *Go Tell It on the Mountain.*

Capote, Truman. *Breakfast at Tiffany's.* New American Library, 1958. The moving story of a glamorous madcap adrift on the Upper East Side in the 1950s.

Crane, Stephen. *Maggie, A Girl of the Streets.* New York: W.W. Norton & Company, Inc., 1979. Crane's impressionistic, ground-breaking first novel—published at his own expense in 1893—was one of the first to make slum dwellers and social problems the subject of literature.

Doctorow, E.L. *Ragtime.* New York: Bantam Books, 1980. Rich white, Harlem black, immigrant Jew—Doctorow writes of three families whose lives converge in early 20th-century New York. A deft weaving of fictional characters and real people, including Emma Goldman and Stanford White.

Dreiser, Theodore. *Sister Carrie.* New York: New American Library, 1980. The classic novel of an innocent girl set adrift in a corrupt city, *Sister Carrie* begins in Chicago but comes to its harrowing conclusion in the bleak, heartless streets of New York.

Ellison, Ralph. *Invisible Man.* New York: Vintage Books, 1990. The classic 1952 novel follows a nameless protagonist from his home in the Deep South to the basements of Harlem. A masterpiece of African American literature that chronicles the effects of bigotry on victims and perpetrators alike.

Finney, Jack. *Time and Again.* New York: Simon & Schuster, 1970. A cult classic that time-travels back and forth between the present and the 1880s, when New York was little more than an overgrown small town.

Gaitskill, Mary. *Bad Behavior.* New York: Vintage Books, 1988. A fierce, original collection of stories about life in the bedrooms of the urban fringe.

Hijuelos, Oscar. *The Mambo Kings Play Songs of Love.* New York: Farrar Straus Giroux, 1989. A rich and deeply resonant novel that re-creates the world of immigrant Cuban musicians living in New York post-WW II.

James, Henry. *Washington Square.* New York: New American Library, 1979. One of James's shorter and more accessible novels, *Washington Square* is an engrossing tale of the manners and mores of upper-crust 19th-century New York.

McCarthy, Mary. *The Group.* New York: Harcourt Brace Jovanovich, 1982. One of America's foremost women-of-letters uses her acerbic wit to chronicle the lives of eight Vassar graduates living in New York in the '30s.

McInerney, Jay. *Bright Lights, Big City.* New York: Vintage Books, 1984. A young man immerses himself in the excesses of 1980s New York—the clubs, the drugs, the after-hour hot spots—until brought to an abrupt reckoning.

Morrison, Toni. *Jazz.* New York: Penguin Books, 1993. The Pulitzer Prize-winning author sets her latest novel in Harlem in 1926. This tale of passion, jealousy, murder, and redemption begins when a door-to-door salesman of beauty products shoots his lover.

Paley, Grace. *Enormous Changes at the Last Minute.* New York: Farrar Straus Giroux, 1974. Quirky, funny, sad, combative, vulnerable Paley, who grew up in immigrant New York in the '20s and '30s, captures the soul of New York in one of her best collections of stories.

Parker, Dorothy. *The Portable Dorothy Parker.* New York: Penguin Books, 1976. Poems, stories, articles, and reviews by that most quotable of New York/*The New Yorker* writers.

Petry, Ann. *The Street.* Boston: Houghton Mifflin Company, 1974. Both a historical document and a novel, this bleak and poignant classic takes place in poverty-torn Harlem in the late 1940s.

Powell, Dawn. *The Wicked Pavilion*. New York: Vintage Books, 1990. A comic masterpiece set in the 1940s in a dingy yet fashionable cafe frequented by small-time hacks, hustlers, and poseurs. Among Powell's other novels set in New York is *Angels on Toast*.

Roth, Henry. *Call It Sleep*. New York: Farrar Straus Giroux, 1991. A classic coming-of-age novel of immigrant life, first published in 1934 and set on the Lower East Side.

Thompson, Kay. *Eloise*. New York: Simon & Schuster, 1955. The heroine of this beloved children's book is a six-year-old who lives in the Plaza Hotel.

Wharton, Edith. *The Age of Innocence*. New York: Collier Books, 1986. The first book written by a woman to win the Pulitzer Prize is a subtle, elegant portrait of desire and betrayal in moneyed Old New York. Among Wharton's other books set in the city are *The House of Mirth, A Backward Glance,* and *Old New York.*

Wolfe, Thomas. *The Bonfire of the Vanities*. New York: Bantam Books, 1988. The extravagant, hyperbolic tale of a greedy Wall Street bond trader who takes a wrong turn in the Bronx.

Poetry
Among the many poets who have written extensively on New York City are Walt Whitman, Langston Hughes, Hart Crane, Allen Ginsberg, Djuna Barnes, and Frank O'Hara.

INDEXES
ACCOMMODATIONS INDEX

RESTAURANT INDEX

GENERAL INDEX

Page numbers in *italics* indicate information in maps, charts, and special topics.

ABOUT THE AUTHOR

Christiane Bird has courted *wanderlust* since age four, when she and her family lived in Iran and sojourned throughout the Middle East. An ardent fan of New York City, she is a former travel writer for the New York *Daily News,* the author of *The Jazz and Blues Lover's Guide to the U.S.* (Addison-Wesley, 1991; rev. ed. 1994), and the co-author of *Below the Line: Living Poor in America* (Consumer Reports Books, 1987), a photography book by Eugene Richards. Her articles have appeared in major national magazines, and her short stories in *Antaeus* and *The Southern Review.* She is also author of Moon's *New York Handbook.* A graduate of Yale University, she lives in Greenwich Village with thoroughbred racing consultant Jerry Brown and their two cats.

Order Directly from Moon and Save!

Stay up to date and save 25% with Moon's new Handbook upgrade offer!

Starting April 1, 1998, just mail us the cover from your old edition of a Moon Travel Handbook with your order for the current edition of the same title, and save 25% off the retail price of the current edition.*

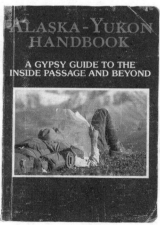

*Normal shipping rates apply. Offers #1 and #2 may not be combined with one another, or with any other offer.

To order, call 800-345-5473, fax 530-345-6751.

www.moon.com

Enjoy our travel information center on the World Wide Web (WWW), loaded with interactive exhibits designed especially for the Internet.

ATTRACTIONS ON MOON'S WEB SITE INCLUDE:

ATLAS
Our award-winning, comprehensive travel guides cover destinations throughout North America and Hawaii, Latin America and the Caribbean, and Asia and the Pacific.

PRACTICAL NOMAD
Extensive excerpts, a unique set of travel links coordinated with the book, and a regular Q & A column by author and Internet travel consultant Edward Hasbrouck.

TRAVEL MATTERS
Our on-line travel zine, featuring articles; author correspondence; a travel library including health information, reading lists, and cultural cues; and our new contest, **Destination X,** offering a chance to win a trip to the mystery destination of your choice.

ROAD TRIP USA
Our best-selling book, ever; don't miss this award-winning Web guide to off-the-interstate itineraries.

Come visit us at: **www.moon.com**

MOON TRAVEL HANDBOOKS

LOSE YOURSELF IN THE EXPERIENCE, NOT THE CROWD

For 25 years, Moon Travel Handbooks have been the guidebooks of choice for adventurous travelers. Our award-winning Handbook series provides focused, comprehensive coverage of distinct destinations all over the world. Each Handbook is like an entire bookcase of cultural insight and introductory information in one portable volume. Our goal at Moon is to give travelers all the background and practical information they'll need for an extraordinary travel experience.

The following pages include a complete list of Handbooks, covering North America and Hawaii, Mexico, Latin America and the Caribbean, and Asia and the Pacific.To purchase Moon Travel Handbooks, check your local bookstore or order by phone: (800) 345-5473 M-F 8 am.-5 p.m. PST or outside the U.S. phone: (530) 345-5473.

"An in-depth dunk into the land, the people and their history, arts, and politics."
—*Student Travels*

"I consider these books to be superior to Lonely Planet. When Moon produces a book it is more humorous, incisive, and off-beat."
—*Toronto Sun*

"Outdoor enthusiasts gravitate to the well-written Moon Travel Handbooks. In addition to politically correct historic and cultural features, the series focuses on flora, fauna and outdoor recreation. Maps and meticulous directions also are a trademark of Moon guides."
—*Houston Chronicle*

"Moon [Travel Handbooks] . . . bring a healthy respect to the places they investigate. Best of all, they provide a host of odd nuggets that give a place texture and prod the wary traveler from the beaten path. The finest are written with such care and insight they deserve listing as literature."
—*American Geographical Society*

"Moon Travel Handbooks offer in-depth historical essays and useful maps, enhanced by a sense of humor and a neat, compact format."
—*Swing*

"Perfect for the more adventurous, these are long on history, sightseeing and nitty-gritty information and very price-specific."
—*Columbus Dispatch*

"Moon guides manage to be comprehensive and countercultural at the same time . . . Handbooks are packed with maps, photographs, drawings, and sidebars that constitute a college-level introduction to each country's history, culture, people, and crafts."
—*National Geographic Traveler*

"Few travel guides do a better job helping travelers create their own itineraries than the Moon Travel Handbook series. The authors have a knack for homing in on the essentials."
—**Colorado Springs** *Gazette Telegraph*

MEXICO

"These books will delight the armchair traveler, aid the un-decided person in selecting a destination, and guide the seasoned road warrior looking for lesser-known hideaways."

—*Mexican Meanderings* **Newsletter**

"From tourist traps to off-the-beaten track hideaways, these guides offer consistent, accurate details without pretension."

—*Foreign Service Journal*

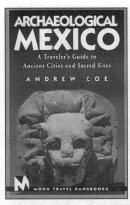

Archaeological Mexico	**$19.95**
Andrew Coe	450 pages, 25 maps
Baja Handbook	**$15.95**
Joe Cummings	380 pages, 44 maps
Cabo Handbook	**$14.95**
Joe Cummings	265 pages, 18 maps
Cancun Handbook	**$13.95**
Chicki Mallan	270 pages, 25 maps
Colonial Mexico	**$16.95**
Chicki Mallan	300 pages, 38 maps
Mexico Handbook	**$21.95**
Joe Cummings and Chicki Mallan	1,200 pages, 232 maps
Northern Mexico Handbook	**$16.95**
Joe Cummings	590 pages, 68 maps
Pacific Mexico Handbook	**$17.95**
Bruce Whipperman	580 pages, 69 maps
Puerto Vallarta Handbook	**$14.95**
Bruce Whipperman	330 pages, 36 maps
Yucatan Handbook	**$15.95**
Chicki Mallan	470 pages, 62 maps

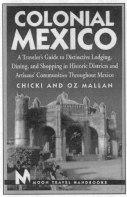

LATIN AMERICA AND THE CARIBBEAN

"Solidly packed with practical information and full of significant cultural asides that will enlighten you on the whys and wherefores of things you might easily see but not easily grasp."

—*Boston Globe*

Belize Handbook	**$15.95**
Chicki Mallan	390 pages, 45 maps
Caribbean Handbook	**$16.95**
Karl Luntta	400 pages, 56 maps
Costa Rica Handbook	**$19.95**
Christopher P. Baker	780 pages, 74 maps
Cuba Handbook	**$19.95**
Christopher P. Baker	740 pages, 70 maps
Dominican Republic Handbook	**$15.95**
Gaylord Dold	420 pages, 24 maps
Ecuador Handbook	**$16.95**
Julian Smith	450 pages, 43 maps
Honduras Handbook	**$15.95**
Chris Humphrey	330 pages, 40 maps
Jamaica Handbook	**$15.95**
Karl Luntta	330 pages, 17 maps
Virgin Islands Handbook	**$13.95**
Karl Luntta	220 pages, 19 maps

NORTH AMERICA AND HAWAII

"These domestic guides convey the same sense of exoticism that their foreign counterparts do, making home-country travel seem like far-flung adventure."

—*Sierra Magazine*

Alaska-Yukon Handbook	**$17.95**
Deke Castleman and Don Pitcher	530 pages, 92 maps
Alberta and the Northwest Territories Handbook	**$17.95**
Andrew Hempstead and Nadina Purdon	530 pages, 72 maps,
Arizona Traveler's Handbook	**$17.95**
Bill Weir and Robert Blake	512 pages,54 maps
Atlantic Canada Handbook	**$17.95**
Nan Drosdick and Mark Morris	460 pages, 61 maps
Big Island of Hawaii Handbook	**$15.95**
J.D. Bisignani	370 pages, 23 maps
British Columbia Handbook	**$16.95**
Jane King and Andrew Hempstead	430 pages, 69 maps

Colorado Handbook	**$18.95**
Stephen Metzger	480 pages, 59 maps
Georgia Handbook	**$17.95**
Kap Stann	370 pages, 50 maps
Hawaii Handbook	**$19.95**
J.D. Bisignani	1,030 pages, 90 maps
Honolulu-Waikiki Handbook	**$14.95**
J.D. Bisignani	380 pages, 20 maps
Idaho Handbook	**$18.95**
Don Root	610 pages, 42 maps
Kauai Handbook	**$15.95**
J.D. Bisignani	320 pages, 23 maps
Maine Handbook	**$18.95**
Kathleen M. Brandes	660 pages, 27 maps
Massachusetts Handbook	**$18.95**
Jeff Perk	600 pages, 23 maps
Maui Handbook	**$14.95**
J.D. Bisignani	410 pages, 35 maps
Montana Handbook	**$17.95**
Judy Jewell and W.C. McRae	480 pages, 52 maps
Nevada Handbook	**$18.95**
Deke Castleman	530 pages, 40 maps
New Hampshire Handbook	**$17.95**
Steve Lantos	500 pages, 18 maps
New Mexico Handbook	**$15.95**
Stephen Metzger	360 pages, 47 maps
New York City Handbook	**$13.95**
Christiane Bird	300 pages, 20 maps
New York Handbook	**$19.95**
Christiane Bird	780 pages, 95 maps
Northern California Handbook	**$19.95**
Kim Weir	800 pages, 50 maps
Oregon Handbook	**$17.95**
Stuart Warren and Ted Long Ishikawa	588 pages, 34 maps
Pennsylvania Handbook	**$18.95**
Joanne Miller	448 pages, 40 maps
Road Trip USA	**$22.50**
Jamie Jensen	800 pages, 165 maps
Southern California Handbook	**$19.95**
Kim Weir	750 pages, 30 maps
Tennessee Handbook	**$17.95**
Jeff Bradley	530 pages, 44 maps
Texas Handbook	**$18.95**
Joe Cummings	692 pages, 70 maps
Utah Handbook	**$17.95**
Bill Weir and W.C. McRae	490 pages, 40 maps

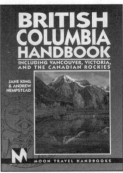

Washington Handbook	$19.95
Don Pitcher	870 pages, 113 maps
Wisconsin Handbook	**$18.95**
Thomas Huhti	590 pages, 69 maps
Wyoming Handbook	**$17.95**
Don Pitcher	610 pages, 80 maps

ASIA AND THE PACIFIC

"Scores of maps, detailed practical info down to business hours of small-town libraries. You can't beat the Asian titles for sheer heft. (The) series is sort of an American Lonely Planet, with better writing but fewer titles. (The) individual voice of researchers comes through."

—Travel & Leisure

Australia Handbook	$21.95
Marael Johnson, Andrew Hempstead, and Nadina Purdon	940 pages, 141 maps
Bali Handbook	**$19.95**
Bill Dalton	750 pages, 54 maps
Bangkok Handbook	**$13.95**
Michael Buckley	244 pages, 30 maps
Fiji Islands Handbook	**$13.95**
David Stanley	280 pages, 38 maps
Hong Kong Handbook	**$16.95**
Kerry Moran	378 pages, 49 maps
Indonesia Handbook	**$25.00**
Bill Dalton	1,380 pages, 249 maps
Japan Handbook	**$22.50**
J.D. Bisignani	970 pages, 213 maps
Micronesia Handbook	**$14.95**
Neil M. Levy	340 pages, 70 maps
Nepal Handbook	**$18.95**
Kerry Moran	490 pages, 51 maps
New Zealand Handbook	**$19.95**
Jane King	620 pages, 81 maps
Outback Australia Handbook	**$18.95**
Marael Johnson	450 pages, 57 maps
Philippines Handbook	**$17.95**
Peter Harper and Laurie Fullerton	670 pages, 116 maps
Singapore Handbook	**$15.95**
Carl Parkes	350 pages, 29 maps
Southeast Asia Handbook	**$21.95**
Carl Parkes	1,000 pages, 196 maps

South Korea Handbook	**$19.95**	
Robert Nilsen	820 pages, 141 maps	
South Pacific Handbook	**$22.95**	
David Stanley	920 pages, 147 maps	
Tahiti-Polynesia Handbook	**$13.95**	
David Stanley	270 pages, 35 maps	
Thailand Handbook	**$19.95**	
Carl Parkes	860 pages, 142 maps	
Vietnam, Cambodia & Laos Handbook	**$18.95**	
Michael Buckley	720 pages, 112 maps	

OTHER GREAT TITLES FROM MOON

"For hardy wanderers, few guides come more highly
recommended than the Handbooks. They include
good maps, steer clear of fluff and flackery, and offer
plenty of money-saving tips. They also give you the
kind of information that visitors to strange lands—on
any budget—need to survive."

—*US News & World Report*

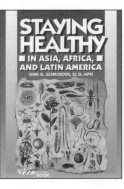

Moon Handbook	**$10.00**	
Carl Koppeschaar	141 pages, 8 maps	
Moscow-St. Petersburg Handbook	**$13.95**	
Masha Nordbye	259 pages, 16 maps	
The Practical Nomad: How to Travel Around the World	**$17.95**	
Edward Hasbrouck	575 pages	
Staying Healthy in Asia, Africa, and Latin America	**$11.95**	
Dirk Schroeder	197 pages, 4 maps	

MOONBELT

A new concept in moneybelts.
Made of heavy-duty Cordura
nylon, the Moonbelt offers
maximum protection for your money
and important papers. This pouch,
designed for all-weather comfort, slips under your shirt or waistband, rendering it virtually
undetectable and inaccessible to pickpockets. It features a one-inch high-test quick-release
buckle so there's no more fumbling around for the strap or repeated adjustments. This
handy plastic buckle opens and closes with a touch but won't come undone until you want
it to. Moonbelts accommodate traveler's checks, passports, cash, photos, etc.
Size 5 x 9 inches. Available in black only. **$8.95**

ROAD TRIP USA

Cross-Country Adventures on America's Two-Lane Highways

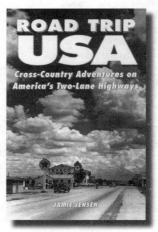

$22.50   800 pages

"For those who feel an adrenaline rush everytime they hear the words 'road trip,' and who understand that getting there is at least half the fun, this is quite simply the best book of its type ever published."
—*Conde Nast Traveler* **web site**

"Just might be the perfect book about hitting the summoning highway . . . It's impossible not to find something enticing in *Road Trip USA* to add to your next cycling expedition. An encyclopedia of roadside wonders."   —**Harley Davidson** *Enthusiast*

"For budding myth collectors, I can't think of a better textbook."
—*Los Angeles Times*

"A terrific guide for those who'd rather swat mosquitoes than take the interstate."
—**Colorado Springs** *Gazette Telegraph*

"Jensen is well-versed in travel, has an enjoyable yet informative style and will guide you along each mile. Don't leave home without it!"   —*Mobilia*

"Zany inspiration for a road Gypsie in search of off-the-beaten-path adventure."
—*The Toronto Globe and Mail*

"A historic journey into the heart and soul of America."
—*Route 66 Magazine*

"Jamie Jensen and the 12 intrepid contributors to *Road Trip USA* have been everywhere and seen everything compiling this exhaustive, delightful, destination-anywhere guide to American road-tripping."

—*Citybooks,* **Washington D.C.**

"Not only a fantastic guide . . . a great companion!"

—*The Herald,* **Columbia S.C.**

THE PRACTICAL NOMAD

✈ TAKE THE PLUNGE

"The greatest barriers to long-term travel by Americans are the disempowered feelings that leave them afraid to ask for the time off. Just do it."

✈ TAKE NOTHING FOR GRANTED

"Even 'What time is it?' is a highly politicized question in some areas, and the answer may depend on your informant's ethnicity and political allegiance as well as the proximity of the secret police."

✈ TAKE THIS BOOK

$17.95   576 pages

With experience helping thousands of his globetrotting clients plan their trips around the world, travel industry insider Edward Hasbrouck provides the secrets that can save readers money and valuable travel time. An indispensable complement to destination-specific travel guides, *The Practical Nomad* includes:

airfare strategies

ticket discounts

long-term travel considerations

travel documents

border crossings

entry requirements

government offices

travel publications

Internet information resources

WHERE TO BUY MOON TRAVEL HANDBOOKS

BOOKSTORES AND LIBRARIES: Moon Travel Handbooks are distributed worldwide. Please contact our sales manager for a list of wholesalers and distributors in your area.

TRAVELERS: We would like to have Moon Travel Handbooks available throughout the world. Please ask your bookstore to write or call us for ordering information. If your bookstore will not order our guides for you, please contact us for a free catalog.

> **Moon Travel Handbooks**
> **P.O. Box 3040**
> **Chico, CA 95927-3040 U.S.A.**
> **tel.: (800) 345-5473, outside the U.S. (530) 345-5473**
> **fax: (530) 345-6751**
> **e-mail: travel@moon.com**

IMPORTANT ORDERING INFORMATION

PRICES: All prices are subject to change. We always ship the most current edition. We will let you know if there is a price increase on the book you order.

SHIPPING AND HANDLING OPTIONS: Domestic UPS or USPS first class (allow 10 working days for delivery): $4.50 for the first item, $1.00 for each additional item.

Moonbelt shipping is $1.50 for one, 50 cents for each additional belt.

UPS 2nd Day Air or Printed Airmail requires a special quote.

International Surface Bookrate 8-12 weeks delivery: $3.00 for the first item, $1.00 for each additional item. Note: We cannot guarantee international surface bookrate shipping. We recommends sending international orders via air mail, which requires a special quote.

FOREIGN ORDERS: Orders that originate outside the U.S.A. must be paid for with an international money order, a check in U.S. currency drawn on a major U.S. bank based in the U.S.A., or Visa, MasterCard, or Discover.

TELEPHONE ORDERS: We accept Visa, MasterCard, or Discover payments. Call in your order: (800) 345-5473, 8 a.m.-5 p.m. Pacific standard time. Outside the U.S. the number is (530) 345-5473.

INTERNET ORDERS: Visit our site at: www.moon.com

ORDER FORM

Prices are subject to change without notice. Be sure to call (800) 345-5473,
or (530) 345-5473 from outside the U.S. 8 a.m.–5 p.m. PST for current prices and editions,
or for the name of the bookstore nearest you that carries Moon Travel Handbooks.
(See important ordering information on preceding page.)

Name: _____ Date: _____

Street: _____

City: _____ Daytime Phone: _____

State or Country: _____ Zip Code: _____

QUANTITY	TITLE	PRICE

Taxable Total_____

Sales Tax (7.25%) for California Residents_____

Shipping & Handling_____

TOTAL_____

Ship: ☐ UPS (no P.O. Boxes)   ☐ 1st class   ☐ International surface mail

Ship to: ☐ address above   ☐ other _____

Make checks payable to: **MOON TRAVEL HANDBOOKS**, P.O. Box 3040, Chico, CA 95927-3040
U.S.A. We accept Visa, MasterCard, or Discover. **To Order**: Call in your Visa, MasterCard, or Discover number,
or send a written order with your Visa, MasterCard, or Discover number and expiration date clearly written.

Card Number: ☐ **Visa**   ☐ **MasterCard**   ☐ **Discover**

☐ ☐ ☐ ☐   ☐ ☐ ☐ ☐   ☐ ☐ ☐ ☐   ☐ ☐ ☐ ☐

Exact Name on Card: _____

Expiration date:_____

Signature: _____

New York, New York

The Empire State.

$19.95
784 pages
95 maps

$13.95
300 pages
19 maps

The Big Apple.

Moon Travel Handbooks brings you both.

Two exciting destinations.
Two new, vigorously
comprehensive titles from
MOON TRAVEL HANDBOOKS.

MOON
TRAVEL
HANDBOOKS